CW01064735

Animalism

Animalism

New Essays on Persons, Animals, and Identity

EDITED BY
Stephan Blatti
and Paul F. Snowdon

OXFORD
UNIVERSITY PRESS

OXFORD
UNIVERSITY PRESS

Great Clarendon Street, Oxford, OX2 6DP,
United Kingdom

Oxford University Press is a department of the University of Oxford.
It furthers the University's objective of excellence in research, scholarship,
and education by publishing worldwide. Oxford is a registered trade mark of
Oxford University Press in the UK and in certain other countries

The moral rights of the authors have been asserted

First Edition published in 2016

Impression: 2

Published in the United States of America by Oxford University Press
198 Madison Avenue, New York, NY 10016, United States of America

British Library Cataloguing in Publication Data
Data available

Library of Congress Control Number: 2016930898

ISBN 978-0-19-960875-1

Printed in Great Britain by
CPI Group (UK) Ltd, Croydon, CR0 4YY

Contents

List of Contributors   vii

1. Introduction   1
    Stephan Blatti and Paul F. Snowdon

Part I

2. We Are Not Human Beings   31
    Derek Parfit

3. Animalism vs. Constitutionalism   50
    Lynne Rudder Baker

4. Constitution and the Debate between Animalism and
    Psychological Views   64
    Denis Robinson

5. Remnant Persons: Animalism's Undoing   89
    Mark Johnston

6. Thinking Animals Without Animalism   128
    Sydney Shoemaker

Part II

7. The Remnant-Person Problem   145
    Eric T. Olson

8. Headhunters   162
    Stephan Blatti

9. Thinking Parts   180
    Rory Madden

10. Four-Dimensional Animalism   208
    David B. Hershenov

Part III

11. Animalism and the Varieties of Conjoined Twinning   229
    Tim Campbell and Jeff McMahan

12. A Case in which Two Persons Exist in One Animal   253
    Mark D. Reid

split-brain cases, severed
corpus-collosum

13. Animalism and the Unity of Consciousness: Some Issues   ?   266
    Paul F. Snowdon

14. Animal Ethics   ✗   283
    Jens Johansson

15. The Stony Metaphysical Heart of Animalism   ✗   303
    David Shoemaker

Index   329

List of Contributors

Lynne Rudder Baker, University of Massachusetts, Amherst

Stephan Blatti, University of Memphis

Tim Campbell, Institute for Futures Studies

David B. Hershenov, University at Buffalo

Jens Johansson, Uppsala University

Mark Johnston, Princeton University

Rory Madden, University College London

Jeff McMahan, University of Oxford

Eric T. Olson, University of Sheffield

Derek Parfit, University of Oxford

Mark D. Reid, Wilkes University

Denis Robinson, University of Auckland

David Shoemaker, Tulane University

Sydney Shoemaker, Cornell University

Paul F. Snowdon, University College London

1

Introduction

Stephan Blatti and Paul F. Snowdon

The purpose of this collection is to gather together a group of chapters that are inspired by three central questions: What is animalism? What implications does it have? Is animalism true? The aim is to push the debate about these questions forward. Most of the chapters are new. The two that are not—those by Parfit and by Campbell and McMahan—are recent and highly important essays that raise fundamental questions about animalism, and we feel they deserve a place in this collection. We also wanted to collect together good work from different intellectual centres around the world, in North America, the UK, and Australasia, but also work from philosophers of different ages and at different stages. Some chapters represent forceful and novel presentations of relatively well-known viewpoints, whereas others move the debate along totally new directions. No view is dominant, and different chapters focus on different aspects of the debate. We, the editors, are both animalists (which is not to say that we are animalists of precisely the same kind), but our main hope with this collection is that it will stimulate new discussion, not that we shall make converts to our own view. It takes time for debates in philosophy to deepen and to sort the wheat from the chaff, but we hope this collection will help those things to happen in the next stage of debate about animalism.

In this introduction we shall sketch the background to the current debates and try to relate the chapters here to that background. It is impossible for us to pick out every issue or argument in all the chapters that we regard as important. All we can do is to highlight some of them. As with all philosophical subjects, properly sorting out the issues is a task for those who wish to think about them.

One way to think of animalism is as a view about the relation between us, persons, and animals. According to it we are identical with some animals. We can, then, regard the background question as—what is our relation to animals? It is interesting to note that this general question has risen to prominence not only in the analytic philosophical tradition, but also in the continental tradition (e.g. in the work of Derrida) and in various areas of interdisciplinary inquiry (e.g. animal studies). The issues discussed here, then, provide one example of intellectual convergence between multiple philosophical traditions and areas of investigation.

1.1. 'Animalism'

As is the wont with -ism's in philosophy, not everyone will define 'animalism' in the same way. But a way that seems true to its use by many people is that it stands for the claim that we, each of us, are identical to, are one and the same thing as, an animal of a certain kind. That kind is what is called *Homo sapiens*. Putting it less technically, each of us is a human animal. According to this proposal we can say that at various places there is both an animal and one of us, and those things are in fact the same thing.

Now, it is often convenient to have a noun picking out those things that we have so far picked out as 'us', or as 'one of us'. We shall talk of the 'person' and of 'persons'. In using this venerable noun we are not committing ourselves to our usage being the same as that of the normal usage. But using this noun, so interpreted, we can formulate the claim as 'each person is an animal'.

Formulating it in these ways leaves plenty of important interpretative questions unexplored, to which we shall return, but it suffices to fix the central thesis. And putting the thesis this way renders it an answer to the question 'What are we?' or 'What is our nature?' These questions are ones that have perennially gripped us, and to which many intellectual traditions have given their answers.

1.2. Recent History

We shall begin with a brief and schematic history of the recent emergence of this approach in philosophical thinking about ourselves.

In post-war analytical philosophy the problem of personal identity received considerable attention from a succession of highly talented and creative philosophers, including Strawson, Williams, Shoemaker, Parfit, Nagel, Mackie, Lewis, Unger, and Noonan, to name only a few of those involved in the debates. One striking thing about these debates was the almost total absence in them of any mention of the notion of an animal. People in the debate simply assumed that an interest in the nature of ourselves was an interest in the analysis of what it is to be a *person*. The term 'person' was, that is, taken to express or stand for our basic nature. With that as a background assumption, thinking about our persistence over time—called, of course, the problem of personal identity—tended to start by considering the proposal that persons are tied to their bodies, a proposal that was defended by Bernard Williams. However, this view was more or less universally rejected by philosophers, a rejection based primarily on the power of brain transplant arguments, initially and very effectively developed by Shoemaker. This dismissal was usually very rapid and taken to be more or less obvious. The debate then resolved itself, very roughly, into a choice between increasingly sophisticated versions of the type of approach originally proposed by Locke—a development led with great ingenuity by Shoemaker and Parfit—and the proposal that we are tied in our persistence requirements to our brains, a view articulated, among others, by Nagel and Mackie. Although the debates continued to regard these as the two main alternative ways to think about our persistence, they were enriched and complicated by two further developments. The first was the extraordinary popularity within American and Australian philosophy, and subsequently in British philosophy, of thinking about what is called identity over time within a framework of four-dimensionalism. David Lewis's work had a major influence in moving the debate in that direction, of course. This meant that new ways to formulate the basic ideas were inserted into the debate, and some new and fairly technical issues emerged. The second new direction resulted from the very important work of Parfit who took what was basically a sophisticated Lockean approach and tried to derive from it some radical claims in value theory about the importance of facts about personal identity, captured, no doubt rather crudely, in the slogan that 'identity is not what matters'. Parfit's ideas about value and his linking of the personal identity debate to value theory generated a rich discussion, and this linkage remains present in more recent debates, and indeed in some contributions to this volume.

There is an important question that can be raised here, on the assumption that the foregoing is more or less correct: Why was the idea of an animal conspicuously absent in this classical period of debate? To answer this question we need to return to Locke's famous discussion of personal identity, in which the notion of an animal was central.[1] One of Locke's purposes was to affirm that the person—one example, as we might say, being Locke himself—is not the animal but has persistence conditions which are quite different, and is therefore a different item. Locke exercised great care in specifying the different ideas for which the words 'animal' and 'person' stood. A reasonable conjecture, or proposal, we suggest, is that Locke's treatment of these two terms and notions was so effective that it generated in people engaging with the problem the conviction that the notion of a person is the central one fixing the type of thing the problem is about, with the consequence that the notion of an animal was lost to sight. The centrality of the notion of person represented what we might call a basic framework assumption in the very formulation of the problem.[2]

Whatever the truth in that hypothesis, it is surely hard to escape the conviction that, despite the richness of these debates, the invisibility in them of the notion of an animal represented a gross impoverishment and oversight. This conviction struck a number of philosophers, whose styles and metaphysical inclinations were otherwise quite diverse, more or less simultaneously and independently in the 1980s (or perhaps earlier). Among the philosophers who endorsed this conviction were David Wiggins, Michael Ayers, Paul Snowdon, and Eric Olson in the UK, and Bill Carter and Peter van

---

[1] See Locke 1975, II.xxviii.3, 5–8, 12–15, 21, 29. In these sections Locke regularly alludes to animals and humans in his efforts to settle the nature of personal identity. Currently the interpretation of Locke's discussion is a matter of considerable controversy, but Locke's role in relegating the notion of animal can be acknowledged whichever side one is on in this debate.

[2] The invisibility of the notion of 'animal' in what we are calling the classical period was not of course total. In influential discussions by both Shoemaker and Johnston, the notion does surface. What is striking is how rare this engagement is, and, moreover, how—even when the notion of an animal attracted attention—the assumption was that, of course, the animal is not what we are.

Inwagen in the USA. Although this is not true of all those listed in the previous sentence, the emergence into the debate of the notion of an animal was tied to three basic convictions: first, that where each of us is, there is an animal, a thing belonging to a kind that represents one of our most fundamental categories we operate with; second, that given what seem to be the properties that the animal in question has (in particular, its *psychological* properties), there is something close to a paradox in denying the identity between the animal and the person, and hence there is something close to a paradox in the major views that the dominant tradition was exploring; third, in the light of the force of that type of consideration, we should search very hard for ways to counter the arguments that philosophers provide for denying the identity, since those arguments give the appearance of leading us astray. The initial and shared reason for thinking that there is something close to a paradox in the denial of the identity acquired the name of the 'two lives objection'.[3]

These developments in philosophy were driven primarily by responses within that discipline to the arguments that were taken to be powerful by its practitioners, but other disciplines provided what we might call 'aid and comfort' for the new ideas. Criticisms of what came to be called 'anthropodenial' (i.e. the denial that we are animals) in the writings of such ethologists as Frans de Waal strongly supported animalism.

Once this animalist approach came to the notice of philosophers more generally, and the idea of an animal ceased to be so invisible to philosophers, the debate became much richer, in a way that was dictated by the basic structure of the early animalist writings. One area of debate was the attempt by anti-animalists to discredit the so-called two lives objection.[4] Another area of debate has been the development of anti-animalist arguments that did not surface in the initial period of discussion.[5] However, on the pro-animalist side of the debate, new arguments are emerging and new difficulties in the opposition views are being constructed.[6] We shall spell some of these out in more detail in Section 1.3. The work in the present volume bears testimony to these critical and constructive developments.

1.3. Objections to Animalism

We have emphasized that animalism can be described as an identity thesis (each of us is identical to an animal) and this, we shall argue, illuminates the structure of the debates about it. The fundamental commitment of an identity thesis is that, since the entities in question are supposed to be the same thing, they must have the same properties. So the argumentative strategy of opponents to the claim will be to find a

[3] For early expressions of this line of thought see Carter 1989, Snowdon 1990, Ayers 1991.
[4] See Noonan 1998, Baker 2000, Shoemaker 1999.
[5] See, e.g., Baker 2000, McMahan 2002, Johnston 2007.
[6] See Blatti 2012, Snowdon 2014.

property which one entity has but the other lacks. If that can be found, then however closely they are related, they are not *identical*. Now, if we simply compare in a superficial way ourselves with the animals located where we are, what is striking is how much overlap there is in our properties. We would say that the two things have the same physical properties (e.g. we weigh the same, look the same, etc.), and we share the same biological features (e.g. the two of us are alive, digest food, breathe, reproduce, and so on).[7] So, how might someone argue that there is property difference? One cannot argue that the animal is an animal, but that we are persons, since any animalist will agree with that but claim that what follows is that there is an animal which is a person, and there is no obvious reason to object to that as a possibility.

What supposed differences do philosophers think they have located which support the denial of this identity? One traditional reason for rejecting this identity emerged in the writings of Descartes. He combined the claim that we rational creatures are non-physical selves, or egos, with the further claim that animals are purely physical systems running according to physical-mechanical laws. The conjunction of these claims implied that we things which are selves are not the self-same things as animals. However, in the tradition of debate that the chapters in this volume are situated, this Cartesian conception of an alleged difference in properties has not really had any serious influence. Further, part of Descartes' reasons for thinking that we are non-physical egos is that he believed that a purely physical system is very limited in what it can do, whereas we are capable of an almost unlimited range of achievements due to our rationality. This supposed contrast in capacities, however, is doubly unjustified. First, Descartes really has no good reason to think that he knows what powers purely material things can possess. Either he should have held that he was ignorant of the powers of material things, or, maybe, he should even have inclined to the idea that some matter has very advanced capacities. This latter idea would have amounted, so to speak, to an early discovery of that amazing physical thing, the central nervous system. Second, Descartes had no grounds for supposing he knew what *our* cognitive powers are. Maybe they are much more limited than he knew. The anti-animalists in this volume are not really inspired by such Cartesian reasons.[8]

The supposed property differences between us and the human animal occupying the same space that have seemed to occur to most philosophers are differences in what should be counted as happening to us and to the linked human animal in certain

[7] To anyone who has spent any time on safari, what is most obvious is how the activities and processes that fill the lives of the animals observed there are ones that fill our time too, such activities as cleaning oneself and others, feeding, drinking and excreting, resting, searching for food, etc. These similarities between us and them are what is most striking, though the precise way we, for example, acquire food is different to the way they acquire it. Of course it is also striking that we devote time to things they do not engage in—like writing philosophy, making clothes, and putting up buildings!

[8] Although writers in the present volume do not belong to the Cartesian tradition, there is in current philosophy an approach to the problem of personal identity, known as the Simple View, which, in many of its expositions, resembles the Cartesian approach in its conclusions and its style of argument. Presentations and criticisms of this approach can be found in Gasser and Stefan 2012.

supposedly possible circumstances. Putting it very broadly, these alleged differences between us the animal where we are are modal differences, that is, differences between what is possible for us and what is possible for the human animal. The assumption behind this is that such modal differences are *genuine* differences in properties. This seems to us, and to most people in the debate, a reasonable assumption.

Now, one way to describe these candidate cases is to say that they represent potential disassociations between us and the animal. In traditional discussions these disassociations are of two basic kinds. In one kind of case, the disassociation takes the form of a potential development allegedly resulting in the presence of the animal but not of the original person. End of life cases supply examples that some would describe this way. Suppose some trauma has resulted in permanent loss of mental capacity. Some describe this result as consisting in the human animal remaining but the person as having gone. There are, of course, other candidate cases that elicit this description from some people considering them.

In the second dominant kind of dissociation case, the idea is that a potential sequence of events results in the presence of the person—the thing of our kind—but not of the animal. The best-known and strongly influential example of this sort of case is that of a brain transplant. When most people think about brain transplant examples, making the assumptions that they do, their verdict is that the process preserves the person with the brain, but the animal does not go with the brain and could even be destroyed if, say, what is left of the body minus the brain were destroyed.

Since brain transplant cases have been so influential, they have been the focus of considerable debate, including debate within this volume. The crucial task for anyone using such an argument against animalism is to persuade us that we can say with confidence that the outcome for the person is different from the outcome for the animal. The task for the defender of animalism is to make a convincing case for supposing that we cannot say this with confidence. Now, one point that has emerged is that it is not at all obvious that concentrating within the debate on what are solely brain cases is justified. It might seem that head transplants ground the same pair of dialectically significant contrasting verdicts about the person and the animal. In Chapter 2, Parfit's argument starts with a head transplant case, though he also relies on brain transplant cases too. It would also not be inaccurate to describe Chapter 11, by Campbell and McMahan, as centrally concerned with the philosophical consequences of things that can happen to human heads.

Another issue concerns the basis that people who employ such transplant arguments have for making their judgements about the outcome. Standardly and originally the basis was thought of, and described as, intuition. On hearing the description of the outcome, we simply judge that the person is still there but that the animal need not be. Such relatively immediate judgements were called (philosophical) intuitions. Anyone with any inclination to accept animalism will naturally ask whether such intuitions are reliable. A very interesting viewpoint on this is the one developed by Mark Johnston, some aspects of which figure in Chapter 5 in this volume, according to which there is no good basis to trust our relatively immediate reactions to the description of cases when tracing the fate of the persons involved, but that there are relatively well-established metaphysical principles that support the verdict about the survival of the person upon which the brain transplant argument rests. In contrast, in chapter 9 Rory Madden expresses scepticism about this proposal. It needs pointing out, also, that such transplant arguments rely on our being accurate about what happens to the animal. Are we entitled to be confident about that?

1.4. Animalism and Personal Identity

We have been arguing that animalism can be regarded as an identity thesis, and that this understanding of it illuminates the character of what have been the main types of objections to it. Such dissociation cases are not, of course, the sole type of objection to it, and we shall return to some of those shortly. On the present understanding of animalism, there is a significant contrast between it and what is called Lockeanism (either ancient or modern). The contrast is that animalism is not per se a theory of what is normally called personal identity, whereas Lockeanism is such a theory. When people talk of personal identity, they mean facts about the persistence over time of things that are persons. A theory of personal identity is, then, some attempt to spell out in an informative way what is involved in, or essential for, such facts obtaining. The Lockean answer is that facts about personal persistence are constituted by facts about psychological relations over time. The animalist identity claim does not purport to pick out such essential elements in personal identity. It at most implies that, whatever those facts are, they will be the same as the facts that are constitutive of the animal (with which the person is identical) remaining in existence. Animalists can disagree radically about what those facts are. It is therefore a serious mistake for philosophers to describe a particular approach to personal identity as *the* animalist approach, even if practically all animalists agree with it. For example, it is in principle an unsettled issue what the relation is between animal persistence and life. Most animalists hold that the end of life marks the end of the existence of the animal, but that is a separate and further claim from the core animalist thesis that the person is identical with the animal. Further, whether or not life is essential for animal, and, therefore, personal survival, it is far from clear to what degree something that is an animal of the human kind can lose its parts and remain in existence. Obviously it can lose parts, such as limbs and some organs, and equally obviously it cannot remain in existence after all its parts, say the atoms of which it made, are separated and dispersed. What can we say about other cases though? A serious task for animalism is to make progress with these questions. However, since the notion of an animal is shared between the supporters of the animalist identity thesis and its opponents, this task is also a shared one. Objections to animalism equally rely on assumptions about animals.

Although drawing the contrast between animalism as an identity thesis and animalism as a thesis about *personal* identity is important because it makes the central thesis more precise, doing so also encourages us to think about the basic thesis in broader ways. Thus, if each of us is a human animal and we count ourselves as subjects of experience, it is implied that a human animal is a subject of experience. The question then is: Are there conditions on being single subjects of experience that human animals might fail to satisfy? This is the question that Snowdon engages with in Chapter 13, especially in relation to the idea of the unity of experience, and perhaps cognition, that single subjects must enjoy.

We have argued in this section that animalism per se is not a theory of personal identity, but also that it has a generality that certainly makes it a much broader proposal than being merely a theory of personal identity.

1.5. Issues and Motivations

We want to investigate briefly four other aspects of the content of animalism and to make some remarks about its appeal. The first is what its epistemological status is. We can compare it with the supposed status of standard theories of personal identity. In what we have called the classical period of debate, the working assumption was that we can determine in some suitably a priori manner what our requirements for persistence are. The method was that of classical conceptual analysis, in which intuitive verdicts on described cases were taken to be the method of adjudicating between alternative proposals. Mark Johnston engagingly called this 'the method of cases'.[9] What needs remarking is that the animalist identity thesis is not committed at all to its being an a priori discernible truth. The idea is simply that it is a true identity. One consequence of this status is that proponents of the identity are not committed—when considering supposed counterexamples where there are alleged property differences—to convincing their opponents that simply thinking about their example ultimately will reveal that there is no property difference. The proponent is committed only to convincing the opponent that he or she is not entitled to think they have located a property difference. Requiring more simply reveals a failure to grasp the real status of the proposal.[10]

A second issue concerns the employment of the first person plural pronoun in stating the thesis. Why has that been adopted? One point is that formulating it that way reflects the fact that the basic source of interest in these questions is an interest in our own nature. Each of us naturally asks: What am I? But we also naturally accept that we as a group share a nature, and so we ask: What are we? This represents one justification

---

[9] See Johnston 1987.

[10] The philosopher mentioned earlier as an early animalist who did not see things this way is Wiggins. For him the notion of an animal can be discerned in the best analysis of the notion of a person. His view seemed to be that it is obvious that we are persons, and that philosophy can reveal that the proper analysis of 'person' builds the notion around that of a type of animal. Most animalists, by contrast, do not regard the identity as defensible by that sort of reasoning.

for putting the thesis this way. But, further, there is no obvious noun that picks out the group we wish to talk about. It might seem that the animalist identity could be expressed by saying that (all) persons are animals. But there is no reason to suppose that this picks out the right group. One problem is that—at least according to one standard use of 'person' encapsulated in Locke's famous definition that a person is a being with reason and reflection that can consider itself the same thinking self in different times and places—there is no ground for supposing there could not be persons who are not animals (say, gods, angels, pixies, etc.). On the other hand, if we are interested in what *we* are, there is no reason to exclude from the extension of 'we' creatures like us who lack the psychological faculties that Locke deems necessary for personhood. Of course, there may be other nouns that could be used than 'person', but there seem to be problems with these alternatives as well.

If it is thought that we have a reason to employ the first-person plural pronoun in stating the identity, then a question needs posing and facing. The problem arises because pronouns like 'we' and 'us' do not have strict rules governing their reference. If a speaker uses the word 'we' to pick out a group, it seems that it must include the speaker, but who else it includes is left open simply given the use of 'we'. So, a philosophical identity thesis employing the word 'we' or 'us' raises the question: Which group is meant by 'we'? Our aim here is not to answer that question, but rather simply to highlight it as one that ultimately needs a proper treatment within this debate.

The third issue we want to highlight is that our formulation of animalism as an identity thesis has made no commitment to the claim, which animalists typically endorse, that, as we might put it, if something is an animal, then it is essentially and fundamentally an animal.[11] This way of speaking is surely familiar, even if it is hard to explain in a much fuller way if it is challenged. Another way of putting it is that 'animal' is a high-level sortal term. Let us call this the 'animal as sortal' thesis.

It is clear that the basic identity thesis does not entail the 'animal as sortal' thesis. It is quite obvious that there is no reverse entailment, since many deniers of the identity assume that the 'animal as sortal' thesis is true. Locke seems to have been a prime example. It needs, then, to be recognized that it is possible to hold the identity thesis with or without the 'animal as sortal' thesis.

That leaves two important questions to be faced. The first is whether the sortal thesis is true or not. The second is whether the position that affirms the identity without affirming the sortal thesis is interesting and important or not. We are not proposing to answer those questions here, but simply to point them out as ones that hang over the debate about animalism. Chapter 5 by Mark Johnston engages with this problem.

The fourth area to which we would like to draw attention is the relation between animalism and value theory. Although the question 'What are we?' (and the proposed answers to that question, for example, that we are animals) are not directly about value, it is natural to see links between them. There are various examples of philosophers

---

[11] For an endorsement of this claim see Snowdon 1990, Olson 1997.

proposing links here. For example, Locke's original discussion of personal identity stresses that 'person' is a forensic term, that is, a notion the application of which has implications about responsibility. His arguments frequently appeal to intuitions about responsibility and about concern.[12] More recently Parfit has defended the radical idea that 'identity does not matter' on the basis of an argument resting on aspects of a theory of personal identity. In his case, the assumed account of our persistence conditions is neo-Lockeanism. Further, in some discussions of animalism, when defending it against some objections, appeal has been made to such ideas.[13] So, one general theme, currently somewhat limited, in the literature about animalism has been its links to values (in the broadest sense). Several of the chapters in Part III address themselves to these links.

What are the issues here more generally? One general question is whether there are arguments from claims about value which count against animalism, or such arguments which count for animalism. An example of a line of thought against animalism, deriving from Locke's approach is based on two claims: first, if person x is the same person as y, then x is responsible for everything that y did; and second, to be responsible for an action, a person must be mentally linked to the action, say, by way of remembering it. If both these claims are true, then animalism is in trouble. But in reply it is perfectly reasonable to deny both claims. A person is not necessarily responsible for what he or she did, and there is no rigid prohibition on someone counting as responsible for an action that is not remembered. A further general issue is whether the animalist thesis might clarify our thinking about value. If animalism is correct does that undermine the arguments that Parfit advances to support his claims about value? Or does the idea that we have an animal nature help us to identify what is of value in our lives? These are questions that need investigation. In this volume Chapter 14 by Jens Johansson provides an illuminating and original discussion of some of these issues.

Although it is not our aim to make converts to animalism, nor to argue for the position here, there are some features of the position that seem to us to warrant not simply abandoning it in the face of a few typical philosophical objections. That is to say, we should test such objections thoroughly. Here are four reasons for regarding it this way. First, once one rejects animalism it becomes difficult to propose an account of our nature and persistence conditions that will be complete and intelligible, and which has any chance of generating agreement. Even if neo-Lockeans have satisfactorily answered the standard objections to their view, they seem to have no route to filling in the details of the required psychological links that will look plausible. Those who favour a view based on the notion of the continuance of neural structures enabling consciousness either are tempted to identify us with those inner neural structures, in which we have a self-conception that is more or less incredible, or they identify us in normal times with the larger surrounding entity, but they still face the task of specifying

[12] For one development of the idea that such value concerns are central to Locke, see Strawson 2011.
[13] See Olson 1997, ch. 3.

what neural bundles are necessary and sufficient for persistence, which it is hard to believe can be done in a way that generates agreement. It may be that we have to go in such directions but there is considerable attraction in trying to avoid that. Second, animalism has the singular advantage of being the view that many scientifically know-ledgeable people assume and work within. It should give philosophers some pause when they deny what many people take as more or less obvious.[14] Third, although philosophers have concentrated on analysing the conditions for us remaining in exist-ence over time, we should also aim to achieve some understanding of our spatial extent at a time. Why are these limbs and organs part of me, but, say, my clothes are not? Most so-called theories of personal identity shed no light on this question. We have, though, a well-grounded and clear grasp of the extent at a time of animals. Animalism prom-ises to explain (or illuminate) both our persistence conditions and our spatial extent. Fourth, animalism seems to make available to us explanations of many of our basic features. Thus, if we are animals we can explain why the world contains us in terms of ordinary evolutionary theory. And, we assume, we can explain why we have special concerns about our own futures, and why we are drawn to sex, and eating, and so on, in terms of our nature as animals. There is an explanatory simplicity built into the view.

These points do not force us to accept animalism, but they surely give some support to being reluctant to give up such a view without a real fight. Anyway, the chapters that follow need to be carefully weighed, if these attractions are real.

1.6. Contents

We now wish to highlight some of the issues raised by the contributors, and point to some questions that need asking in light of them. Our approach has to be very select-ive, and we cannot pick out everything that is of significance.

We have arranged the chapters into three broad groups: those that are principally concerned with criticizing animalism (Part I), those that are principally concerned with defending animalism (Part II), and those that are principally concerned with exploring animalism's practical applications (Part III). Of course, this is not the only way the chap-ters might have been arranged, and even by the classifications we adopted, individual chapters might have been grouped differently. (Chapter 11 by Campbell and McMahan, for example, is *both* critical of animalism and an exploration of animalism's implica-tions.) In any case, the reader should follow her interests in determining the sequence in which she moves through the volume; the chapters certainly need not be read in the order in which we have arranged them. A second purpose of this section of our intro-duction, then, can be seen as guiding the reader's determination on how to proceed.

---

[14] For a characteristic affirmation of animalism by a scientist, here is the opening of psychologist Thomas Suddendorf's recent book (2013: 1): 'Biology puts beyond doubt that you are an organism. Like all living organisms, humans metabolize and reproduce. Your genome uses the same dictionary as a tulip and overlaps considerably with the genetic makeup of yeast, bananas, and mice. You are an *animal*.'

Part I

In Chapter 2, Derek Parfit provides an important contribution in presenting his current thinking on animalism, Lockeanism, and the fundamental nature of human persons. Parfit observes that the whole human animal thinks only derivatively, i.e. only in virtue of having a proper part that is directly engaged in thinking. The part of the animal that thinks nonderivatively is not the head, since the head thinks only in virtue of having a thinking brain as a part. Nor is the animal's brain a nonderivative thinker, since it thinks only in virtue of including a thinking cerebrum. And while Parfit never tells us precisely what thing it is that thinks nonderivatively, ultimately there must be a smallest proper part of a human animal that does so: the cerebrum itself maybe, or perhaps some still smaller part. And whatever brain part it is that nonderivatively satisfies Locke's definition of a person ('a thinking intelligent Being, that has reason and reflection, and can consider it self as it self, the same thinking thing in different times and places'), this thing, Parfit says, is what we are. He calls this the 'embodied person view' because this proper part of your animal is a person and this embodied person is you.

Parfit's extended argument for this position consists in demonstrating its utility. For example, this view preserves our intuition about transplant cases: when the part of your brain that thinks nonderivatively is removed from one animal body and implanted into another animal body, you (i.e. the person you are) are thus relocated. The embodied person view can also answer various challenges that the animalist has put to the Lockean. For example, the too many thinkers objection makes the point that the Lockean distinction between persons and animals carries the absurd implication that every thought is had by two thinkers: the person and the animal. But the Lockean who affirms the embodied person view has the resources to avoid this problem: unlike the person who thinks nonderivatively, the animal thinks only by having a part that does. Furthermore, Parfit presents his view as 'an obvious solution' to the thinking parts objection to animalism. For each human animal, there is only one thing—one small part of the animal's brain—that is nonderivatively a Lockean person. To the extent that proper parts of the animal are thinking parts, they are not thinkers in the most important sense. As a result, you can know that you are not an animal because you are whatever thing it is that thinks nonderivatively, and that thing—that person—is not an animal.

Parfit's embodied person view is innovative and represents an important contribution both to the debate over personal identity generally and to the discussion of animalism specifically. Indeed, it is for this reason that we wanted to include this essay in the volume, despite its having appeared in print previously. Nevertheless, the embodied person view relies on some distinctions that will require further scrutiny. One such distinction is the derivative–nonderivative distinction itself. It is unclear, for instance, precisely what conditions a thing must satisfy in order to qualify as being directly involved in thinking. In the absence of this precissification, animalists may suspect that any plausible candidate for being a nonderivative thinker will include as a proper part something that is not directly involved in thinking. The embodied person view also relies on a distinction between two usages of the first-person pronoun. In defending his view against an important objection, Parfit distinguishes the 'Inner-I' used to refer to the Lockean person and the 'Outer-I' used to refer to the human animal. Parfit is certainly not the first Lockean to draw this distinction; Baker (2000, 2007), Noonan (1998, 2001), Strawson (2009), and others have done so as well. But nor is it a distinction that has escaped controversy.[15]

In Chapter 3, Lynne Rudder Baker usefully and carefully presents her distinctive and well-known view of the relation between persons and animals, which is anti-animalist, and which holds that, in standard conditions, the animal constitutes, but is not identical with, the person. She sketches her distinctive elucidation of the constitution relation and its links with predication and truth conditions. She then employs these ideas to try to rebut the core pro-animalist arguments, and finally she adds two new reasons to favour her approach. Her response to the pro-animalist arguments raises the question why we should operate with the logic that she sketches. This is a question that has already received considerable attention, and the conduct of that debate will benefit from her clear and concise presentation. With her novel anti-animalist arguments one rests on the conviction that it is possible to preserve a person while totally replacing the constituting organic matter by inorganic matter, hence removing the animal while preserving the person, and one crucial question is why we should concede that is possible. This question has, at least, two sides. Can we be confident that a non-organic construct can sustain mentality? The other issue is whether we are entitled to be confident that if such an entity is possible it should count as being the person. The other argument rests on the conviction that persons will survive bodily death, a central religious conviction in the Christian tradition, but not something all of us are inclined to think. The argument also relies on the principle that if something is in fact to exist eternally it must be incorruptible. It might seem to those on the outside of the religious debate that God's supposed omnipotence might unlock this problem. However, this interesting argument illustrates the way in which debate about animalism can be, and has been, broadened by its links to theological considerations.

In Chapter 4, Denis Robinson's ambitious aim is to persuade us that what he calls psychological views of our fundamental nature fit well within what we might call a plausible metaphysics of the natural world. In particular, Robinson aims to counter the claim, promoted by Ayers and Olson, that it is a difficulty for non-animalist accounts if they employ the notion of constitution. He starts by engaging with the thought that animalism is more commonsensical than the psychological alternative. Robinson holds that the psychological view implies that entities of different types can coincide, but he suggests that this possibility is one that is not repugnant to common sense, since

---

[15] For discussion, see Noonan 2012 and Olson 2002, 2007: 37–9.

it seems to be an implication of standardly recognized cases in which we start with something, A, and things happen to A resulting in the emergence of a new thing, B, without A ceasing to exist, so that A and another thing B end up coinciding. In such cases there is often a sense in which B emerges gradually, which fits the way in which, supposedly, the human animal develops into a person. The psychological theorist should take 'person' as a substance concept, and, it is argued, the popularity of responses to thought-experiments that favour the psychological account should be granted as evidence that we do indeed operate with such a concept.

Setting aside worries specifically about employing the notion of constitution in the theory of persons, Robinson investigates the general notion, or notions, of constitution. One notion is that of 'minimal constitution' (or 'm-constitution') which applies when two items are constituted at a time by the same material elements. This is contrasted with a more limited notion of constitution linked to the employment of the term by Baker. Robinson's aim is to develop an account of m-constitution, which though not specifically tied to four-dimensionalism, can easily accommodate it. He develops his account by giving a series of suggested examples of m-constitution. For the purpose of this summary, the first example will have to suffice. Robinson has a normal car, from which the doors are removed. Cars without doors can be regarded as a new type of thing called a pre-car, suitable for beach driving. This pre-car has never had doors, but Robinson's old car—which is still there without its doors—did have doors, so the pre-car and the old car are not identical but they are composed of the same matter. In the next section, however, Robinson expands his account to cover what are the important cases of substances in the debate about personal identity, namely substances which are dynamic, constantly evolving and changing their matter (e.g. human animals and perhaps persons). In setting up his account, he also prepares an answer to the query, posed by Olson, as to how there can be different substances with different modal properties composed of the same matter at the same place and time. It is remarked that the categories we employ in describing the world involve lots of ones which merely approximate to full substance concepts, but nonetheless there are good examples of substance concepts. In developing his account of substances of this sort, Robinson alludes to the way of speaking (endorsed by Wiggins, for example) which links substance concepts to principles of activity as insightful, but he tries to make it more precise by bringing in the fundamental notion of immanent causation, operating at different levels. The idea of coincident substances simply represents the idea that two substances constituting processes can happen to converge at a time so that the material base sustaining the appropriate processes are grounded in the same material base. This, it is claimed, does not generate any puzzles.

Robinson ends by acknowledging that there are many uncovered complexities here, some to do with the way that 'person' might be a psychological substance concept, but he suggests that, despite the strong link between human animals and persons of our kind, there can be room for individual human persons to leave behind their animal origins.

Robinson's highly metaphysical and original analysis can, perhaps, be examined at two levels. The first is whether the metaphysical nature of substance concepts and puzzles about them have been properly resolved. The second is whether he has located solid evidence that in discussions about our nature and persistence conditions we need to regard 'person' as a separate substance concept.

In Chapter 5, Mark Johnston provides an extremely rich and multifaceted evaluation of animalism, leading to the conclusion that it is false. This conclusion Johnston regards as the point at which we need to begin the interesting task of saying what we really are, but that is, sadly, a task that he does not attempt in this chapter. The shape of the overall negative argument is familiar from some of his earlier attempts to face up to the problem of personal identity, but the present chapter develops the argument in novel, wide-ranging, and powerful ways, which this summary is barely able to indicate.

Johnston's discussion starts by fixing the target—animalism—as requiring not simply that we are animals, but that we cannot cease to be animals. As he puts it, this latter requirement can be expressed by saying that animalism requires that the kind 'animal' is a substance kind. Johnston begins with the important question: How can we determine whether animalism is true? One candidate method is what Johnston calls 'the method of cases', which is really the method of testing proposed accounts by whether they fit our intuitions about various imagined scenarios. This is taken to be the method of old-fashioned conceptual analysis. Standardly this method is taken to work against animalism, given the normal intuitive verdict on brain transplants (and other cases). In the section 'Some New Worries About the Method of Cases', Johnston opposes this method in the present case. One new argument is that whether dualism is true is an empirical question, so we cannot settle what our basic nature is by an a priori method of cases. A second and new argument is that the best model for the way we apply general concepts is that we rely on 'generic' connexions, which are not exceptionless principles, so our conceptual resources, on which the method of cases relies, does not contain data to determine verdicts about the type of cases that philosophers imagine. This section of argument raises the issue of whether either line of thought does discredit reliance on the method of cases. If Johnston is right then some dialectical benefit accrues to animalism since this method usually is taken to supply counterarguments to animalism. In Johnston's view, though, this relief is merely temporary.

Johnston suggests a new method. At a general level it is to use 'all relevant knowledge and argumentative ingenuity'. With that there could be no quarrel. But at a more specific level Johnston stresses that the kind of thing that we are must be a kind that our ordinary methods of tracing do actually trace. He proposes that his idea initially indicates that we are animals. A significant question is whether there is even this initial link.

The crucial question, though, is whether the type animal is a substance type. After discussing whether 'homo sapiens' is a substance type, and arguing that it is not, Johnston focuses on the central question about 'animal'. Johnston makes two initial points. The first is that ordinary brain transplant arguments, pioneered by Shoemaker, do not settle this question, being examples of the discredited method of cases. The second is that the well-known too-many-thinkers argument for animalism merely shows that we are animals and not that animal is a substance kind. It does not, therefore, support animalism.

This second critical conclusion is correct. The too-many-thinkers argument does not show that animal is a substance kind. However, it is well worth asking (1) whether it remains a significant argument since not everyone, unlike Johnston, does think we are animals; and (2) whether in the original context (and perhaps the abiding context) in which it was proposed the idea that animal is a substance type was more or less taken for granted, in which case it would take us all the way to animalism.

In the rest of the chapter Johnston argues that some fundamental principles about the creation and destruction of persons means that animal is not a substance notion. These principles force us to describe certain cases as ones in which a person who was an animal remains in existence but ceases to be an animal. One of the principles is called No Creation and it says: you do not cause a person to come into being by removing tissue, unless that tissue is suppressing the capacity for reflective mental life. Johnston claims that if this is correct then cases like brain transplants on standard assumptions about the role of the brain in the generation of consciousness and reflection will be examples which merit the above verdict. Johnston himself proposes the gruesome example of a guillotine that chops off heads but also crushes and eviscerates the rest of the body. It should be pointed out that Chapter 9, by Rory Madden, contains a response to this type of argument, and a crucial question is whether that reply seems strong.

In the rest of the chapter Johnston considers and rejects different responses to this problem proposed by van Inwagen and by Olson, and also the proposal that such severed heads can count as animals. This part of the discussion is interesting and forceful, and each significant claim deserves scrutiny. Johnston leaves us at this point, longing to know what he thinks we are, which, of course, he is entitled to in a volume focussed on animalism.

In Chapter 6, Shoemaker continues his defence and elucidation of a modified Lockean account of personal identity, further amplifying a tradition of thought to which he has already made many significant contributions. It is extremely valuable having his recent thinking on this in the volume.

Shoemaker wishes to say that persons are animals with psychological persistence conditions, but that in the space each of us occupies, there is also what he calls a 'biological' animal, which is an entity with biological persistence conditions. He regards this as meaning that 'animal' is ambiguous. Shoemaker follows Unger in holding that what we call animals (e.g. the cats and dogs we have as pets) are animals with psychological persistence conditions, but they themselves also coincide with biological animals. On Shoemaker's reading of the animalist view, it says that persons are animals with biological persistence conditions. The aim of his chapter is to explain how his complex view can escape the so-called 'too many minds' objection to it, which is supposed to support animalism. In Shoemaker's view, the objection arises because we accept physicalism, which seems to imply that physically identical things have the same mental properties, and since the psychological animal and the biological animal have the same physical properties, they will have the same mental life. Shoemaker's response, therefore, is to devise a metaphysics of properties that gives an interpretation of physicalism which blocks this derivation.

Shoemaker's account is centred on the distinction between thick and thin properties. Thin properties (e.g. shape) can be shared by entities of different kinds, whereas thick properties (e.g. mental properties) can be shared only by entities of the same kind. Shoemaker takes properties to be individuated by causal profiles. He distinguishes between causal roles that are defined in terms of effects generated in the entity itself and those that are not defined that way. A possible illustration of this distinction, not given by Shoemaker, is that being radioactive is not defined particularly in terms of effects on the entity itself, whereas being angry is, perhaps, defined in terms of continuing processes within the thing possessing the property. A further aspect of this distinction put forward in Section 6.3 is that a thick property 'partly determines the possessor's persistence conditions'. Shoemaker claims that mental properties are thin in this sense. Then, in Section 6.4, the notion of realization is clarified so that just because an entity possesses the properties which fix that there is a mental property present does not mean that that thing has the mental property. With these clarifications in place, Shoemaker proposes that he has avoided ascribing mental properties to biological animals. Further, in Sections 6.5 through 6.7, he employs the machinery that he has set up to explain the embodiment of psychological subjects, and also to explain and defend talk of bodies and corpses.

The metaphysics that Shoemaker constructs around the concepts described above defies any brief summary and also any brief assessment. The challenge for a reader is to test the approach out as thoroughly as possible.

Part II

Olson devotes Chapter 7 to analysing a key objection to animalism and to assessing the prospects for a satisfactory animalist response to that objection. The objection he considers—the 'remnant persons objection', first developed by Mark Johnston (2007: 45)—is a twist on the more familiar transplant objection. In this case, instead of imagining your cerebrum being installed in the cerebrum-less skull of another human animal, Johnston invites us to consider your cerebrum mid-transplant: removed from your skull, but artificially sustained—in the fabled vat, say. This organ, we can assume, is not only capable of thought in general, but is psychologically just like you. Johnston calls it a 'remnant person'. Animalism, of course, is committed to denying that this remnant person is you, since a cerebrum is not an animal. The official animalist line has it that you are the cerebrum-less organism left behind.

But even beyond this counter-intuitive commitment, animalists face the further challenge of explaining the origin of a remnant person: When does it come into existence? As Olson notes, the person does not exist before the operation, since this would mean that there must have been two persons prior to the procedure: 'you, who according to animalism became a brainless vegetable, and the remnant person, who became a 'naked brain'. And yet the alternative answer—that the person came into existence when your cerebrum was removed from your skull—looks to be equally problematic. First of all, it seems absurd to think that a person could be *created* simply by cutting away sustaining human tissue. A further problem emerges once we imagine what the animalist must say about the fate of remnant people in transplant operations. When your cerebrum is installed in my body, I do not become you, the remnant person. According to animalism, I am the same organism that previously lacked a cerebrum; I was never a cerebrum in a vat. But this suggests that, by animalism's lights, the result of the transplant is the *destruction* of the remnant person. Consequently, neither answer to the origin question appears to be open to the animalist. Claiming that the person existed prior to the cerebrum's removal commits the animalist to affirming the existence of multiple persons for each human animal, while claiming that the person came into existence when the cerebrum was removed commits the animalist to the two absurdities just described.

Olson devotes the remainder of his chapter to exploring several possible strategies whereby an animalist can avoid these absurdities while still accounting for the 'sort of thing the remnant person would be, where she could come from, what would happen to her at the end of the operation and why, and how she would relate to you and me'. He rules out the possibility that the remnant person could be you after considering three ways that an animalist might defend this claim—'accidentalism', 'scattered animalism', and Madden's (2011) 'remote-thought hypothesis'—and finding all of them unconvincing. And Olson's objections to the proposal that the remnant person could be your cerebrum—what he calls 'remnant cerebralism'—are equally withering. The last strategy that Olson explores appeals to van Inwagen's (1990) answer to the special composition question in denying the existence of a remnant person. Olson calls this proposal—'brain eliminativism'—'drastic', but offers no further criticism, and one has the sense that, of the various strategies open to the animalist, this is the one that Olson regards as the least unpromising, as it were.

Nevertheless, Olson concedes that he can see no really satisfying animalist solution to the remnant-person problem, but that this constitutes reason to reject animalism 'only if our being animals is the source of the problem'. And in the final section of the chapter, Olson argues that this is not the case, i.e. that the remnant persons problem represents a challenge to animalism no more than it does to nearly all of animalism's main rivals. The one exception, Olson recognizes, is the brain view, according to which we *are* our brains (or, perhaps, our cerebrums).

In Chapter 8, Stephan Blatti focuses on what might be called the standard objection to the standard argument. The standard argument for animalism—the 'thinking animal argument'—was developed and refined over the years by Ayers, Carter, McDowell, Snowdon, and Olson. This argument registers the implausible multiplication of thinkers to which anyone who denies animalism's identity thesis is thereby committed. According to one formulation of the standard argument, since animals think, and since you think, if the identity thesis is false, then there must be two qualitatively identical mental lives running in parallel: yours and that of the animal located where you are. But since this is absurd, we should accept the identity thesis. The standard objection to this argument—one that animalism's supporters and critics alike regard as posing a formidable challenge—points out that an analogous line of reasoning seems to recommend the opposite conclusion. Since thinking is plausibly attributed to many of an animal's proper parts—e.g. its undetached head, its brain—what entitles the animalist to suppose that each of us is the whole thinking animal rather than any one of the animal's many thinking parts? This sceptical question reflects the 'thinking parts problem'.

Blatti's aim is not to solve this problem, but to outline several strategies that animalists might pursue further in attempting to escape the thinking parts problem without renouncing the thinking animal argument. According to one of these strategies, the animalist answers the sceptical question directly by appealing to Tim Williamson's (2000) recent attack on the 'phenomenal conception of evidence' and its role in sceptical scenarios like the one envisioned by the thinking parts problem. According to this conception, a subject's phenomenal state just is her evidentiary state. But, Blatti suggests, if Williamson is correct that this conception is false because knowledge is factive, then the sort of evidence to which we would ordinarily appeal in ascribing thinking to the whole animal (e.g. the fact that the sensory, proprioceptive, and kinesthetic experiences that your proper, thinking parts have are detected in parts of the whole animal that are not parts of themselves) *does* in fact ground our claim to know—indeed, consists in our knowledge—that each of us is the whole thinking animal rather than any of its thinking parts.

The second main strategy that Blatti explores involves short-circuiting the thinking parts problem by challenging the attribution of thinking to proper parts in the first place. Here he distinguishes Wittgensteinian from non-Wittgensteinian resistance to such ascriptions. For the Wittgensteinian, to ascribe psychological activities to a proper part is to subsume under the concept *human animal* something that does not fall under that concept. Thinking cannot intelligibly be attributed proper parts like heads and brains, on this view, because the criteria for the ascription of thinking lie in the behaviour of a whole animal, and proper parts do not behave. The non-Wittgensteinian diagnosis that Blatti sketches reaches the same conclusion by a different route. Rather than pointing to conceptual confusion as the culprit, he urges us to reflect on the contexts in which attributions of thinking are ordinarily made: not in isolation, let alone in the course of philosophical argument, but embedded in practices of agential understanding and moral concern. In other words, it is in our attempts to describe, explain, praise, and blame one another's actions that we credit ourselves with various cognitive and affective capacities. This, Blatti suggests, is the reason why animalism's critic is mistaken in attributing thinking to a human animal's parts: because the only behaviour eligible for agential understanding and moral concern is the behaviour of the whole animal.

The aim of Blatti's paper is not to pursue any one of these strategies as far as they go, but to provide a roadmap for other animalists to do so. Nevertheless, it must be admitted that, for all of the strategies Blatti sketches, the devil lurks in the details, and some of those details—such as Williamson's conception of knowledge as evidence and Wittgenstein's account of conceptual criteria—are highly contentious indeed.

In Chapter 9, Rory Madden's very rich contribution starts from a recently devised problem for what he calls the naïve thesis, which is the idea that we are things which have a human shape, and that the things within that shape are our parts. This is summarized in the words that we are humanoids. As he points out, this thesis is not the same as animalism, since it is possible to hold that we are constituted by the animal where we are, even though we are not identical to that animal, but we would then share the animal's shape. Clearly, though, animalists are committed to the naïve thesis. The problem in its initial formulation is epistemological. It relies on a number of assumptions and so takes some time to formulate properly, even in summary form.

It starts from the naturalistically inspired thesis that the parts of us that are responsible for generating consciousness and thought are just a small part of us. Most of us would say that these parts, which Madden calls our T-parts, are more or less the same as the brain. To this can be added the idea that just as our T-parts are what enable us to have a viewpoint, our T-parts are also parts of other entities, whose existence we seem to recognize. Thus my T-part is also part of my head, and of my upper body, etc. Now, it would seem that if I have a viewpoint in virtue of the processes in the T-parts that I contain, then anybody who contains those same T-parts thereby also acquires a viewpoint, indeed the same viewpoint. So this means that my head has a point of view, as does my upper body, as does anything that overlaps with my T-parts. If that is right, then our knowledge that *we* are humanoids is threatened. The reason is, roughly, that it is not implausible to say that it is a condition on a ground for a belief to count as knowledge-generating that it will not generate errors in most subjects who form beliefs on its basis. However, most of my overlappers will form the false belief that they are humanoid on the basis of the experiences which lead me to think I am humanoid. Given this epistemological principle, it would seem to follow that I do not know that I am humanoid. In which case it also seems to follow that I do not know that I am an animal. Madden remarks that he agrees with Olson in thinking that this is a far more troublesome problem for animalism than the familiar traditional anti-animalist arguments.

In Madden's engagement with this argument a rich and very interesting range of responses are developed and explored. What stands out is that the argument relies on a fair number of diverse assumptions, allowing a wide range of potential replies. One response he mentions is what he calls 'eliminativism', the view that there are no such things as undetached parts of us. If there are no overlappers then the problem vanishes. Some philosophers affirm this negative ontological claim. Madden's response is not to affirm categorically the existence of overlappers, but to suggest, surely plausibly, that it is hard to feel confident that there are no such things as my head or my hands or my fingers. Indeed, such a response is almost as paradoxical as the original sceptical conclusion. We are to save the idea that we know we are humanoid by being sceptical that there are such things as heads, knees, and toes.

Conceding then that there might be overlappers, there is the rough distinction, introduced by Olson and followed by Madden, between potential solutions that query the epistemological assumptions and those that reject the psychological assumptions relied on in the argument. The first epistemological response he sets out is to deny that the fact that my overlappers on the basis of the same grounds as I have will go wrong and so discredit the idea that I have knowledge about my shape and parts. The suggestion is that it is not at all obvious that I and my overlappers are basing our convictions on what should be thought of as the same grounds. Madden calls this move 'evidential-externalism'. Madden's view is that more needs to be said if this response is to look persuasive, but he does not rule some such addition out. Madden then develops what he calls a thought-theoretic response. The proposal to be explored starts from the idea that to entertain thoughts about oneself one needs to be acquainted with oneself, which involves having genuine channels of information about oneself. What Madden then explores is the thought that this requires mechanisms that have the natural function of supplying such information. If something like this is true then there is a reason to disallow that the so-called overlappers have acquaintance with themselves, since it would be very implausible to claim that there are mechanisms in our bodies with such a natural function. The third potential response that Madden articulates (in Section 9.3) proposes that the elucidation of what a mental subject is—that is to say, being a thing with a point of view and consciousness—involves the idea that the grounds of consciousness within it must have the proper natural function of interceding between the inputs and the outputs of the things itself. To this can be added the suggestion that the neural structures within humans have that function for the human, and not for the overlappers. The consequence would be that the overlappers are not in fact minded, even though they contain within themselves structures that ground consciousness. Madden carefully explores this proposal and suggests ways of developing it.

Finally, Madden engages with the remnant persons problem as proposed by Johnston and Parfit. He points out that this objection is not the same as the main one he is considering. His response to this consists in giving counterexamples to the basic assumption in the way that problem is set up, which is that shrinking an entity cannot create a new thing of the same sort as you started with. Madden's example comes from biology.

This summary leaves out most of the fascinating details of Madden's discussion. His chapter does raise many questions. One is whether the general idea of function plays the roles in our understanding of knowledge and of having a mind that his response to the main sceptical argument requires. Another important question is whether there might be other responses than the ones Madden explores. Overall, Madden's discussion encourages animalists in their suspicion that the sceptical argument rests on too many assumptions to be genuinely convincing.

In Chapter 10, David B. Hershenov engages with a very important question about animalism, which can be expressed in these words: How does animalism stand within a four-dimensionalist approach to ontology? Most supporters of animalism work in a non-four-dimensionalist framework, and perhaps, as one might put it, simply hope that the view's status is not affected by the choice of a different basic metaphysics. Hershenov's discussion aims to make a case for the truth of this claim or hope by critically examining the arguments of Hud Hudson, whom Hershenov describes, as having 'thought longer and harder about this topic' than anyone else he knows. Hershenov proceeds by picking out two lines of thought that Hudson proposes and trying to counter them. The first is, roughly, that according to the animalist the person has early stages which are mindless, but since according to the dominant type of four-dimensionalism there will be countless objects with early stages that are mindless, this will mean that there are 'an infinite number of entities that are persons', which is absurd. The second argument that Hudson proposes is that stages of animals contain elements that are not involved in thinking, whereas it is less arbitrary to restrict person stages to bits that are directly relevant to the production of thought. To the first argument Hershenov replies, roughly, that it is not at all arbitrary to have a view according to which persons have stages which are 'unminded', since these early stages have a crucial causal role in the final generation of the minded stages, when what we have is a developing animal. To the second argument Hershenov replies that it is far less easy than philosophers assume to restrict the generation of mindfulness to the brain. This is bold, and is clearly not a point the significance of which solely concerns the particular purposes of Hershenov's chapter. In the final two sections, Hershenov argues with considerable forcefulness that our judgements (or intuitions) about our persistence—as revealed, for example, in our attitude of prudential concern—indicate that what we are best regarded as tracking are the human animals we are (according to animalism). This part of his argument links to and contrasts with Johansson's treatment of prudence. It is clear that Hershenov has, in this chapter, contributed in a major way to two debates. The first debate is the one mentioned earlier about the status of animalism within a four-dimensionalist ontology. The second debate is, of course, the general assessment of the arguments which are critical of animalism and which can be presented within other more standard ontologies. Of particular importance here is his attempt to oppose some of the pressures to shrink the person to something more or less like the brain.

Part III

In Chapter 11, Tim Campbell and Jeff McMahan do two very important things. They construct what they see as counterexamples to the animalist identity based on the cases where either there are what might be called two-headed animals and cases where there are what might be called two animals sharing a single head. About these cases they claim that either they involve two subjects or selves and a single animal—in which case both subjects cannot be the animal, hence one is not an animal—or they involve one subject and two animals, and since there is no reason to identify the self with one of the animals rather than the other, it cannot be either animal. These cases are extremely interesting, and one issue is whether Campbell and McMahan adjudicate them correctly. But the second crucial issue is what it would show if they are right about these cases. They simply assert that we—standard and typical humans—are the same sort of thing as the selves in these odd cases. But is that a legitimate assumption? The second thing they do is to develop a conception of ourselves according to which we either are brains or are constituted by brains (or parts of brains). A very basic question is whether this conception is supported by consideration of the examples, but also whether such an approach has any plausibility.

Mark D. Reid begins Chapter 12 by surveying what he calls counterexamples to animalism which 'involve duplication', and he concludes that the standard ones are 'inconclusive'. Reid proposes a new potential counterexample, which he urges us to regard as 'conclusive'. His extremely ingenious and novel case in effect combines brain splitting (with a severed corpus callosum) plus a process called 'Intracarotid Amytal Procedure', in which one cerebral hemisphere is in effect disabled by the selective injection of some substance leaving the other hemisphere capable of operating. Reid envisages that what happens is that on one day one hemisphere is disabled and then on the next day the other hemisphere is disabled, and so on. This is envisaged as happening from birth (or even earlier). Reid's claim is that the best description of the result is that there are two distinct persons created in a single animal, whom we might call 'Lefty' and 'Righty'. Each sleeps during the day the other is awake. In his paper Reid carefully develops and evaluates the issues that are involved in this case. Looked at in a general way there are two big questions the imagined case raises. The first concerns the overall logic. Suppose we agree with Reid's description of what has happened, namely the creation of two persons in a single (human) animal. Is that a serious problem for animalism? This issue arises for the argument developed in Campbell and McMahan, and so we shall not spell it out again. The second issue is whether Reid's description of what this case involves is correct. We need to remind ourselves that, if we think about the case in terms of what is happening to the single human animal, then we have to count it as involving a single functioning entity, the animal, which is being damaged by a complex surgical procedure. Having to think that way about the animal, it seems fair to say, must have some weight in deciding how we are to describe it in terms of 'persons' and 'subjects'. However, this new case merits careful scrutiny.

In Chapter 13, Paul Snowdon attempts to broaden the exploration of animalism. The chapter tries to work out what implications animalism has about the conditions for different mental states to belong to a single subject. When we are talking about experiences this might be called the unity of consciousness. Focussing on the example of split-brain cases, it is argued that animalism is committed to a singularist verdict; that is, the verdict that the post-operative states are states of a single subject, despite the functional disunity among them. It is then argued that no contradiction can be generated in psychological theories for such single subjects, nor are there principles of interpretation (of a kind proposed by Davidson) that such a psychological theory must flout. Nor are there, contrary to what Tim Bayne proposes, any principles about inferences a single subject must make in relation to first-person beliefs, which create difficulties for this account. When the debate focuses on experiences it is argued that no reason exists not to count the various experiences that the post-operative patients enjoy as experiences of a single subject. Nagel, it is claimed, fails to unearth any principle that rules this out. In conclusion, it is proposed that the question as to what degree of unity the mental states of a single subject must possess is an empirical one, and there are no reliable a priori principles that we can discern.

Various questions can be raised about this argument. Does the chapter really explain how to avoid problems for singularism in relation to split-brain cases? Does it seriously disarm the Nagelian intuition that the experiences of a single subject must have some strong degree of functional unity? Are there perhaps other more difficult cases for the singularism to which animalism is committed?

Jens Johansson starts Chapter 14 by helpfully clarifying the animalist thesis. Having done that, the paper aims to analyse and evaluate some problems for animalism that arise out of our attitudes to prudential concern and moral responsibility. One can say, therefore, that Johansson's chapter belongs in the general category of considering issues about animalism that relate to value theory. In particular, Johansson engages with replies, suggested by Olson (1997), to some possible arguments of this sort that are critical of animalism. These issues arise from both the nature of what is called 'prudential concern' and from assumptions that we make about moral responsibility, though here we shall restrict the summary to the case of prudential concern. That is meant to be the special sort of concern that someone feels about something that is taken by them to be going to happen to *them*. The problem for animalism arises from two assumptions. The first assumption, which might appear truistic given the previous characterization, is that if, say, X is reasonably prudentially concerned about the future occurrence of E then E must be happening to X, i.e. X is the person to whom E will be happening. This links (reasonable) prudence to personal identity. The second, more controversial assumption, is that if looking ahead X knows that the person undergoing E will be linked psychologically to X in the way that a cerebrum transplant from X into some other object will bring about then it will be reasonable for X to be prudentially concerned about the occurrence of E. If that is granted then it implies that transplanting the cerebrum of X preserves and takes with it the person X, a proposition that is normally thought of as inconsistent with animalism. Olson's clever response to this line of thought is to deny the first and apparently truistic claim that proper prudential concern requires identity with the person undergoing E. Olson points out that Parfit and Shoemaker have already made a convincing case against this. Johansson agrees, but adds that Olson has not *shown* that there are no related principles about prudence that can be used to generate an anti-animalist conclusion. Johansson's clever and novel move to break this logjam is to suggest that we focus on the entity that is agreed to be the animal present in the scenarios. Two things now seem true. First, we know (or we can assume) that the animal does not go with the cerebrum and whatever psychological connexions it generates. But if it is plausible to say that the person is reasonably prudentially concerned about the future occurrence of E it seems equally plausible to say that the animal is also reasonably prudentially concerned. If both things are granted then it turns out that the range of reasonable prudence does not conflict with animalism. In this move Johansson is attempting to make progress, as he himself points out, in a way that animalists have done in other areas in the debate, which is to ask participants to think about what we should say about the animal which is agreed to be present. This provides, or appears to provide, a significant anchor to speculation about what should be said. The important question that now arises if there still is to be debate about these issues is whether Johansson's judgements about the animal are correct. But another important issue is whether someone trying to deny animalism and sustain the person/animal contrast can do that plausibly once we remember that both fall in the domain of practical reason. Has Johansson here provided us with a strengthening of the so-called 'two-lives' argument?

Like Johansson, David Shoemaker is also concerned with animalism's normative import. In Chapter 15, he addresses animalism's apparent inability to account for the practical concerns of human persons. Shoemaker formulates this objection as an argument against the plausibility of animalism, as follows: '(1) animalism lacks the proper fit with the set of our practical concerns; (2) if a theory of personal identity lacks the proper fit with the set of our practical concerns, it suffers a loss in plausibility; thus, (3) animalism suffers a loss in plausibility (in particular to psychological criteria of identity)'. In response to this objection—which he labels 'Challenge'—Shoemaker considers three possible replies, each of which is extrapolated from recent work by David DeGrazia (2005), Marya Schechtman (2010), and Olson (1997).

According to Shoemaker, both DeGrazia and Schechtman would reply to Challenge by denying (1). In DeGrazia's case, (1) is rejected on the grounds that, as far as what is known about the actual world, the persistence of human animals is at least a necessary condition for the possession of those psychological characteristics which, in turn, ground such practical concerns as moral responsibility, prudential concern, and the like. By DeGrazia's lights, this fact is enough to block the inference to (3)—i.e. to prevent animalism from suffering any loss in plausibility. Schechtman too would contend that animalism is perfectly capable of accounting for the practical concerns of human persons. But on her view, the route to (1)'s rejection is more ambitious, involving appeal to an expansive notion of personhood—what she calls a 'person-life'—which 'incorporate[s] the metaphysical insights of animalism in a way that allows that theory to produce the desired practical implications'. Ultimately, however, Shoemaker finds that neither DeGrazia's nor Schechtman's denials of (1) result in what an adequate response to Challenge really demands, which is an explanation of the justificatory role played by identity *qua* necessary condition for our practical concerns, where that explanation is both robust and informative (in senses that Shoemaker describes).

More promising, Shoemaker argues, is Olson's reply to Challenge, which involves denying not (1), but (2). According to Olson, the intuition many of us report concerning familiar brain-transplant scenarios—i.e. that persons go where their psychological-continuity-preserving organs go—may not track any particular theory of personal identity, but *only* our practical concerns. And in that case, animalism may be true regardless of its failure to explain adequately our practical concerns.

But as Shoemaker points out, even if Olson is correct that the transplant intuition *may* reflect only our practical concerns and thus *can* be divorced from any particular account of personal identity, it does not follow that the plausibility of a theory of personal identity is not impacted by the degree to which it jibes with our practical concerns. As a result, Olson's attack on (2) is not sufficiently strong. On Shoemaker's view, what is required in order to undermine (2)—and, thereby, to block the inference to (3)—is a defence of the claim that '*none* of the relations or elements in which numerical identity consists matter, so that the correct theory of personal identity will contain nothing of relevance to our practical concerns'. This is precisely the claim that Shoemaker proceeds to defend in the concluding section of the chapter—what he calls the 'Identity Really *Really* Doesn't Matter View.'

We are very grateful to the contributors for the chapters they have produced. Their work, we feel, is testimony to the richness of the debate about animalism that already exists, but we also believe and hope that it will act as a stimulus to enrich the debate beyond its present bounds.[16]

References

Ayers, M. R., 1991, *Locke*, 2 vols, London: Routledge.

Baker, L. R., 2000, *Persons and Bodies: A Constitution View*, Cambridge: Cambridge University Press.

Baker, L. R., 2007, *The Metaphysics of Everyday Life*, Cambridge: Cambridge University Press.

Blatti, S., 2012, 'A New Argument for Animalism,' *Analysis* 72: 685–90.

Carter, W. R., 1989, 'How to Change Your Mind,' *Canadian Journal of Philosophy* 19: 1–14.

DeGrazia, D., 2005, *Human Identity and Bioethics*, Cambridge: Cambridge University Press.

Gasser, G. and Stefan, M., 2012, *Personal Identity*, Cambridge: Cambridge University Press.

Johnston, M., 1987, 'Human Beings,' *Journal of Philosophy* 84: 59–83.

Johnston, M., 2007, '"Human Beings" Revisited: My Body is Not an Animal,' in *Oxford Studies in Metaphysics*, vol. 3, D. W. Zimmerman (ed.), Oxford: Oxford University Press, 33–74.

Locke, J., 1975, *An Essay Concerning Human Understanding*, P. Nidditch (ed.), Oxford: Clarendon Press.

Madden, R., 2011, 'Externalism and Brain Transplants,' in *Oxford Studies in Metaphysics*, vol. 6, K. Bennett and D. W. Zimmerman (eds), Oxford: Oxford University Press.

McMahan, J., 2002, *The Ethics of Killing: Problems at the Margins of Life*, Oxford: Oxford University Press.

Noonan, H. W., 1998, 'Animalism versus Lockeanism: A Current Controversy,' *Philosophical Quarterly* 48: 302–18.

Noonan, H. W., 2001, 'Animalism versus Lockeanism: Reply to Mackie,' *Philosophical Quarterly* 51: 83–90.

---

[16] We also thank Nicolle Brancazio for her assistance in preparing the Index.

Noonan, H. W., 2012, 'Personal Pronoun Revisionism: Asking the Right Question,' *Analysis* 72: 316–18.

Olson, E. T., 1997, *The Human Animal: Personal Identity Without Psychology*, New York: Oxford University Press.

Olson, E. T., 2002, 'Thinking Animals and the Reference of "I",' *Philosophical Topics: Identity and Individuation* 30: 189–208.

Olson, E. T., 2007, *What Are We? A Study in Personal Ontology*, New York: Oxford University Press.

Schechtman, M., 2010, 'Personhood and the Practical,' *Theoretical Medicine and Bioethics* 31: 271–83.

Shoemaker, S., 1999, 'Self, Body, and Coincidence,' *Proceedings of the Aristotelian Society: Supplementary Volume* 73: 287–306.

Snowdon, P. F., 1990, 'Persons, Animals, and Ourselves,' in *The Person and the Human Mind: Issues in Ancient and Modern Philosophy*, C. Gill (ed.), Oxford: Clarendon Press, 83–107.

Snowdon, P. F., 2014, *Persons, Animals, Ourselves*, Oxford: Oxford University Press.

Strawson, G., 2009, *Selves: An Essay in Revisionary Metaphysics*, Oxford: Oxford University Press.

Strawson, G., 2011, *Locke on Personal Identity*, Princeton, NJ: Princeton University Press.

Suddendorf, T., 2013, *The Gap: The Science of What Separates Us from Other Animals*, New York: Basic Books.

Van Inwagen, P., 1990, *Material Beings*, Ithaca, NY: Cornell University Press.

Williamson, T., 2000, *Knowledge and Its Limits*, Oxford: Oxford University Press.

PART I

2

We Are Not Human Beings

Derek Parfit

2.1.

We can start with some science fiction.[1] Here on Earth, I enter the Teletransporter. When I press some button, a machine destroys my body, while recording the exact states of all my cells. This information is sent by radio to Mars, where another machine makes, out of organic materials, a perfect copy of my body. The person who wakes up on Mars seems to remember living my life up to the moment when I pressed the button, and is in every other way just like me.

Of those who have thought about such cases, some believe that it would be I who would wake up on Mars. They regard Teletransportation as merely the fastest way of travelling. Others believe that, if I chose to be Teletransported, I would be making a terrible mistake. On their view, the person who wakes up would be a mere Replica of me.

This disagreement is about personal identity. To describe such disagreements, we can first distinguish two kinds of sameness. Two black billiard balls may be qualitatively identical, or exactly similar. But they are not numerically identical, or one and the same ball. If I paint one of these balls red, it will cease to be qualitatively identical with itself as it was; but it will still be one and the same ball. Consider next a claim like, 'Since her accident, she is no longer the same person'. This claim involves both senses of identity, since it means that *she*, one and the same person, is *not* now the same person. That is not a contradiction, since it means that this person's character has changed. This numerically identical person is now qualitatively different.

When people discuss personal identity, they are often discussing what kind of person someone is, or wants to be. That is the question involved, for example, in an identity crisis. But I shall be discussing our numerical identity. In our concern about our own futures, that is what we have in mind. I may believe that, after my marriage, I shall be a different person. But that does not make marriage death. However much I change,

---

[1] This chapter is taken from material written with the support of a Foundational Research Grant from the Ammonius Foundation, for whose generosity I am very grateful. I hope to publish other parts of this material elsewhere. I have been much helped by comments from Eric Olson, Sydney Shoemaker, and Ingmar Persson.

I shall still be alive if there will be someone living who will be me. And in my imagined case of Teletransportation, my Replica on Mars would be qualitatively identical to me; but, on the sceptic's view, he wouldn't *be* me. *I* shall have ceased to exist. That, we naturally assume, is what matters.

In questions about numerical identity, we use two names or descriptions, and we ask whether these refer to the same person. In most cases, we use descriptions that refer to people at different times. Thus, when using the telephone, we might ask whether the person to whom we are speaking now is the same as the person to whom we spoke yesterday. To answer such questions, we must know the *criterion* of personal identity over time, by which I mean: the relation between a person at one time, and a person at another time, which makes these one and the same person. We can also ask what kind of entity we *are*, since entities of different kinds continue to exist in different ways.

Views about what we are, and how we might continue to exist, can be placed, roughly, in three main groups. On some views, what we are, or have as an essential part, is a soul: an immaterial persisting entity, which is indivisible, and whose continued existence must be all-or-nothing. Even if we don't believe in immaterial souls, many of us have some beliefs about ourselves, and personal identity, that would be justified only if some such view were true. Though such views make sense, and might have been true, I shall not discuss them here, since we have strong evidence that no such view is true.

Of the other views, some can be called *Lockean*. Locke famously defined a person as 'a thinking intelligent being that has reason and reflection and can consider itself as itself, the same thinking thing in different times and places'.[2] Lockean criteria of identity appeal to the kind of psychological continuity that, in my imagined case, holds between me and my Replica. On the Lockean view that I have earlier defended, which I called

the Narrow, Brain-Based Psychological Criterion: If some future person would be uniquely psychologically continuous with me as I am now, and this continuity would have its normal cause, enough of the same brain, this person would be me. If some future person would neither be uniquely psychologically continuous with me as I am now, nor have enough of the same brain, this person would *not* be me. In all other cases, there would be no answer to the question whether some future person would be me. But there would be nothing that we did not know.

On this view, my Replica would not be me, since he would not have my brain. That, I claimed, would not matter, since being destroyed and Replicated would be as good as ordinary survival. I shall later return briefly to that claim. The other main kind of view appeals not to psychological but to biological continuity, and is now often called *Animalist*.

In considering this disagreement, I shall first describe some animalist objections to the various Lockean views that were put forward, in the 1960s, 1970s, and 1980s, by such people as Shoemaker, Quinton, Perry, Lewis, and me. As Snowdon, Olson, and

---

[2] John Locke, *Essay Concerning Human Understanding*, Book II, Chapter XXVI, Section 9.

other Animalists pointed out, we Lockeans said nothing about the human beings—or to use a less ambiguous phrase, the human animals—that many of us think we are.

If persons are, in the Lockean sense, entities that can think about themselves, and whose continued existence essentially involves psychological continuity, a human embryo or fetus is not a person. But this embryo or fetus is, or becomes, a human animal. This animal's body, Lockeans claim, later becomes the body of a Lockean person. Animalists ask: What then happens to the human animal? It would be convenient for Lockeans if this animal retired from the scene, by ceasing to exist, thereby leaving its body under the sole control of the newly existing person. But that is not what happens. Most human animals continue to exist, and start to have thoughts and other experiences. So if Lockeans distinguish between persons and human animals, their view implies that whenever any person thinks some thought, a human animal also thinks this thought. Every thinking of a thought has two different thinkers. That conclusion seems absurd. As McDowell writes: 'surely there are not two lives being led here, the life of the human being... and the life of the person'.[3] We can call this the *Too Many Thinkers Problem*.

There may also be an *Epistemic Problem*. If there are two conscious beings thinking all my thoughts, the person and the animal, how could I know which one I am? If I think I am the person, Animalists object, I might be mistaken, since I may really be the animal.

There is a third problem. Snowdon pointed out that, on Locke's definition, human animals qualify as persons.[4] So if Lockeans distinguish persons from human animals, they must admit that, on their view, all of our thoughts and other experiences are had by two persons, one of whom is also an animal. This objection may seem decisive, by undermining the whole point of this Lockean distinction. We can call this the *Too Many Persons Problem*.

Several Lockeans have suggested answers to these objections. Shoemaker, for example, argues that, if we claim animals to be entities whose criterion of identity is biological, and requires the continued existence of much of their bodies, such animals could not think, or have other mental states, since the concepts that refer to mental states apply only to entities whose criterion of identity is psychological. Though these human animals might seem to have thoughts and experiences, that would not really be true.[5]

Baker argues that the animal and the person are both constituted by the same body, which gives them an ontological status that is in between being one and the same entity and being two, separately existing entities. For that reason, Baker claims, though there

---

[3] John McDowell, 'Reductionism and the First Person', in *Reading Parfit*, edited by Jonathan Dancy (Oxford: Blackwell 1997) p. 237.

[4] 'Persons, Animals, and Ourselves', in *The Person and the Human Mind*, edited by Christopher Gill (Oxford: Oxford University Press, 1990) p. 90.

[5] 'On What We Are', in *The Oxford Handbook of the Self*, edited by Shaun Gallagher (Oxford: Oxford University Press, 2011). In what follows, I shall not be rejecting Shoemaker's view, but proposing another, simpler way of thinking about ourselves.

are, strictly, two different thinkers thinking each of our thoughts, we can count these thinkers as if they were one.[6]

We can next distinguish between concepts which are *substance sortals*, in the sense that they apply to some persisting entity whenever it exists, and *phase sortals,* which apply to some entity, in the present tense, only while this entity has certain properties. Two such phase sortals are 'teenager' and 'caterpillar'. When we reach the age of twenty, we cease to be teenagers, but we don't thereby cease to exist. Nor do caterpillars cease to exist when they become butterflies.

I have earlier suggested that, in response to these animalist objections, Lockeans should claim that the concept of a person is another phase sortal. [7] On this view, we are human animals who began to exist as an embryo or fetus though we were not then persons in the Lockean sense. And if we suffered brain damage which made us irreversibly unconscious, we would continue to exist, though we would have ceased to be persons. One of Locke's aims was to describe persons in the way that makes most sense of our practical and moral beliefs. 'Person', Locke writes, 'is a forensic term', applying only to responsible rational beings. We could keep this part of the Lockean view if we claim that we have certain reasons, and certain principles apply to us, only while we are persons. For example, I might point to an ultrasound image of an embryo or fetus, saying 'There I am. That was me', but adding that, since I was not then a person, it would not have been wrong for some doctor to kill me. We might make similar claims about the concept of a human being. We might say that, just as an acorn with one green shoot sprouting is not yet an oak tree, an embryo is not yet a human being. And some other moral principles apply to us, we might claim, only after we become human beings.

Lockeans, I now believe, need not retreat to any such claim. There is another, stronger Lockean view that can answer the Animalist objections that I have described. This view also avoids some problems that face Animalist views. So I shall next describe these other problems.

2.2.

Most Animalists believe that we shall continue to exist if and only if our bodies continue to exist, and to be the bodies of living animals. Williams even claimed that persons *are* bodies.[8] But suppose that, in   ✳

Transplanted Head, my body is fatally diseased, as is Williams's brain. Since we have, between us, only one good brain and body, surgeons bring these together. My head is successfully grafted onto the rest of Williams's headless body.

[6] Baker, Lynne Rudder, *Persons and Bodies* (Cambridge: Cambridge University Press, 2000).
[7] In my 'Persons, Bodies, and Human Beings', written around 1992, published in *Contemporary Debates in Metaphysics*, edited by John Hawthorne, Dean Zimmerman, and Theodore Sider (Oxford: Blackwell, 2008).
[8] Bernard Williams, 'Are Persons Bodies?' in *Problems of the Self* (Cambridge: Cambridge University Press, 1973).

On Williams's view, he would wake up with my head, being psychologically just like me and mistakenly believing that he was me.

Most of us would find that claim incredible. Suppose that you knew both Williams and me, and you visit the resulting person in the post-operative recovery room. You see my head on the pillow, and have a long conversation with someone whom you assume to be me. If some nurse then lifted the blankets on the bed, and you saw the rest of what you knew to be Williams's body, you wouldn't conclude that you *weren't*, as you had assumed, talking to me. You would believe that the person with my head would be me. As many animalists concede, this widely held belief, which some call the *Transplant Intuition,* provides a strong objection to their view.

Olson suggests that Animalists can explain why most of us find this objection plausible.[9] In all actual cases, Olson claims, when some present person is psychologically continuous with some past person, that is strong evidence that these people have the same body, thereby being one and the same person. So it is not surprising that we mistakenly believe that, if our brain and psychology were transplanted into a different body, we would wake up in that other body. We would find this Brain-Based Psychological Criterion just as plausible, even if, as Animalists believe, this criterion is false.

These claims do not, I believe, answer this objection to Animalism. When we compare different proposed criteria of identity, we should consider cases in which these criteria would conflict. If in such imagined cases Criterion A seems much more plausible than Criterion B, we cannot defend B by saying that A seems plausible only because, in all or most actual cases, A coincides with B. Suppose that, on the *Finger Print Criterion*, some future person would be the same as some present person if and only if these people have qualitatively identical finger prints. In rejecting this view, we could point out that, if some plastic surgeon remoulded the tips of someone's fingers, we would all believe that this person would continue to exist, with the same brain and psychology, though with different finger prints. Finger Printists might reply that, if this Brain-Based Psychological Criterion seems more plausible when it conflicts with the Finger Print Criterion, that is only because, in nearly all actual cases, people with the same brain and psychology also have the same finger prints. That would be a weak reply. If the Finger Print Criterion seems much less plausible when these criteria conflict, that *is* a strong objection to this criterion. Similar remarks apply to the Transplant Intuition. If it seems very plausible that the person with my head but the rest of Williams's body would be me, that is a strong objection to the Animalist claim that this person would be Williams.

Some Animalists assume that all animals have the same criterion of identity over time. Since many animals, such as oysters, do not even have psychologies or brains, these Animalists could not accept a Brain-Based Psychological Criterion of animal

---

[9] 'Animalism and the Remnant Person Problem', henceforth 'Animalism', sections 1 and 2, in *Metaphysics of the Self,* edited by J. Goncalves (Oxford: Peter Lang, forthcoming).

identity. But other Animalists might claim that different kinds of animal continue to exist in different ways, and with different criteria of identity. At least in the case of human beings, they might say, the animal goes with the brain. These Animalists would then agree that, in *Transplanted Head*, the resulting person would be me.

This version of Animalism may now seem to coincide with this Lockean view, thereby ending this disagreement. But that is not so. We should distinguish between our cerebra, or upper brains, and our brain stems. It is our cerebrum on which all of our distinctive mental activity depends. The brain stem controls the functioning of our body in other ways. Most Animalists believe that, if our cerebrum were destroyed, but our brain stem continued to maintain the functioning of our heart, lungs, and most of our other organs, we the human animal would continue to exist, though in an unconscious vegetative state, or coma.

We can therefore add some details to our imagined case. We can suppose that, in *Transplanted Head*, my brain stem would be left behind. It is only my head and cerebrum that would be successfully grafted onto William's brain stem and the rest of Williams's body. With its brain stem retained, my body would then continue to be the body of a living though unconscious animal. It would be implausible to claim that this would now be a *different* animal, because the animal that used to have this body had gone with its cerebrum into a different body.

Suppose next that in another case, which we can call

Surviving Head, my head and cerebrum are not grafted onto someone else's brain stem and body, but are kept alive and functioning by an artificial support system.

As before, you visit the post-operative recovery room, see my head on the pillow, and talk with what you take to be me. If the nurse lifted the blankets on the bed, and you saw not a human body but an artificial support system, you wouldn't believe that the conscious being to whom you had been talking *wasn't* me. Some Animalists might claim that this conscious being would be the same animal as me. But there is now a different objection to this view. This conscious being would be a person, in the Lockean sense. But this person, whose physical basis is only an artificially supported head, would not seem to be an animal.

To strengthen this objection, suppose that, in

Surviving Cerebrum, what is removed from my body is not my head, but only my cerebrum, which is then kept functioning by an artificial support system. The resulting entity is conscious, as the neuro-physiological evidence shows. There is also some device which enables this conscious being to communicate with the outside world, since the brain activity involved in certain voluntary mental acts enables this being to spell out the words of messages to us, and some other device enables us to send replies. In this way you have conversations with this conscious being, who claims to be me, seems to have all my memories, and starts to dictate the rest of my unfinished book.

As before, this conscious rational being would be a Lockean person, whom many of us would believe to be me. But it would be harder for Animalists to defend the claim that this conscious being, whose physical basis is only a cerebrum, is an animal, and the same animal as me.

It is worth supposing, however, that some Animalists make this claim. These people might say that an early embryo is a human animal, though it lacks most of the properties of a living organism. The same would be true, they might claim, of my detached, artificially supported cerebrum.

If Animalists made this claim, their view would cease to be an alternative to Lockean views. On the Lockean Brain-Based Psychological Criterion, some future person would be me if this person would be uniquely psychologically continuous with me, because he would have enough of my brain. This criterion implies that, in *Surviving Cerebrum*, the conscious being would be the same person as me. When Animalists entered this debate, their main claim was that such psychological criteria of identity are seriously mistaken, because we are human animals, so that our criterion of identity must be biological. If these Animalists now claimed that, in *Surviving Cerebrum*, the conscious rational being would be a living animal, who would be me, these people would be claiming that the true criterion of identity for developed human animals is of this Lockean psychological kind.[10] Since these Animalists would now be Lockeans, I shall here consider only those other, Non-Lockean Animalists who would believe that, in *Surviving Cerebrum*, the conscious being, though a Lockean person, would not be an animal.

This fact, these Animalists might say, is compatible with their view, which claims only that most persons are animals. There might be some conscious beings that are Lockean persons but aren't animals. But we could then ask: How would this conscious being be related to the human animal, Parfit, who used to have this cerebrum?

Animalists have two alternatives. They might claim that, when my cerebrum is detached from the rest of my body, a new conscious rational being comes into existence. But, as Johnston and Olson write, that claim would be hard to believe. It is hard to see how we could create a new conscious being merely by disconnecting my cerebrum from the rest of my body.

Suppose next that, after this conscious being spends many days communicating with us, my cerebrum is detached from its artificial support system and successfully grafted onto some other human animal's brain stem and body. The resulting being would then be a human animal. But what would happen to the conscious being which existed for a period on its own, as a non-animal? It would be convenient for Animalists if this Lockean person, who is not an animal, would cease to exist when my cerebrum was grafted into the rest of someone else's body. But it is hard to see how, merely by connecting this conscious being to the rest of this body, we would thereby cause this being to cease to exist. Animalists object to the way in which, when Lockeans describe how a young human animal becomes a person, Lockeans implausibly assume that the animal then retires from the scene. The same problem arises here the other way round.

---

[10] These Animalists would be adding only that these Lockeans had failed to point out that their criterion also applies to human animals. That would be no objection to this Lockean view.

Animalists cannot plausibly assume that, when my cerebrum is grafted into this animal's body, this Lockean person would retire from the scene. As Olson writes:

Animalism seems to imply that the detached brain would be a person who comes into being when the brain is removed and ceases to exist when the brain goes into a new head. And that seems absurd.[11]

Olson calls these the *Creation and Destruction Problems*.

To avoid these problems, Animalists might instead claim that this conscious being already existed when my cerebrum was in my body, and that this being would continue to exist both while it is artificially supported, and after it is grafted into another human animal's body. But if Animalists made this claim, they would face another version of the Too Many Thinkers Problem. As well as the human animal thinking my thoughts, there would be another conscious being that was not an animal, thinking all the same thoughts. This problem, moreover, isn't raised only by this imagined case. It applies to every actual fully developed human animal. On this version of the Animalist view, all of any human animal's thoughts are also thought by another, different conscious being.

Animalists, Olson writes, therefore face this dilemma: 'if your brain thinks now, there are too many thinkers; if it doesn't, things can gain or lose mental capacities in an utterly baffling way'.[12]

Olson calls this the *Thinking Parts Problem*. This problem, he writes, is 'considerably more serious than animalism's unintuitive consequences in brain-transplant cases', adding that 'it has no obvious solution'.[13]

2.3.

This problem has, I believe, an obvious solution. According to some Lockeans, as I have said, the person and the animal are both constituted by the same body, in a way that makes them, though not numerically identical, not wholly separate either. On this view, though it is strictly true that each thought is thought by two thinkers, the person and the animal, we can count these thinkers as if they were one.

According to another, better view, we are not animals, or human beings. We are what McMahan calls the conscious, thinking, and controlling *parts* of human beings. We can call this the *Embodied Part View*. The Thinking Parts Problem has a thinking parts solution.

On this view, the Creation and Destruction Problems disappear. If my cerebrum were detached from the rest of my body and artificially supported, no new conscious being would mysteriously come into existence. Nor would a conscious being mysteriously disappear if my cerebrum were later successfully grafted into another human body. The same conscious being would exist throughout, first as the thinking,

---

[11] 'Animalism', abstract.   [12] 'Animalism', end of section 5.
[13] Eric Olson, *What Are We?* (Oxford: Oxford University Press, 2007) 216.

controlling part of one human animal, then existing for a while on its own, then becoming the thinking, controlling part of a different human animal.

This view also avoids the Too Many Thinkers Problem. Animals digest their food by having a part, their stomach, that does the digesting. Animals sneeze by having a part, their nose, that does the sneezing. These facts do not create a Too Many Digesters or Too Many Sneezers Problem. Human animals think, we can similarly claim, by having a part that does the thinking. There are not too many thinkers here.

Some Animalists consider this Embodied Part View. Olson writes: 'If we are neither animals nor material things constituted by animals, we might be parts of animals.' But Olson then rejects this view, calling it 'a desperate ploy', and doubting whether anyone 'seriously advocates' this view.[14]

Olson rejects this view because he assumes that an animal's thinking part would have to be claimed to be its brain. Though Olson calls it 'just about conceivable that the brain view might be true', he does not include this view among the 'live options' that are worth considering. Johnston similarly claims that, if we accept the view that brains can think, we shall be led to absurd conclusions.[15]

What Olson calls the brain view is, however, only one version of the Embodied Part View. This version is not, I believe, absurd. Some other Animalists claim that, rather than having bodies, we *are* bodies. On that view, it is our bodies that have our experiences, and think our thoughts. If these other Animalists came to accept the Embodied Part View, they might claim that the animal's conscious thinking part is not its body but its cerebrum or upper brain. Rather than saying, for example, that Einstein's body discovered the theory of general relativity, they would say that Einstein's brain made this discovery. Many people would find that claim more plausible. In a well-known radio quiz programme, people compete for the title *Brain of Britain*. And Hercule Poirot says, tapping his forehead 'These little grey cells. It is "up to them".'

If we are Embodied Part Theorists, however, we need not make such claims. The thinking part of a human animal, we could say, is related to this animal's cerebrum or upper brain in a way that is roughly similar to that in which this animal is related to its whole body. Most of us distinguish between ourselves and our bodies. If we deny that human animals *are* their bodies, we could similarly deny that the thinking part of these animals is their upper brain.

In what seems to me best of the few published defences of the Embodied Part View, McMahan claims that we are the *minds* of human animals. McMahan calls this the *Embodied Mind View*.[16]

---

[14] 'Animalism', start of section 7.

[15] Mark Johnston, 'Human Beings Revisited: My Body is Not an Animal', in *Oxford Studies in Metaphysics*, Volume 3, edited by Dean Zimmerman (Oxford: Oxford University Press, 2007), pp. 54–5.

[16] Jefferson McMahan, *Killing at the Margins of Life* (Oxford: Oxford University Press, 2002), chapter 1. The Embodied Parts Proposal was independently suggested by Ingmar Persson, in 'Our Identity and the Separability of Persons and Organisms', *Dialogue* 38 (1999). But Persson rejected this view, on what seem to me overly sceptical grounds. See also his 'Self-Doubt: Why We Are Not Identical to Things of Any Kinds', *Ratio* 17 (December 2004), and his magisterial *The Retreat of Reason* (Oxford: Oxford University Press, 2005).

Some Animalists come close to accepting this view. Carter imagines a case in which President Nixon's brain is transplanted into the empty skull of Senator McGovern. Nixon's mind, Carter claims, would then become McGovern's mind. And Carter writes: 'McGovern's mind may...remember being part of a person who stepped onto a certain helicopter after resigning as President.'[17]

If we transferred Nixon's brain into McGovern's body, Carter adds, McGovern might bear some moral responsibility for Nixon's decision to bomb Cambodia, since the mind that used to be Nixon's but is now McGovern's would be 'the mind that once decided to do this awful thing'.

Since Carter claims that our decisions are made by our minds, we might expect him to claim that we, the decision-makers, *are* these minds. On that view, in Carter's imagined case, we would not unjustly hold McGovern responsible for Nixon's earlier decisions. But Carter rejects this view, writing 'since people have arms and legs and minds don't, people can't be identified with minds'.[18]

Some other people would object that, just as we shouldn't claim that *brains* think, or make decisions, we shouldn't claim that *minds* think, or make decisions. Johnston, for example, writes: 'If we are saying that something is...thinking...the subject of predication should be an animal or person.'[19]

Embodied Part Theorists can make similar claims. On a third version of this view, human animals think by having a conscious thinking part which is a person in the Lockean sense. We can call this the *Embodied Person View*. This, I believe, is the best version of the Embodied Part View.[20]

Though Olson claims that the Thinking Parts Problem has no obvious solution, this problem, he writes, 'is no reason to prefer any other view to Animalism'.[21] That is not so. This problem is a strong reason to prefer the Embodied Part View, since this is the only view on which the Thinking Parts Problem disappears.

Nor is this view merely a philosophical invention, since it states more clearly what many non-philosophers already believe, or would after reflection believe. Olson writes, 'no one thinks that we are heads'.

No one, we should agree, thinks that we are *just* heads. But we might be *embodied* heads. And most of us would believe that, for us to survive, it would be enough that our head survives, and continues to be the head of a conscious being. The body below the neck is not an essential part of us.

[17] William R. Carter, 'How to Change Your Mind', *Canadian Journal of Philosophy* 19 (May 1989): 13.
[18] Carter, 'How to Change Your Mind', 7 note 9.
[19] Mark Johnston, 'My Body is Not an Animal', in *Oxford Studies in Metaphysics*, Volume 4, edited by D. Zimmerman (Oxford: Oxford University Press, 2006), p. 54. There is much highly relevant material, which I hope to discuss elsewhere, in Johnston's *Surviving Death* (Princeton, NJ: Princeton University Press, 2010).
[20] Though we can also apply the Embodied Part View to such animals as dogs, whose conscious, thinking and controlling parts are not Lockean persons.
[21] Olson, *What Are We?*, p. 216.

We can next mention the actual cases of those conjoined twins who share all or most of the same body below the neck, but have two heads, and have different thoughts and other experiences. No one doubts that these are the heads of two different people.

It may be less obvious that, for us to survive, it would be enough that our cerebrum survives. If those who love me, rather than seeing my head on a pillow, saw only an artificially supported cerebrum floating in a vat, they might doubt that I was still there. But as the dictated messages would show, the conscious being based on this cerebrum would be psychologically just like me, seem to have all my memories, etc. After reflection most of us would believe that I *was* still there. Whether I have continued to exist could not depend on whether my functioning cerebrum retained its outer covering of bone and skin, so that this conscious being still looked like me.

There are many actual cases of another relevant kind. One such case is that of Nancy Cruzan, whose cerebrum ceased to function, but whose brain stem maintained her body in a vegetative state for seven years until a US Supreme Court ruling granted her parents' request to have an artificial feeding tube removed. On Cruzan's gravestone her parents had inscribed:

Departed January 11 1983 At Peace December 26 1990.

When Cruzan's cerebrum died, her parents came to believe, Cruzan the person departed from her body, though the human animal continued to exist with its heart beating and its lungs breathing until, after the feeding tube was removed, the heart stopped and the animal was at peace.

Nor are we merely appealing to such intuitions. We have reasons to make such claims. While defending Animalism, Olson writes:

if there are now two things thinking your thoughts, one doing it on its own and the other such that its thinking is done for it by something else, you are the one that thinks on its own.[22]

But this plausible *own-thinker principle* supports, not Animalism, but the Embodied Person View. The animal's thinking *is* done for it by something else, the part whose physical basis is the cerebrum. This human animal could not think on its own, since without this part it could not think at all. But the conscious thinking part *can* think on its own, as it would do in some of the imagined cases that we have been considering. If, as Olson claims, we are 'the one that thinks on its own', we are not the animal but this conscious thinking being, the Lockean embodied person.

When Johnston discusses these cases, he appeals to something like the own-thinker principle. Johnston considers the suggestion that, though the person and the animal think the same thoughts, that is not puzzling, since there are not two separate thinkers here. On this view:

(1)   the person 'counts as a thinker derivatively', since the person thinks only '*because* the animal does'.

---

[22] 'Animalism', section 5, quoting from Roderick Chisholm *Person and Object* (Chicago: Open Court, 1976) 104.

Johnston rejects this view, claiming that it 'gives the wrong result'. In his words:

if I had to pick which of two things I am identical with, the person or the animal, a good rule would be: Pick the thing which is *non-derivatively* the subject of mental acts. And on the present proposal... it is the animal, and not the person, that is non-derivatively the subject of mental acts... But the result we wanted is that I am identical with the person.[23]

Since this proposal gets things the wrong way round, the obvious next suggestion is that:

(2)   we are identical, not with the animal, but with the person, which is the non-derivative thinker, and the subject of our mental acts.

Johnston comes close to accepting (2), since he discusses the view that any human animal has 'a mental organ dependent on its brain, whose operation constitutes the animal's thinking', and he also claims that, as persons, we should take ourselves to be 'the non-derivative or primary source of the thought in us'. These claims support the view that:

(3)   we, who are persons, are the part of the animal that does the thinking.

Johnston, however, rejects (3). Summarizing what is shown by the Too Many Thinkers Problem, Johnston writes: 'Olson has a sound argument here... one that must condition all further discussion of personal identity. *We are animals.*'[24]

Johnston adds only that we, who are persons, are not *essentially* animals, since he believes that, in cases like *Surviving Head* or *Cerebrum*, we would continue to exist as persons, though we would have ceased to be animals. Though Johnston's other claims imply that we are the part of the animal that does the thinking, Johnston's belief that we *are* animals leads him to reject that conclusion.

2.4.

I turn now to possible objections to the Embodied Part View, whose best form I have claimed to be the Embodied Person View.

One objection is that, as Carter claims, we can't *be* our minds, since we have arms and legs and our minds don't. Discussing the view that we are brains rather than minds, Olson similarly writes: 'Is it really a serious view... that we are about four inches tall and weigh about three pounds?'[25]

We can call this the *Physical Properties Objection*. On this objection, we have many physical properties which cannot be had by our conscious thinking part, whether we claim this part to be a brain, or a mind, or a Lockean person. Since we have such physical properties, we must be human animals, rather than some part of these animals.

[23] Johnston, 'My Body is Not an Animal', 50.
[24] Johnston, 'My Body is Not an Animal', 48.   [25] Olson, *What Are We?*, p. 76.

This objection can be answered. If we are *embodied* persons, as I believe, we can explain how and why we can intelligibly claim ourselves to have the physical properties of our bodies. We already do that now if we distinguish between ourselves and our bodies, as when I say that I am 6 foot tall and weigh 160 pounds because my body has these properties.

We sometimes use 'I' and 'me' more widely, to refer to more than our bodies. I might say, for example, that I have been splashed with mud, though it was only my trousers that were splashed. And if I were a veiled Islamic woman, I might say that someone had seen me, though this person saw only my clothes. If we are the conscious controlling part of an animal, we are very closely related to the rest of this animal's body, in which we can feel sensations, and with which we can see, hear, smell, and touch the world around us. As Descartes wrote, while defending his soul-involving version of the Embodied Part View, this controlling part is not lodged in our body merely in the way in which a pilot is lodged in a ship. Since we can explain how and why, on the Embodied Part View, we can claim ourselves to have the properties of our bodies, the Physical Properties Objection fails.

We can next return to the Epistemic Problem, which is held to count against all views which distinguish between a person and a human animal. On such views, Olson writes:

how could you ever know which one you are? You may think you're the person. But whatever you think, the animal thinks too. So the animal would . . believe that *it* is a person...Yet it is mistaken. If you *were* the animal and not the person, you'd still think you were the person. So for all you know, you're the one making the mistake.[26]

Olson here assumes that pronouns like 'I' and 'you' are unambiguous, and must always refer to the same thing.

That is not, I believe, true. We use 'I' in different senses, or ways. It is often claimed that the word 'I' unambiguously refers to the speaker of the sentence in which 'I' is used, or to the thinker of an I-involving thought. But this claim itself illustrates the ambiguity. The speaker of any sentence may be a human animal. But when we think I-involving thoughts, we may not be intending to refer to a human animal. We can think of ourself as the direct thinker of these thoughts, whatever this thinker is. This thinker might be, not the animal, but the part of the animal that does the thinking, which I am calling the Lockean person.

If our pronouns are in this way ambiguous, the Epistemic Problem partly disappears. In describing this problem, Olson writes: 'Suppose you were the animal rather than the person.'

But we can't usefully *suppose* either that we are the animal, or that we are the person, since we would then be supposing falsely that the words 'I' and 'we' must always refer to the same thing. Some uses of these words may refer to an animal, and others to a person. The names of nations have a similar ambiguity, since they may refer to a nation

---

[26] Eric Olson 'Thinking Animals and the Reference of "I"', *Philosophical Topics*, Spring 2002.

state, as in the claim 'France declared war', or to a part of the Earth's surface, as in the claim 'France is roughly hexagonal'. We shouldn't claim that France must be either a nation state or a part of the Earth's surface, though we don't know which.

It will help to make our pronouns more precise. In our thoughts about ourselves, we can use the phrase 'Inner-I' to refer to the Lockean person, and 'Outer-I' to refer to the human animal. We can use similar senses of Inner- and Outer- me, you, he, she, we, and us. Suppose next that someone thinks both

(A)   Inner-I am the person, the conscious, thinking, controlling part of this animal, which is directly thinking this thought,

and

(B)   Outer-I am the animal that is indirectly thinking this thought, by having a part, Inner-I, that does the thinking.

On the Embodied Person View, the person and the animal both think both these thoughts. And, as thought by either thinker, both thoughts are true.

It might be objected that, when the animal believes that

(A)   Inner-I am the person,

the animal would be falsely believing that *it* is the person, since it would be using the pronoun 'Inner-I' and the verb 'am' to have a belief about itself. But that is not so. The animal would understand these new, more precise pronouns, by having a part that understands them, and the animal believes (B) as well as (A), by having a part that does the believing. If these uses of the word 'am' seem misleading, we could restate these thoughts as

(C)   Inner-I *is* the person that directly thinks these thoughts, and Outer-I *is* the animal that indirectly thinks them.

We can use 'is' rather than 'am' when thinking about ourselves, as General De Gaulle did whenever he thought 'De Gaulle is the saviour of France'. As before, whether (C) is thought directly by the person, or indirectly by the animal, (C) is true.

Return now to Olson's claim that, if there were two thinkers of all our thoughts, the person and the animal, neither thinker could know which one it was. When Olson presents this objection, he discusses the version of Teletransportation which I called the *Branch Line Case*.[27] Suppose that the new improved replicator scans my brain and body without destroying them, and then makes a Replica of me, in a room that is just like mine. Olson claims that, because I and my Replica would be exactly similar, in exactly similar surroundings, each of us would believe that he was me, and neither could know which of us was right. Similar remarks apply, Olson claims, to the Lockean view which distinguishes between the person and the animal. But this analogy is

[27] Eric Olson, 'Personal Identity', section 6, *Stanford Encyclopaedia of Philosophy*, 2002.

misleading. When I and my Replica both believe ourselves to be me, and then wonder who is right, these are two different conscious mental processes, or episodes of thinking. No such claim applies to the Lockean view. On this view, just as there is only a single episode of sneezing when the animal sneezes by having a part, its nose, that does the sneezing, there is only a single episode of thinking when the animal thinks by having a part that does the thinking.

Consider next Johnston's claim that we should take ourselves to be 'the *non-derivative* or primary source of the thought in us'. We can distinguish two kinds of derivative thinking. Some of our thinking is derivative in the sense that we are merely thinking again what someone else thought first, and led us to think. Platonists, for example, might derivatively think what Plato thought. The Moon similarly shines at night, in a derivative way, by reflecting light that comes from the Sun, which is the Solar System's non-derivative or primary source of light. But no such claim applies to the animal and its conscious, thinking part. When a human animal thinks by having a part that thinks, there is nothing that corresponds to the derivative shining of the Moon. There are not two thinkers here, one of whom thinks in a derivative way by thinking again what the other thinks. The animal's thoughts are derivative in a second, stronger sense. When Inner-I the Lockean person thinks some thought, we can truly say that Outer-I, the animal thereby thinks this thought. But the animal does not itself do any thinking. The animal cannot think in what Olson calls the *strict* or non-derivative sense.

On the objection that we are discussing, if there was both a person and an animal which think all the same thoughts, neither could know whether it was the animal or the person. This objection can now be answered. When Descartes asked what he could know, despite the arguments for scepticism, he thought: 'I think, therefore I am.'

Descartes concluded that he could know that he was an immaterial thinking substance. As Lichtenberg objected, Descartes should have thought only: 'This is the thinking of a thought, so at least some thinking is going on.'

Descartes' *Cogito* leaves it open in what sense, or way, any thought must have a thinker. This question we can also leave open here. We can assume that any conscious being that can think about itself, and its identity, is at least a person in the Lockean sense, whatever else this being may be. We are supposing that someone thinks

(C)   Inner-I is the person that is directly thinking these thoughts, and Outer-I is the animal that is indirectly thinking them, by having a part that is doing the thinking.

To explain the meaning of the pronoun 'Inner-I', we can claim that, when used in some thought, this pronoun refers to the person that is the direct thinker of this very thought. When any direct thinker uses 'Inner-I', knowing what this phrase means, this thinker knows that it thereby refers to itself. So in thinking (C), Inner-I the person would know that it is not the animal but the person.

We can next ask what the animal could know. Just as the animal thinks some thought only by having a part, the Lockean person, that does the thinking, the animal can know something only by having a part, the person, that knows this thing. Since the person knows that Outer-I is the animal that indirectly thinks these thoughts, the animal thereby knows, in its derivative way, that Outer-I is this animal. Nor could the animal be mistaken, since the animal cannot make any mistake except by having a thinking part that makes this mistake, and this part, the Lockean person, would not be mistaken.

There is, I conclude, no Epistemic Problem. And if Lockeans appeal to the Embodied Person View, they can answer the other Animalist objections to Lockean views. Since the animal thinks only by having a part that thinks, there are not too many thinkers here. And since the animal is a person only in the derivative sense of having a Lockean person as a part, there are not too many persons here.

2.5.

The title of this chapter claims that we are not human beings, in the sense that means: human animals. Some of my remarks may seem to have undermined that claim. If our pronouns are ambiguous, as I have suggested, how can I hope to show that *we* are not human beings, or animals, but are the conscious, thinking, controlling parts of these animals?

I have not undermined that claim. If we resolved the ambiguity of our pronouns, by distinguishing the inner and outer senses, these senses would not have equal status, or equal importance in our conceptual scheme.

Return to my imagined case in which my head and cerebrum would be successfully grafted onto someone else's brain stem and the rest of that person's body. My own brain stem would maintain the functioning of the rest of my body, which would remain the body of a living but unconscious human animal.

Most of us would believe that, in this case, it would be I who would later wake up, with my head and the rest of this other person's body. If we used these more precise pronouns, we would then be believing that it would be Inner-I, the Lockean person, who would wake up, and continue my life with a new body below the neck. Outer-I the human animal would continue to exist in a vegetative state. But that would not affect Inner-Me, the person. And if we imagined ourselves about to undergo this operation, most of us would believe that we would be the person who woke up again, not the animal that lingered on in a vegetative state.

Since the inner senses of pronouns have more importance, we can now express these senses in the old familiar, briefer way. I hereby announce that, from now on, I shall use the word 'I' in the different, more precise sense that I have expressed with the phrase 'Inner-I'. I invite Inner-you, the other Lockean persons reading this chapter, to do the same. We can then truly claim that we are not human beings in the sense that refers to human animals, but are the most important parts of these animals, the parts that do all the things that are most distinctive of these human animals, as conscious, thinking, rational beings.

Olson considers the objection that, since our pronouns are ambiguous, there is no single answer to the question of which entity we are. Though he is an Animalist, Olson then writes:

If the word 'I' in my mouth sometimes refers to a thinking thing and sometimes to an unthinking thing…[such as my body] then our concern is with the thinking thing. Never mind the referential role of personal pronouns. This is an essay in metaphysics. Our question is about the nature of the beings holding the enquiry. So we can rephrase our question.…What sorts of beings think our thoughts?[28]

The answer, I have claimed, is: Lockean persons. Olson also writes:

Surely it couldn't turn out that there is something other than me that thinks my thoughts, whereas I myself think them only in some loose, second-rate sense? [29]

That is true, since Olson is such a Lockean person, the part of a human animal that thinks Olson's thoughts in the strict, first-rate sense.

If, as I have argued, we are not the animals that we call human beings, what difference does that make?

The most direct moral implications apply to the first part of every human being's life, and to the last part of many human beings' lives. According to the Catechism of the Catholic Church, 'Human life must be…protected absolutely from the moment of conception. From the first moment of his existence, a human being must be recognized as having the rights of a person…The first right of the human person is his life' (1992). Many people make similar claims.

If we, who are Lockean persons, are not human beings, these claims do not apply to us. Nor do such claims apply when our cerebrum has died, so that we have ceased to exist, though our brain stem keeps the human animal alive. As McMahan claims, neither early abortion, nor removing a feeding tube from such a human being, would kill one of us. Though such acts raise moral questions, they do not violate the rights of persons.

If we are not human animals, that in one way makes little theoretical difference. In a book whose final proofs I corrected a few months ago, my first sentence is: 'We are the animals that can both understand and respond to reasons.'[30]

It was only while preparing this chapter that I came to believe that we *aren't* animals, but are the conscious, thinking, controlling parts of these animals. But though my book's first sentence is, I now believe, misleading, I would not revise that sentence, but would only add a qualifying note. My sentence is close enough to being true. We are each part of a human animal, and we make this animal able, in a derivative way, to understand and respond to reasons. Outer-We are, in that sense, rational animals, because Inner-We are rational persons.

---

[28] Olson, *What Are We?*, p. 13.   [29] Olson, *What Are We?*, p. 79.
[30] Derek Parfit, *On What Matters* (Oxford: Oxford University Press, 2011).

There are some other theoretical implications. For those who believe that we don't have souls, in the sense of persisting immaterial substances, one of the main recent philosophical disagreements has been between Lockean or psychological theories, and Animalist or biological theories. Animalism, Shoemaker writes, 'presents a powerful challenge to neo-Lockean views'. The 'crux of the current debate...[is] whether this challenge succeeds'.[31] I have tried to show that it does not. Animalists rightly claimed that Lockeans should not ignore the question whether we are animals, and Animalists put forward forceful objections to most Lockean views. But if Lockeans revise their claims, by turning to the Embodied Person View, these objections can, I have claimed, be answered. And this view also avoids some strong objections to Animalism. If Animalists also turned to this view, this disagreement would be resolved, and we together would have made philosophical progress.

I shall end with a more personal remark. In my earlier writings about these questions, my main aim was not to defend a Lockean criterion of personal identity, but to argue that, in our thoughts about our identity, or what is involved in our continuing to exist, most of us have, at some level, various false beliefs. We believe, for example, that if we are about to lose consciousness, it must either be true, or be false, that we shall wake up again. Such beliefs, I argued, are mistaken. Personal identity is not as deep, and simple, as most of us take it to be. Even if we did not know whether we would ever wake up again, we might know the full truth about what was going to happen. Since we have such false beliefs about what is involved in our continued existence, we may misunderstand the rational and moral importance of personal identity. On the true view, I claimed, though we have reasons for special concern about our future, these reasons are not given, as we assume, by the fact that this will be *our* future. Nor will our death be as significant as most of us believe. In my somewhat misleading slogan, personal identity is not what matters.

In defending these claims, I appealed in part to the imagined case in which two future people would be psychologically continuous with me as I am now, because each person would have one half of my cerebrum. But this is only one example. And I have found it hard to convince some people that, in other cases, personal identity is not what matters. I cannot persuade these people, for example, that if they were about to be destroyed and replicated, it would not matter that their future Replica would not be them, so that they would never wake up again.

If Animalism were true, it would be easier to defend these claims. Suppose again that, because your body below the neck is fatally diseased, as is someone else's cerebrum, doctors will successfully graft your head and cerebrum onto this other person's brain stem and headless body. According to Animalists, it would be this other person who would later wake up with your head, being psychologically just like you, and mistakenly believing that he or she was you. If we accepted this Animalist view, it would be easier to see that personal identity is not what matters. It would be clear that,

[31] Shoemaker, 'Persons, Animals, and Identity', *Synthese* 162 (2008): 315.

if someone would later wake up with your head, and would be psychologically just like you, it would have no practical or moral importance that this person would not be you. While defending his biological, Animalist view, Olson similarly writes:

In divorcing our identity from psychological continuity, the Biological Approach would entail that these relations of practical concern are even less reliably connected to with numerical identity than Parfit and Shoemaker have argued.[32]

If, as I have argued, Animalism is not true, I cannot defend my claims about what matters by appealing to this imagined case. That gives me a reason to *wish* that Animalism were true. But this is not a reason to *believe* that Animalism is true. So I regret that Animalism—a view that is highly plausible, widely accepted, and was strangely neglected until Snowdon, Olson, and others gave it the prominence that it deserves—seems not to be true.

[32] Eric Olson, *The Human Animal* (Oxford: Oxford University Press, 1997), pp. 71–2.

3

Animalism vs. Constitutionalism

Lynne Rudder Baker

Animalism and Constitutionalism are rival answers to metaphysical questions: "[W]hat are we, metaphysically speaking? What are our most general and fundamental features? What is our most basic metaphysical nature?" (Olson 2007: 3). "What are we, most fundamentally?" (Baker 2007a: 4).

Animalism is the metaphysical thesis that "each of us is numerically identical with an animal: there is a certain organism, and you and it are one and the same"(Olson 2007: 24). Or to put it slightly differently, "[w]e are identical with, are one and the same thing as, certain (human) animals" (Snowdon 1990: 71). An Animalist, then, endorses propositions expressed by sentences of the form: "I am identical to an organism," "you are identical to an organism," "Obama is identical to an organism," and so on. According to Animalism, our persistence conditions are third-personal.

Constitutionalism is the metaphysical thesis that each of us is identical to a person, who is initially constituted by (but not identical to) an animal and who has a first-person perspective essentially (Baker 2007a). According to Constitutionalism (at least my version of it), our persistence conditions are first-personal.

The fact that Animalism and Constitutionalism are *metaphysical* theses has certain consequences. For Animalism: If, *metaphysically* speaking, you are identical to a certain organism—call it "O"—then (i) there is no time at which you exist and O fails to exist; (ii) there is no time at which O exists and you fail to exist; (iii) there is no time at which you have a property—modal, indexical, whatever—and O fails to have it then; (iv) there is no time at which O has a property and you fail to have it then.[1]

For Constitutionalism: If, metaphysically speaking, you are identical to a certain person—call it "P"—then (i') there is no time at which you exist and P fails to exist; (ii') there is no time at which P exists and you fail to exist; (iii') there is no time at which you have a property—modally, indexically, whatever—and P fails to have it then; (iv') there is no time at which P has a property and you fail to have it then.

---

[1] I am making certain assumptions that I have argued for elsewhere: (a) some properties may be had essentially (Baker 1997); (b) certain entities (like you and organisms) exist at some times and not at other times (Baker 2007a: 228–31); some entities have properties at some times and not at other times (Baker 2007a: 166–9).

It further follows from the fact that Animalism is a metaphysical thesis that (v) our persistence conditions are the persistence conditions of animals—third-personal conditions. Finally, if Animalism is true, then (vi) "*any* of us could exist at a time without having any mental properties at that time, or even the capacity to acquire them" (Olson 2007: 44, emphasis mine). And it further follows from the fact that Constitutionalism is a metaphysical thesis that (v') our persistence conditions are the persistence conditions of persons—first-personal conditions. Finally, if Constitutionalism is true, then (vi') *none* of us "could exist at a time without having any mental properties at that time, or even the capacity to acquire them."

I shall assume that Animalism is the metaphysical thesis expressed by "you are identical to an animal," and that Constitutionalism is the metaphysical thesis expressed by "you are identical to a person." Each thesis is elucidated, respectively, by (i)–(vi) and by (i')–(vi').

After briefly sketching my theory of persons, I shall present a series of arguments for Animalism, and show how Constitutionalism can deal with them; then I shall present two arguments for Constitutionalism, and defend them. The upshot, I hope, will be that on a number of fronts, Constitutionalism is superior to Animalism as the ontology for human beings.

A Constitution View of Persons: A Brief Sketch

Every concrete object that exists is of some primary kind or other. X's primary kind is the answer to the question: What, most fundamentally, is x? What we are most fundamentally are persons. There are no sufficient, subpersonal conditions for personhood: persons are basic entities. We may have evolved by natural selection; but when we did evolve, a new kind of entity appeared. Biologically, we are continuous with the rest of the animal kingdom; ontologically, we are unique (Baker 2007a).

What makes us unique is that persons are essentially first-personal: we have rudimentary or robust first-person perspectives essentially. We persist as long as our first-person perspectives are exemplified. (To allow for temporal gaps, I should say that a person exists whenever her first-person perspective is exemplified.) Consciousness is required for a rudimentary first-person perspective; a unique conceptual ability is required for a robust first-person perspective. The unique conceptual ability is the ability to refer to oneself as oneself, without any name, description or third-personal referring device. A robust first-person perspective is manifested by thoughts like "I wish that I were a movie star," "I'm glad that I study philosophy," and "I believe that I am eligible for social security."

Not only are persons essentially first-personal, but also human persons are also essentially embodied. However, we do not necessarily have the bodies that we do have; we could exist with nonorganic bodies as long as the bodies provide the mechanisms that support their person-level activities and states. We are constituted by our bodies, and the bodies that constitute us now are organisms. With enough neural implants and prosthetic limbs, we may come to be constituted by nonorganic bodies.

The relation of constitution is exemplified everywhere: genes are constituted by sums of DNA molecules, which are constituted by sums of cells and so on down to physical microparticles; driver's licenses are constituted by pieces of plastic, which are constituted by certain kinds of molecules, and so on. Constitution is a time-bound relation: the Bayeux Tapestry is constituted by one sum of threads at one time, and after a minor repair, by a different sum of threads at another time. (So, "x constitutes y" is elliptical for "x constitutes y at t.")

Although constitution is not identity, it *is* a relation of unity. Constitution is not merely spatial co-location. The constitution relation allows the constituted object and the constituting object to share instantiations of properties by what I call "having properties derivatively." The intuitive idea is simple: if x constitutes y at t, then some of x's properties at t have their source (so to speak) in y, and some of y's properties at t have their source in x.

I'll illustrate with the example of a driver's license, which is constituted by a piece of plastic. The driver's license has the property of being rectangular only because it is constituted by something that could have been rectangular even if it had constituted nothing. And the piece of plastic has the property of satisfying the TSA officer only because it constitutes something that would have satisfied the TSA officer (a valid driver's license) no matter what constituted it. So, we have a driver's license constituted by a piece of plastic. The "source" of its property of being rectangular is in the constituting piece of plastic. The "source" of its property of satisfying the TSA officer is in the constituted license.

Now we can distinguish having a property nonderivatively from having a property derivatively. I'll say that the driver's license has the property of satisfying the TSA officer nonderivatively, and the property of being rectangular derivatively; the piece of plastic that constitutes my driver's license has the property of being rectangular nonderivatively, and of satisfying the TSA officer derivatively. I have defined these terms rigorously in Baker (2007a). Not all properties may be had derivatively, but I'll skip the details here.[2] Enough properties can be had derivatively to see how constitution is a relation of unity.

Even primary-kind properties may be had derivatively. Something may have a primary-kind property without having that property as *its* primary-kind property. There are two ways to fall under a primary-kind sortal: to be essentially of that kind or to be

---

[2] Several classes of properties are excluded from being had derivatively: they are not shared. The excluded classes contain: (1) properties expressed in English by locutions using "essentially," "necessarily," "possibly," "primary kind," and the like (e.g. being a pencil essentially); (2) properties of being constituted by x, or being identical to x (e.g. constituting a pencil); (3) properties rooted outside the times at which they are had (e.g. having been quarried in 1500); (4) certain combinations of properties (e.g. being a granite monument). In (Baker 2007a), I define parthood—ordinary parthood—in terms of constitution as well as of mereology. So, the property of having part P at t is excluded since it is defined in terms of constitution. The property of having P as a part at t may not be had derivatively.

contingently related by constitution to something that is essentially of that kind (see Wasserman 2004). Since *chair* is a primary kind, your chair is a chair essentially, but the sum of particles that make it up is only a chair contingently, in virtue of constituting the chair. The sum of particles is not a chair unless there is a chair that it constitutes. If the chair is smashed to smithereens and no longer exists, the sum of particles that once constituted the chair still exists, but no longer constitutes a chair. So, something (e.g. a sum of particles) may have a primary-kind property contingently when suitably related to something (e.g. a chair) that has it essentially.[3] The chair is a chair nonderivatively, but the sum of particles is a chair derivatively—in virtue of constituting something that is a chair nonderivatively. Call the distinction between having a property nonderivatively and having a property derivatively the "Key Distinction."[4]

The Key Distinction is useful in illuminating a distinction made by Aristotle. Aristotle distinguished sameness in number (numerical sameness) from sameness in being (identity) (Aristotle 1941, *Topics*, Bk. I, Ch.7). The Key Distinction shows how such a distinction as Aristotle's can work: a chair is a chair nonderivatively and the sum of particles that constitutes the chair at t is a chair derivatively; if x constitutes y at t, and y is an F nonderivatively but x is an F derivatively, there is only one F. The chair and the sum of particles that constitutes it at t are numerically the same but not the same in being. Similarly for a person and her body at t. Persons and bodies have different persistent conditions.

Now let us turn to arguments against Constitutionalism from the point of view of Animalism.

Animalist Arguments against Constitutionalism and their Rebuttal

1. A "Reductio Argument." Snowdon offers a version of this argument in favor of animalism, understood as the truth of "I am an animal." In Snowdon's terms, "I am an animal" is to be interpreted as

(A)   I am identical to an animal.[5]

---

[3] Many properties (unrelated to this discussion) may be had essentially by some things and nonessentially by other things. A planet has the property of having a closed orbit essentially; a comet that has a closed orbit has that property nonessentially. (This assumes that planets are planets essentially; otherwise it is only a *de dicto* necessity that planets have closed orbits.)

[4] Critics never argue against the Key Distinction. They either ignore it (Johansson 2009) or assume that it is absurd (Kearns 2009) or profess not to understand it (Olson 2007: 61). But it is rigorously defined (Baker 2007a: 167–8), and it does important work in the theory. For ease of reading, I do not make the distinction explicitly when I think that there is no risk of confusion. The default is "nonderivatively."

[5] Snowdon 1990: 91. Any Animalist who wants to join the issue with me *must* interpret (A) as an identity statement. On my view, I am not identical to an animal (I am not an animal nonderivatively), but I am an animal derivatively—now, when I am constituted by an animal. Many critics simply do not acknowledge my Key Distinction.

Under that interpretation, on my view, (A) is false. (On my view, "I am an animal" is to be interpreted as "I am an animal either nonderivatively or derivatively," or equivalently, "I am either identical to, or constituted by an animal" and hence is true.) Here is a version of Snowdon's argument, which Snowdon calls the Reductio Argument.

The Reductio Argument

(1) If A is false, then when I say, "I am an animal," that remark is false.
(2) Animals—and hence H [the animal that, according to Animalism, I am identical to]—have evolved the capacity to use "I."
(3) If (2), then remarks using "I" made through the mouth of H are remarks in which H speaks of itself.
(4) If remarks using "I" made through the mouth of H are remarks in which H speaks of itself, then the remark on occasion O ("I am an animal," made through the mouth of H) was true.
∴ (5) (A) is true.[6]

This argument looks unassailable to its proponents, but given the tenets of the constitution view, it is unsound. I agree that animals—and hence H—have evolved the capacity to use "I." But, according to Constitutionalism, the animals that developed the capacity to use "I" came to constitute beings of a new kind—persons—and when a person-constituting animal uses "I," the referent is the person (the person-constituted by-the-animal). No animal that does not constitute a person uses "I" meaningfully.

When a human organism (around birth?) develops a rudimentary first-person perspective (with sentience, intentionality, the ability to imitate), a new kind of being (a person) comes into existence. The person then has a first-person perspective nonderivatively, and the organism has it derivatively.[7] The rudimentary first-person perspective of a human infant then typically develops into a robust first-person perspective as the toddler learns to use "I" to refer to herself without any name or description. What makes a human person ontologically unique is the development of a robust first-person perspective from a rudimentary first-person perspective.

An animal that constitutes a person is a person only derivatively. "I" is a personal pronoun and always refers to the (nonderivative) person constituted by an animal. Every use of "I" out of the mouth of an animal refers to the (nonderivative) person that the (nonderivative) animal constitutes. (Chimpanzees do not constitute persons and do not use "I" to refer at all.) So, contra (3), the animal was not referring to the animal;

---

[6] From 2,3 MP, we get 3*—remarks using "I" made through the mouth of H are remarks in which H speaks of itself. From 3*,4 MP, we get 4*—the remark on occasion O ("I am an animal," made through the mouth of H) was true). From 1,4* MT, we get 5.

[7] For details, see (Baker 2007a). The reason for this two-step is to make room for human infants to be persons.

the person spoke of herself—a person not identical to, but constituted by, an animal. Since (3) is false, the argument for (5) is unsound.

I am not postulating an ambiguity in the use of "I." When "I" is used sincerely and comprehendingly, it refers to a nonderivative person—that embodied person. If I say, "I have a headache," I (the nonderivative person) am referring to my head (part of the body that constitutes me now, a body that is a person derivatively now). But "I" does not refer to my head; "I" in my mouth always refers to me, the embodied person. Nevertheless, I need not deny that H is a person derivatively—as long as H constitutes me, a person nonderivatively. So, on my interpretation, "H is a person" means "H is a person nonderivatively or derivatively," and is thus true; but "H is a person" does not mean "H is identical to a person."

The first-person perspective may well be a product of natural selection. Here is a just-so story to show that a Constitutionalist need not deny that persons evolved naturally. Eons ago, there evolved a species of primates whose mentality was determined by their brains in interaction with each other and with their environments. They were social beings who had (perhaps) routinized social interactions of grooming, feeding the young, and so on. The range of their cognitive states was limited to those concerning their local present environments and survival and reproduction. At some later time, beings of this species experienced a "cognitive inflation" (my term), similar to the expansion of the physical universe after the Big Bang. Cognitive inflation was a period of remarkable cognitive innovation. At the end of this period of cognitive inflation, beings of this species had acquired spoken and written language, art, and government. Their lives and thoughts were products, not just of biology, but also of learning, culture, and technology. We are their descendants (this is a variation on Mithen 2004).

With my own philosophical preoccupations, here is what I take from this just-so story. Before the period of cognitive inflation started, there were animals with rudimentary first-person perspectives, but no human persons. Somewhere along the line, they developed language. My speculation is that with the development of language came the development of concepts, environmental and social, and this linguistic development triggered a new stage of the first-person perspective—the robust first-person perspective—the capacity to conceive of oneself *as* oneself, in the first person. At this point in evolutionary history, human organisms came to constitute human persons.

With the development of language came an explosion of the kinds of thoughts that could be entertained—modal thoughts about necessity and possibility, normative thoughts about what makes a good person, counterfactual thoughts about what might have been, abstract thoughts about numbers and properties, and first-person thoughts about oneself and one's desires, intentions, and beliefs. The development of language and the first-person perspective also made possible law-governed societies, institutions of all sorts, the sciences, and technology.

The rudimentary first-person perspectives of human infants tie persons to the animal kingdom; the robust first-person perspectives that we develop make persons ontologically unique. But my ontological claim—that persons, in virtue of their first-person perspectives, are an ontologically distinct kind of being—is fully compatible with biology. This is so because, again, first-person perspectives, robust as well as rudimentary, may well have evolved by natural selection. Ontology need not follow biology.

2. The "Too Many Persons" (or "Too Many Minds") Objection. Now the Animalist may charge that Constitutionalism violates a very plausible principle:

(VPP)   If x is a person and y is a person and *x is not identical to y*, then there are two persons.

However, the Key Distinction allows us to make an Aristotelian distinction between identity and sameness and define "the same F at t" like this:

x and y are the same F at t $=_{df}$ x is F and either x = y or x constitutes y at t or y constitutes x at t.[8]

This extension of "the same F" to constitution underwrites another very plausible principle:

(VPP*)   If x is a person and y is a person and *x is not the same person as y*, then there are two persons.

(VPP*) is likewise very plausible. Moreover, it does philosophical work in my theory. So, we have good reason to replace (VPP) with (VPP*). So, although H and I are both persons at t and nonidentical, there are not two persons where I am.

Olson says: "I don't know what Baker means when she says that A [the animal that constitutes me now] and I, though numerically different, are one person" (Olson 2007: 61). But as we just saw, I distinguish identity from sameness, and since A and Olson are the same person (A derivatively and Olson nonderivatively), there is just one person.

On my view, there are two ways to be nonidentical: x and y are nonidentical if and only if either: there is some time at which x and y are constitutionally related or x and y have separate existence; x and y have separate existence if and only if there is no F and time t such that x and y are the same F at t. (This is well defined in Baker 2007a: 170.) Another way to put it is that if x constitutes y or y constitutes x, then x and y are nonidentical without being numerically different.

3. The "thinking-animal" problem. The thinking-animal problem is a variation of the "too-many-thinkers" problem: if both A and I have thoughts, we must have the same thoughts; in that case, how could we not be identical (Olson 2007: 29)? Olson says, "Friends of the constitution view will want to solve the thinking-animal problem by denying that human animals can think, or that they can think in the way that we think" (Olson 2007: 62).

---

[8] I am assuming here and elsewhere that F is a property that can be had derivatively, a nonexcluded property. This definition is an extension to constitution of Perry's definition of "the same F" (Perry 1970).

I believe that nonhuman animals can think, but that they are limited in the kinds of thoughts that they can think. They are limited by their lack of a language, and consequent paucity of concepts with which to think. Most of all, they are limited by their lack of a robust first-person perspective. Primates have only rudimentary first-person perspectives, and can entertain no thoughts of the form "I believe [or other psychological or linguistic verb] that I* am F." A and I share a brain (I have it derivatively), but the brain is not a thinker. Some thoughts—perhaps expressible by "Danger over there"—may be had by higher animals, but the thoughts characteristic of mature people (e.g. "I wonder how I* am going to die") cannot be had by animals except derivatively, when an animal constitutes a person.

Olson asks, "What could give us identity conditions different from those of human animals?" After all we have the same microstructure (Olson 2007: 63). I have already given the answer: the in-hand ability to develop a robust first-person perspective. I think that it is a metaphysical error to suppose that what something most fundamentally is always depends on microstructure. What makes a clock, say, the thing it is depends on its intended function: to tell time. Similarly, what makes a person the thing she is depends on a unique conceptual ability that animals do not have (except derivatively when they constitute persons). What makes us persons is that we are of a kind that typically develops robust first-person perspectives. (Theists can take the analogy with artifacts further: what makes us the things that we are depends on our Maker's intentions.)

4. An Argument from a Theory of Composition. Olson thinks that "animalism leads very naturally to a certain sort of theory of composition" (Olson 2007: 228). The theory that animalism leads to is van Inwagen's view that "things compose something if and only if their activities constitute a biological life" (Olson 2007: 226). Let us turn to Olson's claim that "theory of composition would tell us what we are" (Olson 2007: 232).

Van Inwagen's theory of composition that leads to an ontology exhausted by simples and animals is, of course, a threat to Constitutionalism, which recognizes a broad pluralistic ontology. By itself, this is no problem for a Constitutionalist, who can just reject the theory of composition.

But Olson thinks that his theory of composition—which all agree is incompatible with Constitutionalism—raises a problem for the Constitutionalist. Olson asks the Constitutionalist what he takes to be a fatal question: "Under what circumstances do particles compose something other than a mass?" (Olson 2007: 231).

But there is an easy answer available to the Constitutionalist. Universalism: particles *always* compose a sum, but sums are mere aggregates; they are not identical to any ordinary objects (like chairs, trees, or people). "Sum" is just a singular label for a plurality.[9] Sums may *constitute* objects, but they are not identical to the objects that they

---

[9] David Lewis explained that mereology is "innocent." "[W]e have many things, we do mention one thing [a sum] that is the many taken together, but this one thing is nothing different from the many" (Lewis 1991).

constitute. You now are constituted by a human animal, which in turn now is constituted by a particular sum of particles. Last month, the same sum of particles existed but did not constitute you then.

Universalism as an answer to the composition question does not bloat ontology beyond Constitutionalism alone; sums are ontological "freebies" that are nothing but the items that they contain referred to by a singular term. The important point is that constitution and composition are two different relations. It is a significant (though popular) misstep for metaphysicians to try to make do with composition alone. A theory of composition would tell us what we are only if what we are is identical to a mereological sum. But it is no part of Constitutionalism to hold that any ordinary object, animal or not, is identical to a mereological sum.

There are independent reasons to reject an ontology of material things that holds that the "only material things are simples—presumably elementary particles—and things with lives" (Olson 2007: 226). First, whether or not there exist simples is an open empirical question (Schaffer 2003). Second, there is good reason to think that artifacts exist and are ontologically on a par with "natural" objects (Baker 2008; Baker 2004). In light of the fact that exclusive reliance on theories of composition leads to a wildly implausible metaphysics, it is a profound mistake to suppose that "a theory of composition would tell us what we are" (Olson 2007: 232).

In sum, according to Animalism (and van Inwagen's theory of composition), there is no *ontological* distinction between us and earthworms. By contrast, I think that metaphysics should tell us about what is fundamental to our being the kind of thing that we are (as opposed to earthworms), and about what is significant about us. Constitutionalism, at least on my view, holds that composition cannot suffice for ontology. To get "real objects" of the sorts we are familiar with from science and common sense, we need constitution.[10]

Arguments for Constitutionalism and Their Defense

1. An argument from biotechnology. It is no secret that biotechnology has made amazing strides in recent years. Pacemakers, artificial knees and hips, arms and legs, are only the beginning. Now cochlear implants allow deaf people to hear, and brain–machine interfaces will soon allow totally paralyzed people to operate robotic limbs by their thoughts. Monkeys have been trained to feed themselves by operating a realistic prosthetic arm (Whalley 2008; Moritz et al. 2008). There is no stopping progress on the replacement of organic parts of a body with nonorganic devices that allow paralyzed

---

[10] For discussion of limitations of algebraic theories of composition, see (Simons 2006). Peter van Inwagen has formulated a temporally indexed mereological theory that is to allow for objects (like animals) that change their parts. But his view has the counterintuitive consequence that there can be identical sums that share no parts: e.g. the sum that composed you when you were born (sum$_1$) is identical to the sum that composes you now (sum$_n$)—even though there is no part that sum$_1$ and sum$_n$ have in common (van Inwagen 2006).

people with, say, spinal cord injuries to function. The artificial devices are integrated with the organic parts in such a way that the devices contribute to (and make possible) cognitive processing.

Consider a case of a paralyzed person P who survives the implantation of a nonorganic mind–brain interface connected to robotic limbs which P can move "at will." Either the animal A associated with P before the operation survives the implantation operation or not.

Suppose that A does survive. After the operations integrating the neural implant and the robotic limbs, the patient's body includes artificial devices: she is no longer constituted by an animal but by the sum of an animal and certain artificial devices. Moreover, she can now move her robotic limbs. According to Olson, "[N]o animal could be partly or wholly inorganic" (Olson 2003: 321). So, the neural implant and robotic limbs cannot be parts of the animal A. But without the neural implant and robotic limbs, the animal cannot move. So after the operation, the person has a property—ability to move limbs—that the animal lacks. Now recall the third consequence of the thesis of identity of person P and animal A: there is no time at which the person P has a property—modal, indexical, whatever—and the animal A fails to have it then. So, the third consequence of the thesis of identity of person and animal is violated. It follows that the person is not identical to the animal.

Now suppose that animal A does not survive the operation. Suppose that the operation interferes with the biological unity of the human animal to such a degree that the animal does not survive the operation. But the person, who can move her limbs at t', does survive the operation. Recall the first consequence of the thesis of identity of person P and animal A: there is no time at which P exists and A fails to exist. This consequence is violated by this branch of the dilemma, according to which we suppose that the animal A does not survive the operation. Thus, again, the person P is not identical to the animal A.

So, whether the animal survives the operation or not, the success of biotechnology seems to up-end the Animalist. However, the Constitutionalist has no difficulty explaining the situation. On Constitutionalism, the person is necessarily embodied, but does not necessarily have the body that she has at a particular time. At time t, after the paralysis sets in but before the operations, the person is constituted by an animal and cannot move. At time t', after the operations, the person is constituted either by the sum of an animal and certain artificial devices or by the sum of organic and inorganic items (depending on whether the animal survives the operation). Either way, the person can move. At t, person P is constituted by an animal; at t', person P is constituted either by the sum of an animal and artificial devices or by the sum of organic and inorganic items. You and the person to whom you are identical have all the same properties at the same times. All the consequences of Constitutionalism (i')–(vi') hold.

Someone may object that I have "proved too much." The same reasoning of my argument from biotechnology against the identity of a person and animal can also show that the monkey is not identical to an animal. And that is obviously false; a monkey is paradigmatically identical to an animal.[11] But I need not deny that a monkey is identical to an animal. When the paralyzed monkey is operated on, either both the monkey and the animal go out of existence or both the monkey and the animal survive the operation. There is no time at which the monkey exists and the animal fails to exist.

On the one hand, suppose that the animal/monkey does not survive the integration of the neural implant and robotic limb. This would be the case on the Animalist assumption that animals can have no inorganic parts. On that assumption, the post-operation being is a new kind of creature—an organic-nonorganic hybrid. On the other hand, on the assumption (denied by many Animalists) that animals can have inorganic parts, the monkey/animal survives, and can move its limbs. In either case, the monkey and the animal are identical.

So, I can hold on to the view that the monkey is identical to an animal, but that the person is not. The reason that the person survives the operation is that her first-person perspective is still exemplified. On my view, it is irrelevant whether or not an animal can have inorganic parts. If an animal cannot have inorganic parts, then the person after the operation is no longer constituted by an animal, but rather by the sum of certain organic and inorganic parts. If an animal can have inorganic parts, then in the near future, there will be operations after which the person is no longer constituted by an animal, but by a sum of mostly inorganic items. So, if we recognize first-personal persistence conditions for persons, and third-personal persistence conditions for animals, we get a plausible account of how a person paralyzed at t can move at t', without denying that a monkey is an animal.

Notice that I am not relying on dubious thought experiments requiring brain transplants, or mental-state transplants. The scenario I just sketched is not only physically possible, but it is close to being actual.[12]

Other developments in biotechnology have implications for Snowdon's Link Thesis. Here is the Link Thesis:

If an individual is to be credited with possession of the concept of a person, then for any negative personal-identity judgment with the content "Person 1 at place p_1 and time t_1 is not identical with person 2 at p_2 and t_2," that individual accepts the corresponding negative animal-identity judgment with the content "Animal 1 at p_1 and t_1 is not identical with animal 2 at p_2 at t_2," must also be accepted. (Snowdon 1990: 81)

Suppose that person 1 is paralyzed and during the operation at t_1 to integrate the neural implant, something goes wrong and—as in the case of Terri Schiavo—the cerebral parts of the brain that regulate higher-level functioning are permanently destroyed.

---

[11] I would say that a monkey (in contrast to a person) is an animal nonderivatively.

[12] Perhaps in the more remote future, enough artificial replacements will be developed so that we would hold that a person still existed, yet there was no animal; if the biological functions of metabolism were performed by nonorganic mechanisms, and the essential organs (e.g. heart) were replaced by artificial devices, and the patient survived, then there would be a person constituted by an nonorganic body, with few organic parts left, or none at all.

However, with the aid of technology—ventilator, feeding tube, etc.—the animal is kept alive. There are great controversies here, but they do not seem to involve insufficient grasp of the term "person." Suppose that person 1, who dies at t_1, is not identical with any person at t_2. According to the Link Thesis, anyone who has the concept of a person will accept that animal 1 at p_1 and t_1 is not identical with animal 2 at p_2 and t_2. But is that so? Surely, one can accept a criterion of higher "brain death" for persons and not for animals without failing to understand the concept *person*. Regardless of the Link Thesis, the progress of biotechnology has made the ontological thesis that persons are identical to animals implausible.

2. An Argument from the Possibility of Bodily Resurrection. Resurrection in the Christian tradition requires the identical person who lives before death also to live after death. If bodily resurrection is possible and if Animalism is true, then the same living organism lives both before and after death—into eternity. But it is impossible that a pre-mortem living organism lives eternally after death. A pre-mortem living organism is corruptible; anything that is eternal is incorruptible. Corruptibility and incorruptibility are persistence conditions, and thus are had essentially. Therefore, no single individual can be corruptible during part of its existence and incorruptible during some other part. So, no pre-mortem living organism lives eternally, and Animalism is at odds with the Christian doctrine of resurrection. (This argument appears in detail in Baker 2007b.)

The Constitution view avoids the consequence for Animalism by taking personal identity to be a matter of sameness of first-person perspective over time. I give an Argument from Providence—based on the traditional idea of God's having natural knowledge and free knowledge—to show how it is within God's power to bring about the state of affairs in which Smith (the person with Smith's first-person perspective) can in eternity be constituted by an incorruptible body. There is a fact of the matter as to which person in eternity is Smith (Baker 2007b: 28–30).

In an online paper, Peter van Inwagen has taken issue with my view (van Inwagen 2006). As I understand him, van Inwagen has two criticisms: (1) I have given no noncircular informative definition of the words "x and y have the same first-person perspective" (van Inwagen 2006: 12); and (2) I do not show how there can be physical continuity between "the person who dies in the present age of the world and the person who is raised on the day of resurrection." Let me reply:

In response to (1), I agree. Any informative noncircular definition of persons or of personal identity over time must *ipso facto* be reductive. Since I believe that we are not reducible to nonpersonal or subpersonal items, of course I cannot give an informative noncircular definition of what makes us persons. Persons are fundamentally different kinds of beings from anything else in the natural world. I say a lot about human persons, but it does not amount to a noncircular informative definition (Baker 2011).

In response to (2), I do not think that physical continuity need be shown. In virtue of what is *Smith's* first-person perspective exemplified in the resurrection? The answer is

God's free decree.[13] According to a Christian version of Constitutionalism, it is within God's power to bring about Smith's existence in the resurrection without any physical continuity between Smith-constituted-by-his-earthly-body and Smith-constituted-by-resurrection-body-1. Smith exists in the resurrection in virtue of God's free decree that brings about both the exemplification of the first-person perspective that is Smith's and the state of affairs that the person (Smith) whose first-person perspective is exemplified is constituted by a certain resurrection body (Baker 2011).

It is not surprising that a discussion of resurrection appeals to God's powers without saying how He brings things about. We have no idea how God effects any of that which He freely decrees, from creation *ex nihilo* on. All that metaphysics can do is to leave room for a miracle—which is not explainable. Nobody—whether materialist or not—can explain how God brings about resurrected people. By not requiring bodily identity for personal identity, Constitutionalism—unlike Animalism—has conceptual room for a miracle.

Van Inwagen (2006) thinks that materialists have a special problem about resurrection. He thinks that "if human persons are physical substances, nothing but physical continuity can ground the identity of human persons across time." Since I don't know what van Inwagen packs into the notion of a physical substance, maybe I don't think that human persons are physical substances in his sense. I call myself a materialist (about the natural world), because I believe that every object and property exemplified in the natural world is either a physical object or property (i.e. recognized by theories of physics) or is constituted by physical objects or properties. There are no immaterial souls. If this is not enough to be a materialist, well, call me something else—just not a mind-body dualist.

In any case, believers in bodily resurrection are better off as Constitutionalists than as Animalists. In contrast to Animalists, Constitutionalists do not take being a person to be just a contingent and temporary property of beings that are fundamentally non-personal (organisms). Indeed, on the Animalist view, our having first-person perspectives (or any mental states at all) is irrelevant to the kind of being that we are (Baker 2007b: 30–1).

Conclusion

I have rebutted a series of Animalist arguments against Constitutionalism:

1. A Reductio Argument.
2. A "Too-Many Persons" (or "Too-Many Thinkers") Argument.
3. A "Thinking-Animal Argument."
4. An Argument from Composition.

---

[13] What God knows by his natural knowledge is that a particular exemplification of a first-person perspective would be Smith's (this is a necessary truth); what is a matter of God's free decree is whether or not that particular exemplification occurs.

And I have presented and defended two arguments on behalf of Constitutionalism:

1. An Argument from Biotechnology.
2. An Argument from the Possibility of Resurrection.

I hope to have shown that Constitutionalism is superior to Animalism as an onto-logical view of persons.

Bibliography

Aristotle. 1941. *The Basic Works of Aristotle*. Richard McKeon, ed. New York: Random House.

Baker, Lynne Rudder. 1997. Why Constitution is Not Identity. *Journal of Philosophy* 94: 599–621.

Baker, Lynne Rudder. 2004. The Ontology of Artifacts. *Philosophical Explorations* 7: 99–111.

Baker, Lynne Rudder. 2007a. *The Metaphysics of Everyday Life*. Cambridge: Cambridge University Press.

Baker, Lynne Rudder. 2007b. Persons and the Metaphysics of Resurrection. *Religious Studies* 43: 333–48.

Baker, Lynne Rudder. 2008. The Shrinking Difference Between Artifacts and Natural Objects. *American Philosophical Association Newsletter on Philosophy and Computers* 7, no. 2.

Baker, Lynne Rudder. 2011. Christian Materialism in a Scientific Age. *International Journal for Philosophy of Religion* 69, no. 1: 1–12.

Johansson, Jens. 2009. Review of *The Metaphysics of Everyday Life*. *Philosophical Quarterly* 59: 365–8.

Kearns, Stephen. 2009. Review of *The Metaphysics of Everyday Life*. *Philosophical Review* 118, no. 4: 533–5.

Lewis, David. 1991. *Parts of Classes*. Oxford: Basil Blackwell.

Mithen, S. 2004. Review Symposium of Andy Clark's Natural-Born Cyborgs. *Metascience* 13, no. 2: 163–9.

Moritz., Chet T., Steve I. Perlmutter, and Eberhard E. Fetz. 2008. Direct Control of Paralysed Muscles by Cortical Neurons. *Nature* 456, no. 07418: 639–42.

Olson, Eric T. 2003. An Argument for Animalism. In *Personal Identity*, ed. Raymond Martin, and John Barresi, 318–35. Malden, MA: Blackwell Publishing.

Olson, Eric T. 2007. *What Are We? A Study in Personal Ontology*. Oxford: Oxford University Press.

Perry, John. 1970. The Same F. *Philosophical Review* 79: 3–21.

Schaffer, Jonathan. 2003. Is There a Fundamental Level? *Noûs* 37: 498–517.

Simons, Peter. 2006. Real Wholes, Real Parts: Mereology Without Algebra. *Journal of Philosophy* 103, no. 12: 597–613.

Snowdon, Paul F. 1990. Persons, Animals and Bodies. In *The Person and the Human Mind*, ed. Christopher Gill, 83–107. Oxford: Clarendon Press.

Van Inwagen, Peter. 2006. I Look for the Resurrection of the Dead and the Life of the World to Come. Unpublished—online Word doc. <http://philosophy.nd.edu/people/all/profiles/van-inwagen-peter/documents/Resurrection.doc> accessed February 2016.

Wasserman, Ryan. 2004. The Constitution Question. *Noûs* 38: 693–710.

Whalley, Katherine. 2008. Brain–Machine Interfaces: Getting to Grips with a Robotic Arm. *Nature Reviews Neuroscience* 9, no. 499. <http://www.nature.com.silk.library.umass.edu:2048/nrn/journal/v9/n7/full/nrn2447.html>.

4

Constitution and the Debate between Animalism and Psychological Views

Denis Robinson

We begin with a section discussing Animalism's claim to be naturally favoured, by common sense, over Psychological views. This provides an opportunity also to introduce the idea of the need for Psychological views to believe in some sort of relation of coincidence or "constitution" between distinct material entities, and some attendant *prima facie* difficulties. The following sections further discuss constitution relations, specially a generic and minimalist version, and related issues in the ontology of material entities. A naturalistic physicalism is presupposed, setting aside both supernaturalist and Substance Dualist views, while aiming to limit essential appeal to ontological assumptions which go beyond those reasonably attributable to common sense.

Animalism's Distinctive Status, and the *Prima Facie* Acceptability of Psychological Views

Almost inevitably, materialists holding Psychological views *must* claim that non-identical common-sense material entities can at times coincide. The more plausible that *generic* claim can be made, the more appropriate it must be to see generic perplexities arising out of it as problems for everyone, hence *not* as reasons for preferring Animalism *per se*. A main task of this chapter is to argue that that generic claim is plausible, and to explore matters bearing on or arising out of it. That main business will begin in earnest in the next section.

This section will pave the way by reviewing the question of the *prima facie* plausibility—from the point of view, if you like, of common sense—of neo-Lockean views. Should Psychological views, once we grasp what they involve, be greeted with an "incredulous stare", so that even apparently conclusive arguments in their favour should be treated grudgingly and with suspicion? Or should they be regarded as plausible and unsurprising?

Why should we even raise such questions (of *prima facie* or common-sense plausibility) or enter the inevitably vague and controversial territory they involve? Appeals
to common sense are rarely decisive in metaphysics, and there is no prospect of them
being so here. The claim that G.E. Moore (and everyone else!) had no hands has been
thought arguably sufficiently repugnant to common sense to doom any theory
implying it. But more typically, metaphysics deals in dry and technical issues—matters
on which common sense can reasonably be held to have no opinion firmer than a
bemused shrug, and for which, even if a firmer opinion existed, it would be of little
account. However, although neither side in this debate is likely to claim "Moorean"
certainty, it is not to be seen as inherently dry and uninteresting to non-specialists.
After all, it concerns the essential characteristics and existence-conditions for ourselves, the very beings conducting the debate.

A more specific reason for caring about the overall intuitiveness (or otherwise) of
Psychological views is that they rely significantly on intuitions about cases, perhaps
arising out of "common sense" or some close relative of it. The status of such appeals is
controversial. We should ask whether Psychological views are inherently much more
counter-intuitive than Animalism, from a common-sense standpoint, since if they are,
intuitions about particular cases might risk suffering a *modus tollens* defeat by those
counter-intuitions.

Animalism says familiar human persons are strictly and metaphysically identical
with human animals. A human animal *becomes* a person—so comes to be *identical
with* that person—merely through acquiring the usual powers and accomplishments
of its species: capacities for self-conscious awareness, planning, intention, regret, psychological judgments, and communicative skills to match.

Sometimes differences between Animalism and its diverse competitors command
our attention: in religious warfare, persecution of blasphemers, or disputes relating to
abortion, conception, euthanasia, and the disposal of remains. Yet often we—even we
philosophers, when off work—forget those differences. This surely is partly because
our mundane interpersonal dealings tend to be homogenized by an ever-present
"human–animal interface". Proverbially, our generic fate is to live in a state of embodied
conflict between our generic *animal* nature and the effects of that social acculturation
which our distinctive *human* nature makes natural for us. These invariances, and that
social nature, mask from us the risk of being at cross-purposes, implicit in viewing
others as entities of quite different kinds from the entities they take themselves to be.

Alternatives to Animalism must acknowledge this distinguished role of human animals in our lives, while carrying some surplus burden of proof in the form of ontological and epistemic commitments beyond those of Animalism. (To put it bluntly,
non-Animalists must make it plausible that we are both acquainted with and identical
with entities not identical with those animals we are so well acquainted with and from
which we are, at least under mundane circumstances, so inseparable.) For these
reasons alone, human persons seeking a view of their own nature and persistence-
conditions might well think Animalism goes naturally to the head of the queue. Or,

more to our present purposes, they may think this to be so *at least* conditionally on rejecting Substance Dualism. So should the ease with which many people seem to accept Psychological views be seen as some sort of systematic error? This chapter is intended, not to demonstrate, but to improve the plausibility of the view that despite the *prima facie* handicaps, it is reasonable and coherent to favour Psychological views.

Let's return to the topic of "becoming a (human) person". In saying that according to Animalists, a human creature typically *becomes* a person through normal processes of maturation, it was necessary to add "and so comes to be *identical with* that person", because the form of words "an X becomes a Y" can mean different things with significantly different ontological import: they imply different things about comings, and ceasings, to exist.

We'll focus on the slightly more precise form of words "an X, the individual A, becomes a Y, the individual B". Where X is "human animal" and Y is "person", on an Animalist interpretation, A does not cease to exist, and though there comes to be a Y present, no new entity comes into existence in order to bring this about since A itself comes to be a Y: A is *identical with* B. (Call this "Type 1 Becoming".) A very different kind of example is one in which a pile of building materials becomes a house. In this case A, the pile of materials (that is, the *pile*, not the materials), ceases to exist in the course of this process, and a distinct entity B, the house, comes into existence, *replacing* A. (Call this "Type 2 Becoming".) In a third kind of case (the possibility of which is questioned by some, Olson[1] among them), a new entity B *does* come to exist, and it is that entity which is a Y, but nevertheless A is *not* replaced, but *continues* to exist, and moreover, subsequently coincides precisely with the newly existing B, and is composed of exactly the same ingredients as it. (Call this "Type 3 Becoming".)[2]

On Psychological views, a human animal's becoming a human person is *a case of Type 3 Becoming*. Persons *begin to exist when* a suitably continuing psychology first arises, and *cease to exist when* the relevant psychological connections, or the possibilities for continuing them, come to an end. Because our diverse psychological capacities arise gradually, and often fade gradually away, it's natural to think of a psychologically individuated person's coming into or going out of existence as a gradual event with quite vague boundaries. But existence does not come in degrees! Psychological views thus require us either to accept that each of us is an objectively vague entity (a view I'll entirely set aside), or to assume that one or another of the "multiple candidate" or "multiple precisification" stories about vagueness applies here, accepting that much thought and talk about particular human persons derives its truth from facts involving many slightly differing competing, or cooperating, truthmakers. This commitment—to *many* entities

---

[1] Olson has written so vigorously in defence of Animalism, most notably in Olson 1997, that it is seems entirely appropriate to refer to him in a chapter on these topics. It is only fair to Olson to note, though, that Olson 2007—to which this chapter refers several times—projects a much less partisan and more agnostic viewpoint than the earlier work.

[2] As will be noted later, there are ways of ceasing to be an X which are time-reversed analogues of these three ways of becoming an X.

differentiated merely by *slight* changes in the emerging or waning *mental* capacities of animals—is not one which Animalism shares. But is that commitment so costly that it pushes Psychological views back down the queue? Are these implications alone enough to give Psychological views a ranking of "last resort" when compared to Animalism?

We have long understood that vagueness runs through all discourse about commonplace entities, there being a myriad of highly similar, well-qualified competitors for being "precisely delineated" instances of such things as clouds or cats. The temporal boundaries of animals themselves are certainly vague. Is "dead" like "fake", so that a *dead* animal is necessarily *not* an animal? If *so*, and an animal ceases to exist when it dies, we may ask: *is there a precise instant of death*? If *not*, we must ask if there is a precise instant at which a dead animal ceases to exist. "No" is the plausible answer, either way. Even a millisecond is not an instant, and it's hardly clear that there's a difference of *principle* here hinging on how much longer than an instant such processes take. If Animalists must accept that their lives end with—and perhaps also begin with—gradual processes, taking longer than an instant, the cost to Psychological theorists of having to believe in perhaps long drawn-out, gradual processes at the beginnings and ends of their lives is arguably not a massively worse cost than comparable costs faced by Animalists. Arguably, then, there is no reason here to try to avoid Psychological views at all costs. It is important to note, for present purposes, that insofar as *prima facie* cases of Type 3 Becoming seem quite commonplace, they also *typically* appear to have this gradual character.

Let's turn briefly to noting the ease with which an Animalist perspective may be displaced. Here we should reflect on Locke's contribution (Locke 1975, Book 2, ch. 27). Whatever his exact intentions—and I am certainly no historian—it seems to me that Locke's discussion of personal identity *can* be read as mixing only mildly revisionist with descriptive (or "hermeneutic") elements, reminiscent of "explication" in a Quinean sense. What follows is meant to emphasize the extent of the apparently *descriptive* element.

Locke is plausibly read as advocating some regimentation of usages of words like "man" and "person", supported by *reductios* of alternatives, based on appeals to intuitions which suggest he believes he is mobilizing and clarifying *a pre-existing shared concept* rather than stipulatively introducing a new one. He seems to expect readers to recognize and endorse his conceptual claims. His optimism has been at least partly borne out: improved and amended ideas descended from Locke's have taken root and developed a considerable philosophical following. Crucially, *there have been many people ready to accept, in effect, the idea that "person" is a substance-concept* (and a distinctly non-biological one).

The notion of a "substance-concept" will be crucial in what follows. As the term is here used, such a concept is a sortal or "kind" concept so associated with *essential persistence-criteria* that something can begin or cease falling under it *only* by beginning or ceasing to exist. This entails that in most cases it is *a concept which comes to apply only through Type 2 or Type 3 Becoming.* In the context of animal-to-person becoming,

Type 2 Becoming seems not to be an option—no one thinks the human animal ceases to exist in becoming a person—so in this context, taking "person" to be a substance-concept is effectively equivalent to regarding becoming a *human* person as *Type 3 Becoming*. The fact that many find post-Lockean views plausible, then, seems good evidence that Type 3 Becoming, *per se*, does not offend common sense. Substance-concepts are importantly related to, but different from, "phase-sortal concepts", which are typically associated with Type 1 Becoming. More will be said about these import-ant notions in later sections.

There are further implications of Lockean views which might be seen as going against common sense, but which Locke and many following him do not seem to have resiled from: specially, the possibility of purely material, spatio-temporally discon-tinuous and intermittently existing persons. Locke was after all attempting to establish the possibility of Judgment Day resurrection *whether or not* persons are purely mater-ial beings, so you might say the crowning claim of his enterprise was the possibility of discontinuous, at least partly material, existence for such beings. Setting aside the reli-gious *motif*, the same point is illustrated by Locke's examples of the Day Man and the Night Man, and the prince and the cobbler (Locke 1975, Book 2, ch. 27, paras 23, 15). These consequences of Locke's position are explicit and obvious, but many readers have failed to throw up their arms in dismay over them.

This might seem like a point on which Animalist and neo-Lockean doctrines are on a par, since Animalists too might accept the possibility of discontinuous existence for animals, through the fantasy of teleportation and the like. Acceptance of such possibil-ities is not the domain of Psychological theorists alone. But the point can be sharp-ened. The *range* of such neo-Lockean possibilities *for persons* which people seem comfortable envisaging—for instance, having one's mental states transferred to a non-biological realizer such as a computer or android—cannot readily be accounted for simply by conjoining Animalism with the assumed possibility of discontinuous existence for animals and other ordinary material objects. This idea of persons as *real-izable by* successive, possibly distinct entities—even by entities of quite different kinds!— is, I believe, Locke's truly radical doctrine, and this is what underlies the pos-sibility, given Locke's views, of a distinctive kind of intermittent or discontinuous exist-ence for persons. If any consequence of Psychological views were to offend against common sense, it might be thought to be this one. In fact though, not only readers of Locke, but millions of viewers of popular entertainment, have little problem with programs—*Star Trek* is the best-known example—premised on a thoroughly neo-Lockean understanding of personal identity.[3]

---

[3] Of course, all fantasy fiction requires knowing suspensions of disbelief, and many fantasies portray people magically transported in a twinkling from one place—or body—to another. But such narratives depend on explicitly supernaturalistic back stories. *Star Trek* and its descendants instead present an idea of human (and other) persons as reconstructable by transfer of suitable information, an in principle natural-istic conception of a kind that many familiar with both philosophy, and *Star Trek*, have found eminently compatible with post-Lockean thought.

Mark Johnston, in an important critique of the "method of cases" (appealing to intuitions when constructing philosophical views), says

Our intuitive reactions to the puzzle cases should be able to be taken as manifestations of our grasp of…necessary and sufficient conditions, and not as overgeneralizations from the everyday run of cases or manifestations of a particular conception of people, be it a religious conception…or some more inchoate secular counterpart. (Johnston 1987: 60)

Without following Johnston in his wholesale antipathy to "the method of cases" and to Psychological accounts of personal identity, we should contemplate one of his gentler morals, namely that we should not attach too much importance to intuitions until we have persuaded ourselves that they are not due to some unconscious distorting influence stemming from the cultural remnants of some officially abandoned doctrine. The obvious candidate for such a distorting influence, religious or secular, on "common sense", is in this case Substance Dualism. Forms of Substance Dualism have been widespread and popular for millennia, and arguably they have marked human cultures so deeply that neither in Locke's time, nor since, has it been easy for us to resist falling under the spell of intuitions which, perhaps beneath the table-top of consciousness, trade on such views, even while we consciously disavow them. The suggestion has some credibility, and Locke does employ the notion of the soul in setting up his prince and cobbler example. (Indeed students, in my experience, sometimes protest that Locke's use of this example is illegitimate precisely because it brings into play intuitions having Dualist origins.) But the suggestion is essentially speculative. There are no clear grounds for believing that, had Locke known of radio transmission, he would have been less satisfied with an example in which devices involving an information-bearing radio signal were used to do the job.

In fact, we could ask whether the historic—or rather prehistoric—order of derivation was in fact the reverse of what is here suggested. If an inchoate and unanalysed ur-concept of personhood of a broadly Lockean kind were to have developed in the early millennia of human history, we can easily enough imagine how it might have been transmogrified into Substance Dualism, perhaps through a combination of primitive theorizing about the role of breath, and an anticipation of Descartes' early fallacy of inferring the immaterial nature of the self from the possibility of doubting the existence of all that is material without doubting the existence of oneself.[4] But given that there is no real prospect of reconstructing the actual history of these matters, the moral to be drawn from these reflections in this chapter will be a partly coherentist one. Neo-Lockeans need not worry too hard about the provenance of the intuitions which seem to support our theories, provided the theories themselves are coherent and yield a satisfying account of how the concept of a person can be seen as integrated into our ordinary thought and practice about selves and others. Nothing in this section has established that Psychological views should be considered positions of last resort. On that note, we move on to the next section.

---

[4] *Discourse on Method*, Part IV.

Constitution

Many anti-Animalist Materialists describe the relation between human persons and human animals by saying the person is *constituted* by the animal. Olson calls this "the constitution view" (Olson 2007: ch. 3). Some problems he raises for it, such as his challenging "thinking animal" or "too many thinkers" problem, are specific to the case of persons (Olson 2003: 35; 2007: 60). But he also raises issues for *constitutionalism* itself. This is simply the view that (non-identical) material things *can* stand in the relationship of *constitution*. Olson emphasizes the importance of this issue, saying, for instance:

Whether the constitution view is right depends largely on the truth of constitutionalism in general. If constitutionalism is false, so is the constitution view. *If constitutionalism is true, on the other hand, and if we are material things, it will be hard not to accept the constitution view.* (Olson 2007: 52, my italics)

This remark seems to justify setting aside for present purposes, Olson's more specific challenges, and here concentrating on issues about constitution. To clarify the project, we can begin with some points about usage of the word "constitution". The word (as a technical term of philosophy) has evolved over the past four and a half decades, and some inconsistencies of usage have developed, along with some possibly misleading habitual taxonomies of positions. This chapter aims to defend the plausibility of a "constitution view"; but the view defended will not be quite the view Olson discusses under that label.

An English-language "is" of constitution was recognized and named in Wiggins (1967), using examples like "the portico *is* wood and stucco", and "the jug *is* the collection of china-bits"(Wiggins 1967: 10). It was essential to Wiggins' agenda to distinguish this term from the "is" of identity. The term "constitutes" came to figure in 1970s discussions of semantics for mass terms, most commonly as an introduced technical term, or primitive predicate in a formal language, to denote a relation between material objects, and either "Quantities" of matter (in Helen Cartwright's technical sense, which I'll capitalize), or stuffs like snow or gold, construed as individuals (Cartwright 1970; Burge 1975). Allan Gibbard also used "constituted of" as a synonym for "made of", and suggested a shared temporal parts account of this relation, in his seminal "Contingent Identity", with its discussion of a statue made from a lump of clay (Gibbard 1975: 192). Usage of the term in Robinson (1982a; 1982b) derives from such sources. Thus Robinson (1982a) defended the view of constitution as sharing of temporal parts, following both Gibbard (1975) and Lewis (1976), though Lewis *named* the relation, not "constitution", but "identity-at-a-time".[5]

---

[5] There are two prima facie different uses of the term "constitution", exemplified by the two examples from Wiggins: i.e. (i) in relating material individuals like lumps of clay, aggregates of china bits, Quantities of gold, or statues to one another; and (ii) in relating such individuals to "stuffs" construed as spatio-temporally widespread individuals, e.g. Gold, Snow, Porridge, Wood, and Stucco. But these can be so analysed as to reveal a single underlying concept of constitution, if one is prepared to equate, e.g., "This ring is gold" with

Subsequently the usage has diversified. Depending on context, some continue to use the word in a *generic* way more in line with its usage over the first couple of decades of its technical philosophical use, while others have in the past couple of decades refined its use, restricting its denotation to a *more narrowly* defined relation.

First, the *generic* use. This is typically in play when people classify puzzle cases as instantiating "problems" (or "puzzles" or "paradoxes") "of (material) constitution". These are cases of which it can be argued, rightly or wrongly, that *both members of a pair of non-identical material entities, at or over some time, are composed of exactly the same matter and hence share many important properties, including occupying exactly the same spatial region.* This relation (when real and not merely apparent) is "constitution" in the most generic technical philosophical sense of that term.[6] Because this notion imports minimal assumptions about the *nature or analysis* of the constitution relation, it will henceforth be called "minimal constitution", or for short "m-constitution". "Minimal constitution-alism", or "m-constitutionalism", then, is the doctrine that, however they are to be described in further detail, cases of constitution in this sense are really possible. We should immediately note (a) that if m-constitutionalism is false, Type 3 Becoming is impossible, and (b) that putative examples of Type 3 Becoming are *not* by any means the only kind of examples which it may be tempting to regard as cases of m-constitution.

One reason for viewing such cases as "paradoxical" is their apparent clash with the popular saying that "two things can't be in the same place at the same time".[7] But this saying is interpreted most sensibly (and most charitably to common sense) as implicitly qualified, meaning something like "two material things can't be in the same place at the same time *unless* (at that time) *they share their matter*".[8] So construed, the "truism" merely draws attention to matter's well-known resistance to the passage of other matter. This interpretation is most charitable to common sense because it allows common sense to acknowledge without inconsistency the possibility of Type 3 Becoming. This chapter accordingly defends the *m-constitutionalist viewpoint*, in opposition to *strict deniers*, who deny the very possibility of m-constitution, and hence of Type 3 Becoming.

Second, *more specific* notions of "constitution" arise because occasions of m-constitution can be analysed or further characterized in diverse ways. Over the past couple of decades it has become common to restrict the "constitution" label to relations which fit a favoured, more detailed analysis. One influential voice in this trend has

---

"For some x, x is a Quantity of Gold and x constitutes this ring", in other words, by viewing the constitution of entities by stuffs, as mediated by Quantities of those stuffs.

[6] A small caveat: people differ over what to say about the limiting case where the entities have exactly the same lifetime. Some of us say that such cases are "limit cases" of constitution, so that constitution is neither an irreflexive nor an asymmetric relation. Others vigorously oppose that view.

[7] In Olson's words: "We can increase the tension by noting the apparent truism that no two material things can be in exactly the same place at once. If we know anything about material things, we know that they compete for space and exclude one another" (2007: 48).

[8] The reconciliation with common sense is even easier if we say—as four-dimensionalists and other believers in constitution typically do say—that in ordinary synchronic counting we usually count, not by identity, but by constitution.

been Lynne Rudder Baker (e.g. in Baker 1997; 2000), who has vigorously defended a view she sometimes calls "the Constitution View" (note the definite article): many others have followed her in this usage. Thus "constitution" is now often understood to denote only relations along the lines of those picked out by Baker's favoured account. The resultant narrower version of constitutionalism is committed to various essentialist theses, doctrines about "primary kinds", and *inter alia* insistence that constitution is an asymmetric—hence irreflexive—relation. Henceforth "n-constitution" (for "narrowly defined constitution") will be used for those relations which fit Baker's more specific account, or something similar. An important point bearing on the strategy which follows is the following. Any instance of n-constitution will be *a fortiori* an instance of m-constitution (not vice versa!). Hence any sustainable claim about m-constitution in general will apply *a fortiori* to the narrower class of instances of n-constitution.

Olson 2007 introduces the idea of constitution with the following remarks:

The claim, then, is that two or more things can be made entirely of the same matter at the same time. For technical reasons it will be useful to recast this idea in slightly different terms. (Olson 2007: 49)

The first sentence is a simple statement of m-constitutionalism. The "technical reason" Olson cites for not resting with that formulation is that four-dimensionalists "say that two things can be made of the same matter at once, but they don't mean it in the sense that is relevant here" (Olson 2007: 49, n. 1). Olson 2007 accordingly gives "constitution" and "temporal parts" a separate chapter each.

Though there is a distinctive four-dimensionalist take on constitution, I think Olson is seriously mistaken to give such a reason for treating four-dimensionalism and constitutionalism as contraries. Recent constitutionalists such as Baker do give the word "constitution" a meaning which goes *beyond* "two or more things being made entirely of the same matter at the same time", but that doesn't imply that they change the ordinary meaning of the latter words. And there is no reason at all to say that four-dimensionalists are required to change the ordinary meanings of these words. Contrary to some prevalent misunderstandings of four-dimensionalism, it need not be an eliminativist, nor a reductionist, doctrine! (Compare Lewis 1983: postscript B.) Four-dimensionalism simply offers a neat analysis of m-constitution as sharing of temporal parts.

Where A and B stand in the m-constitution relation at or over time t, the four-dimensionalist can say that A and B *share their temporal parts* at or over t. This is equivalent to saying that A's t-part and B's t-part are identical. This in turn has resulted in some terminological muddying of the waters, associated with the slogan "Constitution is Identity", which originally came into play as a way of referring to the doctrine that m-constitution between entities *over the whole of their joint lifetime* entails that they are identical—something which follows from that very shared-parts doctrine.[9] As so used, the slogan never implied that the constitution relation is the

---

[9] See Johnston 1992 and Noonan 1993.

identity relation (merely that they overlap in certain "limit cases"), just as the claim that things have a shared part is not equivalent to an identity claim. But the boundary has become blurred between that original interpretation and a use of the slogan to mean straightforwardly that constitution and identity are indeed the very same relation. This has been costly to the image of four-dimensionalism, since it blurs the line between a doctrine which *strictly denies* the possibility of Type-3 Becoming, and a doctrine which provides for it. In a similar way a terminology of "pluralism" versus "monism" has evolved which sometimes classifies four-dimensionalism as a "monist" view (because in the limit case a single entity, as it might be both a lump of clay and a statue, is present) although such a classification thereby associates four-dimensionalism, which permits Type-3 Becoming, with views which strictly deny it (by saying, in effect, that "creating" the statue by modelling the lump provides a case either of Type 1 or Type 2 Becoming). Kit Fine (2003) has a useful terminology which at least subdivides "monisms": strict deniers are called "extreme monists" and the four-dimensionalist view here considered is called "strictly moderate monism" (Fine 2003: 199). Such writers as Harold Noonan (2008) and Penelope Mackie (2008) also use this or related terminology, which though not self-explanatory preserves important distinctions. Many writers, unfortunately, do not follow them.

N-constitutionalism and four-dimensionalism, in any case, provide different options for defending the viability of Psychological views by allowing for Type-3 Becoming. Chapters 3 and 5 of Olson (2007) raise a variety of difficulties for these options, and like all the chapters of that book, they are worthy of a detailed critique. But this is not the place for so ambitious an enterprise. An alternative approach will instead be pursued in what follows. Though I believe four-dimensionalism is a plausible ontological approach and says little which, properly understood, conflicts with common sense, I also believe the prospects are good for a defence of m-constitutionalism—including a useful exploration of some of the deep issues about sortal concepts, substances, the "grounding" of sortal properties, and associated issues of modality—which is "ecumenical" in the following sense. It abstains from invoking either the doctrine of unrestricted temporal partition, which I take to be the *sine qua non* of four-dimensionalism properly so-called, or the further claims which n-constitutionalism typically adds to basic m-constitutionalism. What follows attempts to make a start on this project. Such commitments as eventually come will be consonant with a four-dimensionalist view but will not use four-dimensionalist apparatus.[10]

One virtue of this ecumenical approach is that, since both n-constitutionalist and four-dimensionalist accounts of particular cases typically entail that they fit the conditions for m-constitution, any "ecumenical" conclusions which can be drawn

---

[10] An important caveat: in order to avoid ambiguities and confusions easily generated by reliance on ordinary English tenses, particularly associated with cases that involve dynamic systems, such as organisms which continuously change their matter, I shall frequently make use of explicit relativization to times. I believe quantification over times (both moments and periods) is itself commonsensical and commonplace, but in case it seems questionable, it is worth pointing out that it is at least distinct from full-fledged four-dimensionalism.

about m-constitution will be available for adaptation into those other frameworks. Most importantly, if good reasons can be established for requiring a viable materialist ontology to allow for m-constitution, they may be seen as undermining the viability of strict denials either of m-constitutionalism or the possibility of Type-3 Becoming. Debates and problems about how to flesh out a bare m-constitutionalist account will then be best viewed, arguably, as in-house disputes within generic materialist ontology, not to be seen as automatically undermining the plausibility of Psychological views of personal identity.

This is a good point at which to refine slightly the account of m-constitution, in a way suited to the recognition that, as remarked earlier, it may relate entities of a dynamic nature and constantly changing material composition. I define *momentary co-composition*, as a relation MCC(x,y,t) obtaining between material entities x and y relative to a *moment* t iff *x and y exist at t* and *the fundamental physical constituents of x at t are all and only the fundamental physical constituents of y at t*.[11] The relation m-const(x,y,t) ("x minimally constitutes y relative to t") is the relation which obtains between x, y, and t iff *either t is a moment and MCC(x,y,t) or t is a period and for every moment t* within t, MCC(x,y,t*)*.[12]

I'm comfortable with m-constitution being an equivalence relation. Its reflexivity does not limit it to cases of identity, and its symmetry does not preclude its having interestingly asymmetric instances. (Furthermore, this lets us acknowledge the multiple occupancy view—defended in Robinson 1985—that cases of fission symmetrically exemplify this relation, though this unpopular claim hardly suits my more ecumenical purposes.)[13]

Let's now contemplate some examples of m-constitution.

---

[11] I take it that material entities are a proper sub-set of physical entities, not assuming that all fundamental physical constituents of a material entity—such as quarks—need be material. I purposely avoid the messiness which gunk could inject into this discussion.

[12] Anyone who cannot swallow my use of "m-constitution" is welcome to substitute the term "co-composition". There's a trivial ambiguity in how four-dimensionalists should interpret the above definition, when either x or y may be brief or momentary stages of longer-persisting things. Should we think of the "fundamental constituents" mentioned in the definition as likewise brief or momentary stages of longer-lasting entities like electrons? Or as the longer-lived entities themselves? Not a problem! Either answer will do, one condition necessarily being met just if the other is. There is nothing wrong for a four-dimensionalist in saying that relative to t—at or over t—one of the constituents of x is an electron, however brief t is: this will be true just if that electron's t-part is equally a constituent of x relative to t. Thus the definition does not violate our ecumenical aim by precluding four-dimensionalism. Note that Sider's idiosyncratic "stage theory" might not fit all the things said here about four-dimensionalism, but space does not permit discussing either Sider's view or Gallois' so-called "occasional identity" view.

[13] It's crucial to distinguish "constitution", *qua* technical term in metaphysics, from the ordinary-language homonym it descends from. The same goes for "Identity": henceforth, as a constant reminder, I shall capitalize the latter technical term. Neither "Constitution", in its technical sense, nor Identity, is unambiguously expressed by ordinary language expressions like "is", "is the same as", "is the same thing as", "is physically identical with", or other variants, in part because ordinary language does not systematically distinguish Constitution relations from Identity. It's important to beware of intuitions about the relations designated by the technical terms which may originate in their ordinary-language ancestry. I think the idea that "Constitution" must be asymmetric stems from ordinary language: but here we need an apt technical term, not ordinary-language conceptual analysis.

Examples of M-Constitution

Examples like the following, I claim, make generic m-constitutionalism *per se* not merely plausible, but well-nigh inescapable. An important point about these examples is that although some count as cases of Type-3 Becoming, some do not. Claims that putative cases of Type-3 Becoming may, with varying degrees of difficulty, be reinterpreted as cases of Type-1 or Type-2 Becoming (and ditto for their temporally reversed twins, the various kinds of Ceasing), must tend to become otiose if there are cases crying out for an m-constitutionalist description which are not on any view instances of Type-3 Becoming. In the context of the debate between Animalist and Psychological views, where it is precisely the possibility of Type-3 Becoming which is at issue, these other examples may seem of questionable relevance. But the agenda of this chapter is to argue on the contrary that we should be happy to treat the ontology of Persons and their relations to Animals in a manner which is integrated with our broader materialist ontology, and if the latter involves cases of m-constitution it is not clear why the former should not also invoke the same relation.

Example 1: car, doors

Suppose the doors of my ten-year-old car are removed and melted down for scrap. Afterwards I use my car as a beach buggy. There is a *bona fide* material object which was previously a proper part of my car. In fact, the factory might produce such items whole, calling them "pre-cars", only fabricating and screwing on doors immediately prior to delivery. The pre-car now coincides with my car. By Leibniz's law, they cannot be Identical, since the doors were once part of my car, but were never part of the pre-car. Therefore this is an example—thoroughly commonsensical, I claim—in which a pair of everyday material objects come to be related by m-constitution.

Countless similar examples are available. Robinson (1982a) uses the example of a cloak composed of a single piece of cloth, and a single button. After losing the button, the cloak is m-constituted solely by the piece of cloth, which never had a button as a part. Richard Cartwright's classic (1975) uses the example of a matchbook from which a single match is torn. Lewis (1986) has an example involving the Great Western Railway. Geach has a version of an ancient "Amputation Puzzle", concerning an amputee cat Tibbles, and Tib, the tail-less cat-complement (Wiggins 1968). A chief difference between my examples and the case of Tibbles is that the parts which come to coincide with wholes are *articulated* parts (delineated by non-arbitrary physical boundaries), indisputably material objects in their own right, whereas some may quibble over, for example, the pre-amputation existence of the entity Tib. But the difference is slight given the sensible view that we continually extend the notion of "part" to non-articulated parts.

Examples 2A, 2B: boulder, mountain

These develop an example from Robinson (1982a). They may defy geological knowledge but I don't believe they defy common sense.

VERSION A

Molten lava flows into the seabed, solidifying within a giant undersea sinkhole to form an enormous boulder. Over geological time mud and detritus are continually added to the sea floor. The boulder becomes enveloped in sedimentary rock. Subsequent tectonic forces raise the solidified seabed and the sea retreats. As it does so the softer sedimentary rock is eroded by the weather. Eventually a mountain consisting of a single enormous boulder rests on an eroded sedimentary plateau. Finally thermal stress due to an ice age causes the boulder to fragment into a million small pieces. The mountain remains. The boulder exists before the mountain, the mountain exists after the boulder ceases to exist, the boulder was once beneath the sea, the mountain never was, and the mountain comes to be composed of many loose fragments, which the boulder never was. Mountain and boulder are non-Identical. For several million years they stand in the m-constitution relation. This example is structurally different from many others, in that the entities in question have overlapping lifespans. The mountain thus cannot in this case be viewed as "merely a phase" of the boulder—nor vice versa!

VERSION B

This case starts with a mass of congealed sandy sediment forced upwards through tectonic pressure. The viscosity of this sediment is due to the presence of a certain sticky mineral. Eventually the mass becomes a mountain. Drying and warm weather trigger chemical reactions, the sticky mineral turns to cement, and the mountain solidifies into a single giant boulder. From then on, the example resembles the previous version.

Despite differences, Version B has a structural similarity to the case of the ordinary (not teleported or brain-transplanted) human person, on a Psychological view. The shorter-lasting object (the boulder) comes to exist through gradual internal physical and chemical changes within the longer-lasting object (the mountain), and coincides with the latter until ceasing to exist through another sequence of internal changes.

Example 3: gold/ring/brooch

Great-Aunt Mary bequeaths a gold ring to Aunt Jane, who has it melted down and made into a small brooch. The brooch and ring are distinct material objects which never coexist. The Quantity of gold persists over the entire period. It is not Identical with either ring or brooch. So long as the ring exists it stands in the m-constitution relation to the gold; ditto for the brooch.

When considering these examples, important points to note include the following:

(i) Cars and pre-cars, boulders, mountains, rings, and brooches are material objects, but in none of these cases do coinciding entities "compete for space and exclude one another".

(ii) My car's doors are *inessential* parts: removing them doesn't "replace" my car with another. It's not plausible that the pre-car ceased to exist when the doors were screwed on. *Cases of potential m-constitution can be as wide-spread as cases of objects having inessential parts!* Note too that if we take the pre-car to be a car all along, the act of adding the doors will produce a case of the so-called "paradox of increase", a kind of time-reversed version of the case here presented.

(iii) It's not plausible in either example that the mountain's creation destroys the boulder, or vice versa.[14]

(iv) Relevant temporal boundaries in the boulder/mountain examples are vague. This in no way negates the claim that for a time, there is m-constitution between mountain and boulder.

(v) Quantities of stuff are *bona fide*, common-sense material entities which persist and may be reidentified over time, may be created and destroyed, and which are as an ontological category distinct from material objects. *To acknowledge this fact is to acknowledge that there is a proliferation of cases of m-constitution involving such entities.* It is not plausible to say that the gold ceases to exist at any point in Example 3.

(vi) It is not plausible to say that the ring still exists when Aunt Jane is wearing her brooch.

(vii) Some of the claims could be challenged in various ways familiar in the literature. For instance, the gold ring and the gold brooch might be said merely to be perturbations in the form of the Quantity of gold, not *bona fide* substances at all. Something similar might even be said about the mountain examples, viewing both boulder and mountain as stages in the life of a Quantity of mineral stuffs. Briefly, there are several reasons for setting aside at least some such challenges in the present context. First, they fly in the face of common sense, seeming to be *ad hoc* manoeuvres which in effect threaten to leave us likely to be often unable to judge when we are or are not referring to a temporally bounded entity as opposed to some longer-lasting object or Quantity. Second, they do not generalize to all cases. That is the point of example 1. Third, if there are *any* kinds of case which are much more plausibly described as cases of m-constitution than any other way, such motivation as might be mustered for forcing accounts of these cases into anything but an m-constitutional account will be at least largely undermined. The project here is to see what a plausible overall materialistic ontology looks like, not to rule on individual cases in relative isolation.

Compared to these examples, one of the most popular—indeed hackneyed—examples of m-constitution, where a "lump" of clay comes to coincide with a statue, provides a somewhat regrettable choice of model.[15] "Lump" is not a paradigmatic sortal, being too

[14] Compare Burke 1994, section II, where it is argued that when a piece of copper is used to make a statue, the piece of copper is destroyed and replaced with another which is identical with the statue. This is one instance where solutions to supposed "puzzles" of constitution can arguably be seen as *ad hoc* and not readily generalized, once a sufficiently wide variety of examples is considered.

[15] It's a rather convenient example given the agenda of Gibbard 1975, but ironically, most people who use it don't share Gibbard's agenda, and often ignore Gibbard's precise version of the example where, most unusually, the two entities never fail to coincide.

vague in its usage to determine persistence-criteria not hostage to argumentative fortune. If I melt a lump and allow it to congeal, do I have the same lump? If I roll it as thin
as filo pastry, then knead it together again, do I have the same lump? I don't know, and
it rarely matters. Because it is so unclear that these questions have principled answers,
I assimilate lumps to *nondescript material entities*. This is by no means to say that such
entities are not real! But "nondescript material entities", as I shall use the phrase,
are perforce individuated in part by *ad hoc* means, in the absence of paradigmatic
substance-kinds to which they belong and which determine relatively determinate
identity- and persistence-conditions for them. This means that intuitions about lump/
statue cases can easily waver and judgments can seem arbitrary. It also helps engender
the attitude that in any case of constitution, one entity is, by its kind, "subordinate to"
the other. "Substances" in some strong sense are taken as "paradigmatic" material
entities, and cases of m-constitution involving "inferior" entities like masses, lumps,
and heterogeneous aggregates are segregated from cases like our boulder/mountain
cases where both parties to the relationship carry "substantial" ontological weight. But
the latter cases are more *a propos* in the debate over Animalism.

Compare Quantities. If some gold goes missing, there are fairly determinate truth-
conditions for the claim that *that* gold has been recovered. Common sense is well aware
that some gold can be divided for concealment into many portions, some being sent to
each of five continents, but later reunited in a single ingot, without *that* gold ever ceasing
to exist, even though philosophers, despite Helen Cartwright's best efforts, seem loath
to allow Quantities equal status with objects in the materialist scheme. "Lump" (with its
unlovely relative "hunk") sits uneasily between fully fledged object sortals like "boulder",
"ring", and "mountain", on one hand, and "Quantities" on the other. So those reluctant to
acknowledge m-constitution may all too easily suggest *ad hoc* alternatives—like "the
lump does not survive the making of the statue"—which just do not plausibly generalize
to the earlier examples. ("Quantity" may not be ideal for the requisite technical term.
Dean Zimmerman's "masses" (1995) would be equally good, though both terms have
misleading ordinary language connotations. In an ideal world the ontological category
would be properly acknowledged and well understood, not treated as "second rate", and
a relatively neutral label would be standardly used for it.)

This completes my argument for the extreme common-sense implausibility of
denying m-constitutionalism. Next I shall briefly sketch some approaches to some of
the most basic questions raised by the acceptance of m-constitution as *bona fide* and
pervasive, with some reference to the case of human persons, set in the context of some
suggestions about the ontology of material entities.

Kinds, Sortals, Substances, and Materialist Ontology

The discussion at the end of the immediately preceding section reflects in part the view
that the category of "substances", in a sense which at least roughly correlates with the
conceptual category of "substance concepts", is too often given pride of place in thought

about materialist ontology. The Heraclitean aspects of our world, to which such categories do not readily apply, are too pervasive to be brushed into the margins. That view is maintained in this section. Somewhat as the perfect circular motions of Aristotelian cosmology needed to be replaced by the functions and derivatives of Newtonian dynamics in order to cope with the complex movements resulting from free fall in a space permeated by variable, continuous fields of force, so the continuities, heterogeneities, and dynamism of the physical world set limits to the descriptive reach of those substance-oriented categories. But that view is consistent with and complemented by the views, also taken here, that the world contains entities to which something like a traditional notion of "substance" applies; that we constantly employ, with great cognitive benefits, "substance concepts" in something like the sense that term has been given in recent decades; that animals and persons are reasonably viewed as substances in something like the relevant sense; and that "person" is in a relevant sense a substance-concept. None of these categories is however free from vagueness, gradual transitions, and borderline cases.

Within the context of continuing to sketch some elements of the kind of approach to materialist ontology here favoured, we can now explore a couple of the familiar problems for constitutionalism. Olson refers to some of them when he says:

In each of these [proposed cases]... numerically different objects not only coincide materially, but also differ in important... respects... The objects differ in *kind*... in their *modal properties*... [and] have *different persistence conditions*. (Olson 2007: 30, my italics)

These differences between identically composed entities in respect of kind, modal properties, and persistence-conditions, are aspects of the "grounding problem" (Bennett 2004): they are salient and important, and arise with m-constitution cases as well as with the stronger relation Olson discusses. How are they to be explained? I'll discuss differences in *kind*, and *persistence conditions*. The discussions are linked and interwoven. (Differences in modal properties have been to my mind well dealt with by Gibbard 1975, Lewis 1971, Noonan 1991, and many others. What follows is meant to be consonant with the approach taken by those authors, specially Lewis 1971.)[16]

Our discussion of *kinds* begins with a (brief and incomplete) explanation of *sortals*, and some related notions, specially *mass nouns*. Sortals may be words or concepts. A paradigm *substance-sortal* F is associated with persistence-conditions which entail that something is an F at all, or none, of the times at which it exists. A *phase-sortal* is logically equivalent to the addition of some contingent or temporary requirement to criteria associated with an actual or possible substance-sortal.[17] "Associated" covers

---

[16] There are further apparent property-discrepancies which generate further aspects of the "grounding problem", not to be addressed here. For instance, it may be said that in the case of Gibbard's example of the lump of clay Lumpl and the always-coincident statue Goliath, Goliath has a value as an artwork that Lumpl lacks. Issues about both modality, and the opacity of intentional contexts, obviously arise here, and space does not permit addressing any of them in the present chapter.

[17] Four-dimensionalism is not excluded by the invocation of these notions: to the contrary, they can be used to avoid misunderstandings and misrepresentations of four-dimensionalism's consequences. Braddon-Mitchell and Miller 2006 provide an excellent discussion of these issues.

two cases: those where knowledge of the associated conditions is required for ordinary communicative understanding of the term or grasp of the concept, and those (typified by natural kind and "twin-earthable" terms) where it is not, and the conditions are best seen as part of some empirically discoverable "real essence".

Paradigm mass nouns are similarly associated with persistence-conditions, but paradigm sortals, unlike paradigm mass nouns, are *also* associated with *synchronic counting conditions*. If, for sortal "F", at time t x is an F and y exists at t, then criteria associated with "F" suffice to determine in principle whether or not x and y are properly counted at t as one F.[18]

Substance sortals, phase sortals and mass nouns provide useful but coarse-grained and incomplete tools for materialist taxonomy. Given the Protean character of language, not every sortal determines a class of substances, and not every mass term applies to paradigm Quantities of stuff, even when abstract nouns are set aside. "Furniture" and "doggerel" behave like mass nouns, "chess-game" and "tornado" like substance-sortals. This is why I refer to *paradigm* substance sortals and mass nouns. Furthermore, as already noted, the material world is strewn with *nondescript material entities*, not easily classified in these terms: chalk marks, flames, ripples, rivers, patches of gum, drifts of household dust, remainders of servings of fish and chips, and many more.

There is a well-known neo-Aristotelian tradition keen to flesh out the definition of substance sortals, or of substances, in terms like the following:

f is a substance-concept only if f determines either a principle of *activity*, a principle of *functioning* or a principle of *operation* for members of its extension. (Wiggins 2001: 72)

Consonant with the Aristotelian tradition, we may further require that the essence of a complex substance involves a form or principle of unity, a relation among its possibly varying parts which is such that if it holds at a given time then the substance exists at that time, and has a power of self-maintenance, development and persistence (at least relative to its natural environment). (Johnston 2007: 64)

It's questionable whether the variability and vagueness of the categories of "substances", and of "substance-sortals", permit us to make a clean matchup between these ontological and representational domains through use of such refinements. Wiggins (2001) suggests that true Identities involving material *objects* need "covering" by substance-sortals. But *all* entities are self-identical, and the more conditions we add to these notions, the more numerous the material entities they will be forced to exclude as "not objects", hence as "nondescript" entities (even setting aside Quantities) somehow excused from those rules. But that said, and despite these limits, we do get good service from our widespread use of terms or concepts fitting the general patterns I have described, largely due to their association with distinctive kinds of persistence-conditions.

---

[18] This clause works well without modification, for multiple occupancy cases where synchronic counting is by m-constitution rather than by identity.

"Power of self-maintenance" is somewhat grand language, given that a snowflake, and possibly a radioactive lithium atom with a half-life of milliseconds, might count as substances. But there's a useful less grand notion in the neighbourhood. When a pebble sits on a table top and is still there five minutes later, it's in virtue of moment-to-moment causation over this period, as the pebble by its earlier presence causes the same pebble to be there later. This is *immanent causation*. I suggest an improved taxonomy of material entities would make use of a taxonomy of *kinds*, *degrees*, and *layerings* of immanent causation. I shall not supply these taxonomies, merely make a few brief comments (see also Zimmerman's very helpful 1997).

The hard-to-match notions of "substance" and "substance concepts" provide somewhat blunt tools in metaphysics. An idea which the above formulations are in part attempting to capture is that substances have *ontological autonomy*, but the search for necessary and sufficient conditions for the latter may be Quixotic given that it surely comes in types and degrees. Various kinds of unity, and independence, contribute to it. The relevant unities, temporal and spatial, are largely causal. The temporal unities, at least, are essentially forms of immanent causation, the hierarchy of its varieties corresponding, roughly, to a layering of substrate or realization relations.

Chalk marks are not substances, being too dependent on blackboards and such to give them stability and persistence. (Is a blackboard in Johnston's terms a chalk mark's "natural environment"?) Paradigm Quantities are not substances because they need have neither autonomous spatial boundaries, nor spatial unity. They exhibit *highly localized* immanent causation, permitting point-by-point tracing over time. Termini of collections of the causal lines so traced mark temporal boundaries of Quantities.

Paradigm substances which are *objects* do have autonomous *spatial* boundaries (permitting synchronic counting criteria): a richer kind of immanent causation, preserving overall form, is associated with their spatial unity. This can be as simple as a pebble's persisting, because its material components persist and mutually adhere, retaining their configuration. Or it can be as complex, for a living creature, as a combination of trillions of conjoined chemical factories. The homeostatic stability underlying animal life supervenes on the persistence through immanent causation of even vaster numbers of haemoglobin molecules, sodium ions, strands of DNA, and a myriad other kinds of entities, processes involving them, and the stability of such articulated parts as membranes, bones, muscles, nerve fibres, and the rest. This is an example of the "layering" of immanent causation. Here the "natural environment" must include immediate access to oxygen and frequent access to water and food. Note that macroscopic "form" changes with an animal's every movement, and the microscopic internal changes are vastly more complex.

Something like the Sun, on the other hand, is a borderline case of a material substance: a ball of plasma comprising a giant nuclear furnace, retaining overall form not by rigidity of structure but by dynamic equilibrium of physical forces. Nevertheless, the Sun is vastly more "autonomous"—because less dependent on input from a fine-tuned "natural environment" for its continuance—than an animal. Perhaps we should dub the Sun a "Heraclitean substance".

All these issues are relevant to the notion of *"persistence-conditions"*. The persistence-conditions associated with a paradigm substance-sortal F constrain not just outer form, but inner structure, and the causal relations involved in the persistence and evolution of those aspects of "form". Here I echo Johnston's words (see earlier), but with greater emphasis on the *layering* of kinds of causal unity, the consequent *variety of kinds* of "form", and the *kinship* between substances and Quantities. Note that *persistence-conditions*, in virtue of specifying what it takes for entities of the relevant kind to begin, to continue, or to cease existing, *subsume existence-conditions*. Existence-conditions for Fs will include *synchronic* or *momentary* conditions: hence there is at most only partial separation between synchronic and diachronic identity-conditions.

The idea of existence-conditions is helpful in making a logical point about all these conditions: *they have no causal roles.* That means they are no more caused than they are causes. If the causal unfolding of the world results in the conditions for Fs to exist being satisfied, then Fs exist. We cannot ask how the existence conditions caused an F to exist: they are not among its causes. Nor can we sensibly ask how an F, by existing, is causally responsible for its persistence-conditions. This helps explain why entities of identical composition at a given moment can have different persistence-conditions. The Fs include only things which satisfy persistence-conditions for Fs. And if the causal unfolding of the world results in the conditions coming to obtain for both an F and a G to exist, bearing the m-constitution relation, then an F and a G bearing that relation do exist (and this remains true even if the conditions are apt for their exactly coinciding in time as well as in space). Asking how the F and the G manage to generate different persistence-conditions for themselves would be a confused piece of putting the ontological cart before the logical horse, like asking how the three-sidedness of a triangle brings it into being. The same goes for the genesis of the so-called different "dispositions" (capacities to survive squashing, and so on) of entities related by m-constitution. In different courses of events different existence-conditions cease to be satisfied, that is all. It's misleading to think of this as the "manifestation" of a disposition, like glowing upon heating.

Is "person" a natural kind term? Putnam has taught us how to answer that: we consult intuitions about Twin Earth scenarios (Putnam 1975). The crucial issue is whether there could be beings ("Twin Persons") which satisfy our usual *constitutive* (not merely evidential) criteria for being persons, but which might lead us astray because of being, nevertheless, *not* persons due to having the wrong, unknown, "real" essence. Human culture is replete with thoughts, fictions, beliefs, and speculations about non-human persons. I don't believe any of that suggests "person" *is* twin-earthable. I see it as akin to a (non-teleological) *functional* notion. Once we set aside Substance Dualism, we are left with few hints (beyond inconclusive worries about qualia) that genuine personhood hinges on any real essence more "hidden" than having suitable mental states and capacities. A person *realizes* the "person" role. "Realization" is not a *bare* fact, which is why we here refer to *human* persons.

But this does not settle whether "person" is, as Psychological theorists claim, a substance-concept! (Compare "predator".) It's striking that there's no philosophical consensus on this point. The agenda of this chapter is to explore the coherence of Psychological views, not to prove them outright. So at this point I am *assuming* that "person" is a substance-concept, to explore the viability of that view. If it is, *constitution* is the relevant form of realization. There is no way though that "person" can be anything but one of the vaguer substance-terms, if psychological views are to be correct, given the proliferation of different kinds of psychological connectedness and continuity which might be counted as central, and the different degrees of weight they might be accorded. This is why this chapter mainly uses the plural: "Psychological views".[19]

Persons as represented by Psychological views risk not being thought substances because they need realizers of unrivalled complexity—in the cases we are sure of, living humans having mature and fully functional brains—so their ontological autonomy may seem correspondingly slight. This stems partly from the mistake of thinking that persons are on this view *distinct* from their realizers—the things which *constitute* them. But constitution is not like distinctness, in any ordinary sense, even when it is not Identity, and *ordinary human persons psychologically viewed are flesh and blood beings.* Their distinctive "person-suitable" kind of higher-level immanent causation may itself be mistakenly thought evanescent, but *qua* the foundation of human agency it is what largely shapes human history. This psychological continuity and connectedness, piggy-backing on the structures and processes in our brains and nervous-systems, but in principle capable of crossing boundaries between different realizers, is what Psychological theorists insist on as the *sine qua non* of personal persistence. The neo-Lockean approach to personal identity, and the functionalist approach to mental states, are two parts of the metaphysical jigsaw which make an easy fit.[20] On a functionalist approach, mental states require realizers, centrally provided in our case by the human nervous system and the sense organs and musculature with which it interacts. The *functional states* so realized are so only in virtue of belonging to a suitably complex system. When such a system is realized, at least in a suitably integrated and persisting manner, a person is thereby realized.

There's more to be said here about constitution and kinds. Consider substance-sortals "F" and "G", entities x and y, where F(x) and G(y), x exists over period t(x), y exists over period t(y), t(y) falls wholly within t(x), and m-const(x,y,t(y)). *Over t(y),*

[19] Robinson 2004 argues that the lack of a canonical way of resolving differences between rival accounts of personal identity (even when all the rivals are psychological accounts), together with the great moral and prudential relevance of such differences, makes some such differences "radical disagreements" closely akin to radical moral disagreements.
[20] A point of which Sydney Shoemaker has been a primary exponent (e.g. in Shoemaker 1984). (This is not to say that Shoemaker's entire metaphysical standpoint is embraced in this chapter.)

x and y must be intrinsically similar, surely, being material entities having just the same physical constituents. Over that time, x and y are of different substance-kinds. If substance-kinds are *intrinsic*, how can that be? Indeed, since things' extrinsic properties are, plausibly, a resultant of purely external relations with other things, together with the intrinsic properties of the various *relata*, and given that the relevant external relations are spatio-temporal and causal—so, you might think, shared by x and y over t(y)—it's not totally clear how x and y can differ even in extrinsic properties over t(y).

It's natural to think a thing's intrinsic properties closed under a suitable notion of supervenience: properties supervening on intrinsic properties are themselves intrinsic. But what is the minimal supervenience base? Here we need to talk about properties which are intrinsic to things *relative to* times. I'll assume that the relevant supervenience *base* in this case is properties which are intrinsic relative to *moments*. Now we need to distinguish *two kinds* of relativity to a time—two ways in which properties may be *tensed*—I'll call them "superficially tensed" and "deeply tensed" properties. This is an important general distinction.

Consider the grandfather relation. My maternal grandfather died before I was born. *When* was he my grandfather? He *was* my grandfather, I *am* his grandchild. The difference in tense signals no difference in the time of the relationship. We use present tense when I'm the grammatical subject, because I still exist; past tense when my grandfather is a grammatical subject, because he no longer exists.

It's similar with substance-sortals. Consider the substance-sortal "mountain". We say "Everest *is* a mountain, and Krakatoa *was* a mountain". Here too I suggest the different tenses merely reflect different times of existence. We should say that the time-relative predicate "Mountain(x,t)" has underlying logical form "Mountain*(x) & Exists(x,t)", where "Mountain*" is an untensed one-place predicate of, if you like, our informal metaphysical metalanguage. So "mountain", like all substance-sortals, is *superficially tensed*—because *necessarily* true of a thing *always* or *never*—whereas, e.g., "snow-covered" is *deeply tensed*, because a mountain may be snow-covered one day, not the next. This aligns with the idea that substance-sortals tell us, in some deep sense, "what a thing *is*"—not merely *what it became* or *what it will become*. It is part of what is captured in the four-dimensionalists' idea of an F being a "maximally R-related aggregate of temporal F-parts", with R an F-suitable relation, as in Lewis's classic definition of "person" (Lewis 1976).

So all properties in our supervenience base are deeply tensed. A thing may obviously have deeply tensed intrinsic properties which supervene on, but are not, momentary: for instance, the property of having mass m over a period of a minute. And a thing may have *global* intrinsic properties, which supervene on a thing's momentary intrinsic properties over no less than the whole of its existence. In our schematic example of an F and a G, t(x) differs from t(y), so despite their limited match of intrinsic (and supervening extrinsic) properties, x and y must differ in their *global* intrinsic properties. (Note that this is consistent with a constitution as part-identity view.)

So can we say that substance-sortals like "F" and "G" are *temporally global* (*as opposed to momentary) intrinsic properties*? No!—for at least two related reasons. (i) A property is only *superficially tensed* in my intended meaning if it *necessarily* always or never applies to an individual. A property—like always being warmer than −5°C—may be *contingently globally intrinsic* to an entity, but nevertheless deeply tensed. Substance-sortal properties are only *superficially* tensed because they *necessarily* apply to individuals always or never. (ii) Substance-sortal properties are at best *near-intrinsic* because they are *temporally maximal* or *boundary-respecting*. If we posit an entity z made of the same matter at the same time as a pebble, but which begins existing a millisecond later than and ceases existing a millisecond earlier than the pebble, many of z's intrinsic properties will be very similar to the pebble's. Whether or not that entity exists, it cannot be another *pebble* because pebble-persistence-conditions do not count *those* times as beginnings or ceasings of *pebble*-existence, since pebbleoid processes of immanent causation act across them. *Not* failing this condition is not an *intrinsic* property of a pebble: it is *minimally extrinsic*, dependent on what exists beyond the pebble's temporal boundaries.[21] (Here we abstract away from complexities about vague boundaries: but vague boundaries may be real and natural, like the boundary you cross in walking from a plain onto a mountain.)

To sum up, *substance-sortal properties are temporally-maximal properties which things have essentially if at all.* If the foregoing is correct, they are superficially tensed (we could say, "deeply untensed") properties of things which supervene on their global intrinsic properties *together with* facts about their immediate (or at least close) boundaries and surrounds. (Synchronic counting criteria, of course, impose requirements on *spatial* boundaries also.) When an F and a G coincide over a time t, but have different lifetimes, their substance-sortal properties will supervene on correspondingly different sets of intrinsic and minimally extrinsic properties, not *just* on their common intrinsic properties *over* t.

Thus I offer a minimal generic answer to the question of how our x and y *could* be of different kinds F and G even though m-constitution (or if you prefer, co-composition) obtains between them over t(y)—though perhaps on pain of accepting constitution as part-identity (so that in limiting cases we have a single entity which satisfies both the conditions for F-hood and for G-hood). That seems like one *good* reason to do so!

Coda

With "human animal" and "human person" in place of generic "F" and "G" things will be more complicated. Since "human animal" is a *biological* kind, many will say the *kind*-essence of its members must include the right evolutionary aetiology. If so,

---

[21] This point is closely related to Lewis's 1976 inclusion, in a four-dimensionalist context, of the term "maximally" in the definition of "person" referred to above.

biological substance-*kinds* are *strongly* extrinsic: the relevant aetiology reaches back hundreds of millennia.

Further analysis here in principle calls for a complete theory of the constraints, or lack of them, governing essential properties, specially those of human animals and human persons, and their relations to sortals. Can we say "the distinct kinds determine distinct essential properties"? Or "distinct essential properties determine distinct kinds"? Must human *persons* inherit a biological essence from their animal realizers, and when or where does it stop? A panoply of intricate further issues, about modality, and about essences, here present themselves, so it's hard to push the "ecumenical" approach any further. Instead, this chapter will close with a couple of sketchy suggestions for further thoughts—and attitudes—aimed in the general direction of those issues.

I am no fan of the post-Kripkean fashion of populating the world with real essences at the drop of a predicate. That is why I like the Lewisian multiple-counterpart-relations approach to *de re* modality, and the doctrine of constitution as part-identity. In classifying nondescript material entities—"chalk mark", "splash", "flame"—we clearly ascribe *nominal* essences to them, and there is no reason why some substance-sortals (perhaps "sand-hill" and "dust-bunny") should not work similarly. I took care to allow for that, in specifying my use of "sortal". It's not *clear* to me that non-twin-earthable or "functional" sortals do not *all* belong in that nominal-essence-bestowing category.

Crucially, the debatable but commonly alleged essential extrinsic properties invoked by the doctrine of "the necessity of origin" (originating from, e.g., given parents, zygote, quantity of wood, etc.) involve *individual* essences, *not* kind essences. "Helicopter", "sand-hill", perhaps "person", might have merely nominal kind-essences, without threatening the claim that each *instance* of those kinds has its own individual essence including facts about origin. (Note that one way to try to argue for including evolutionary history in the real essences of species is to assimilate species to individuals.) So *individual human* persons *might* have individual essences derivative on their animal origins. Nevertheless they might, *qua* belonging to the kind "persons", be metaphysically capable of leaving their animal nature behind. What is an essential fact about a thing's origins need not translate into something which governs its entire future career.[22]

Bibliography

Baker, L. R. 1997. Why Constitution Is Not Identity. *Journal of Philosophy* 94: 599–621.
Baker, L. R. 2000. *Persons and Bodies: A Constitution View*. Cambridge: Cambridge University Press.

[22] For helpful advice and comments on various versions of this chapter, leading to significant improvements, I am greatly indebted to several people, including specially David Braddon-Mitchell, Frederick Kroon, Daniel Korman, Kristie Miller, Daniel Nolan, and the editors of this volume.

Bennett, K. 2004. Spatio-Temporal Coincidence and the Grounding Problem. *Philosophical Studies* 118 (3): 339–71.

Braddon-Mitchell, D. and Miller, K. 2006. Talking About a Universalist World. *Philosophical Studies* 130: 499–534.

Burge, T. 1975. Mass Terms, Count Nouns, and Change. *Synthese* 31: 459–78.

Burke, M. B. 1994. Preserving the Principle of One Object to a Place. *Philosophy and Phenomenological Research* 54: 591–624.

Cartwright, H. M. 1970. Quantities. *Philosophical Review* 79: 25–42.

Cartwright, R. 1975. Scattered Objects. In K. Lehrer ed., Analysis and Metaphysics. Dordrecht: Reidel.

Fine, K. 2003. The Non-Identity of a Material Thing and Its Matter. *Mind* 112: 195–234.

Gibbard, A. 1975. Contingent Identity. *Journal of Philosophical Logic* 4: 187–221.

Johnston, M. 1987. Human Beings. *Journal of Philosophy* 84: 59–83.

Johnston, M. 1992. Constitution Is Not Identity. *Mind* 101: 89–105.

Johnston, M. 2007. Human Beings Revisited: My Body Is Not an Animal. In Dean Zimmerman, ed., *Oxford Studies in Metaphysics*, Vol. 3. Oxford: Oxford University Press.

Lewis, D. 1971. Counterparts of Persons and Their Bodies. *Journal of Philosophy* 68: 203–11.

Lewis, D. 1976. Survival and Identity. In A. Rorty, ed., *The Identities of Persons*. Berkeley: University of California Press.

Lewis, D. 1983. Postscripts to "Survival and Identity". In Lewis, *Philosophical Papers*, Vol. 1. New York: Oxford University Press.

Lewis, D. 1986. *On the Plurality of Worlds*. Oxford: Blackwell.

Locke, J. 1975. *An Essay Concerning Human Understanding*, ed. P. Nidditch. Oxford: Clarendon. (2nd ed. published in 1994.)

Mackie, P. 2008. Coincidence and Identity. *Royal Institute of Philosophy Supplement* 62: 151–76.

Noonan, H. 1991. Indeterminate Identity, Contingent Identity, and Abelardian Predicates. *Philosophical Quarterly* 42: 183–93.

Noonan, H. 1993. Constitution Is Identity. *Mind* 102: 133–46.

Noonan, H. 2008. Moderate Monism and Modality. *Analysis* 68 (1): 88–94.

Olson, E. 1997. *The Human Animal*. New York: Oxford University Press.

Olson, E. 2003. An Argument for Animalism. In R. Martin and J. Barresi, eds, *Personal Identity*. Malden, MA: Blackwell.

Olson, E. 2007. *What Are We?* New York: Oxford University Press.

Putnam, H. 1975. The Meaning of "Meaning". In Putnam, *Philosophical Papers*, Vol. 2. Cambridge, Cambridge University Press.

Robinson, D. 1982a. Re-Identifying Matter. *Philosophical Review* 91: 317–41.

Robinson, D. 1982b. *The Metaphysics of Material Constitution*. PhD dissertation, Monash University.

Robinson, D. 1985. Can Amoebae Divide Without Multiplying? *Australasian Journal of Philosophy* 63: 299–319.

Robinson, D. 2004. Failing to Agree or Failing to Disagree? *The Monist* 87: 512–36.

Shoemaker, S. 1984. Personal Identity: A Materialist's Account. In S. Shoemaker and R. Swinburne, *Personal Identity*. Oxford: Blackwell.

Wiggins, D. 1967. *Identity and Spatio-Temporal Continuity*. Oxford: Blackwell.

Wiggins, D. 1968. On Being in the Same Place at the Same Time. *Philosophical Review* 77: 90–5.

Wiggins, D. 2001. *Sameness and Substance Renewed*. Cambridge: Cambridge University Press.

Zimmerman, D. 1995. Theories of Masses and Problems of Constitution. *The Philosophical Review* 104: 53–110.

Zimmerman, D. 1997. Immanent Causation. *Noûs* Supplement s11: 433–71.

5

Remnant Persons
Animalism's Undoing

Mark Johnston

My topic is animalism, understood not as the relatively uncontroversial doctrine that we are animals—as opposed say to plants, angels, or separable immaterial souls—but rather as the stronger and more interesting doctrine that we are always animals, and that no one of us can cease to be animals without thereby ceasing to be. More exactly, animalism is, or is at least committed to, the following thesis:

Animal is one of our substance kinds, i.e. every human person is always in fact an animal, and there is no possible future deviating from any point in his or her existence in which they are not animals.[1]

This is the view that, if not precisely endorsed by David Wiggins' *Sameness and Substance* (1980), is strongly encouraged by a close reading of that important book; and it was the view defended my *Particulars and Persistence* (1984).[2]

The latter work was rightly confined to oblivion by its author in part because there was a sound argument that shows that even if we are presently animals, we can, nonetheless, cease to be animals without thereby ceasing to be. This is the argument from "remnant persons": in short, if we suppose that we cannot cease to be animals without thereby ceasing to be, then we are saddled with a repugnant consequence, namely that

---

[1] Compare Paul Snowdon "I shall simply stipulate that it [animalism] involves *two* claims. The first is that we are identical with certain animals. But it is also a part of the view that our persistence conditions are those *of animals,* animals being regarded as one fundamental kind of thing. So the second claim, which I shall treat as at least partly elucidatory of this thought, is that anything which is an animal must be an animal, and the self-same animal, at all the times it exists. Given that the view claims both things, it is committed to the claim that we must be animals, and the self-same animals, at all times we exist." This is taken from "Personal Identity and Brain Transplants" in David Cockburn (ed.), *Human Beings* (Cambridge University Press, 1991), p. 111.

[2] David Wiggins, *Sameness and Substance* (Harvard University Press, 1980). *Particulars and Persistence* (Doctoral Thesis, Princeton University, 1984) argues for the even stronger view that we are essentially human organisms, and this is defended against the brain transplanting intuition—you go where your brain goes—in the same way as animalists like Eric Olson later defended animalism against that intuition.

there are very strange ways for persons to come into existence; specifically, simply as the result of the removal of non-neural tissue.

Initially, animalism should be taken very seriously as an account of our conditions of identity over time, for at least two reasons. For one thing, there is considerable evidence that we are not (even in part) separable immaterial souls, and so the supposed entity that led many to think that we are either distinct from animals or very, very distinctive animals is not, so the evidence suggests, actually there. For another, the fact that reliance on the method of appealing to intuitions about imaginary cases (i) delivers the result that we go where our brain goes in a case of brain transplantation and (ii) favors to some degree the result that we would survive teletransportation and the like, should not really worry the friends of animalism, despite the fact that these "intuitions" are at odds with the central claim of animalism, namely that we could not cease to be animals without ceasing to be. This is because the ideology behind the method of cases is deeply problematic, as is shown by a variety of considerations, only some of which will be canvassed here.

How Could There Be Such a Topic "Personal Identity"?

The first question that should be discussed in any lecture course on personal identity is: How can there be such courses on personal identity? What is so distinctive about persons, such that their identity at a time and over time is a topic of interest? Would anyone propose a course on sponge identity or on rhododendron identity? Obviously not, for the answers would be immediately forthcoming, and occasion no serious dissent. You have the same sponge just in case you have the same animal organism, and you have the same rhododendron just in case you have the same plant organism. That is, pretty much, the end of each course. And you can't earn a living like that!

Animalism encourages a deflationary answer to the first question: if we were clear-headed, then there would be no sensed need for such courses. It is only because of our resistance to the naturalistic idea that we are animals that there seems to be a difference between the sponges and us.

That, it will emerge, is definitely the wrong answer.

Setting aside our well-known fascination with our own species, the right answer to the question of why there are courses on personal identity obviously has something to do with the human imagination. We appear to be able to imagine ourselves surviving the destruction of our bodies, either as separable immaterial souls, which may then be re-embodied, or as teletransported persons, who after a period of non-existence come to have a new body made from ambient matter. What is taken to survive in such imagined cases is something (at least partly) mental, either an entity or a series of events and states. In either case it is something that continues to exist even though the original organism, and the original animal, ceases to exist. So the imagination tells us that we do not have the same conditions of identity over time as mere organisms, or mere animals. (By that phrasing in terms of identity *conditions,* I mean what would also be said by saying that Organism and Animal are not substance kinds, i.e. the sorts of kinds whose members cannot migrate into or out of.)

The Method of Cases and the Evidential Status of the Imagination

The second question that should be discussed in the course on personal identity is whether the imagination is really telling us any more than this: we can *imagine* being disembodied and we can *imagine* coming to have a new body. But why should we think that the imagination is a reliable guide to what we could *in fact* survive? What is the evidential status of imagination?

The old answer that once structured and dominated the literature on personal identity had at least one virtue; it was easily stated. Philosophy is the analysis or articulation of the conditions of application of our concepts. As masters of these concepts—a curiously gendered phrase—we have at least an implicit grasp of their application conditions; this tacit knowledge of when they apply and when they should be withheld can be manifested equally well in real and imaginary cases. This must be so, since the master of a concept is antecedently armed with a capacity to tell whether or not to apply the concept, however reality might turn out to be (perhaps within certain limits of normality). The method of imaginary cases articulates our tacit knowledge of the application conditions of our concepts.

In the best case, the method delivers an "analysis"; that is, an account of a special sort of necessary and sufficient condition or set of conditions for the application of the relevant concept, namely a necessary and sufficient condition or set of conditions that could be recognized as correct simply on the basis of a certain sort of ideal reflection on our tacit understanding of when to apply and when to withhold the concept in question.

Therefore, the relevant verdicts and the resultant analysis could be delivered from the armchair, i.e. without any significant empirical investigation. So it was sometimes said that the relevant analyses could be known *a priori*; roughly, in a condition approximating blissful ignorance of the empirical facts.

There were a few promising victories for this kind of method, but they were skirmishes rather than major battles. The analysis of the concept of knowledge was, at least for at while, considered a paradigm of this kind of investigation, one which neatly exemplified how the method of cases could lead us to an analysis of a concept. "Intuitions"—that is judgments—as to whether the case at hand was, or was not, a case of knowledge were collected by visiting real and imaginary cases alike, and then those intuitions were brought into some sort of reflective equilibrium that bore on the question of the necessary and sufficient conditions for someone's knowing some arbitrary proposition. Imagined cases were naturally treated as on a par with real cases; for if we are interested in articulating our tacit understanding of the application conditions of our concept it would be odd to restrict our evidence base to the adventitious experiments of nature, when we could also avail ourselves of the full range of ingeniously designed thought experiments. Wouldn't that be like only considering the moves that have been made in actual chess games, rather than the full range of moves that *could have been* made?

As in chess, so with our concepts: imagination is a reliable guide to what could happen, and it therefore provides us with cases which are just as helpful as the actual cases so far as rendering explicit our implicit understanding of the application conditions of our concepts, as it might be the concept of a checkmate in four or of a case of knowledge.

This ideology behind the method of cases thus offers to explain how the imagination can have a probative status, how it can have a kind of evidential significance, which mere fancy could not. The imagination's philosophically interesting function is to generate a wider than actual range of cases, across which our conceptual competence can express itself.

For a good while, this method looked attractive when it came to the concept of personal identity. We were to collect "intuitions" about real and imaginary cases of personal survival and ceasing to be, and then bring those intuitions into some sort of reflective equilibrium that bore on the question of the necessary and sufficient conditions for an arbitrary person's survival. The result would be the filling in of the details of the relation R in an a priori (and necessary) bi-conditional of this form:

> x, considered at t, is numerically the same person as y, considered at t*, if and only if xRy.

Thus arose the old analytical question: Is R a matter of x and y having the same body, or being the same organism, or having the same consciousness, or having the same mind (however that mind might be embodied), or having the same separable immaterial soul? Now the course is—or at least *was*—underway.

Some New Worries About the Method of Cases

There are many worries that have and can be raised against this whole approach to the question of personal identity, but here is one that has not yet been noted.[3] Consider the widely believed claim that there are separable souls that at death leave the bodies they animated and begin a journey in the underworld or the overworld, souls that can be reincarnated in new bodies or—in an alternative version—re-embodied in their resurrected bodies. A large majority of human beings over the last 2,500 years have believed in the separable soul. If this belief were true then it would have a controlling impact on

---

[3] For some others, see Kathleen Wilkes, *Real People* (Oxford University Press, 1988) along with my "Human Beings", *Journal of Philosophy*, 84 (1987) and *Surviving Death* (Princeton University Press, 2010) pp. 44–7.

any satisfactory account of the conditions of personal survival. That is, if it were true then it would significantly constrain the filling out of the details of R. But if the proper upshot of the study of personal identity is an a priori bi-conditional of the above form, and if the truth or falsehood of the soul hypothesis radically constrains the details of R, then the truth or falsity of the hypothesis that we are separable souls must then be an a priori matter.

The problem with this whole approach is that the hypothesis that we are separable souls is manifestly not an a priori matter. It is an empirical question that cannot be settled by reflection on the application conditions of our concepts. Whether we are (at least in part) separable souls is an a posteriori question that cannot be answered by mere intuition delivered from the armchair.

The relevant empirical facts, not available to us if we simply loll around in the armchair, are these. As we know more and more about the brain, even the highest mental functions seem to have definite brain functions as their condition *sine qua non*. The intriguing specificity of cognitive loss, depending often on the precise location and extent of this or that brain lesion, continually confirms that brain function cannot be overridden as a source of mental capacity. Even in cases of recovery from the specific cognitive losses produced by local brain damage, there is, significantly, no reported phenomenology of memories of an intact thinking soul being "locked inside" an inept, because damaged, brain and body. The thoughts and mental capacities were just not there, it seems. Yet an immaterial bearer of these mental capacities and thoughts need not be damaged just because the brain is damaged.

To develop this line of thought just a little, consider trepanation, one of the oldest surgical procedures, in which holes are made in the skull and through the durus, the tissue surrounding the brain, in order to drain a stroke-induced hematoma that has been putting pressure on the brain, thereby often causing unconsciousness, or at least all the bodily signs of unconsciousness. Many victims of unconsciousness caused by a subdural hematoma now recover full consciousness as a result of successful trepanning, or "craniotomy" as it is now called.

Why, then, are there no reports of the phenomenology of "being locked in" when the victim "wakes up" after craniotomy?

Contrast the genuine cases of being mentally "locked in" thanks to almost complete bodily paralysis. Such reports arise because in such cases the higher centers of the brain remain intact. But on the substantial dualist conception even these higher centers are mere instruments by which thoughts have their effects. There are, as it were, still "higher" centers, located in the soul or independent spiritual substance that drives the brain, centers that brain damage would leave intact.

Yet temporary brain damage leading to unconsciousness is not, as it happens, phenomenologically like bodily paralysis, contrary to what the hypothesis that our mental life is the life of a separable immaterial soul would predict, at least given natural auxiliary assumptions. Does the blood that leaks out under the durus in subdural hematoma, also somehow leak into the soul?

This kind of point goes beyond the mere correlations revealed by lesion work and MRIs. In the face of all the bodily signs of unconsciousness found in severe cases of subdural hematoma, the natural dualist expectation would be that if and when the pressure on the brain was relieved and the patient awoke, he or she would report having been "locked in" to a bodily prison. This is just what we do not find.

I do not say that there are no alternative auxiliary hypotheses that would make the facts concerning the phenomenology of recovery from subdural hematoma *consistent* with the hypothesis of the separable soul. I just say that any friend of this hypothesis should be surprised and slightly dismayed by such facts.

On the other side of the ledger, there are the startling reports, more or less spontaneously produced in roughly 10 to 15 percent of resuscitated cardiac arrest cases, of what are now called "out-of-body" experiences. The experiences, which seem to their subjects to be happening during a period that coincides with the clinical death of their own bodies, involve such things as the sense of leaving one's body and of looking down at the medical personnel pumping one's chest in their attempts at resuscitation. As the experience develops, one seems to be traveling through a tunnel to a bliss-inducing white light. As one moves in the light, dead relatives, and even old pets, are encountered, and in some cases one is presented with a review of one's life. This, of course, would represent the beginning of an empirical vindication of the soul hypothesis.

Here is what I take to be least controversial in this controversial area. There is a genuine phenomenon that goes under the name of the "out-of-body experience." However, in investigating this phenomenon, one does not find *robust* evidence of distinctive knowledge of the external world that could only be gleaned from the ostensible vantage points of the disembodied subject. If one has left one's body and is looking down upon it, then one could be expected to take in facts about, say, the emergency room that are not available to the normal viewers, there on the floor. Experiments have indeed been proposed, even partly performed, but what we do not have is a decisive case that clearly passes the obvious test. I have in mind a cartoon that effectively presents the obvious test: we see an emergency room in which a cardiac arrest patient is being resuscitated by doctors. Mounted high up on the back wall of the emergency room is a sign whose message is visible *only* from near the ceiling of the room (Figure 5.1).

What if such obvious tests were frequently passed by the resuscitated patients? What if they reported reading such signs as "You're Dead!" "Eat at Joe's!" "Medicare Won't Be Covering This!" or whatever happens to be displayed at the moment of their deaths. And suppose we could rule out collusion and suggestion and remote cognition from the hospital bed? What then?

I must confess that this would be enough for me. We should seriously consider the idea of locating our mental lives in independent substances, substances whose mental functioning can outlive the functioning of their associated brains. So far no such disturbing reports have been collected in any well-controlled setting; but they might turn up or they might not turn up. (My *bet* is that they won't, but that is based on other

Figure 5.1. If You Can Read This...

empirical evidence of the sort cited earlier.) All of this serves to highlight what should anyway be obvious, namely that the separated survival of the soul is an empirical question. It remains an empirical question even if, as many think, it is an entirely settled empirical question.

The point is that this is the death knell of the old "analytic" approach to the problem of personal identity. For it shows that the correct filling out of R in the bi-conditional

x, considered at t, is numerically the same person as y, considered at t* if and only if xRy

is an a posteriori or empirical matter. And this means that it is not accessible simply by way of articulating our tacit understanding of the application conditions of the concept of being the same person. Our intuitions about cases of personal survival, be those cases real or imaginary, are just beliefs we have, and they may well be false, especially in the *recherché* cases designed precisely to tease apart the very things—the persistence of the body, mental continuity, the persistence of the individual personality—which go together in the central core of ordinary cases that dominate our experience of the continued existence of persons.

(We shall later consider the thought, developed in detail by Robert Nozick, that we can introduce a close successor to our concept of personal identity, one that has a chance of applying to situations even though there are no souls to trace, and then analyze *that* concept, thereby producing an a priori bi-conditional appropriate to it. This too, it will be shown, misrepresents the nature of our conceptual competence.)

There is a natural weakening of the target bi-conditional that might seem responsive to this objection from the a posteriori or empirical status of the proposition that we are (at least in part) separable immaterial souls. Given the ideology behind the method of cases, the right-hand side of the bi-conditional has to include a series of a priori conditionals, conditions underwritten by our implicit conceptual knowledge; for example:

If we are (at least in part) immaterial souls then Q is the relation that has to hold between x and y.

If we are not (even in part) immaterial souls then S is the relation that has to hold between x and y.

So now, so the response goes, we can see that the method of cases can proceed as intended, as long as we understand our initial target relations as various—including say Q and S—with our ultimate choice among them resting on the empirical evidence of the sort already cited.

The original objection now takes its definitive form when we ask: just how various are the initial target relations left open by what we know a priori, that is to say in the armchair reflecting only the knowledge which drives our concept of being numerically the same person? Notice that there seems to be no specific relation S such that the following bi-conditional is both non-trivial and knowable a priori:

If persons x and y are not even in part separable immaterial souls and xSy then x = y.

For, clearly, there are various distinct conditions of identity for various kinds of "soul-free" persons. If we are always minded animals, and could not cease to be such without ceasing to be, then one relation—one close to that specified by the bodily criterion—will be relevant. However, if we are always somehow-or-other embodied consciousnesses and could not cease to be such without ceasing to be, then another relation—one close to that specified by the psychological criterion—will be relevant. So are we minded animals or embodied consciousnesses? The deliverances of the method of cases give out precisely here; hence the unresolved dispute between what was called the bodily and the psychological criteria of personal identity. Anyone who claims to have resolved that dispute by the method of cases will simply find "differing intuitions" on the other side. So here too we must resort to empirical means, we must use all we collectively know and all of our capacities for argumentative ingenuity to settle the question.

What is coming into clear view here is that we really wanted to know the answer to this question: What is it that we are? Are we (at least in part) always, and must we always continue to be (at least in part), immaterial souls? Are we always, and must we always continue to be, minded animals? Are we always, and must we always continue to be, embodied consciousnesses? Or are we something else entirely? The method of cases, properly thought through, is impotent to decide between such questions. The most it can do is explore some fairly direct consequences of one or another of these hypotheses, when they are assumed to be true. But we wanted to know which hypothesis *is* true.

Why did we philosophers overestimate the power of the method of cases, understood as a way of articulating our tacit "conceptual" knowledge? Why did we think we could resolve hard cases based on the articulation of the application conditions of our concepts?

One suggestion, due to Sarah-Jane Leslie, is that it is because of a tendency on the part of philosophers to misrepresent "conceptual knowledge" as tacit knowledge of necessary universally valid necessary and sufficient conditions; that is, tacit knowledge of universally quantified bi-conditionals that hold in all possible worlds. As against this, there is a growing body of empirical evidence that application conditions of our concepts do not take the form of exceptionless necessary and sufficient conditions, but rather rely on generic connections among concepts, connections that admit of exceptions *that are nonetheless not counterexamples.*[4]

Some philosophers might say that each concept by its nature either applies to a given situation or does not apply, so that if our conceptual knowledge is exhausted by such generic connections then the right thing to say is that we are employing many concepts of personal identity, namely all of those which accord with the verdicts entailed by the relevant generics, but differ over the remaining cases. Psychologists do not as yet talk this way; but there lies no great sin. They can clearheadedly say that the proper word for what those philosophers are calling "concepts" is instead "property." Given this translation manual, one can hold to two very natural theses; there is *an* ordinary concept of a persisting person, and yet it underdetermines exactly which property we have in mind.

So it may be that according to our ordinary concept of a persisting person the generic to the effect that persons survive if their individual minds continue on, and the generic to the effect that persons will survive if their bodies are kept alive and functioning, are both true. Notice that a negative verdict on our prospects of surviving teletransportation does not yield a counterexample to the first generic, but only an unusual exception. It can seem to be a counterexample because we sometimes misconstrue generic connections as universal quantifications, perhaps with restricted antecedents. While a white raven is a counterexample to "All Ravens are black" it is not a counterexample to "Ravens are black." Male kangaroos are counterexamples to "All normal Kangaroos carry their young around in pouches" but they are not counterexamples to "Kangaroos carry their young around in pouches."

---

[4] Sarah-Jane Leslie, *Generics and Generalization*, forthcoming with Oxford University Press.

Accordingly, the opinion that a person does not survive in a persistent vegetative condition is not at odds with the generic that persons survive if their bodies are kept alive and functioning, because that opinion concerns an exceptional case, which only became very salient with the rise of advanced life-support technology. Generics allow for just such exceptions, and so if our "a priori or conceptual knowledge" of the conditions of personal survival is exhausted by such generics then the analytic method of cases with its focus on the persistent vegetative condition, teletransportation, and the like was just a mistaken attempt to exploit our conceptual competence precisely where it delivered no verdict, namely the very cases which that competence simply ignored.

That would predict that even an ideal and exhaustive application of the method of cases would leave the "hard cases" unresolved. Is this not what we actually find when we consider teletransportation and the like? The bodily criterion and the pure or "wide" psychological criterion differ over whether the very same organism or brain has to survive in order for the very same person to survive, and no amount of clever marshaling of intuitions seems to decide this issue.

The hypothesis that our "a priori or conceptual" knowledge *at best* provides generic connections between personal survival and certain bodily and psychological continuity also makes trouble for the sophisticated conceptual approach to personal identity presented by Robert Nozick.[5]

Nozick's account of personal identity has two stages, the first of which is often ignored. He rightly observes that if there were immaterial human souls then their persistence or continued existence would be at least highly relevant to the persistence or continued existence of human persons. But, Nozick supposes, there are no such souls, and so he believes we should fall back on a successor concept of personal identity, one in which both bodily and psychological continuity are given weight in deciding which future individuals are good enough continuers of a person identified at an earlier time. Then, so Nozick's theory goes, the closest of these good enough continuers is identical with the person identified at an earlier time.

This "closest continuer theory" is an ingenious suggestion, but the crucial observation is that it only delivers results about the hard cases in which bodily and psychological continuity come apart if we smuggle in one or another further premise, namely one of these:

You can have a close enough continuer in the absence of one of either bodily or psychological continuity

or

You can't have a close enough continuer in the absence of one of either bodily or psychological continuity.

---

[5] See chapter 2 of his *Philosophical Explanations* (Belnap Press, 1981), "The Identity of the Self".

However, both of these premises do go beyond our conceptual or a priori knowledge, if that knowledge just consists in generics like:

Persons survive if their bodies are kept alive and functioning.

Persons survive if their minds continue on (in the typical sorts of ways, which involve significant sorts of mental continuities).

From this perspective, Nozick's ingenious theory is ultimately just alchemy, i.e. a way of mistakenly trying to transmute ignorance into knowledge. This happens precisely at the point where he assumes one of the two premises above, namely that you can have a close enough continuer in the absence of one of either bodily or psychological continuity. However, neither of the premises are things we know; no amount of analysis of our concepts or articulation of our "conceptual" knowledge can validate either premise, if that knowledge is generically structured in the way just described.

The error of turning ignorance into supposed knowledge—the error of overdescribing what our concept of personal identity proscribes and prescribes—is also found among both the advocates of the so-called bodily criterion and of the so-called "wide" psychological criterion. Each provide their differing and opposing answers to the hard cases in which bodily and psychological continuity come apart—teletransportation most notably—precisely by overestimating our "conceptual" knowledge." In effect, they make the mistake of representing the generics cited above as universal quantifications, indeed universal quantifications holding in all possible situations or worlds. This is, at the very least, a massive overestimation of our conceptual knowledge.

The Alternative Method

Should the course on personal identity stop there, in a kind of self-accusing despair? Not at all; for the appeal to our conceptual knowledge, available more or less in the armchair, was self-consciously an appeal to a *restricted* range of knowledge, namely knowledge which could plausibly be deemed the special province of philosophy, as opposed to the empirical sciences. All the preceding discussion suggests is that this knowledge, if it exists, is even more restricted than philosophers of the analytic school supposed.

The proper method in philosophy is not to limit oneself to the impoverished realm of conceptual or a priori knowledge, knowledge somehow deriving from, or embedded in, our competence with concepts, or alternatively, knowledge deriving from our competence with meaningful terms of our language. The proper method is to use *all* one knows and all one can find out, in the most ingenious ways one can. Philosophy is integrative theoretical vision combined with argumentative ingenuity, deployed at a fairly abstract level. Philosophy has no special province; but so far from marginalizing philosophy, this liberates it. On the other hand, this means that we philosophers are now under a clear obligation to learn a lot more science than the analysts of old deemed relevant. We need to get out of the armchair and look into things.

The considerations that prompt the change in method also require a change in the question. The question worth asking is not "What are the necessary and sufficient conditions for correctly applying the concept *numerically one and the same person*?" The question of interest is instead a question about *which changes we can undergo, and which conditions we can be found in.*

Elsewhere, I posed that question as the question of what we essentially are, more precisely, as what the most specific account of our essence is.[6] But there are other ways of getting at the idea that involve slightly less in the way of theoretical commitments; in particular, I think we need not mention essence, and so we need not take a view on whether there is a remote possible world in which I come into existence as a parrot or a cyborg. After all, how would all that we know give us an answer to that? (By including insight into essence, of course—but what kind of knowledge is that? I don't despair here; the point is rather that the philosophy of personal identity is hard enough without the further question of essence entering in.)

Essence aside, the more limited question concerns what changes you or I, as representatives of *us*, could undergo, or be around—that is exist—after. Could I, for example, given that I am presently a human animal, turn into a parrot or into a patient in a persistent vegetative condition or... you name it? Is that possible; would it really be *me*, or would I simply have ceased to exist and been replaced by a parrot or by a patient in a persistent vegetative condition or by... you name it?

One way of posing the question about what changes I could undergo or be around after is to ask what kind of thing we are, in one restricted sense of "kind" made clear by David Wiggins. Wiggins reminded us of the distinction between phase kinds, kinds like *adolescent* and *senator*, which we can migrate in and out of, and kinds like *concrete (as opposed to abstract) being*, which we cannot migrate into or out of.[7] You can become and then cease to be a senator without yourself ceasing to be, but you cannot cease to be a concrete being and continue to exist. Wiggins called the kinds you can't migrate into or out of, "substance kinds," and using that terminology we can ask "What is the most detailed substance kind to which we belong?"

That is a reasonable philosophical refinement of the old question "What is it that we are?" Answering it promises to provide an account of the limits on the ways we could change compatible with our continuing to exist. I don't say that it is obvious when a kind is a substance kind. However, I do think that there is something like a proof that Homo sapiens, and indeed Animal, are not substance kinds.

[6] *Particulars and Persistence*, and more recently "'Human Beings' Revisited" in Dean Zimmerman (ed.), *Oxford Studies in Metaphysics*, Vol. 3, 2007.
[7] Despite his use of these terms in a statement of a thesis that seems at odds with this claim, I do not believe that Timothy Williamson in his *Modal Logic as Metaphysics* (Oxford University Press, 2013) really intends to deny the claim I have in mind. No one thinks that a number or a shape or a color or a magnitude could become a grain of sand, or that they themselves could become a number or a shape or a color or a magnitude. Perhaps, here, it would be less misleading to speak of the kinds *particular* and *predicable* as kinds whose members cannot migrate into or out of.

It should be noted that "substance kind" is in one respect unfortunate terminology, for it is reminiscent of a quasi-Aristotelian theory of substances, a theory for which Wiggins himself had considerable affinity. That association should be set aside in what follows, for Aristotelianism about persistence represents a particular and controversial theory of what prevents migration into and out of the kind in question.

How then do we get going on the question of the most detailed, specific, or restrictive substance kind to which we belong? At one level, it can be none other than the method of using all of the relevant knowledge and argumentative ingenuity we can muster. But there is a promising place to start; namely with the humble and ubiquitous activity of tracing ourselves and others over time, an activity whose manifest success places significant constraints on the kind of thing we are. Whatever kind it is that we are, you won't get very far saying that it's a kind whose members we would find it very hard to trace in the easy and offhand ways in which we seem to trace ourselves and others. For the cost of saying that comes close to severing all connection with the topic of personal identity, precisely because it makes our unproblematic knowledge of facts of personal identity deeply problematic.

Just to recall these easy and offhand ways in which we have knowledge of personal identity: I seem to have rich knowledge of a host of humdrum facts of personal identity over time as I observe my students in class, and yet, often enough when they are not speaking, I bear no more complicated epistemic relationship to them than I do to the deer in my backyard. That is, I trace them over time by way of carefree observation of bodily continuity, sometimes augmented by observing some sort of consistency in bodily behavior.

Still, I have massive knowledge of my students' identities over time without, it seems, relying on auxiliary hypotheses concerning regular connections between the kind of things I observe, namely animals of a certain sort, and metaphysically more exotic entities such as souls, let alone bare subjects of experience who could survive any amount of bodily and psychological discontinuity. During the lulls in class discussion when the students fidget, or daydream, or look to their teacher and try simply to take in what he is saying, I am still in a position to notice persisting animals of a certain sort and thereby come to have knowledge that, for example, the person before me in *that seat* is numerically one and the same person that I saw just a minute or so earlier.

It seems that if I go by any rule in arriving at such knowledge, it is the simple (generic) rule: same human animal, same person.

Taking this fact seriously makes it very difficult to go on to maintain that what we ultimately turn out to be are *bare* subjects of experience; that is, simple beings whose continued existence is not constrained either by bodily or by mental continuity.

Even if such things were to turn out to exist, they are not the things that we are tracing when we trace persons. Otherwise, our offhand methods would hardly deliver massive knowledge of facts of personal identity. Relative to our easy and offhand methods of tracing persons, judgments about the persistence of bare subjects would be highly adventurous conjectures. Nevertheless, we do have rich, if humdrum, knowledge of personal identity over time, at least in the massive core of ordinary cases. Indeed, it is among the most secure sorts of knowledge that we possess.

So the suggestion is that our point of departure in theorizing about personal identity should be the hypothesis that we are members of some substance kind that is "epistemically ready to hand"; that is, a kind whose members are easily traceable in the undemanding ways in which we trace ourselves and others. A very good place to start then would be with the biological kind Homo sapiens, and with the concomitant thought that we are certain kinds of animals. That point could be reinforced by observing that much of our tracing of our fellows through time is strongly analogous to the tracing of cats by dogs, or dogs by dogs, or dogs by us. Similar perceptual and cognitive mechanisms appear to be involved. And in all these cases, the object of attention is unquestionably another animal.

Animalism as the Point of Departure

In saying these things, I find myself in significant agreement with what is now called "animalism," the thought that our conditions of survival are just those of a certain sort of animal. When I read the works of "animalists," such as Michael Ayers, Richard Wolheim, William Carter, Paul Snowdon, David Mackie, and Eric Olson, they seem to me to be—in large part—sane revivals of what we ordinarily know over against the farrago of so-called "intuitions" pumped out of imaginary cases.[8]

Outside of philosophy, most biologists, certainly all of my acquaintance, accept the view that our conditions of survival are those of a certain sort of animal as an obvious consequence of biology, and are astounded, even perhaps scandalized, that there is a subject that purports to have *more* to say about what we are in the relevant sense.

Animalism is then definitely the place to start in discussions of personal identity. Even so, as will emerge, it is not the place to end up. And certainly animalism does not follow from the facts of biology; indeed, a blank reading of those facts does not itself support the form animalism usually takes, namely that our *most specific* substance kind is Homo sapiens. After all, most animalists would deny that I could continue to exist as a sponge or a worm, even though these are members of the animal kingdom.

That we are members of the species Homo sapiens, and so members of the animal kingdom is, of course, a fact of biology that no sane and informed person would deny. (Notice that someone who believed that we are composites of immaterial souls tied to

---

[8] Michael Ayers, *Locke*, 2 vols. (Routledge, 1991); William Carter, "Our Bodies, Our Selves", *Australasian Journal of Philosophy*, 66 (1988); "How to Change Your Mind", *Canadian Journal of Philosophy*, 19 (1989), "Will I Be a Dead Person?" *Philosophy and Phenomenological Research*, 59 (1999); David Mackie, "Animalism vs. Lockeanism: No Contest", *Philosophical Quarterly*, 49 (1999); Eric Olson, *The Human Animal: Personal Identity Without Psychology* (Oxford University Press, 1997); "An Argument for Animalism" in J. Barresi and R. Martin (eds.), *Personal Identity* (Blackwell, 2003); Paul Snowdon, "Persons, Animals, and Ourselves" in Christopher Gill (ed.), *The Person and the Human Mind* (Oxford University Press, 1990); "Personal Identity and Brain Transplants" in David Cockburn (ed.), *Human Beings* (Cambridge University Press, 1991); "Persons, Animals, and Bodies" in José Luis Bermúdez, Anthony Marcel, and Naomi Eilan (eds.), *The Body and the Self* (MIT Press, 1995); Richard Wolheim, *The Thread of Life* (Cambridge University Press, 1984).

an organism would also locate us in this very same species; they would simply have a distinctive view about the constitution of members of Homo sapiens. This seems to be Aquinas's view for example.)

Are we then done; is the course on personal identity finally over?

Not yet. At least one further question obviously remains: Is this species the most detailed or determinate substance kind to which we belong? Is there a still more restrictive substance kind to which we belong, one which imposes more restrictive conditions on our continued existence over time? For example consider the kind, Always Minded Homo sapiens, where this more restrictive kind requires that its members have mentality at all times at which they exist, so that its members cannot migrate into a persistent vegetative condition or from the mindless condition of an (as yet unquickened?) embryo. The mere highlighting of that real possibility makes the "liberal" and "conservative" approaches to the subject of "medical ethics" look equally shaky, in the sense that both depend on things that we do not know, and indeed do not know how to investigate, short of reverting to the rather limited method of cases.

Is Homo sapiens a Substance Kind?

There is also a less obvious, but more important question than the question of specificity: is the species Homo sapiens itself a substance kind? Is it true that none of those who are members of the species could migrate into it or out of it? Here biology surprises us, both with respect to migration in and migration out.[9]

On migration in, consider the animals of an earlier species that were the lucky "sports" who actually came to be the first members of Homo sapiens. Like all sports, they were produced by random genetic mutation. The overwhelming majority of sports will not make for a new species, but are simply "dead-enders" in the old species. This is because their genetic differences will prevent them from interbreeding with their parental population, and from occupying the same ecological niche as their parental population. However, in the lucky case there are enough similar individuals around to form a distinct interbreeding population and occupy a new ecological niche, and so the sports in question thereby come to be the first members of a new species. So it was with the true Adam, the true Eve, and all the rest. They were not born members of the species Homo sapiens, instead they *became* the first members of that species. In that sense they "migrated in." Like most migration, it was an adventitious matter, depending in part on external circumstance. The most likely outcome for a sport is to remain an infertile and dysfunctional member of its parent's species. So species, Homo sapiens among them, are not substance kinds.

---

[9] The following discussion is drawn from work by Joseph LaPorte and Samir Okasha; see LaPorte, "Essential Membership", *Philosophy of Science*, 64, 1997; *Natural Kinds and Conceptual Change* (Cambridge University Press, 2004); Okasha, "Darwinian Metaphysics: Species and the Question of Essentialism", *Synthese* 131, 2002.

When it comes to migration out, the dominant species concepts in biology have the following consequence: old species *cease to exist* when speciation events occur; as when, for example, a population becomes reproductively isolated due to one or another factor. So, if a population of humans becomes reproductively isolated from the rest, interbreeds, and finds a new niche, then two new species come into being—one comprising the population that recently became reproductively isolated, the other comprising the remaining populations—and the species Homo sapiens ceases to exist. The former extant members of Homo sapiens will then count as members of one or another new species. All that is a matter of extrinsic circumstance, it could happen while we're sitting on the couch. Does it then follow that you can "migrate out of" a species like Homo sapiens, so that we have here another indication that species are not substance kinds? It does follow if you cease to be a member of a species that has ceased to exist, which is the assumption most often made in the biological literature on species.

There does seem to be something to be said in favor of the view that you presently can't be a member of a defunct species. You can see the point when it comes to other groups. There once was a noble Australian Rules Football Club known as South Melbourne, second only in greatness to Geelong. The South Melbourne Football Club fell on hard times and no longer exists; it was replaced by a dodgy, corporate-driven outfit called "The Sydney Swans." As it happens, I know of several people in the old neighborhood of South Melbourne who still regard themselves as members of the South Melbourne Football Club. I deeply admire their loyalty, but I think they are confused. What could their present membership in the South Melbourne Football Club consist in? You don't retain your membership in a club once it ceases to exist, and likewise, it is natural to suppose, you don't retain your membership in the species you were born into when it ceases to exist and you go on. So, the thing to conclude is that there can be cases of migrating out of the species Homo sapiens.

Notice that even if you do retain membership in the species you're born into even when the species ceases to exist, species membership is still not an essential feature of the members of the species. Consider an infant Homo sapiens born right before a speciation event; that infant is a Homo sapiens. But surely that infant could have been born somewhat later, say after the speciation event, in which she would not be a Homo sapiens.

I do not, at the end of the day, want to rest the claim that Homo sapiens is not a substance kind just on these points about the nature of species, and on migration in and out of species. There are many competing species concepts, I have only detailed one or two, but that is enough at least to suggest that biologists do not regard themselves as under the obligation to conceive of species so that species membership is essential.

The main argument will be that Homo sapiens is a substance kind only if Animal is a substance kind, and Animal is not a substance kind. The points about migration in and migration out are simply meant to be cautionary tales. They caution us that the classificatory facts of biology do not themselves provide an account of what we are in the sense of what changes we could survive, undergo, or be around after. For actual answers to those questions, we need to determine further just which of the kinds we are members of are substance kinds.

Biology is not in any way required to think about and answer the question "What are the substance kinds?" The various notions of a species it finds useful are not *required* to be notions of a substance kind. (A fortiori, and contrary to the theory of reference of natural kind terms made famous by Saul Kripke and Hilary Putnam, biology is under no obligation to serve up kinds that sort things by their "scientifically discoverable essences." That is just a psychologically very natural, but nonetheless false, essentialist picture of biology, imposed on it from without.[10])

What then of the higher taxa; can their actual members migrate in and out of them? Are there reptiles that are extrinsically and accidentally reptiles, and so potentially non-reptiles? That is harder to see; and one might reasonably think that once one eventually arrives at a *kingdom*, like Animal, then the possibility of members of this kingdom migrating in or out of it is much harder to sustain. But, again, I take it that most animalists will deny that I could become a sponge or a worm, even though sponges and worms are as much animals as I am.

Animalism and Brain Transplantation

One seductive argument that Animal is not really a substance kind naturally emerges from Sydney Shoemaker's influential appeal to the method of cases in the following passage from *Self-Knowledge and Self-Identity*:

It is now possible to transplant certain organs ... in such a way that the organ continues to function in its new setting. ... [I]t is at least conceivable ... that a human body could continue to function normally if its brain were replaced by one taken from another human body. ... Two men, a Mr. Brown and a Mr. Robinson, had been operated on for brain tumors, and brain extractions had been performed on both of them. At the end of the operations, however, the assistant inadvertently put Brown's brain in Robinson's head, and Robinson's brain in Brown's head. One of these men immediately dies, but the other, the one with Robinson's head and Brown's brain, eventually regains consciousness. Let us call the latter "Brownson." ... When asked his name he automatically replies "Brown." He recognizes Brown's wife and family ... and is able to describe in detail events in Brown's life. ... Of Robinson's past life he evidences no knowledge at all.[11]

As a matter of statistical fact, by far the most common "intuitive" reaction to this case is to suppose that Brownson is Brown. The intuition seems all the more compelling if we add that Brown's brain was kept alive and functioning during the operation, so that

---

[10] For an extended discussion of this point see John Dupre, *Humans and Other Animals* (Oxford University Press, 2002) and Sarah-Jane Leslie, "Essence and Natural Kinds: When Science Meets Preschooler Intuition" forthcoming in *Oxford Studies in Epistemology*, Tamar Gendler and John Hawthorne (eds.).

[11] *Self-Knowledge and Self-Identity* (Cornell University Press, 1963), pp. 23–4.

there was continuous consciousness subserved by that brain while it was in transit from Brown's body to Robinson's body. Brown goes where his brain goes according to the widespread and strong intuition. If we treat this intuition as evidence, we can then reason this way. Brownson is not the same organism or human animal as Brown. In fact, Brown's de-brained body—let's call it "Brownless"—could be provided with enough in the way of brain stem tissue, transplanted from still another source, so as to be kept alive in a persistent vegetative condition. It can seem that this human "vegetable" Brownless is identical with the very *animal* that once exhausted Brown's bodily nature. Brownless is that animal in a surgically mutilated condition.

Brown has not only ceased to be the animal that he was, but during the transit he simply consisted of a brain. But a brain is an organ, not an animal organism. No brain is an animal. So Brown migrated out of the condition of being an animal, therefore Animal is not a substance kind.

Notice, however, that this argument turns on a classic appeal to an intuition about an odd case, a case which is *precisely designed* to tease apart mental continuity (holding between Brown and Brownson) and the organic physical continuity (holding between Brown and Brownless) that secures the survival of a human animal. As argued earlier, we have good reason to reject the sheer appeal to such cases as probative, on the obvious ground that in separating out mental and physical continuity the presentation of such cases may well undermine the precondition of our being good judges of personal identity, namely the convergence of the two forms of continuity which in everyday life we take to be the reliable signs of personal identity.

Moreover, even if we grant that something like the principle that persons survive if their minds survive does lie behind the application conditions of our concept of being the same person, say in the sense that we are guided by this generic in evaluating the ordinary cases of personal identity over time, that is the massive range of cases where mental and physical continuity line up, then it would still be fallacious to reason the following way about the brain transplanting case:

1. Persons survive if their minds survive.
2. Brown's mind survives when only his brain is kept alive and functioning.
3. So, Brown survives when only his brain is kept alive and functioning.
4. A brain is not an animal.
5. So, Animal is not a substance kind for Brown.

The second premise can seem quite plausible, given that the supervenience of mind on brain functioning is widely accepted. In the ordinary case, the continued existence of a mind is secured by the continued functioning (of the relevant sort) of the associated brain, and it is natural to suppose that this would continue to be so even if the brain was kept alive and functioning (in the relevant way) by advanced medical procedures.

However, even granting all that, the conclusion does not follow, since the first premise is a generic, plausibly understood as governing what characteristically happens in the ordinary run of things. Unfortunately for the proposed argument, the case at hand is precisely designed to fall outside the ordinary run of things, since it separates out mental and physical continuity.

Still, Shoemaker's case does at least serve to highlight the importance of the question: Is the kingdom Animal a substance kind? If so, animalism is at least on the right track in answering our main question. (The question of specificity would remain.) If not, the obvious fact that we are all, as presented constituted, animals (and not say plants or angels or brains in vats, or brains in transit to other bodies, or disembodied souls) takes us very little distance toward answering the central question of personal identity.

An Argument for Animalism?

Eric Olson, in "An Argument for Animalism," presents the following straightforward case for something he calls "animalism." In some quarters it has become a sort of master argument for animalism. (It is anticipated by Carter and Snowdon, but Olson gives it a particularly forceful presentation.)

I turn now to my case for Animalism. It seems evident that there is a human animal intimately related to you. It is the one located where you are, the one we point to when we point to you, the one sitting in your chair. It seems equally evident that human animals can think. They can act. They can be aware of themselves and the world. Those with mature nervous systems in good working order can anyway. So there is a thinking, acting human animal sitting where you are now. But you think and act. You are the thinking being sitting in your chair.

It follows from these apparently trite observations that you are an animal. . . . and there is nothing special about you: we are all animals. If anyone suspects a trick, here is the argument's logical form.

6. $(\exists x)(x$ is a human animal & x is sitting in your chair)
7. $(\forall x)((x$ is a human animal & x is sitting in your chair) $\to x$ is thinking)
8. $(\forall x)$ (x is thinking & x is sitting in your chair $\to x =$ you)
9. $(\exists x)$ (x is a human animal & x = you).[12]

The motivating thought here is that animals, especially highly evolved human animals, can think; that is, they can be subjects of belief, desire, feeling, and sensory experience. But if you are not identical with such an animal, then there are, bizarrely, at least two thinkers occupying your chair. For there is an animal there and animals are thinkers, and then you are, indisputably, another thinker.

Olson supposes that resistance to his argument will take one of three forms: either there are no human animals, or human animals can't think, or there are indeed two thinkers there.

Forced to choose among these options, the choice that least disrupts common sense is a version of the third. This is because the term "thinker" is polysemous—it has a

---

[12] In J. Barresi and R. Martin (eds.), *Personal Identity* (Blackwell, 2003). The argument is taken from pp. 325–6 (the premises have been renumbered).

number of related, but not identical meanings—and so can be applied to (at least) two quite different things; namely to a person, that is to a rational *animal*, who is the subject of thought, and to a thing, some of whose characteristic operations constitute thoughts, for example in our case, to an organ of mentation, namely the brain.

True, the brain is not sitting in the chair, but it is in the near vicinity of the chair. There may also be larger units genuinely there in the chair, part of whose functioning includes thoughts, units such as short-lived "hunks of matter," which come and go as the organic body of the animal undergoes (and so survives) matter exchange. If there are such things they could be deemed "thinkers" in the sense of things, some of whose operations *constitute* thoughts. These extra "thinkers" do not threaten the idea that in the case at hand only the (rational) animal *really* thinks, in the sense of being the subject of thought.

Still, if that were all there is to be said against the argument, we could quickly arrive at the conclusion that we are animals, by adding two further "trite" observations; one to the effect that we are not brains, even though we have them and they are indisputably our organs of mentation, and the other to the effect that we can survive the loss or destruction of some of the matter that makes us up.

Having said that, the next thing to note is that it is just not very plausible that these four "trite" observations—

10.   There are human animals
11.   Human animals can think
12.   We are not brains
13.   We are not short-lived hunks of matter that cannot survive the removal or destruction of any of their material parts—

could *entail* that Animal is a substance kind, i.e. that we could not cease to be animals without ceasing to be.

This point is further reinforced by a rather obvious parody of Olson's argument, the "let's avoid too many eaters argument." Informally, the argument goes like this: there is only one thing now in your chair eating a sandwich and there is an animal in your chair eating a sandwich, so you are that animal, so you are an animal. More formally, we can rearrange the argument so it precisely parallels Olson's argument, as follows:

14. $(\exists x)(x$ is a human animal & x is sitting in your chair$)$
15. $(\forall x)((x$ is a human animal & x is sitting in your chair$) \to x$ is eating$)$
16. $(\forall x)$ $(x$ is eating & x is sitting in your chair $\to x =$ you$)$
17. $(\exists x)$ $(x$ is a human animal & $x =$ you$)$.

Offhand, one might think that this is a *better* argument for Olson's conclusion than Olson's original argument, in at least one respect.

It is not too outlandish a barbarism to claim that the brain thinks; after all, you do find it in some neuroscience texts. Still, here is a thing to say that has some appeal: 8. in Olson's original argument is not obviously true; since "thinking" is polysemous, there is a person thinking and there is his hunk of organic matter thinking and there is his brain thinking. In strong contrast, "eating" is not in this way polysemous. To say that when an animal eats, its hunk of organic matter also eats and its digestive system also *eats* is really grating! It is a good candidate to violate what Wittgenstein called the rules of "logical grammar"! In fact, if you think about it, the hunk of organic matter is not around long enough to eat, since it ceases to be if it loses a part! So 16. is more clearly true than 8., so the "let's not have too many eaters" argument is the better argument!

This is, evidently, just a bit of fun. The main thing to see is that these trite observations "there is only one thing now in your chair eating a sandwich and there is an animal in your chair eating a sandwich, so you are that animal, so you are an animal" could not themselves entail that Animal (let alone Human Animal) is a substance kind with us as members. No argument for animalism is forthcoming from these obvious points.

This means that Olson's argument is not an argument for animalism either. *Animalism is intended to be a distinctive view in the philosophy of personal identity, a view which would give an answer to the question of what changes we can survive. So it had better imply not just that we are animals, but also that we could not cease to be animals without ceasing to be. But nothing like this follows from Olson's argument.*

To see just why animalism does not follow from Olson's argument, consider this variant on the argument, directed at an adolescent sitting in her chair:

18. (∃x)(x is an adolescent & x is sitting in your chair)
19. (∀x)((x is an adolescent & x is sitting in your chair) → x is thinking)
20. (∀x) (x is thinking & x is sitting in your chair → x = you)
21. (∃x) (x is an adolescent & x = you).

No one should deny that there are adolescents! No one should deny that adolescents can (in the relevant sense) think! And no one is really tempted to think that when a person is an adolescent there are really two things—the person and the adolescent—in the same place at the same time, each doing his own bit of thinking.

Clearly, nothing of much interest about personal identity is delivered by the adolescent argument. The conclusion is obviously consistent with the fact that an adolescent can survive the process of ceasing to be an adolescent and becoming an adult. The same thing applies to Olson's argument. The conclusion is obviously consistent with the possibility that an animal can survive a process which involves it ceasing to be an animal. There is no argument for animalism here, only an argument to the conclusion that we are animals. (And, as the "let's avoid too many eaters" argument shows, there are in fact a host of arguments to that conclusion.)

There remains one obvious difference between the adolescent argument and Olson's argument. Adolescent is transparently not a substance kind. Adolescence is obviously a phase you can survive, even though it may not seem that way when you are in it. "Adolescent" applies to a thing only during a certain phase of that thing's existence. What obviously isn't true is:

22. If x is an adolescent then x cannot survive ceasing to be an adolescent.

Animalists may have just implicitly assumed:

23.   Animal is a substance kind; that is, if anything is an animal then it is necessarily always an animal.

However, this assumption is not in any way reinforced by Olson's argument; for the argument is identical in structure to the adolescent argument, and the adolescent argument goes no way toward suggesting that Adolescent is a substance kind.

Once we see this, 23. looks like quite an embarrassing assumption to have made in the context of a discussion of brain (or cerebrum) transplants. For, the animalists' opponents, some of them at least, are suggesting that during the transplant, while the brain (or cerebrum) is kept alive and functioning the original person has been reduced to the condition of a brain (or cerebrum). And that view could be put this way: before the transplant the original person was a human animal, and during the transplant he is not an animal. (No brain or cerebrum, and indeed no head, is or wholly constitutes an animal.) This alternative view entails that:

24.   Animal is not a substance kind, for there are animals which could cease to be animals.

So far then, we have a standoff, one that is not in any way resolved either by Olson's argument or by appeal to the method of cases. Indeed, the "let's avoid having too many thinkers" argument is not an argument for animalism at all, any more than the adolescent argument is an argument for adolescentism, the view that actual adolescents can't survive ceasing to be adolescent and so can't survive into adulthood.

Are we then to conclude the course on personal identity with a standoff between those who take Animal to be a substance kind and those who do not? We can, I think, do better; we can provide an argument from general truths we know to the conclusion that Animal is not a substance kind. Animalism, understood not as the banal claim that we are animals, but as the interesting claim that we could not come to be non-animals, can be shown to be false.

Remnant Persons

Here is a conviction that many will share, one which organizes some of our thinking about persons and physical reality, in particular what we now know about the neural basis of consciousness: you can't bring a person into being simply by removing tissue from something, and then destroying that tissue, unless that tissue was functioning to suppress mental life or the capacity for mental life. A developing fetus might have a massive tumor in its developing brain, which suppresses its mental life, and perhaps even its capacity for mental life. Given that, we can understand how removing the tumor could allow a person in Locke's sense—a thinking reflective being that can consider itself as itself at various times and places—to be present for the first time. But you do not bring a person into existence by removing an arm, or a leg, or even a sustaining torso. A person's coming into being is not that kind of extrinsic matter. Nor is this a merely generic truth; rather it holds universally.

In responding to an earlier version of my argument from remnant persons, Olson helpfully pointed out that there is also a plausible principle concerning ceasing to be, which we can approach in this way. Suppose some person is constituted by some organic structure, say a brain in a vat. We may genuinely have a person—that is, in Locke's way of putting it, a thinking reflecting thing that can consider itself as itself at various times (if not places)—in the vat. Could you make that person cease to exist by surrounding him or her with tissue?

I suppose the answer could be yes, if that tissue serves to undermine the person's capacity for reflective mental life. But suppose instead that the tissue simply helps to sustain the brain, and has no negative effects on its functioning. Could that make the person cease to be? No, a person's ceasing to be is not that kind of extrinsic matter.

The following principles organize a good deal of empirically driven thinking about the effects of medical interventions, and in particular what we now know about the way in which our having a mental life of the sort sufficient for personhood depends just on our on our neural functioning:

(No creation) You don't cause a person to come into being by removing, disabling or destroying tissue, unless this positively causally impacts the neural basis of a capacity for reflective mental life, for example by removing a suppressor of that capacity.

(No destruction) You don't cause a person to cease to be by adding tissue, unless adding that tissue negatively causally impacts the neural basis capacity for reflective mental life.

The principles are thus not upshots of the armchair application of the method of cases. They are empirically motivated denials of certain sorts of occult effects; respectively, the creation at a distance of the kind of mentality sufficient for personhood without any effect on the underlying neural functioning, and the destruction at a distance of the kind of mentality sufficient for personhood without any effect on the underlying neural functioning.[13]

---

[13] This is not, and was not when I first formulated it, a principle governing mere removal or "shrinkage" of matter. True, one might suppose that one can cut a doorstopper in half and produce two doorstoppers, neither of which is identical to the original. Here, by mere removal of matter you cause two beings to come into existence. (A case offered by Paul Snowdon.) But that has no bearing on the no-creation principle, which concerns the generation of persons. Still, there may be then the temptation to think that if we already have a separated living brain or cerebrum, and then cut or remove the connective tissue between the hemispheres then we create two people. But the empirically obvious thought is that cutting or removing tissue in this way directly affects the thought constituting capacities of the two, now divided, aggregates of neural tissue, either by removing a masker of those capacities or by bringing into being new capacities. So brain bisection and the like do not provide a counter-example to the principle.

In his *Persons, Animals, Ourselves* (Oxford University Press, 2014) Snowdon has a another nice case, in which enough neural tissue is removed from a person to destroy all memory connection, and we might as well say, all psychological connection, with that person's past, while leaving enough tissue to subserve a

Now it is relatively easy to see that the falsity of animalism follows from the first principle in conjunction with a plausible supervenience principle to the effect that if a brain is artificially kept alive and fully functioning, complex mental life of the sort sufficient for personhood will be maintained, even if that brain comes to be no longer surrounded by a supportive organic body. The supervenience principle implies that in such cases there will be a "remnant person," a person who is obviously not an animal because he is not constituted by a living organic body of the appropriate sort. The no creation principle then implies that the remnant person did not just come into existence, but was there beforehand. But the only person there beforehand was the human animal from which the live brain was taken. So the person who was a human animal survives, i.e. continues to exist, in a condition in which he or she is not an animal.

That is to say, an animal can cease to be an animal without ceasing to be. Animal is not a substance kind, animalism is false, and we would go where our brains go in cases of brain transplantation.

Once again, this last point is crucially not to be established by an "intuition" about Shoemaker's case, but by abstract reflection about the consequences of what we know about causation and supervenience.

The Gruesome Illustration

Let's use an imaginary case, not to pump intuitions, but to illustrate just how the argument works. (I apologize in advance for the gruesome quality of the case; it is the result of trying to set aside one complication of head or brain removal, namely the possibility that the original animal still exists, but in a scattered state—the head here, the torso there. I would appreciate being told of less horrid ways of making the point.)

Really gruesome guillotining:

In the next reign of terror the guillotine returns, but in an even more gruesome form. The aristocrats, otherwise known as the "one percenters," are placed faced down with their heads leaning over a platform. A huge metal block falls from twelve feet above the platform, and completely obliterates the victim's body from the head

reflective mental life that is sufficient for personhood. A friend of the theory that psychological continuity is necessary for personal identity would say that a new person has come into being. But of course in this case there has been a radical intervention in the neural basis of mental life, so the principle does not predict anything at odds with the psychological continuity theory. Thus the principle does not beg the question against the psychological continuity theory.

The nicest case is due to Sherif Girgus. Suppose that a human blastocyst during the pluripotent stage is disposed to twin, but as a result of removal of some cells, twinning is suppressed and a single person develops, one who is (plausibly) neither of the possible twins. Here, at least on certain animalist views, you have caused a person to come into existence simply by removing non-neural tissue. Exercise: explain why this is not relevant to the brain or cerebrum isolation case at the heart of the remnant persons argument. Hint: the isolation case is not a fission case. Fission aside …

down; the head flies forwards, and is caught by an official who quickly attaches it to a medical device which keeps it alive and functioning. The crowds execrate the head for the next few days, until it dies off.

We are to suppose that a hapless aristocrat, who was the victim of this horror, was a human animal; that is, he had an organic body of the relevant sort. This body was obliterated at guillotining, so that the animal that the aristocrat was ceased to exist at just that point. We are also to suppose that the aristocrat's head is kept alive in such a way that the brain of the aristocrat still functions as an organ of mentation; that is, some of its operations are or constitute thoughts, indeed reflective thoughts involving profound despair about the future and the like.

Of course, as things now stand keeping a severed head alive for any significant amount of time may not be medically possible, but it is definitely not metaphysically impossible. Indeed, actual guillotining might well have included the terminal experience of the world spinning around, as one's head rolled into the basket. The brain takes a while to die, so that actual guillotining may not have brought mental life to an immediate end.

So we can legitimately suppose that really gruesome guillotining would leave behind something—something made up of a living head, artificially kept alive—with the active capacity for reflective mental life, something which anticipates a bleak future and frets about this, and so something which is a person.

The supposition that there is still a person around after really gruesome guillotining can be supported by appeal to a certain sort of supervenience claim. While the aristocrat was intact, it was his brain's functioning in a certain sort of way which secured the kind of mentality sufficient for personhood; when only the aristocrat's head survives, that brain might still function in the relevant way for some time, so that it continues to secure the kind of mentality sufficient for personhood. In accepting that, we need not be assuming that it is numerically one and the same person before and after really gruesome guillotining, but only that there is a person—a remnant person—around after really gruesome guillotining, one wholly constituted by a head, or as it might be in even more gruesome variants by a brain, or by a cerebrum.

So there are then two possibilities: either the remnant person is numerically the same person as the original aristocrat, or he is not. Suppose that the remnant person is a numerically different person from the aristocrat. Then either he was there all along, a distinct person from the aristocrat located just where the aristocrat's head was located, or he came into being as a result of really gruesome guillotining. But the only relevant person there beforehand was the aristocrat, whose head, brain, and cerebrum all survived the gruesome event. So it follows that the remnant person was brought into being by really gruesome guillotining. Simply as a result of the (violent) removal of tissue, tissue which was not in any way suppressing a capacity for reflective mental life (but instead helping to sustain that capacity) a person was caused to come into existence.

However this conclusion is at odds with:

> (No creation) You don't cause a person to come into being by removing, disabling, or destroying tissue, unless this positively causally impacts the neural basis of a capacity for reflective mental life, for example by removing a suppressor of that capacity.

So the thing to conclude—the only thing that does not lead to this or that repugnant consequence—is that the aristocrat continues to exist after really gruesome guillotining; he comes to be (wholly constituted by) a head kept alive and functioning. In the even more gruesome versions, he comes to be (wholly constituted by) a brain kept alive and functioning or by a cerebrum kept alive and functioning. So something that was a human animal ceased to be a human animal without ceasing to be. Thus, Animal is not one of our substance kinds, we can survive for a time without then being an animal, so animalism is false.

A Way Out? *not useful SKIP!

Peter van Inwagen has argued that it is not true that whenever you have some things there is another thing that they make up or compose. He has also argued that it cannot be that there are only simples with no compositional structure, because—so his argument goes—he knows himself to be a thinker and not a simple, and a thinker cannot merely be some number of simples, but must be a genuine unit. Van Inwagen is then forced to cast around to find a distinguished kind of complex unit for him to turn out to be; and he finds it in the case of the organism that he is.[14]

In this way, van Inwagen arrives at the conclusion that the only genuine complex wholes we need to recognize are organisms. There are not really tables, there are only simples arranged table-wise, there are not really heads, there are only simples arranged head-wise, there are not really brains, there are only simples and cells arranged brain-wise, and so on and so forth.

On this view, the supervenience principle driving the argument against animalism is false. The argument went wrong when we said:

> While the aristocrat was intact, it was his brain's functioning in a certain sort of way which secured the kind of mentality sufficient for personhood; when only the aristocrat's head survives, that brain might still function in the relevant way for some time, so that it continues to secure the kind of mentality sufficient for personhood.

"There is a further condition," so I imagine someone who wants to exploit van Inwagen's view in the present context saying, "that is required to secure the kind of mentality sufficient for personhood. There must be a genuine unit there to be the person. On van

---

[14] *Material Beings* (Cornell University Press, 1990). It should be noted that van Inwagen has been known to entertain the view that a severed head, an extracted brain, and a removed cerebrum are all organisms. I discuss this view later in the chapter.

Inwagen's view, there is no such thing after really gruesome guillotining. There are simples arranged head-wise, and simples arranged brain-wise, but there is no head or brain or anything else that is constituted by those simples."

Many will find this counter-intuitive, and it is; but van Inwagen will point out that he is led to his conclusions by a telling argument—the one canvassed earlier. Rather than emphasize the counter-intuitive nature of van Inwagen's position, I want to examine how offering this response to the argument against animalism works to undermine the very argument that motivates the response.[15]

Crucially, the response in the spirit of van Inwagen is not giving hostages to scientific fortune. (Otherwise we could just set it aside.) The response can allow that as a result of the particles arranged brain-wise causally interacting in a certain way they will secure something *very like mentality,* indeed something that only falls short of mentality because there is no relevant genuine unit to be the one who has the mental life in question. Perhaps an unfortunate aristocrat summoned up enough calm on the guillotine platform by forcing himself to meditate on Descartes' cogito: "I think therefore I am." Perhaps his remnant head could continue in this philosophical vein, or at least the remnant simples could continue in this philosophical vein, or something which is just like it, *but for the fact that there is no genuine unit in the offing to be the subject of these thoughts.* So much supervenience tells us.

The defender of animalism who wants to rely on van Inwagen's work need not deny this. He can say that there are pseudo-thoughts that can parade before a pseudo-consciousness as thoughts even though they are not thoughts, because they lack a thinker. He can say that this is precisely what happens with the so-called remnant head: there may be pseudo-thoughts there, but there is no genuine unit there to think. There is no thinker, and no person. So there is no violation of no-creation—

(No creation) You don't cause a person to come into being by removing tissue, unless that tissue is suppressing the capacity for reflective mental life—

because there is no remnant person after the guillotining. There is no remnant person because there are no heads, or brains, or cerebrums.

It is noteworthy that this is on its face an extreme defense of animalism. One might have wanted to be an animalist without denying that there are severed heads, but somehow we are now being led to the conclusion that we can't do this.

As against this extreme, last ditch defense of animalism, the question now arises as to whether the fact that we seem to be having thoughts is good evidence for the

---

[15] Here my discussion parallels very closely, and expands upon, what Olson recently wrote about this position, which he calls "brain eliminativism." See his "Animalism and the Remnant-Person Problem" in J. Goncalves (ed.), *The Metaphysics of the Self* (Peter Lang, in press). Olson once was himself a brain eliminativist, and Trenton Merricks still takes this view to be the animalist's best response to the well-known worry that animalism also has a version of the two thinkers problem; since the brain thinks as well as the animal. No it does not, Merricks says; there are no such things as brains. The recognition of polysemy would have been a better way out here.

existence of a genuine unit to be the thinker of those supposed thoughts. There seem to be two possibilities:

> There is a genuine unit in the offing to be the thinker of these seeming thoughts, so that these seeming thoughts are real thoughts.

> There is no genuine unit in the offing to be the thinker of these seeming thoughts, so these seeming thoughts are not real thoughts.

Unfortunately, one is not given any special sign *in thought itself* that the thoughts in question are had by a genuine unit, and so are real thoughts. At least this is so if we follow Hume and set aside the view that thought itself reveals an inner mental thinker, a mental something such as a Cartesian Ego that is the true subject of thought. Of course, that *should* be set aside in the context of defending animalism, since it is directly at odds with animalism; for it would immediately make room for the possibility that I, this Cartesian Ego, might cease to be an animal without thereby ceasing to be.

So we are left with the following strange situation: plausible as van Inwagen's inference from thought to a thinker might be, his resultant very sparse ontology of genuine complex units means that van Inwagen had no right to the premise that he was really *thinking*. Those episodes he was considering could simply have been pseudo-thoughts parading as real thought. There was nothing in what "he" was given from the inside that went any way toward distinguishing his so-called "thoughts" as real thoughts. For all that our mental life reveals, there could just be simples arranged animal-wise enjoying pseudo-thoughts. What then is the residual motivation for a position like van Inwagen's? The argument for the position—in particular for the claim that organisms are the only genuine complex things—now seems self-undermining in a certain way.

Is this not a real worry with van Inwagen's position *as such*, and not just with the adaptation of it in the present context? The position should respect the plausible scientific view that neural activity is a supervenience base for thoughts *and* pseudo-thoughts. It is thought when the relevant neural activity takes place in an organism and it is pseudo-thought when it is merely a pattern found in particles arranged head-wise. But this means that one has to admit that there is something like thought that does not require a thinker. Call this pseudo-thought. How does one then know that "one" has anything more than pseudo-thought? And so, how does "one" then know that there is a genuine unit behind "one's" apparent thinking?

Of course, van Inwagen offered another argument that there are indeed organisms in existence; but that argument just seems to be that being taken up in a life is a quite impressive way in which things can be united. Life deserves a lot of admiration as a process, but why exactly do we need to recognize a further genuine unit, when things are taken up into a life? *Material Beings* provides an argument for that by naturally supposing that there is thinking going on and requiring that a thinker be a genuine unit.

Olson's Reply to the Remnant Person's Problem

Olson has recently replied to my earlier (2007) presentation of the problem of remnant persons.[16] He agrees that the no creation principle is very plausible, and in effect he accepts the supervenience principle. He canvasses various ways out, including the way out inspired by van Inwagen. There he emphasizes the implausibility of van Inwagen's position, involving as it does the denial of the existence of heads and brains, but he also notes its self-undermining character. On these points, we are in complete agreement.

Next, Olson supposes that someone could say that the head or the brain is the same thing as the original animal, on the grounds that an animal might be *accidentally* an animal. The animal that is the hapless aristocrat is only accidentally an animal and so can survive as a severed head or extracted brain. He calls the resultant position "accidental animalism."

This is something of a misnomer, for the resultant position should really be called "phase animalism," for according to this response Animal is a phase kind, not a substance kind. It is not just that I could begin life as a cyborg in another possible situation, so I am accidentally an animal; rather the view is that I could cease to be an animal after having been one. I could become a severed head or a brain.

However, the very idea that phase animalism is an adequate resting place just misconstrues what is at issue in discussions of personal identity over time, where we are precisely interested in what changes we can or can't survive. Accordingly, the suggestion that Animal is a phase kind is not a way out of the remnant persons argument, it is simply the conclusion of the remnant persons argument.

Olson then goes on to describe what he takes to be a better proposal:

> Your brain thinks now, and is the only real thinker there. If it were removed from your head and kept alive in a vat, it would continue to think—though it would then think only for itself, and not for you. Presumably your brain would count as a person while it was detached, but not now while it remains a part of you, even though there would be no change in its mental capacities. Many philosophers will have no objection to this. Orthodox four dimensionalism—the view that all persisting things including ourselves are composed of temporal parts—has a similar consequence: it implies that you think now only insofar as a part of you—your current stage—thinks strictly speaking. And although that stage is not in fact a person, it would be were it not surrounded by other stages psychologically continuous with it, even though there would be no difference in its mental capacities. Yet almost no one takes this to be an objection to four-dimensionalism.[17]

In fact, *Surviving Death*, which appeared after Olson wrote, presents a developed version of this objection as *the* objection to a four-dimensionalist treatment of persons. If four-dimensionalism is true, then a bizarre consequence follows: it is morally wrong to make sacrifices now for one's future benefits.[18] But let's put all of that aside; for there is a more fundamental difficulty that attaches to Olson's proposal.

---

[16] "Animalism and the Remnant-Person Problem" in J. Goncalves (ed.), *The Metaphysics of the Self* (Peter Lang, in press).
[17] "Animalism and the Remnant-Person Problem", p. 8.
[18] *Surviving Death*, pp. 64–5.

On the view Olson proposes, the aristocrat's head or brain becomes a person when it loses its life-supporting tissue. The crucial question is just this: Is *that* person numerically the same person as the aristocrat? Are there two persons here, or one? If there are two persons, then since there were not two persons all along, it follows that a second person has come into being as a result of removing tissue. This is at odds with the no creation principle that Olson and I both find extremely plausible.

Suppose instead that one and the same person is first an animal and then a brain. Then it follows that Animal is not a substance kind, and animalism is false.

So Olson's proposal does not actually engage with or affect the proof that Animal is not a substance kind.

A Problem for Everyone?

Olson has an ingenious final response to the remnant person problem. He believes that there is a very similar problem that almost every theorist of personal identity faces, namely what he calls the "remnant brain" problem. The remnant brain problem begins with a dilemma: Does the remnant brain (or separated head in our example) genuinely think, as opposed to merely being the organ of mentation, the organ some of whose operations constitute the thoughts of the person that the brain (or head) constitutes?

That is a delicate, many would say unsettled, question, which arises within the discussion of mind-brain identity theories. Are the plausible claims in this domain either type or token identities, or instead, merely claims of either type or token *constitution*? Olson argues that on either way of going on this question, there is a problem.

Suppose, to take up one horn of the dilemma, the separated or remnant brain is genuinely a thing which thinks. Then Olson argues it cannot be that it was made a thinker by removing tissue whose only role was to sustain the functioning of the brain. Olson takes this to be a consequence of something very like our principle:

> (No creation) You don't cause a person to come into being by removing, disabling, or destroying tissue, unless this positively causally impacts the neural basis of a capacity for reflective mental life, for example by removing a suppressor of that capacity.

That is, something like:

> (No magical conferring of thought) You can't cause a brain to have the capacity to think by removing tissue, unless this positively causally impacts the neural basis of a capacity for mental life.

But then it follows that the brain was a thinker when it was in its normal surroundings; in our case, in the aristocrat's body. However, the aristocrat was also then a thinker and was not identical with his brain. So there were two thinkers all along, with very different persistence conditions, sharing thoughts. Olson regards this as a consequence to be avoided.

Suppose instead, to take up the second horn of Olson's dilemma, that when your brain is removed from your head it simply remains an organ of mentation, the organ some of whose operations constitute the thoughts of the person that the brain now wholly constitutes. (Notice here that the idiom of constitution is consistently applied; the brain constitutes a person and brain events constitute the thoughts of that person.) As against this position, Olson writes:

Someone might propose that your brain could never think, even when removed from your head. At most it might constitute a thinker: its matter would make up a thinking being other than your brain itself. Your body—an organism—constitutes you now, but if your brain were removed from your head, that organ would then constitute you, or at any rate it would do so for as long as it continued to realize your psychology. (This is Johnston's view, and presumably that of most other "constitutionalists".) But this only relocates the problem. Constitutionalists do not think that your brain now constitutes you, or indeed any other thinking being. You do not weigh three pounds. You—not merely your body, but you yourself—extend all the way out to your skin. It is your animal body that now constitutes you, not your brain. So although removing your brain from your head would not give it consciousness or the power to think, it would give it the power to constitute a conscious, thinking being. Your brain is now prevented from constituting a thinker by its fleshy surroundings, and putting it back where it belongs after its removal would prevent it from doing so once more. Those sustaining tissues "suppress mental life or the capacity for mental life" insofar as they prevent the brain from constituting a psychological being. And that seems absurd.[19]

These remarks, though crucial to Olson's attempt to defuse the remnant person problem, are quite puzzling; and they become more so when we add one thing that is central to the constitution view, namely that while the separated brain *wholly* constitutes the person, the brain in its normal fleshly surroundings only *partly* constitutes the person. Then Olson's complaint against the "constitutionalist" comes to this:

[On the constitutionalist view] it is your animal body that now constitutes you, not your brain. So although removing your brain from your head would not give it consciousness or the power to think, it would give it the power to *wholly* constitute a conscious, thinking being. Your brain is now prevented from *wholly* constituting a thinker by its fleshy surroundings, and putting it back where it belongs after its removal would prevent it from doing so once more. Those sustaining tissues "suppress mental life or the capacity for mental life" insofar as they prevent the brain from *wholly* constituting a psychological being. And that seems absurd.

Given this obvious clarification of the constitutionalist view, Olson's objection thus reduces to a slightly weird statement of the constitutionalist view, with the claim of absurdity simply appended to it. The slightly weird element is the talk of the separated brain being given "the power to wholly constitute a conscious thinking thing." On the constitutionalist view, the separated brain is not in any serious sense given any such power or disposition or capacity; rather it simply *comes to wholly constitute a person,* whereas previously it *partly* constituted a person.

<hr />

[19] "Animalism and the Remnant-Person Problem", p. 11.

Conversely, on the constitutionalist view, when you add appropriate supporting tissue to the brain, say by transplanting it into a receptive and de-brained body, you do not in any serious sense deprive it of any relevant power or disposition or capacity; rather it simply ceases to *wholly* constitute a person.

There is thus no interesting analogy between the constitutionalist's rather banal claim that you can change a person's constitution by adding organic matter to him or her, and the odd idea that you can cause a person to cease to exist by surrounding him or her with tissue that merely supports the person's neural functioning.

The fact that adding organic matter to a thing can sometimes add to the constitution of that thing, and so make what previously wholly constituted that thing now partly constitute that thing is a quite unsurprising idea. It is nothing like a violation of a principle like:

> (No magical conferring of thought) You can't cause a brain to have the capacity to think by removing tissue, unless this positively causally impacts the neural basis of a capacity for mental life.

Take a skin graft, for example; one consequence of a successful skin graft is to make a certain large portion of organic matter cease to *wholly* constitute the person it previously wholly constituted. It *is* absurd to "redescribe" this effect of the skin graft as suppressing the mental life or the capacity for mental life of the original large portion of organic matter. But the absurdity lies in the "redescription" rather than in the banal claim that a skin graft will increase the amount of organic matter that wholly constitutes the recipient of the skin graft. No one would seriously think in the case of a skin graft that you *caused* the original person to lose the capacity to think, just because you added to the organic matter which made him or her up.

Thus the "remnant brain" problem is just not a problem for the constitutionalist view. However, the remnant person problem shows that Animal is not a substance kind, and accordingly, that animalism is false, at least when taken as a distinctive position in the philosophy of personal identity.

Against the "Bodily Criterion"

The remnant person problem also has implications for other views related to Animalism. In particular it can be used, in the obvious way, to show that the bodily criterion of personal identity is false, and it can likewise be used to show that we rational animals are not essentially the organisms that make them up (if this is different from the bodily criterion) and hence that Organism is not a substance kind for rational animals.

But of course, now it will be said that the resultant "constitutionalist" view multiplies thinkers, at the level of the person and the organism or body. I wish people would stop saying that, as if it was an argument for something. "Thinking" is polysemous; we can use it to mean either being the subject of thought, or being a thing some of whose operations constitute the token thoughts of a thinker in the first sense. (Again, the constitution view should be consistently applied *across the board*.)

There are of course two or more "thinkers" here, but that does not mean that there are two or more subjects of thought. Absent a certain surprising resolution of the mind/body problem, no brain, organism, or hunk of organic matter is a subject of thought. And in any case, the clearheaded animalist, will end up saying something like this about the brain as a thinker. Does the brain think; are there then two thinkers, the animal and the brain? Once the polysemy of "thinker" is recognized, that is not really a problem for animalism, any more than the two thinkers argument was a problem for constitutionalism.

What *would* threaten constitutionalism, consistently applied, would be a defense of token/token identities of this form:

> Fred's thinking of such and such = brain process so and so taking place in Fred's brain at time t and location l.

Then we could argue that "thinking" is not really polysemous, and that Fred's brain and Fred's body really think in the same sense as Fred does. (If you don't like talk of different senses, you could try to work with different ways of being a thinker. Here is no great matter, nor was meant to be.)

The moral is—it is also a plea—that the friends of animalism should stop using the two thinkers argument (which is anyway a Trojan horse for them), until we have an actual defense of token/token identities of the above form.

Of course, the defense would have to explain why the corresponding token/token constitution claims won't do as well. Indeed, it would also have to explain how an event constitutively involving the animal Fred can wholly take place in a part of his brain!

An Austere Alternative

Put the constitution view aside for a moment. Is there another way of understanding what is going on in brain transplantation and really gruesome guillotining consistent with avoiding the remnant person problem? One view worth examining is "the pure predicative view"; which simply says that we are predicatively human animals and predicatively human organisms. As a result of really gruesome guillotining we would be predicatively heads, or in the even more gruesome case, predicatively brains. However, none of the following represent our substance kind: Human Animal, Human Organism, Head, Brain; for we can migrate in and out of these kinds.

On this view there seems to be no problem of "too many thinkers," not because of the polysemy of "thinker," but because there is only one thing there, the subject of each of the predications, which also satisfies the predicate "is thinking."

The pure predicative view is not yet a view about personal identity, but it would become one if it was augmented with an account of what our (most restrictive) substance kind is.

Someone might glibly say that Human Person is our substance kind and leave it at that. But if we follow Locke, and understand a person as at least a thinking intelligent being, then the glib remark seems to settle certain controversial questions without argument. Was I once an embryo? Could I live long enough to actually be in a persistent vegetative condition?

Alternatively, we can take the glib remark as just an invitation to say more about what our substance kind is. Perhaps all the extant proposals have simply misidentified crypto-phase kinds as substance kinds!

Are Severed Heads, Brains, and Cerebrums all Human Animals or Human Organisms?

Long ago, I suggested in "Human Beings" (1987) that a separated brain and a severed head would be "radically mutilated" persons, and that we do not determine the extent of an unmutilated person by seeing just how far it can be mutilated. So we are not now, for example, our heads, or our brains, or our cerebrums. This was directed at Thomas Nagel, who once said that we are (now) our brains.

Some animalists have gone further and said that since persons are animals or organisms, a separated brain is an animal or at least a human organism *in a radically mutilated condition*. In some places, van Inwagen takes this view, and recently Joungbin Lim has set about arguing for it, in part by appeal to what I say in the relevant passages of "Human Beings."[20] Is this line of thought, which one encounters from time to time, at all viable?

An animal is an organism of a certain sort. Organisms are marked off from things that are not organisms by their distinctive mode of being. Organisms are marked off from some other living things, like organs, by their distinctive mode of being *alive*. Organisms have the capacity for dynamic self-maintenance of their life functions. These life functions are dispositions to do various things, and when there are a number of such dispositions, we say that we have a living organism.

In the case of a human organism, those life functions include ingestion, metabolism, breathing, oxygenation of the blood, and excretion. So matter is absorbed into the organism, exchanged, and expelled. Hence the dynamic material character of an organism, a feature it shares with organs like livers and brains. But organs and livers are not self-maintaining in the way organisms are. By this I mean that when it comes to the organism, the dynamic exchange of matter with its environment happens within limits, which preserve a continuing basis for those very life functions. The life functions of the organism thereby maintain themselves—they are self-maintaining—because they maintain a physical basis for the very dispositions that they are.

---

[20] Joungbin Lim, *Bodies and Persons* (Doctoral Dissertation, University of Virginia, 2011), chapters 3 and 4.

Organisms, when alive, have the power to dynamically maintain a physical basis for the very dispositions which are constitutive of their life.

The brain may also be said to have life functions as well; sensing is a life function, a function that helps maintain the life of the animal, and more complex mental processes may help maintain the life of the animals that exhibit them. The brain is such that some of its operations—brain events—constitute sensing and thinking, the liver breaks down toxic substances in the blood, and so on. But neither of these organs has the capacity to dynamically maintain within itself a basis for these characteristic life functions. When the organism dies at somatic death, the organs then soon die, precisely because they do not have this capacity for dynamic self-maintenance.

It is important to see that "alive" is polysemous; it is one thing for a brain or a liver to be alive and another thing for an organism to be alive. A brain, as opposed to some of the cells that make it up, is alive only if it is still capable of *carrying out* its characteristic life-function, namely providing the basis for thought; similarly, *mutatis mutandis*, for a liver. An organism is alive if it is still capable of dynamic self-maintenance of its life functions. These are quite different necessary conditions on "being alive." All your organs could be intact, and so yet to die, when you are killed, say by a heart-stopping electric shock.

That point is underwritten by biology's distinction between "somatic death," the death of an organic body or organism, cell death, and organ death, the death of the organism's constituent organs. Somatic death is a global physiological phenomenon; the signs of somatic death are the cessation of heartbeat, breathing, movement, and brain activity. Cell death is a smaller-scale biochemical process in which various cells in various organs lose the capacity to subserve life functions. Cell death sets in some time after somatic death, and with it comes organ death. That is why the organs of the dead can be usefully transplanted into the living if those organs are recovered quickly enough. Cell death in these organs has not progressed to the point where the organs have lost the capacity to subserve various life functions. As it happens, cell death sets in at different times for different types of cells. Left to themselves, brain cells may survive for about ten minutes after somatic death, while those of the heart can survive for about twenty minutes, and those of the liver for about thirty to forty minutes. (Some estimates of these average times are more liberal, others more conservative.)[21]

Since a brain dies by its nature in one way, and an organism dies by its nature in another way, a brain is not an organism. That is the other side of the fact that since a brain is alive in one way and an organism is alive in another way, a brain is not an organism.

---

[21] It is important to remember that capacities or dispositions can be had when they are not operating, and when their manifestations are being temporarily suppressed by other factors; so an organism on life support, say a breathing tube, may not have lost the capacity to breathe; that capacity may simply be suppressed by fluid in the lungs. But when the organism has ceased to have functioning lungs, it has lost one of its life functions. When it loses all of these it is definitely dead.

Could we still say that in the more gruesome variants on guillotining (e.g. the rapid lasering away of all but brain tissue, or all but cerebrum tissue, if that seems to make a difference) the resultant "naked" brain is a still an organism, indeed the original organism, though one in a radically mutilated condition? This is what van Inwagen and Lim do seem to want to say. But as against this, the organism has died, i.e. has ceased to have the capacity for dynamic self-maintenance of life functions like ingestion, metabolism, breathing, oxygenation of the blood, excretion, and mentation, while the brain never had the *capacity for dynamic self-maintenance* of any these life functions, not even mentation, the very life function it subserved.

The same goes for the severed head and the cerebrum; even if they are kept on life support, they *never had the capacity for dynamic self-maintenance of any of these life functions*, including mentation, the very life function they subserved. This is why we should not say that severed heads, and separated brains and cerebrums, are organisms or animals. It is at odds with what biology teaches about the difference between somatic death and organ death, and this is because it is at odds with what biology teaches about the difference between somatic life and organ life.

There remains one thought that may seem consistent with the foregoing; namely that as a result of really gruesome guillotining, in one or another of its variants, we get a radically mutilated and *dead* organism which is now identical to a live severed head, or a live brain or a live cerebrum. There is no direct contradiction here, because "alive" is polysemous. Dead organisms can be live organs or organ containers, like heads. The radically mutilated organism has lost the capacity for self-maintenance, but the remnant has not undergone organ death. Animalism is preserved at the cost of saying that a live head or brain is an animal that was alive but is now dead.

This, however, is not a viable position either. The organism cannot be identical to a live severed head because the organism *was once alive* in a way that no head or brain or cerebrum was ever alive, namely it had the capacity for self-maintenance. The head or brain or cerebrum *never had* this capacity; it had the capacity to sustain certain life functions but not the capacity for self-maintenance. Heads and brains and cerebrums just do not have the right kind of physical structure to ever be loci of the capacity for self-maintenance. But dead animals, if they are the same animals that once were alive, did once have that capacity.

Suppose we instead take the Aristotelian view that the dead animal organism or corpse is not identical with the living animal organism that died and left behind that corpse. (Death, so Aristotle taught, is a substantial change for a living organism, it does not survive that change, even as a thing that has died.) Does that help us to find a viable animalist position to occupy?

No; the resultant view would be that the dead animal, which is identical with a live severed head, is not identical with the live animal. The live animal, which was a person, ceased to be, and left behind as its mutilated corpse another animal which was dead, but still thinking, for a little while. This is a scenario where one thinking animal, indeed one person, ceases to exist, and another thinking thing, indeed another person, one identical with a dead and radically mutilated animal, comes into being. So we still have a violation of no creation.

There could indeed be *something else, besides an animal organism*, that has the following two phases, that of being a live organism and that of being a live head or brain or cerebrum. That was, after all, the thing I called the radically mutilated human being. But, *ex hypothesi*, the existence of that thing is not good news for animalism; for if it exists then Organism, and hence Animal, is not a substance kind. For the thing in question would have migrated out of the kind Organism, and hence out of the kind Animal, for animals are just certain sorts of organisms.

The Proof Set Out

It may be helpful now to set out the whole proof that animalism is false, so that readers can determine just where they might resist:

25.   Animalism, if it is a distinctive view about personal identity, entails that Animal is a substance kind

26.   There are severed heads, and extracted brains and cerebrums (contra van Inwagen)

27.   These are not animals or organisms (contra van Inwagen and Lim)

28.   There are two uses or "senses" of "thinking thing"; one is to pick out a subject of experience, and the other to pick out some part of a subject of experience, a head or brain or cerebrum for example, which is such that some of its operations constitute the thoughts of the "thinking thing" in the first sense

29.   There is a thinking intelligent thing (in the first sense) that can consider itself as itself around after really gruesome guillotining and the like (from supervenience, and the first premise)

30.   You don't bring an intelligent thinking thing (in the first sense) that can consider itself to be itself into being by really gruesome guillotining and the like (the application of the no creation principle)

31.   There are not two overlapping intelligent thinking things (in the first sense) each able to consider itself as itself around before really gruesome guillotining and the like (at least there is nothing to this effect emerging from the level of analysis that is relevant to the problem at hand)[22]

32.   Conclusion: a thinking intelligent thing (in the first sense) that can consider itself as itself—that is, a person—could survive the transition from being an animal or an organism to being a severed head or extracted brain or cerebrum. So Animal is not a substance kind and animalism is false.

[22] For complications, irrelevant to present discussion, see "The Personite Problem" op. cit.

How Does the Proof Go in the Case of Dogs and Frogs?

At a recent symposium on *Surviving Death*, Alex Byrne and Michael Forster pressed me on this question: are human beings special when it comes to the remnant person argument, or can we generate it in the case of other animals? I believe that we can.

Dogs are good candidates to be persons—if you disagree with that think of me as meaning dolphin by "dog." So keeping a dog's head alive and functioning can be keeping alive the locus of a thinking intelligent thing that can think of itself as itself—a person in Locke's sense. That person did not come into being as a result of the removal of tissue, so that living severed head, though no longer a dog, could still be Jasper, albeit in a radically mutilated condition. Dog, or at least Dolphin, is a phase kind.

But frogs, so one might suppose, are another matter. A frog is a minded animal, a thinking thing, but it is not a person, a thinking intelligent thing that can think of itself as itself. So what happens when you sever a frog's head and keep it alive and functioning? I do have some tendency to doubt that here you really have a thinking intelligent thing that can think of itself as itself left, as opposed to a remnant of an animal that had only a rudimentary mental life to begin with. So this kind of consideration does not show that Frog is a phase kind. There is good reason to give your dogs proper names, but not your frogs.

I am kidding; for one thing I do not know where in the evolutionary process we move from the true "frogs" to the true "dogs."

More importantly, I can imagine someone arguing that a frog is at least a thinking thing, and that we do not bring *another thinking thing, period*, into being simply by removing tissue (unless . . .). So in every case where it is barely possible to keep an animal's mental life going by preserving its neural net even after the rest of its body is removed, we might be led to say that we have the same thinking thing, but not the same animal. This will hold true for all minded animals with a certain organic make up, but not for all animals, for there are animals like sponges with no mental life at all.

If we endorse the stronger principle that we do not bring a thinking thing into being by removing tissue (unless . . .), then the result would be that whenever we have minded animals with separable neural nets we have two things, a thinking thing and an animal with different persistence conditions. The thinking thing is only contingently an animal.

Once again, this is not a favorable result for animalism. It is the denial of animalism. At first blush, it may not seem that way, because it seems to strongly vindicate the animalist view that there is little ontological difference between us and other animals; but animalism is more than that (correct, if naturalism is correct) view; animalism is or includes the view that animal is a substance kind.

Where Are We?

The real conclusion that follows from the "let's avoid too many minds" argument—or the *much better* "let's avoid too many eaters" argument—is not actually a view about personal identity over time. It is simply draws our attention to a fact that any view of personal identity must take into account.

After all, the conclusion of those two arguments was just:

(∃x)   (x is a human animal & x = you),

and this is logically equivalent to:

You are a human animal.

However, the latter simply predicates "human animal" of a person. That we are *predicatively* human animals is a fact that every view of personal identity must take into account. Indeed, many views of personal identity, intuitively at odds with animalism understood as a distinctive alternative position in the philosophy of personal identity, have already taken this into account. This means that no distinctive alternative position in the philosophy of personal identity has been characterized by saying that "each of us is identical to a human animal," for that just has (∀y)(y is one of us → (∃x)(x is a human animal & x = y) as it's logical form, which is just logically equivalent to the general *predication*: (∀y)(y is one of us → y is a human animal); that is to say, all of us are human animals. But so what?[23]

On the "wide" psychological criterion of personal identity, according to which we can survive teletransportation, we are all human animals, at least before our first teletransportation, which, I note, none of us have undergone. (We are not plants, we are not souls, and we are not angels.) On the view of Thomas Aquinas, we are presently human animals, which means rational animals, where this in turn entails that the principle of life of the human body essentially includes the capacity for reason, which in its turn, according to Aquinas, entails that our mental functioning is not reducible to bodily functioning, and so can continue on even when we are not animals, as in the interregnum between death and bodily resurrection. Robert Nozick's view of personal identity over time was discussed earlier; need Nozick have denied that we are presently human animals? Of course not.

We must therefore distinguish the view that we are presently animals from the view that we are presently animals *and* Animal is a substance kind. Though the former view follows from the "let's avoid too many thinkers" argument, only the latter view is a distinctive position in the philosophy of personal identity. But reflection on remnant persons shows that this distinctive position is false.

So what then *is* our (most restrictive) substance kind? Now the course on personal identity begins to get really interesting.

---

[23] Recall Snowdon's *two* conditions on Animalism, set out in note 1.

6

Thinking Animals Without Animalism

Sydney Shoemaker

6.1.

Persons breathe, eat, drink, digest food, excrete waste, and in countless other ways do what animals characteristically do. They have organs—hearts, livers, etc.—and reproductive systems characteristic of mammals, and share much of their DNA with other animals. Plainly they are animals. And, of course, since they are (predicatively) animals, they have the persistence conditions of the kind of animals they are.

Is what I have just said an affirmation of animalism? No. What I said implied nothing about what the persistence conditions of animals are. Animalism, as I understand it, is the view that the persistence conditions of persons are biological rather than psychological. And what I said is compatible with their persistence conditions being psychological.

Consider creatures like dogs, whose status as animals should be uncontroversial. As Peter Unger has pointed out, there are thought experiments similar to those that support the claim that the persistence conditions of persons are psychological that support the same claim about the persistence conditions of dogs and other higher mammals.[1] Suppose that transplanting the cerebrum of a dog resulted in the recipient acting just as the donor had done prior to the transplant—it recognizes and shows affection toward the donor's master, knows its way around the donor's home and neighborhood, digs for bones where the donor buried them, knows tricks that were taught the donor, and so on. As Unger points out, applying his "Avoidance of Future Great Pain Test" to this case supports the claim that the recipient is the donor. If we are concerned for the well-being of the original dog, and know that this dog has a cerebrum transplant in its future, we will be willing that it be subjected to mild pain now if we know that this will prevent the recipient from being subjected to much greater pain after the transplant. And, this test aside, it is intuitively plausible that

---

[1] Unger 2000.

given the psychological continuity between them, the donor and the recipient are one and the same dog.

Must someone who accepts this conclusion deny that dogs are animals? Obviously not. What she must deny is that the persistence conditions of this sort of animal are purely biological. But this is not to deny that where the dog is there is an animal whose persistence conditions are purely biological. We can imagine that when Fido's cerebrum is transplanted, there is left behind a "canine vegetable," kept alive by an artificial support system, which has all of Fido's former body except for the cerebrum. And there is certainly a good sense in which this is the same animal as the one that had this body before the transplant. Let's say that it is the same "biological animal." The dog, though certainly an animal, is—prior to the transplant—coincident with but not identical with the biological animal. So on this view the term "animal" is ambiguous. It has its familiar sense, in which dogs, horses, chimps—and persons—are animals, and it has a technical sense in which it applies only to creatures, what I am calling biological animals, whose persistence conditions are purely biological.

If dogs are coincident with, without being identical with, biological animals, the same is true of persons. So a person is an animal with psychological persistence conditions that is coincident with, and in some sense constituted by, a biological animal. Psychological accounts of personal identity are often charged with the implausible denial that animals can think or have mental properties. But obviously the animals persons are can think and have whatever mental properties persons have. It is the biological animals they are coincident with that lack such properties.

If the term "animal" is ambiguous in the way I have suggested, it seems likely that there is a corresponding ambiguity in at least some of the biological predicates that are applied both to persons and dogs, animals in the one sense, and to biological animals. That idea will be developed later.

6.2.

It is compatible with the psychological view that it could turn out that a cerebrum transplant could not yield full psychological continuity between donor and recipient. Perhaps the way mental states are realized in the human body is such that there is no proper part of a human body whose transplantation would yield such psychological continuity. Or perhaps the way these are realized is such that while there is a proper part whose transplantation would yield such psychological continuity, this part is such that if transplanted the biological animal would go with it. (Eric Olson has held that because the brainstem is the biological control center for the human organism, transplanting the whole brain, including the brainstem, could make the recipient the same biological animal, and the same person, as the donor.[2]) What the psychological account is committed to is just the conditional proposition that if a cerebrum transplant yielded

_____

[2] Olson 1997.

full psychological continuity, the person would, in virtue of this, go with the cerebrum. That conditional could be true even if it were biologically impossible for its antecedent to be satisfied. Were this impossible, the biological continuity that constitutes the persistence of the biological animal would be necessary for the persistence of the person. And where there is a person existing at t1 and a person existing at t2, such biological continuity would be sufficient for these persons being one and the same. But on the psychological view, it would still be psychological continuity that constitutes the persistence of the person; what would make biological continuity necessary for the persistence of a person, and in some circumstances sufficient for it, would be just the fact that biological continuity is necessary and sufficient for the psychological continuity that constitutes it.

I know of no reason to think that there is this strong connection between biological continuity and personal identity—no reason to think that a cerebrum transplant could not yield full psychological continuity. But it is worth noting that even if there were this strong connection this would not give us an identity between the person and the biological animal. For the biological animal can exist as a fetus, or as a human vegetable (its cerebrum having been removed), while on the psychological view the person can't—and the psychological view is compatible with there being the strong connection. So on the psychological view the relation between the person and the biological animal has to be coincidence rather than identity, even if the strong connection holds.

It is this sort of coincidence that is the main bone of contention between animalists and proponents of the psychological view. When combined with physicalism about the mental, such coincidence is held to give rise to what I have called the "too many minds" problem, and what Eric Olson has called the problem of "too many thinkers." The idea is that if a person and a biological animal are non-identical but coincident entities, composed of the same matter, they will share the same physical properties and, assuming physicalism, will in consequence share the same mental properties. So, contra the psychological view, the biological animal will have whatever mental properties the person has. Worse, given a plausible view of personhood, the biological animal will itself be a person, which completely undermines the distinction the psychological view tries to draw. And the view has epistemological embarrassments as well—if where I am there are two things thinking my thoughts, how do I know which I am?

The remainder of this chapter will be a reply to this objection. The reply elaborates, and I hope improves, a reply I have made elsewhere.

6.3.

I begin by denying that it is a consequence of physicalism that coincident entities must share all of the same physical properties. We can distinguish what I call "thin" properties, properties that can be shared by things of different kinds, and "thick" properties, properties that can belong only to things of certain kinds. Thickness can vary in degree; properties that can be possessed only by things belonging to a certain species will be thicker than properties that can be possessed only by things belonging to a certain genus. But for present purposes I will work mainly with the dichotomy of thick and thin. Thin properties will be properties like shape, size, and mass that can belong to physical objects of any kind. Coincident objects will share the same thin physical properties, but can differ in their thick physical properties. Mental properties I take to be thick, and the physical properties that realize mental properties, or on which they supervene, are also thick. And it is because coincident entities can differ in their thick physical properties, in particular those that are realizers of mental properties, that it does not follow from physicalism that coincident entities must share the same mental properties.

The thickness here is thickness of causal role. I take properties to be individuated by causal profiles—by the contribution they can make to the production of effects of certain kinds, and to the bestowal of causal powers. What is distinctive about thick properties is that a central part of the causal profile of such a property is the contribution its instantiation makes to influencing the future career of the thing that has it. There is an internal relation between the causal profiles of thick properties and the persistence conditions of the things that have them. To use my favorite illustration of this, it is constitutive of the property of being elastic that if something having this property is subjected to a certain sort of force it, that same thing, will undergo a change of shape, and that when the force is removed it, that same thing, will return to its former shape. And the same will be true of the properties that ground this disposition.

The reason I speak of an *internal* relation here is that not only do the persistence conditions of a property's possessor partly determine the nature of the property, because of the reference to "its future career" built into its causal profile, but the nature of the property, and its causal profile, partly determines the possessor's persistence conditions. To stick with the example of elasticity, if we have a series of thing-stages in which for a while the size of successive stages gets larger and then for a while gets smaller again, and if this change results from a force being imposed and then removed, this will be evidence both that the property of elasticity is instantiated and that the stages are all stages of a single persisting thing. Of course, a persisting thing will have many properties, and what determines whether a series of thing stages constitutes the career of a single persisting thing will be the causal profiles of all of the properties instantiated in these stages and the causal relations that hold between the stages in virtue of the instantiation of these properties. The view here is a version of the view that what constitutes the persistence of objects over time is the holding of causal relations, relations of counterfactual dependence, between property instances occurring at different times. My point here is that the properties whose instantiations are involved in these relations include ones whose causal profiles are such that their instantiation in a thing at a time contributes to the production of later states of that same thing, where the thing's having a career containing these property instantiations and their successor states makes it a thing of a certain sort.

I have said that mental properties are thick properties. The characteristic effects of their instantiation are those mentioned in accounts of their functional roles, and centrally include effects on the future career of the subject. Perceptual and cognitive states lay down memories of themselves, reasoning on the basis of beliefs and desires generates subsequent beliefs, desires, and actions in the same subject, and mental states of many kinds are, at least in the short run, self-perpetuating in the sense that their instantiation in a subject at a time tends to generate instantiations of them in the same subject at later times. What is envisioned in brain transplant cases and the like are cases in which there is a series of mental states in which the functional roles, or causal profiles, of mental states are played out, in the sense that property instances in later stages in the series are successor states of property instances in earlier ones and causally related to them in the ways prescribed by the causal profiles of the instantiated properties, but the earlier stages of the series were of someone having at the earlier times one body while the later stages are of someone having at the later times a different body. In such a case there appears to be a career of a person, or animal of some other kind, which spans portions of the careers of two different bodies and two different biological animals.

6.4.

Thick properties like mental properties do not supervene on, and are not realized by, thin physical properties. But this is not to deny that there is a good sense in which the distribution of thin physical property instances in the world determines the distribution of thick property instances, including mental property instances. My body and my biological animal share all of my thin properties, but do not, I claim, share my mental properties. But my body's having the thin physical properties it has, and its existing in an environment in which various other thin properties are instantiated, determines that there is something here having the mental properties I have. Likewise with my biological animal and its properties: these properties and the environment determine that there is something here having these mental properties. It is just that the "something" having these mental properties is not my body, and not my biological animal—it is me, the person coincident with the body and the biological animal.

Here it helps to think about how property instances are physically realized if physicalism is true. On one notion of realization, property instances are realized by other property instances—e.g. an instance of pain might be realized by an instance of C-fiber firing. I call this *property realization*, and say that the instance of pain is *property realized* by an instance of C-fiber firing. But there is another conception of realization, not in competition with that one, on which every property instance is realized in a microphysical states of affairs, i.e. in certain of the microentities that make up the subject of the property instance being propertied and related in certain ways. The microphysical state of affairs will be of a type having a causal profile which matches that of the realized property. I call this *microphysical realization*.

Some of the microphysical states of affairs will be realizers of thick properties, e.g. mental properties. Consider the microphysical realizer of a particular mental state I am in, say believing that Obama is president. This microphysical state occurs in my career, but it also occurs in the career of my body and the career of my biological animal. I share my matter with my body and my biological animal, and this means that if some of my component microentities are propertied and related in a certain way, so are the same component microentities of my body and of my biological animal. When something's career contains a microphysical state of affairs at a time, that thing has at that time what I call an MSE property, a microphysical-state-of-affairs-embedding property. This will be a thin property. And the thin MSE property bestowed by a microphysical state of affairs will be shared by the coincident entities whose careers contain that microphysical state of affairs. But given that the microphysical state of affairs is a realizer of a thick property—the property of believing that Obama is president—it must be embedded in the career of one of these coincident entities in such a way as to bestow that thick property on the possessor of that career. Let's say that the microphysical state of affairs is *weakly embedded* in the careers of all of the coincident entities, and *strongly embedded* in the career of one of them—the one that has the thick property.

What is it for a microphysical state of affairs to be strongly embedded in a career? Given that it realizes a thick property, and one whose causal profile makes instantiations of it apt to produce certain successor states, the career in which it is embedded must be such as to contain successor states of the appropriate kinds. Consider a case in which a person coincides with a biological animal throughout its career. The career of the person will contain a succession of mental states, each realized by a microphysical state of affairs. The career of the biological animal will contain a succession of biological states, each realized by a microphysical state of affairs. Let's take it that the biological states are instantiations of thick biological properties, ones that can be instantiated only in biological animals and not in persons. (Remember the earlier suggestion that biological predicates are ambiguous and ascribe somewhat different properties when applied to persons and when applied to biological animals.) Both careers will contain both series of microphysical states of affairs—the members of both series will be weakly embedded in both series. But each of the series will have a unity that the combination of the two lacks. Those in the series of mental state realizers will be successor states of earlier members of that series; they will be generated out of those earlier members, together with sensory inputs from outside, in conformance to the causal profiles of the psychological properties they instantiate. Similarly, the microphysical states of affairs in the series of biological state realizers will be successor states of earlier members of that series. It is the occurrence of a series of states of affairs having this sort of unity that constitutes the career of a thing having a series of thick property instances, and what makes a microphysical state of affairs strongly embedded in a career is its occurring in such a series.

Although in the case just imagined the careers coincide, they *could* come apart. The causal profiles of the two sorts of thick properties instantiated in the two series involve different persistence conditions. The careers might, for example, come apart due to a cerebrum transplant, which makes it the case that after a certain time the successor states of the mental property instance occurring prior to that time occur in a different body, while the successor states of the (thick) biological property instances occur in the same body.

6.5.

I should not leave the impression that the career of a person just is a series of mental property instances and their microphysical realizers. For, as I have said, the career of a person will contain, will have weakly embedded in it, microphysical states of affairs that realize instances of biological properties of kinds the person does not have. It will also contain microphysical states of affairs that realize biological properties of kinds the person does have. And it will contain states of affairs that realize instances of thin physical properties the person has.

This raises the question, if, as the psychological view holds, persons are in the first instance subjects of mental properties, how is it that they are also subjects—indeed, essentially subjects—of physical properties and biological properties? As a special form of the question, how is it that a person's career contains not only mental property instances and their microphysical realizers but also instances of physical and biological properties and their microphysical realizers?

Part of the answer is that the mental property instances are property realized in physical and biological property instances. I said earlier that the property realizers of mental property instances are thick physical property instances. This means that their microphysical realizers will belong to series of events having the sort of unity that constitutes the career of a mental subject. But something cannot have thick physical property instances without having thin property instances; something cannot have the sort of neural organization that realizes pain, anger, or thought without having mass and other thin properties.

Many of the thin physical properties we ascribe to persons are in the first instance properties of human bodies. In opposition to at least some animalists, I think that the notion of a human body, as something coincident with but not identical with a person, is a notion in good standing. The first step toward saying what warrants attribution of physical properties of a body to a person is to say what it is for a body to be the body of a particular person. Here there is an account that goes well with the psychological view: a body is the body of a person if it is related in a certain way to the person's psychological states—its sense organs are the source of the person's sensory input, and certain of its movements are under the person's voluntary control.[3] But it can't go without saying that a body's being the body of a person means that the intrinsic physical properties of the body are intrinsic properties of the person. For it could be held

---

[3] See Shoemaker 1976.

that the properties ascribed to the person with physical predicates are not intrinsic physical properties but rather relational properties of a certain kind—e.g. the property of having a body with a certain weight, or height, or size. That is what a Cartesian would say, and it is what someone should say if he thinks that the person is the brain.

Of course, if persons are coincident with their bodies, they will have whatever thin properties their bodies have, and these will include weight, height, shape, etc. But it would put the cart before the horse to give the fact that persons are coincident with their bodies as the explanation of why they share with them these properties; for surely our reason for thinking they are coincident with them is in part that they share with them these properties.

The general answer to our question will have to invoke a general account of synchronic unity—the relation that holds between different property instances belonging to a thing at a time. We saw earlier that the diachronic unity relation for a kind of things—the relation holding between property instances occurring at different times in the thing's career—are reflected in the causal profiles of the properties. The same thing is true of the synchronic unity relation. Oversimplifying a bit, a desire for a drink and a belief that a certain action will get one a drink will result in the doing of that action—if the belief and the desire belong to one and the same person. And arguably, if such a belief and such a desire are so related that they will jointly produce such an action, they and the action they produce will all belong to one and the same person. Here we have a relation, a relation between instances jointly apt to produce a certain sort of effect, that is arguably sufficient for synchronic unity. In this case the property instances are both mental property instances. What we need is a relation, analogous to this one, that can hold between mental property instances and instances of thin physical properties and instances of biological properties.

I think the best place to look for this is in the relation persons have to their body in their capacity of being agents. Intentions and willings typically have as their objects bodily actions or actions that involve bodily actions. The intended results of these actions depend on properties of the body—its mass, and the shapes of such parts as arms and hands. An action will be the joint product of the instantiation of such properties as these and the instantiations of the neural properties that realize the person's willings. Arguably these are synchronically unified. If, in addition, the neural properties instances belong to the person, in virtue of being realizers of the person's willings, then the bodily properties will belong to the person.

Imagine a case in which putting a person's cerebrum into a body resulted only in the body's sense organs being the source of the person's visual and auditory experience, and not in any voluntary control by the person of the movements of the body. I think that we might in this case question whether the person's intrinsic properties include properties of the body. We will be more inclined to say that this is so if in addition to visual and auditory experiences the person has kinesthetic and proprioceptive experiences produced by appropriate states and movements of the body. This will be partly because the person will conceptualize these experiences as of "my arm rising" or "my legs being crossed." But I think that the fact that they are so conceptualized is due to the fact that the normal role of such experiences is to inform the subject of the effects of voluntary actions, and of what actions are possible. Our sense of ownership of our bodies is closely related to their role in implementing our actions—and it is this, I am suggesting, that grounds the synchronic unity of mental and bodily properties.

6.6.

Earlier I suggested that if "animal" has different senses, one applicable to creatures (persons, along with dogs, horses, chimps, etc.) that have psychological persistence conditions, and one applicable only to creatures (biological animals) whose persistence conditions are biological, it seems that biological predicates may also have different senses. We certainly ascribe a wide variety of biological predicates to persons, and the fact that this is so is an important part of the basis for saying that they are animals of some kind. But if the biological properties of biological animals have causal profiles that give them biological persistence conditions, persons (and likewise dogs, etc.) cannot have *these* biological properties. Many of the same biological predicates are applied both to persons and to biological animals. But I suggest that the properties they ascribe are somewhat different in these different applications, because of differences in their causal profiles.

Predicates like "is anemic" and "is immune to smallpox" can be applied to both a person and to the person's biological animal. But consider what happens if the cerebrum of an anemic person who is immune to smallpox is transplanted to a body whose former owner was far from anemic but had never been vaccinated for smallpox. Supposing the person goes with the cerebrum and acquires a new body, and becomes coincident with a different biological animal, the person loses his anemia and his immunity to smallpox. We can suppose that the person's former biological animal is left behind as a human vegetable, kept alive by an artificial support system. It will retain its anemia, and its immunity to smallpox. Evidently, the biological properties of the biological animal are a bit "thicker," more closely tied to the persistence through time of their possessors, than the biological properties of the person that bears the same name.

In saying that the biological properties of the person are less thick than those of the biological animal I don't mean to imply that they are thin. My own inclination is to say that the *body* of the person (and of the biological animal) is not correctly described as anemic and immune to smallpox. The microphysical state of affairs that is the realizer of a thick biological property belonging to the biological animal occurs also in the career of the person and in the career of the body. In the latter it realizes only a thin property (one shared, of course, by the person and the biological animal). In the person it realizes a property that is somewhat thick (not being shared with the body) but less thick than the property it realizes by being strongly embedded in the career of the biological animal.

How can the same microphysical state of affairs realize instances of two thick properties, one thicker than the other? I think the best thing to say here is that the state of affairs that realizes the biological property of the person is not quite the same as the state of affairs that realizes the biological property of the biological animal. The latter state of affairs is weakly embedded in the career of the person, but a proper part of it is strongly embedded in the career of the person, and it is that proper part that realizes the property of the person. Roughly speaking, what is left out of this proper part is that part of the realizer of the biological animal's property that requires states of the human vegetable, in the cerebrum transplant case, to count as successor states of earlier instances of the property in the biological animal's career. This reflects the difference between the causal profile of the person's property and that of the biological animal.

Lynn Rudder Baker has suggested a view according to which biological and physical properties apply nonderivatively to animals (to what I am calling biological animals) and only derivatively to persons.[4] She also applies the derivative/nonderivative distinction in the opposite direction: persons have mental states nonderivatively, while animals and bodies have them derivatively.

Some of what Baker says suggests that having a property derivatively is having the relational property of being coincident with something that has it nonderivatively. For my own part, I do not think that standing in a relation to something having a property should count as a way of having that property—and I think that the physical and biological properties of persons are intrinsic properties of them, not relational ones. In the case of physical properties like mass, shape, and size, I think that the very same properties belong to the person, the biological animal, and the body. In the case of biological properties, I think that slightly different properties are ascribed by the use of the same predicates.

But given that I hold that both persons and biological animals have biological properties, albeit somewhat different ones, why shouldn't I hold that the same is true of mental properties—that is, why shouldn't I hold a view similar to Baker's view that biological animals have, albeit "derivatively," mental properties?

As I have repeatedly pointed out, the career of a person's biological animal has embedded in it, weakly, all of the microphysical states of affairs that are realizers of the person's mental states. There is nothing to prevent someone from defining, for each mental predicate, a "derivative" sense of it in which it ascribes the property of weakly embedding a state of affairs of the kind whose members realize instances of the property which that predicate ascribes when applied to persons. We could then say that the biological animal is angry, bored, thinking about Goldbach's Conjecture, and so on— each of these predicates to be understood in the way indicated. The question is whether there would be any point in doing this. There would be a point in doing this if this were the only way to save the intuition that animals can think and have mental states. But we

____

[4] See Baker 2000.

have seen that it is not the only way of doing this—we can say that persons *are* animals, albeit not biological animals. And there is nothing to be said for doing it that corresponds to what can be said for ascribing biological properties to persons in the way we do. Whether certain biological properties are instantiated in our biological animals affects our futures in ways that are important to us, and are dependent in various ways on our actions. This makes it convenient for us to have a way of ascribing these properties, or closely related ones, to ourselves. No doubt we could make do if biological predicates could only be applied to biological animals; but it would be pointless and inconvenient to limit their application in this way. By contrast, there is no purpose that would be served by having predicates that ascribe to biological animals the properties of weakly embedding the states of affairs that realize instances of mental properties of persons.

6.7.

If a person's body continues to exist as a corpse after death, and if the person ceases to exist at the time of death, then persons and their bodies are numerically distinct, though coincident, entities. In that case there will be as much of a "too many minds" problem vis-à-vis the person and the body as there is vis-à-vis the person and the biological animal. Animalists, who hold that a person's existence does end with death, try to avoid this too many minds problem by denying that a person's corpse is something that existed prior to death. This denial is sometimes supported by the claim that if a corpse were identical with something that existed prior to death it would have to be identical with something that prior to death had biological persistence conditions. The corpse itself does not have biological persistence conditions, so either there is no entity here that exists both before and after death or, if there is, it must be something with disjunctive persistence conditions. And the latter is regarded as unacceptable.

It is not easy to see how one could consistently hold this view without holding that the apple one eats is not identical with one that earlier was on a tree, or that the flowers in a vase are not identical with flowers that were earlier growing in the garden. The apple on the tree is part of a living organism, and presumably its persistence conditions are at least partly biological—it grew from something embedded in an apple blossom, and the events in its career were caught up in a biological process that is part of a life. The apple on the plate or in the pantry is in no sense alive, and is not part of an organism, and the events that occurred in its career subsequent to its being picked are not caught up in a life. The rotting of an apple is no doubt a biological process, but only in the way the decomposition of a corpse is; it is not part of a life.

(A grim counterpart of the case of an apple falling from a tree is that in which an explosion in an airplane sends a man hurtling toward the earth and in which he dies from his injuries on the way down. It would surely seem that *something* fell all the way from the airplane to the ground. But if a man's existence ends with his death, what fell all the way cannot be the man. What can it be if not his body?)

It is clear enough why we regard the apple we eat as the same as one that was earlier on the tree. The career of the earlier apple and that of that later one together form a career that exhibits spatio-temporal and causal continuity. Later stages in this larger career are causally and counterfactually dependent on earlier ones; the blemish on the skin of the apple now is due to something that happened to the apple on the tree, and it is true generally that had the apple on the tree been different in certain ways, e.g. if it had been wormy, the present apple would have been correspondingly different.

The same considerations of course apply to the pre-death body and the corpse. The careers of these form together a career that is spatio-temporally and causally continuous. And there are the same sorts of causal and counterfactual dependence. Scars on the corpse are due to injuries that occurred in the pre-death career. If the pre-death body had not had the name "Lucy" tattooed on its abdomen, the corpse would not now have that name tattooed there.

I have suggested that in the case of coincident objects the persistence of one of the objects consists in a career in which instances of thick properties generate appropriate "successor states" in accordance with their causal profiles. This makes the spatio-temporal and causal continuity that holds in the case of the body/corpse difficult to characterize. The pre-death body will presumably have thick biological properties, but if having these properties requires being alive then the corpse will lack them, and will lack biological states that are "successor states" of instances of these properties. Yet the corpse does have the property of having a heart, liver, kidneys, etc. arranged in certain ways—a property it inherited from the pre-death body. And these are not thin properties—presumably a "swamp corpse," resulting from lightning hitting a swamp and rearranging its matter, which by an astounding coincidence was identical to a real corpse in its thin properties, would not have these biological properties. Evidently the corpse has such properties in part because of its history. A part of it counts as a liver because at an earlier time it performed the functions of the liver. But what makes the corpse's liver the same as the liver of the pre-death body? There is of course spatio-temporal and causal continuity connecting them. But what thick properties does the corpse's liver have whose instantiations are successor states of property instances in the pre-death liver? One thing that will be true of the corpse's liver is that there occur in the earlier parts of its career, before much decomposition has set in, microphysical states of affairs that are similar to, although not identical with, the microphysical states of affairs that realize properties of a functioning liver. Similarly, there will occur in the career of the corpse states of affairs similar to the microphysical states of affairs that realize biological properties of the pre-death body. Whether these should count as realizing thick properties is difficult to say.

However we resolve these matters, I think it is at least as certain that the organs of corpses are identical with organs that existed prior to death, and that corpses themselves are bodies that existed prior to death, as it is that the apple I eat was once on a tree. Does this mean that these entities have disjunctive persistence conditions? It is true that prior to death the persistence conditions of the body seem to be the same as those of the biological animal whose body it is, and to involve continuity with respect to biological properties the corpse lacks. As Olson and van Inwagen like to say, the events in its career are caught up in a life, and this is central to what constitutes its persistence. After death we don't have *this* sort of biological continuity. The continuity we have then consists mainly of property instances perpetuating themselves, to a decreasing extent as decomposition sets in, and the properties in question are either thin properties or analogical counterparts of the thick biological properties of the pre-death body and its organs. But the linkage between the pre-death stages and the corpse stages is not disjunctive. As I have already said, there is a lot that can be said about the persistence conditions of the body/corpse that is not disjunctive; there is the spatio-temporal and causal continuity, and the fact that later stages are counterfactually dependent on earlier ones. This continuity holds throughout the career, but what is important here is that it spans the episode of death; it yields diachronic unity between pre-death stages and post-death stages.

If there is a commonsense view about the matter, it is certainly that human bodies typically survive for a while as corpses—where survival requires identity. This should prevail in the absence of compelling reasons to reject it, and I think that there are no compelling reasons. If we accept it, then unless we are willing to say that the corpse *is* the person, and so that the person survives his or her death, we must accept that persons are non-identical with their bodies, and that we have here a case of coincidence without identity.

6.8.

I think that what makes animalism a *prima facie* plausible position is that it can seem a no-nonsense position that respects both common sense and naturalism. Positions like Cartesian dualism, and bundle theories in the tradition of Hume, do not square well with either common sense or naturalism. And psychological accounts descended from Locke are thought to do no better, because of their supposed denial that we are animals and that animals can think, and because of their commitment to coincident entities, which is seen as raising the too many minds problem. I have tried to show that the supposed advantages of animalism over the psychological view are specious. There is no good reason why psychological theories cannot agree that persons are animals, and that animals can think. And since the psychological view is compatible with physicalism, it cannot be faulted with respect to accord with naturalism. The psychological view is committed to the possibility of coincident entities; but I have tried to show that this commitment is defensible, and that there are reasons for thinking that animalism is saddled with it as well. The advantage of the psychological view over animalism is of course its conformity to strong intuitions about hypothetical cases, including Locke's

Prince-Cobbler case and more recent variants on it that give it a more naturalistic turn by replacing souls with brains.[5]

References

Baker, L. 2000. *Persons and Bodies*. Cambridge: Cambridge University Press.

Olson, E. 1997. *The Human Animal*. Oxford: Oxford University Press.

Shoemaker, S. 1976. "Embodiment and Behavior" in Amelie Rorty (ed.), *The Identities of Persons* (Berkeley and Los Angeles: The University of California Press).

Unger, P. 2000. "The Survival of the Sentient," *Philosophical Perspectives* 14: 325–48.

[5] Thanks to Jennifer Whiting for comments on an earlier draft.

PART II

7

The Remnant-Person Problem

Eric T. Olson

7.1. The Transplant Objection

Animalism is the view that you and I and other normal human people are animals—biological organisms.[1] It is that we are animals not merely in some loose sense—that we have animal bodies, say—but in the simplest and most straightforward sense. There is a certain human animal, and that animal is you.

The most common objection to this view is that it conflicts with widespread and deeply held beliefs about what would happen to us in certain imaginary cases. Suppose your brain were put into my head, and my own brain destroyed. It seems that the resulting being would remember your life and not mine. He would have your beliefs, preferences, plans, and other mental properties, for the most part at least. In other words, he would be *psychologically continuous* with you as you were before the operation. Who would he be: me with a new brain, or you with a new body? (Or someone else altogether?)

Animalism implies that he would be me. That's because the operation does not move an animal from one head to another, but simply moves an organ from one animal to another, just as a liver transplant does. (I return to this claim in Section 7.5.) One animal loses its brain and remains behind as an empty-headed vegetable; another has its brain destroyed and replaced with yours. And according to animalism you are the donor animal and I am the recipient: you get an empty head and I get your brain.

This means that the operation would destroy my knowledge, life plans, preferences, and character traits, and give me yours instead. It would erase all my memories of my own past and replace them with memories of yours: of journeys I never took, conversations I never had, people I never met. It would fill my head with false beliefs, making me convinced that I lived in your house, worked at your job, and was the child of your mother. I should become systematically mistaken about who I am and my place in the

---

[1] By "animals" I mean those organisms that are not plants, fungi, bacteria, or protoctists. Note that Johnston uses the word "animal" to mean something that is *not* an organism, but rather a thing "constituted by" an organism distinct from it (2007: 55).

world. As for you: even if the operation didn't kill you outright, it would deprive you of your knowledge, memories, plans, and preferences—nearly all that matters.

In my experience, those presented with the transplant story have an almost irresistible urge to reject this description. It just sounds wrong to say that putting your brain into my head would give me a new brain full of false memories. Surely the one who got your brain would be *you*. A liver transplant moves an organ from one person to another, but a brain transplant is not really an organ transplant at all, but a "full-body transplant." It moves a person from one organism to another. (As for me: when the surgeons remove my brain before destroying it, they remove me from my own head, just as they remove you from yours.)

But this attractive description is incompatible with animalism. It implies that you and the animal—the one you would be if you were any animal at all—could go your separate ways. And a thing and itself can never go their separate ways. So the alternative description implies that you are one thing and the animal is another. Even if you never have a brain transplant, you have the property that no animal has, namely being such that you *would* move to another animal if your brain did.[2] But a thing cannot both be an animal and have a property that no animal has. Call this the *transplant objection* to animalism.

7.2. A Brief Clarification

Some readers may be assuming that the operation would have to move *some* conscious, intelligent being from one animal to another.[3] That being would start out with the ability to move your limbs and see through your eyes, then become able to move my limbs and see through my eyes (or the limbs and eyes that were once mine) instead. Animalism, the idea goes, simply denies that this conscious being would be you, insisting instead that you would be the brainless organism left behind. That looks unattractive. If some conscious being really did move from your head to mine, and was psychologically continuous with you afterwards, there is good reason to suppose that it would be you.

But no animalist would accept that there is any such being. Why suppose that moving your brain to my head would move a conscious *non*animal—a thinking being in addition to the animal? That is a substantive metaphysical claim, and it gets no support from reflecting on who would be who in imaginary cases. If the transplant objection relied on that claim, it would have to begin with some reasoning for it; yet those who make the objection see no need for such reasoning. That the operation moves a conscious being from one head to another is a consequence of the transplant objection, but not one of its starting points.

---

[2] If there are no such modal properties as this (as counterpart theorists say), or if we don't have them, the argument fails and the objection evaporates.

[3] This assumption is implicit in Shoemaker 1984: 108–11, for example.

7.3. Responses to the Transplant Objection

It can be hard to believe that a brain transplant is metaphysically analogous to a liver transplant. That might make it hard to believe that we are animals.

But this hardly settles the matter. The transplant objection gets its force from the general principle that anyone who is psychologically continuous with you (in the way that the recipient of your brain in the transplant story is) must be you. Yet most opponents of animalism concede that this principle is false.[4] If each half of your brain were transplanted into a different head, both resulting beings would be psychologically continuous with you. Each would be convinced that she was you. Yet they could not both be you: there is only one of you, and one thing cannot be numerically identical to two things. At least one of them would be systematically mistaken about who she is and her place in the world. So the critics of animalism face a transplant objection of their own. If animalism has unwelcome consequences in "single" brain-transplant scenarios, its critics must accept similar unwelcome consequences in "double" transplants. And whatever those critics can say by way of defending their view against the double-transplant objection can be used to defend animalism against the original transplant objection.

Further, if the transplant objection makes it hard to believe that we are animals, other considerations make it at least as hard to believe that we are *not* animals (Olson 2003). There is a human animal sitting where you are. It has your brain, and shares your history (for the most part, anyway). It behaves exactly as you do in both actual and counterfactual situations. That ought to make it conscious and intelligent—just as intelligent as you are. But if you are not an animal, this would make you one of *two* conscious and intelligent beings sitting there and reading this. More generally, there would be two conscious and intelligent beings wherever we thought there was just one—two *people*, if being conscious and intelligent in the way that you are suffices for being a person. Only one of them would persist by virtue of psychological continuity, and would go with its transplanted brain. How could you ever know which person you are—the animal person or the nonanimal person? Any reason you may have to suppose that you are the nonanimal looks like a reason for the animal to think the same about itself. That is something no one would accept. And if for all you know you may be an animal, then for all you know you might not be the one who would get your transplanted brain, undermining the transplant objection.

Opponents of animalism have two possible replies. One is to deny that any human animal (or presumably any other organism) is ever conscious and intelligent, and try to explain why. This would imply that you are the only conscious, intelligent being there. The other is to accept that there *are* two conscious, intelligent beings, and try to

---

[4] Friends of the temporal-parts ontology can accept the principle, or something close to it (Lewis 1976). They say that in "fission" cases, your preoperative temporal parts are shared by two people, who differ in their postoperative temporal parts. There are two of you all along, and the surgeons separate them.

explain how you can nevertheless know you're the one that's not an organism.[5] Either reply will need to include an account of what sort of beings we are, if not organisms. Call this the "thinking-animal problem." It makes the transplant objection look rather insignificant.

7.4. The Remnant-Person Problem

Mark Johnston has pointed out that the transplant story raises another problem for animalism, independent of the transplant objection.[6] Think of your brain in mid-transplant, removed from your head but kept alive. (It has to be composed of living tissue, else the transplant will fail.)

Suppose it's possible for the brain, in this condition, to support thought and consciousness of the sort you had before the operation. This assumption is widely taken for granted: it is the basis for all "brain-in-a-vat" thought experiments. In reality, there is nothing obvious about it. It certainly doesn't follow from the assumption that the brain carries psychological continuity, in that the person who had it at the end of the operation would be psychologically continuous with the donor. Someone ought to offer an argument for this claim. But I will concede it for the sake of argument and see what follows.

If the detached brain supports thought and consciousness, there has to be a being whose thought and consciousness it is. (Otherwise we ought to wonder whether there are any people at all, undermining both animalism and its rivals.) This being would seem to be your brain itself, or perhaps a spatial or temporal part of it. Or it might be something that your brain or a part of it "constitutes." (I will return to constitution later.) Because this thing (we are supposing) would be psychologically more or less like you, that should make it a person—a radically maimed person, we might say. Johnston calls it a *remnant person*. Roughly, someone is a remnant person at a time just if she is a wholly organic person but not an organism or a thing constituted by an organism then, and this condition results from cutting away a portion of a normal human person.

This looks like trouble for animalism. Animalism seems to imply that the remnant person would not be you: you would be the brainless vegetable left behind. The problem is not that the remnant person *seems* to be you. That would be just a variant of the original transplant objection. Nor is the problem that the remnant person would be a person but not an organism. That is perfectly compatible with animalism, which does not say that all people are organisms, but only that we human people are: it allows that there may be immaterial gods or angels. The trouble comes when we ask where the remnant person, if she were not you, could have come from. She could hardly have

[5] Shoemaker (1999, 2011) tries to explain why animals cannot have mental properties; Noonan (2010) tries to explain how we can know that we're not the animals thinking our thoughts.

[6] Johnston 2007. I described a version of the problem earlier (Olson 1997: 120f.), but Johnston develops it much more forcefully.

existed before the operation. If she had, and supposing she was a person then, there would have been two people within your skin at once—you, who according to animalism became a brainless vegetable, and the remnant person, who became a naked brain. We don't want to say that. The alternative seems to be that the operation brings the remnant person into being. But we don't want to say that either.

Why not? For one thing, it seems that there are only two people in the transplant story—you and I—even if we disagree about what happens to them. If the remnant person were someone new, there would be three: you, me, and the remnant person created by removing your brain from your head. Or rather four: if removing your brain creates one new remnant person, then removing my brain to make room for yours creates another. There would be you, me, and the two remnant people created when our brains are removed. That's two too many.

And it's hard to believe that removing someone's brain from her head would create a *new* person. As Johnston puts it:

You can't bring a person into being simply by removing tissue from something… unless that tissue was functioning to suppress mental life or the capacity for mental life. A developing fetus might have a massive tumor in its developing brain, which suppresses its mental life, and perhaps even its capacity for mental life. Given that, we can understand how removing the tumor could allow a person in Locke's sense to be present for the first time. But how could removing a sustaining [head and] torso bring this about? (2007: 47)

If animalism really does imply that the transplant operation would bring a remnant person into being, it violates the attractive principle that you cannot bring a person into being merely by cutting away harmless tissue: call it the *creation principle*.

Now most opponents of animalism will reject this principle as stated (Snowdon 2014: 235f.). Suppose each of your cerebral hemispheres were transplanted into a different head. The result would presumably be two people, each psychologically continuous with you to an extent that would suffice for her to be you (according to the transplant objection of Section 7.1) were it not for the presence of the other. But you could not be both those people, since they are distinct from each other. So the operation must have brought at least one of them into being. It has created a person by cutting away tissue that did not "suppress mental life or the capacity for mental life." If this is a problem, it's not one that can be solved by rejecting animalism.

But we may be able to revise the creation principle to make it consistent with the anti-animalist position that Johnston and others want to promote. Perhaps you cannot bring a person into being merely by cutting away *sustaining* tissue. In the double transplant you don't create a person merely by removing sustaining tissue; you also have to cut the hemispheres apart.

In any event, the problem has another side that Johnston doesn't mention. Imagine once again that your brain is moved from your head to mine and the utilities connected in such a way as to make the resulting person more or less normal. (This is likely to exceed the capabilities of any possible human surgeon, but never mind. Archangels could do it.) If I am an organism, this person is me. But I am not the former remnant person (the one created, or made a remnant person, by removing your brain from your head). *I* was never a detached brain. More generally, nothing can be a detached brain at one time and an organism at another; you can't make a naked brain into an organism by putting it into a new head. Before I was given your brain, I was a brainless vegetable. So according to animalism the remnant person is not me. But then what happens to the remnant person when she goes into my head? Surely she doesn't continue existing but cease to be a person. Nor does she come to be one of two people within my skin. It looks as if she must cease to exist. That would make it impossible to carry out a successful brain transplant without killing someone. And isn't providing a radically maimed person with the parts she was missing a funny way of destroying her? Animalism appears to violate the attractive principle that you cannot destroy a person merely by supplying her with sustaining tissues: call it the *destruction principle*.

So the new objection to animalism is that it violates the creation and destruction principles. You can't create a person just by cutting away sustaining tissues, or destroy one just by providing them. Yet animalism (the objection claims) implies that you *can* do these things. (It also implies that there are four people in the transplant story, whereas there are clearly just two.)

This "*remnant-person problem*" is not merely the original transplant objection put differently. One version of that objection is that the remnant person who would result from removing your brain from your head ought to be you, as she would be psychologically continuous with you. (She would think she was you.) This would rely on the principle that anyone who is psychologically continuous with you must be you, which, as we saw earlier, is doubtful. And animalism can explain why the remnant person would not be you: you are an animal, and no animal can become a remnant person. But Johnston's objection does not require that the remnant person would have to be you. His claim is simply that the operation could not have brought her into being. And animalism does nothing to explain how the operation *could* bring a person into being, or how implanting a remnant person into a new head could destroy her.

To explain how the transplant operation could create and then destroy someone, we should need an account of the metaphysical nature of remnant people—something that would tell us, among other things, when they come into being and pass away. But animalism offers only an account of our own metaphysical nature: that of normally embodied human people. It says nothing about remnant people, who would not be organisms.

(Matters may be even worse than this. If a remnant person would not be an animal, there could be human people who are not animals. In that case we ought to wonder why there is no such nonanimal person associated with each normal human being. If there were, then either there would be two people associated with each human being—an animal and a nonanimal person—or else no human person would be an animal.)

I have no account of why removing someone's brain from her head should bring a new person into being, or why putting it back would destroy one. I like these claims no better than Johnston does. If animalism implied them, this would be more than just a surprising and counter-intuitive consequence. (Every important view has those.) It would be a metaphysical mystery.[7] I think animalists should deny that any remnant person is created or destroyed in the transplant operation. What they need to do is explain, in a way consistent with these constraints, what sort of thing the remnant person would be, where she could come from, what would happen to her at the end of the operation and why, and how she would relate to you and me. I will discuss three sorts of proposals for doing this. One is that the remnant person who would result from removing your brain from your head would be you (Sections 7.5–7.7). The second is that she would be your brain (Section 7.8). The third is that there would be no remnant person at all (Section 7.9).

7.5. Accidentalism

How could the remnant person be you, the donor organism? One thought is that despite appearances, a human organism really would go with its transplanted brain: the operation would not transfer an organ from one animal to another, but pare an animal down to a naked brain and later supply it with new peripheral parts to replace the ones cut away.[8] The claim is not that a detached brain would be a sort of stripped-down organism, but that cutting away your vital organs would temporarily make you a nonorganism.

This is consistent with animalism, which is the thesis that we are organisms, not that we are organisms essentially. Whether an organism must be essentially or permanently an organism is independent of whether you and I are organisms. Because it implies that no remnant person would be created or destroyed in the operation, it would solve the remnant-person problem. For that matter, it would answer the original transplant objection by implying that you would go with your transplanted brain. Both objections would be based on a natural but false assumption about what it takes for a human animal to persist through time. Because the proposal implies that human animals are only accidentally animals (in that they can exist without being animals), I will call it *accidentalism*.

Although this sort of view is sometimes mentioned (Johnston 2007: 51–4; Hershenov 2008), I have never met anyone who actually believed it. It's not hard to see why. No organism would go with its transplanted liver: if you remove an animal's liver, it simply ceases to be a part of the animal. And the brain's role in the persistence of an

---

[7] Aristotelian hylomorphists may see no mystery. On their view, a detached and functioning brain might be a substance but an undetached brain would not be; and a substance is a substance essentially. That would explain why the operation must create and then destroy the remnant person (Toner 2014: 84). This view is hard to understand, and I cannot explore it here.

[8] The proposal would somehow have to avoid the impossible implication that a thing can come to be something that was previously only a part of it—that is, that a thing and another thing can become a thing and itself (van Inwagen 1981).

animal appears little different from that of the liver. If anything, an animal looks *less* likely to go with its transplanted brain than to go with its transplanted liver: the medics say that a human being can survive longer without a brain than without a liver (Shewmon 2001).

But the proposal is not merely unprincipled. Consider that the empty-headed thing remaining after your brain is removed may still be alive. That is, it may be a living organism. In that case it would apparently have the same *life*, in Locke's sense of the word, that the original organism had: the original organism's life-sustaining functions would have continued uninterrupted throughout the operation in the brainless remainder. And if an organism's biological life carries on, we should expect it to continue to be the life of that same organism (van Inwagen 1990: 142–58). How could an organism be outlived by its own biological life? Yet accidentalism implies that this brainless animal would not be the original organism.

That would make it pretty mysterious what the persistence of an organism could consist in. Our usual judgments about what happens to an organism when parts are cut away would be seriously unreliable. Think about how many human animals there are in the transplant story. Everyone takes there to be two: the donor and the recipient of the transplanted organ. But according to accidentalism there are four. One animal—you—starts out full-sized, is then pared down to a brain, and later acquires my noncerebral parts, thereby regaining its previous size. The empty-headed animal left behind when your brain is removed is a second organism. I am a third. Removing my brain to make way for yours reduces me to a naked brain, leaving behind a fourth animal, which then ceases to be an organism (or perhaps to exist at all) when your brain goes into its head.

This would also introduce a new trouble just as pressing as the remnant-person problem. The empty-headed vegetable left behind when your brain is removed could be an organism. Where could it have come from? If it existed before the operation, then either it was a second organism sharing your skin, or else removing your brain made it into an organism. Neither option has any plausibility. The alternative is that the operation brought it into being. But can you really create an organism merely by cutting away what would otherwise have been one of its organs? Or suppose the surgeons put your brain back into your head. According to accidentalism, you then cease to be a naked brain and become a full-sized human animal once more. But what happens to the empty-headed organism into which your brain is implanted? The reimplantation could hardly bring it about that there are two human animals within the same skin. It looks as if the empty-headed organism must cease to exist. But how could you destroy an organism merely by supplying it with the organ it was missing? If we have to say all that, we might as well reject the original creation and destruction principles.

7.6. Scattered Animalism

Here is another view on which the remnant person would be you. Suppose that removing your brain neither makes the animal into a brainless vegetable nor reduces it to a naked brain, but rather changes it from a connected object to a disconnected or "scattered" one. The organism comes to be composed of two detached parts, the brainless vegetable and the naked brain. It may thereby cease to be an organism, making this proposal a variant of accidentalism. The thoughts realized in the brain would then be the thoughts of that scattered object. So the remnant person is not the brain or anything the size of a brain—no such being is ever a person—but a thing composed of the naked brain and the brainless vegetable. If your brain is later transplanted into my head, it then ceases to be a part of the remnant person (you) and becomes a part of me, another organism, and the thoughts realized in it become my thoughts. You then become a brainless vegetable.[9] No remnant person is created or destroyed in the course of the operation, and there would be only two people in the story, you and I, just as there appear to be. Call this "scattered animalism."

It is another friendless view. Like accidentalism, it threatens to imply that there are four human organisms in the transplant story. Two, you and I, become scattered when their brains are removed (and may cease thereby to be organisms). And the two brainless vegetables that this removal leaves behind may also be organisms. That, again, is two too many. Also like accidentalism, it implies that removing your brain could create a new organism—the brainless vegetable—and that putting your brain back in your head would destroy that organism, violating analogs of the creation and destruction principles.

Nor would it solve the remnant-person problem in its full generality. Suppose your brain is removed and that this makes you a scattered object composed of a detached brain and a brainless vegetable. Now let a new brain be implanted into your head. The new brain becomes a part of the object that was previously a brainless vegetable and is now definitely an organism. This makes the new brain a part of you. (The organism of which it is a part is either you or a part of you, and a part of part of something is itself a part of it.) But what about your original brain? Would *it* still be a part of you? Would you have two brains at once? If so, you could have any number: the new brain could itself be put into the vat and replaced with a third, and so on. No one would want to say that. The alternative is that your original brain would cease to be a part of you when a new one is put into your head. (Never mind why.) But in that case your original brain would come to be (or constitute) a remnant person other than you, raising the original problem once more.

7.7. The Remote-Thought Hypothesis

A third view on which the remnant person would be you is consistent with there being just two organisms in the transplant story. When your brain is removed it is no longer a part of you. You stay behind with an empty head. If that organ were later put into my head, it would become a part of me, just as animalism leads us to expect. But

---

[9] Again, the proposal would need to avoid the problem raised in note 8.

the remnant person—the subject of the thoughts realized in the naked brain—is not that brain itself, but you, the now-brainless organism. Although the brain is no longer a part of you, you still use it to think. The thoughts realized in it are not its own—brains don't think—but yours. You think "remotely," in that your thought processes go on entirely outside your boundaries. (Thus thinking and consciousness can be extrinsic properties.) Call this the *remote-thought hypothesis*. It has a real advocate: Rory Madden (2011) proposes it to defend animalism against the transplant objection.

What makes the brainless vegetable the thinker of the thoughts going on in what was once its brain? Madden's idea is that the reference of thoughts and utterances is whatever the best Davidsonian interpretation assigns to them—that is, the best way of assigning them content. And one of the desiderata of such an interpretation is to maximize knowledge. If we took the autobiographical beliefs realized in the naked brain to refer to the brain itself, we should have to conclude that most of them are false and so not knowledge, since most of the things you believe about yourself are not true of your brain. The remnant person might have beliefs she would express like this: I was born in Nether Crozzledene; I attended St. Brutus's Primary School; I am tall enough to reach the light fixture without a ladder. And although these things may be true of you, they cannot be true of your brain: a brain cannot be born or go to school or be tall enough to reach light fixtures. So if we are to interpret these beliefs in a way that would make them true, we must take them to refer to you and not to the detached brain.

Some of the autobiographical beliefs you acquire while your brain is detached may be true if they refer to the brain and not if they refer you, the organism. Suppose your brain is kept for some time in one of those nutrient vats that philosophers like to imagine, and that its keepers enable the remnant person to "see" by attaching the brain to a camera mounted on the edge of the vat. This may give that person a belief she would express by saying, "I am in a room with a vat in it." If this belief referred to you, the brainless vegetable lying in another room without a vat, it would be false, whereas if it referred to the brain it would be true. Still, far more of the remnant person's autobiographical beliefs will count as knowledge if they refer to the organism than if they refer to the brain.

Now if there were a thinking being that shared its matter with the organism until its brain is removed and with the brain thereafter, we might be able to give an even better interpretation by assigning *it* as the reference of the remnant person's autobiographical beliefs. On that interpretation, such beliefs acquired both before and after your brain is removed may come out true. But as we saw in Section 7.2, the transplant story provides no reason to suppose that there is any such being, and no animalist would accept it.

Suppose, then, that the remnant person's autobiographical thoughts would refer to you, the brainless animal. Madden infers from this that they would be your thoughts. In that case you, the animal, would be the remnant person, solving the problem.

The remote-thought hypothesis raises many questions.[10] But even if it's true, it cannot solve the remnant-person problem. As Madden concedes, his proposal implies that if your brain is kept alive in the vat for long enough, and comes to support enough new autobiographical beliefs true of it but not of you (the organism), their reference will eventually shift from you to the brain. At that point the brain will become the thinker of those thoughts and a remnant person distinct from you, reinstating the original problem.

7.8. Remnant Cerebralism

Our question is what animalists can say about the remnant person who would result from removing your brain from your head. So far I have considered views on which the remnant person would be you. Another thought is that she would be your brain—that is, the thing that is now in fact your brain. (Not something constituted by your brain, but the brain itself.) In that case again the operation would not bring a person into being or destroy one, making animalism compatible with the creation and destruction principles. Call this *remnant cerebralism*.

Of course, your brain is not a person now (not according to animalism, anyway). Otherwise there would be two people sitting there and reading this, you (the organism) and your brain. More generally, there would be two people wherever we thought there was just one. Transplanting your brain would transfer the "brain person" to a new organism and leave the "animal person" behind with an empty head (even if she would no longer count as a person in that condition), leaving you to wonder whether you yourself are the brain person, who would go with the transplanted brain, or the animal person, who would not, and how you could ever know. To avoid these troubles, the proposal has to be that removing your brain from your head would change it from a nonperson into a person. And because there would not be two people within my skin after the transplant, putting it into my head would make it a nonperson once more.

So remnant cerebralism replaces the claim that cutting away sustaining tissues can bring a person into existence with the claim that it can make a nonperson into a person. And restoring those tissues would not destroy a person, but merely make her a nonperson. But that's hardly any easier to believe. What's more, the proposal implies that there are four people in the transplant story—you, me, and our two detached brains—yet there appear to be just two.

---

[10] One such question is why first-person thoughts must always refer to the being whose thoughts they are—the one thinking them. Most temporal-parts theorists say that when your current stage thinks, "I fell off the roof," it refers not to itself—the stage didn't even exist when the fall took place—but to the temporally extended person of which it is a part. (I discuss this sort of view in Olson 2007: 37–9, 119–22.) If first-person thoughts need not refer to their thinkers, then the remnant person could be the brain, as she appears to be, even if Madden is right to say that the first-person thoughts she has while in the vat would refer to the brainless organism.

It also raises an urgent question: *Why* is your brain not a person now? The most natural answer is that it hasn't got the right mental properties: to be a person, as Locke said, is to be intelligent and self-conscious, and your brain is not now intelligent and self-conscious. Presumably it has no mental properties at all. But why not? It appears to have all the physical infrastructure needed for mentality: it is connected to its environment via sense organs and motor nerves; and it has the right sort of history to be a thinker, if that matters. It *would* think, according to cerebralism, if it were removed from your head and suitably cosseted. It seems to follow that what prevents your brain from thinking now is nothing more than its fleshy surroundings. An embodied brain is no more sentient or intelligent than a liver, but remove it from its natural habitat and it will blossom instantly into a sophisticated rational being. And putting it back where it belongs would restore it to its former state of oblivion. This would mean that the tissues surrounding the brain really do (as Johnston would say) "suppress mental life or the capacity for mental life." They don't suppress it altogether: they don't prevent the *organism* from thinking. But they prevent the brain from thinking (Hawley 1998). Yet surely you cannot give something the capacity for thought and consciousness merely by cutting away sustaining tissues, or deprive it of that capacity just by providing them. That looks as compelling as the original creation and destruction principles.

Or maybe your brain does now think, and shares all your mental properties. It thinks not merely in some attenuated or derivative sense, by being the organ responsible for *your* thinking, but strictly speaking. Yet it might not be a person now because it is a proper part of you: personhood is "maximal," in that no person can be a proper part of another person.[11] Removing your brain from your head would overcome this obstacle and thus transform it into a person. Though this would still imply that there are four people in the transplant story (the two organisms and the two detached brains), it would at least explain why there are four.

This new proposal is that before the operation, you, the organism, are a person, despite thinking only in the derivative sense of having a thinking brain as a part. Your brain is not a person, even though it thinks nonderivatively. (*Why* you would be a person and your thinking brain would not be, rather than vice versa, is an obvious question left unanswered.) Removing your brain makes you into a nonperson by depriving you of your thinking part, and makes your brain into a person by bringing it about that it is no longer a part of a person. So the operation does not create a person, or enable a previously unthinking being to think; nor would putting your brain into my head destroy a person or render one unable to think. This would explain where the

---

[11] Burke 2003. The idea that personhood is a maximal property is familiar from the ontology of temporal parts, according to which you think at a moment only insofar as the momentary temporal part or "stage" of you located then thinks strictly speaking. Despite now being mentally indistinguishable from you, that stage is not a person—but it would be were it not preceded or followed by stages psychologically connected with it. (This follows from the definition of "person" given in Lewis 1976.) The reason why a person-stage is not a person is simply that it has the wrong neighbors.

remnant person comes from in a way consistent with the creation and destruction principles.

It would follow that no actual person has, strictly and nonderivatively, the mental properties characteristic of personhood (there being in fact no remnant people). And none of the beings that really have got those properties—normal embodied brains— are people. This is at odds with what most of us take the word "person" to mean. It would deprive personhood of any psychological or normative interest. More important, it would make animalism a mere linguistic variant of the view that we are brains. Given that our brains are the true thinkers of our thoughts, the difference between saying that we normal human people are those thinking brains and saying that we are the organisms of which they are parts is merely verbal. It is a disagreement about which beings our personal pronouns and proper names denote and fall within the extension of the word "person," rather than about the nature of those beings themselves. No animalist would accept this. (I will return to the view that we are brains in Section 7.10.)

7.9. Brain Eliminativism

I turn now to the proposal that there is no remnant person in the story. This would be so if a naked brain could not think (or coincide with a thinking being)—but I have conceded for the sake of argument that this is possible. The alternative is to deny that there really are any such things as naked brains. (Whether there would be such things as embodied or undetached brains is left open.) There are particles "arranged cerebrally," but they don't compose anything. (Some things, the xs, compose something y if and only if each of the xs is a part of y, no two of the xs share a part, and every part of y shares a part with one or more of the xs.) So there is no naked brain in the transplant story. The only material things in the vat are particles. But no particle can think. Maybe certain particles could think collectively, even if no individual particle can; but in that case too there is no thinker in the vat, and thus no remnant person. (Or none that is a material thing. I won't discuss the view that remnant people might be immaterial things.) Call this view *brain eliminativism*.[12]

It may be hard to believe that particles arranged cerebrally in a vat would not compose anything. And if they don't, we have to wonder whether particles "arranged organically" compose anything. Yet animalists have to accept that particles arranged organically compose something, namely organisms. If we are organisms, then there must *be* organisms; and whatever Aristotle may have thought, we know that organisms are composed of particles. But why should the inventory of being include human animals but not naked human brains? What's the difference?

As far as I can see, the only way to answer this question is to say in what circumstances particles ever compose something. How, in general, do smaller things have

---

[12] Its advocates include van Inwagen (1990) and Merricks (2001); I discuss some of its consequences in Olson 2015.

to be arranged and situated for them to add up to something bigger? There are two "extreme" answers. Compositional universalism says that any things, no matter what their nature or arrangement, compose something: composition is "automatic." Compositional nihilism says that there are no composite objects, but only mereological simples (things with no parts other than themselves). Animalism is incompatible with nihilism because no organism is a simple; and for reasons I have discussed elsewhere (Olson 2007: 229–32), it sits uneasily with universalism. Animalists need to say that some particles compose something and others don't. But which ones, and why? Very few answers to this question have been proposed. Of those few, the best may be van Inwagen's: that particles compose something if and only if their activities constitute a biological life (1990: 81–97). This implies that the only composite objects are living organisms. That is of course compatible with animalism. And it would explain why there are no remnant people: a remnant person would be neither an organism nor a simple.

Drastic though it may be, brain eliminativism is not obviously any worse than the other solutions to the remnant-person problem.

7.10. The Generality of the Problem

These animalist proposals are a bit wild, and I wish I had a better one. But this is a reason to reject animalism only if our being animals is the source of the problem. I don't think it is.

Consider Johnston's own view.[13] He says that each of us is a nonorganism constituted by an organism, where for one thing to constitute another they must at least be numerically distinct yet made up of the same matter.[14] In the transplant story you are constituted first by an organism, then by a naked brain, then by another organism— the one that previously constituted me, and which your brain becomes a part of. You go with your transplanted brain, avoiding the transplant objection; and the remnant person is you, avoiding the remnant-person problem.

"Constitution" views of this sort are the most popular alternative to animalism. But they face their own variant of the remnant-person problem. If the organism sitting there now constitutes a person, then your brain—the undetached brain now in your head—does not. Otherwise the person it constituted would be a second person in addition to you. More generally, every full-sized human person would contain a brain-sized person within her skull, and you ought to wonder whether you were the big person or the little one. To avoid this trouble, constitutionalists say that normal human

---

[13] Johnston 1987, 2007: 55–8. I'm not certain that I have correctly understood Johnston, but this is my best guess.

[14] Johnston calls the nonorganism a "human being" and an animal, and calls the organism a "body." This is confusing: to most ears, a human being, and certainly an animal, is by definition a kind of organism. It also gives his view a misleading appearance of familiarity. (Parfit is more honest: he puts his rejection of animalism by saying that we are not human beings.) I will describe Johnston's view in my own terms.

animals constitute people—conscious, thinking beings—and undetached brains do not. But your brain *would* constitute a person were it removed from your head and kept alive in a vat. It follows that you can cause a brain to constitute a person merely by cutting away sustaining tissues, and render it unable to do so by providing it with such tissues. That looks about as mysterious as the view that you can create a person by cutting away sustaining tissues and destroy one by supplying them. It also raises hard questions: *Why* would merely cutting away the sustaining tissues cause a brain to constitute a thinking being? Why would restoring them prevent it from doing so? And why doesn't your brain constitute a person now, in its normal state? Constitution views give no clue as to how these questions might be answered; yet they require answers. If this isn't the remnant-person problem all over again, it's a close cousin of it.

Maybe Johnston could explain why your brain would constitute a person in the vat but not in your head (not that he or anyone else has actually done so). In that case animalists ought to be able to explain in the same way why your brain would *be* a person in the vat but not in your head. That would be a version of remnant cerebralism (Section 7.8). It would give animalists a solution to the remnant-person problem about as good as Johnston's (that is, about as good as Johnston's would be if he had an account of why detached but not undetached brains constitute people). I say "about as good" because the animalist proposal would imply that there are four people in the transplant story when there appear to be only two; but it would explain why this was so.

In fact, constitutionalists face a far more difficult explanatory task than animalists do. Animalists have to explain why your undetached brain is not now a person. Constitutionalists have to do that too, since it's part of their own view. As we have seen, they must also account for the additional fact that your brain does not now *constitute* a person. (Animalists, if they are wise, will reject constitution root and branch, and thus need no special explanation for this fact.) Further, constitutionalists need to explain why your brain is not a person when it's in the vat (they say that it merely constitutes one). And of course they need to explain why a normal human organism is not a person or thinking being (but merely constitutes one) and why a normal human person is not an organism (but is merely constituted by one). You and the organism (and you and your brain when you are in the vat) are physically indistinguishable, with the same surroundings, the same history, and the same behavior in both actual and counterfactual situations. Constitutionalists need to explain how such beings can nevertheless differ radically in their mental and biological properties.[15] Compared to these challenges, what to say about remnant people—about a wild science-fiction story based on unargued assumptions about the mental powers of detached organs—looks like a detail.

However troubling the remnant-person problem may be, then, it is not obviously any worse for animalism than for its main rival. One view that really would solve the

---

[15] Shoemaker offers such an explanation (1999, 2011; see also Olson 2007: 60–5). Johnston does not (2007: 55f.).

problem is that we are brains. That is, each of us—each normal person—is literally a three-pound lump of soft, yellowish-pink tissue. I don't mean the view that we are constituted by brains—that would raise the same explanatory challenges yet again—but that each of us really is a brain. Call this the *brain view*. It implies that your brain is a person even now, and removing it from your head would neither make it into a person nor enable it to constitute one. The operation would do nothing more mysterious than change your surroundings. Some have taken the remnant-person problem to support something like the brain view.[16]

The brain view faces many objections (Olson 2007: 84–98). The most relevant for present purposes is that, like animalism, it conflicts with common beliefs about our persistence through time. My brain might be fixed in formaldehyde after my death. (This is a real case, and not science fiction.) It looks as if that organ would still exist in this state. If so, and I *am* my brain, then I too should still exist. It would not be merely a loose manner of speaking, but the literal truth, to say that the brain in the jar is Olson, the author of this chapter. If you don't like animalism's implication that you would stay behind with an empty head in a brain transplant, you won't like the implication that you could become a specimen in formaldehyde either. That may be why almost no one accepts the brain view.

I am not aware of any better solution to the remnant-person problem than those I have discussed.[17]

References

Burke, M. 2003. Is My Head a Person? In K. Petrus (ed.), *On Human Persons*: 107–25. Frankfurt: Ontos Verlag.

Campbell, T. and J. McMahan. 2010. Animalism and the Varieties of Conjoined Twinning. *Theoretical Medicine and Bioethics* 31: 285–301; (Chapter 11, this volume).

Hawley, K. 1998. Merricks on Whether Being Conscious Is Intrinsic. *Mind* 107: 841–3.

Hershenov, D. 2008. A Hylomorphic Account of Thought Experiments Concerning Personal Identity. *American Catholic Philosophical Quarterly* 82: 481–502.

Johnston, M. 1987. Human Beings. *Journal of Philosophy* 84: 59–83.

Johnston, M. 2007. "Human Beings" Revisited: My Body Is Not an Animal. In D. Zimmerman (ed.), *Oxford Studies in Metaphysics*, vol. 3: 33–74. Oxford: Oxford University Press.

Lewis, D. 1976. Survival and Identity. In A. Rorty (ed.), *The Identities of Persons*. Berkeley: University of California Press.

Madden, R. 2011. Externalism and Brain Transplants. In K. Bennett and D. Zimmerman (eds.), *Oxford Studies in Metaphysics*, vol. 6: 287–316. Oxford: Oxford University Press.

Merricks, T. 2001. *Objects and Persons*. Oxford: Oxford University Press.

[16] Campbell and McMahan 2010, Parfit 2012. I say "something like" the brain view because they seem to believe that we are not actually brains, but things constituted by brains. This, like Johnston's view, creates more problems than it solves.

[17] I thank Stephen Cave, Steinvör Arnadottir, Viktoria Knoll, and Alexander Moran for comments on earlier versions of this chapter.

Noonan, H. 2010. The Thinking Animal Problem and Personal Pronoun Revisionism. *Analysis* 70: 93–8.

Olson, E. 1997. *The Human Animal*. New York: Oxford University Press.

Olson, E. 2003. An Argument for Animalism. In R. Martin and J. Barresi (eds.), *Personal Identity*: 318–34. Oxford: Blackwell.

Olson, E. 2007. *What Are We?* New York: Oxford University Press.

Olson, E. 2015. Animalism and the Remnant-Person Problem. J. Fonseca and J. Gonçalves (eds.), *Philosophical Perspectives on the Self*: 21–40. Bern: Peter Lang.

Parfit, D. 2012. We Are Not Human Beings. *Philosophy* 87: 5–28.

Shewmon, D. A. 2001. The Brain and Somatic Integration. *Journal of Medicine and Philosophy* 26: 457–78.

Shoemaker, S. 1984. Personal Identity: A Materialist's Account. In S. Shoemaker and R. Swinburne, *Personal Identity*: 67–132. Oxford: Blackwell.

Shoemaker, S. 1999. Self, Body, and Coincidence. *Proceedings of the Aristotelian Society*, Supplementary Volume 73: 287–306.

Shoemaker, S. 2011. On What We Are. In S. Gallagher (ed.), *The Oxford Handbook of the Self*: 352–71. Oxford: Oxford University Press.

Snowdon, P. 2014. *Persons, Animals, Ourselves*. Oxford: Oxford University Press.

Toner, P. 2014. Hylemorphism, Remnant Persons and Personhood. *Canadian Journal of Philosophy* 44: 76–96.

Van Inwagen, P. 1981. The Doctrine of Arbitrary Undetached Parts. *Pacific Philosophical Quarterly* 62: 123–37.

Van Inwagen, P. 1990. *Material Beings*. Ithaca, NY: Cornell University Press.

8

Headhunters

Stephan Blatti

Advocates of the view known as "animalism" make the following straightforward claim: we are animals. This claim will strike some as hardly worth asserting, let alone defending. But since most contemporary theorists of personal identity still deny animalism, a defense is required after all.

8.1. The Thinking Animal Argument

On its intended reading, the "are" in "we are animals" does not reflect the "is" of non-identical constitution. Nor, on this view, are we animals in the sense of being embodied in animals, or sharing parts or stages with animals. Rather, the "are" in "we are animals" is typically taken to reflect the "is" of numerical identity.[1] The "we" picks out human persons such as you (the reader) and me (the author). And "human animals" refers to biological organisms of the species *Homo sapiens*.[2] Each of us—the walking, talking, thinking entities we are—just is a human animal. So says the animalist.[3]

The standard argument for this view is variously referred to as the "thinking animal argument," the "too many minds objection," the "two lives objection," "too many thinkers problem," and probably several things besides.[4] It was first developed by Michael

---

[1] I use "typically" advisedly here. Olson (2015) has recently argued that it would risk less confusion if the "are" in the animalist's claim were read as the ordinary copula—as reflecting the "is" of predication.

[2] For the purpose of this discussion, I will use "animal" and "organism" interchangeably, though I have come to believe that which of these concepts the animalist appeals to in formulating this claim has significant downstream implications.

[3] The founding advocates of this view include Ayers (1991), Carter (1989), Olson (1997), Snowdon (1990), Wiggins (1980, 2001), and van Inwagen (1990). Other noteworthy proponents include DeGrazia (2005), Hershenov (2005), Mackie (1999), and Merricks (2001). A more synoptic (if already somewhat outdated) overview is given in Blatti 2014.

[4] Respectively, Olson 1997, 2003; Shoemaker 1999; Campbell 2006; Parfit 2012 (also Chapter 2, this volume). How one characterizes the line of reasoning depends principally on one's antecedent disposition toward its conclusion.

Ayers, William Carter, and Paul Snowdon, and later sharpened and popularized by Eric Olson.[5] Here it is:

(P1)   There is a human animal currently located where you are.
(P2)   The human animal currently located where you are is thinking.
(P3)   You are the thinking being currently located where you are.
(C)   Therefore, the human animal currently located where you are is you.

While none of the premises is incontestable, nor is any of them easily denied. Except perhaps for far-reaching metaphysical reasons (e.g. an antecedent commitment to idealism), few would deny the very existence of animals, nor the fact that perfectly good specimens of the species *Homo sapiens* can be found wherever each of us happens to be. So (P1) looks safe.

Concerning (P2), since it would be odd to deny that human animals think while accepting that many nonhuman animals do, and since we can assume that the human animal sitting in your chair is not atypical of its kind, whatever reasons one has for accepting that various nonhuman animals think apply equally to the human animal sitting in your chair.[6] There are those who, in various ways, deny that *any* animal—be it human or not—can think (e.g. Descartes, Shoemaker). But their positions either strain empirical credibility or depend on fairly sophisticated metaphysical machinery (or both). At first glance, anyway, (P2) is much easier to accept.

(P3) is also difficult to resist, since rejecting it would seem to require positing the existence of a thinking being other than yourself that is located where you are. For if (P1) and (P2) are true, and if it is true that you exist and are thinking, then denying (P3) results in the implication that you are but one of (at least) two thinkers thinking your thoughts. Such a view would face a host of difficult questions: practical questions (e.g. which of these beings owns the clothes on your back?), epistemic questions (how do you determine which of these beings you are?), linguistic questions (to which of these beings do instances of the first-person pronoun refer?), ontological questions (what is the relationship between you and the qualitatively identical being with which you are associated?), and so on. These challenges have not passed unnoticed, and serious attempts have been made to address them. But, the animalist says, the trouble can be avoided from the start simply by conceding the truth of (P3).

In sum then, the questions and problems awaiting one who rejects any of (P1) through (P3)—though not necessarily unanswerable or insurmountable—are considerable. So animalism has at least this much going for it.

[5] Respectively, Snowdon 1990: 91; Carter 1988; Ayers 1991, vol. 2: 283; Olson 1997: 106–9; 2003: 325–30; 2007: 29–39. With some slight modifications, the following presentation of this argument rehearses expositions found, first, in Olson 2003 and 2007 and, subsequently, in Blatti 2014.
[6] Note that, here and throughout, terms like "thinking," "cognitive," and "affective" are used to refer broadly and generically to the wide array of psychological events, states, activities, and capacities exhibited by minded creatures: knowing, feeling, believing, experiencing, imagining, suspecting, calculating, guessing, inferring, hypothesizing, reflecting, wondering, understanding, etc.

8.2. The Thinking Parts Problem

Of course, animalism's critics have not just folded their tents and slunk off home. Even notwithstanding the host of positive arguments in support of competing views, there has been much discussion in recent years about the thinking animal argument and what it does or does not show, with a host of philosophers weighing in with alternative theories and explanations.[7]

The response on which I shall concentrate here is typically called the "thinking parts problem."[8] This rejoinder to the thinking animal argument threatens animalism with a line of reasoning that is structurally analogous to the one followed in that argument. In essence, the objection registers the fact that (P1) and (P2) can be replaced with parallel claims concerning other thinking parts. For example:

(P1)′   There is a human head currently located where you are.

(P2)′   The human head currently located where you are is thinking.

To these parallel claims, however, this objection does not add (P3) and draw the inference that you are your head. The problem here involves not one thinking *part*, but thinking *parts* (plural). Moreover, the critic aims to challenge animalism's identity claim—reflected in (C)—not to propose an alternative to that claim.

Instead, what the critic does is to recall the reasons that made (P3) so difficult to reject in the first place: all the ontological, epistemic, linguistic, and practical questions that would need to be answered if (P3) were false. Then she turns the knife by registering all of an animal's proper parts to which thinking is plausibly attributed: besides the head, the brain; the head plus the neck; the animal from the waist up; the whole animal save for the right leg (the right-leg complement); the whole animal save for the left hand (the left-hand complement); the whole animal save for the left hand and one atom in its spleen; the whole animal save for the left hand and a different atom in its spleen; and on and on. The roster of an animal's proper parts plausibly credited with thinking is (it seems) infinitely long. Besides (P1)′ and (P2)′, analogues of (P1) and (P2) could be formulated for all of these parts:

(P1)″   There is a brain currently located where you are.

(P2)″   The brain currently located where you are is thinking.

(P1)‴   There is an upper half of a human animal currently located where you are.

(P2)‴   The upper half of a human animal currently located where you are is thinking.

(P1)‴′   There is a right-leg complement currently located where you are.

(P2)‴′   The right-leg complement currently located where you are is thinking.

---

[7] See, e.g., Baker 2000, Johnston 2007, McMahan 2002, Noonan 2010, and Shoemaker 1999.

[8] The initial presentation of this objection is due to Olson (2007: 215–19). In this case, no one quibbles about the name since anti-animalists and animalists alike recognize it as a formidable challenge.

(P1)′′′′′′   There is a left-hand complement currently located where you are.

(P2)′′′′′′   The left-hand complement currently located where you are is thinking.

Etc.

And since each of these proper parts thinks the same thoughts as the whole animal—including, notably, the mistaken belief that it *is* the animal—nothing appears to entitle the animalist to single out the whole animal, rather than any one of these parts, as *you*. This is the thinking parts problem.

Now, let us assume for a moment that (P1)′ and (P2)′ (and their cognate claims) are true and that the thinking parts problem succeeds in undermining the thinking animal argument. Assuming this to be the case, what exactly would this problem show? Interestingly, it would *not* show that we are not animals. What it would establish, in other words, is *not* that (C) is false. For even the critic must concede that nothing in the thinking parts problem rules out the possibility that the thinking being you are is, in fact, the whole animal. Rather, what the problem does is to reveal how difficult it is for us to *know* that this is more than *merely* possible—how difficult it is, in other words, for us to *know* that we *are* animals. Given (P1)′ and (P2)′, as Olson puts it, "for all you know, you might be your head." Likewise, given (P1)′′ and (P2)′′, for all you know, you might be your brain. And so on, for each of the other pairs of possibilities. The thinking parts problem, then, should be understood as an epistemological problem—a skeptical question that animalism has thus far failed to answer, i.e. "Why suppose, then, that you are an animal, rather than a head or a brain or some other thinking part of an animal?"[9]

But *are* (P1)′ and (P2)′ (and their cognate claims) true?[10] While (P1)′ looks fairly uncontroversial, even animalism's critics should concede that (P2)′ is a peculiar claim. After all, it is almost always the whole human person whom we credit with the exercise of our cognitive and affective capacities. Rarely, if ever, does one say that one's *head* thinks, or that her *brain* knows, let alone that his *left-hand complement* feels. Rather, we say that *she* decides, that *he* experiences, that *we* believe, etc. Of course, linguistic awkwardness and counter-intuitiveness hardly amount to conclusive evidence of a proposition's falsity, so (P2)′ cannot be dismissed solely on this basis. Still, it is a datum that should be registered. In the final analysis, there may be sufficient reason to discount the strangeness of attributing cognition to proper parts of ourselves. But at the outset at least, the burden rests with animalism's critic to supply this reason: to say that the animalist does not have a good reason for not attributing thinking to an animal's proper parts is not to say that there is good reason to do so. In other words, the mere possibility that (P2)′ *could* be true is not enough to motivate the skeptical question raised by the

---

[9] Ibid.: 216.

[10] Hereafter, unless otherwise noted, I will treat "(P1)′" as referring equally to (P1)′ and (*mutatis mutandis*) to its cognate claims, (P1)′′, (P1)′′′, (P1)′′′′, (P1)′′′′′, etc. Likewise, "(P2)′" will be treated as referring equally to (P2)′ and (*mutatis mutandis*) to its cognate claims, (P2)′′, (P2)′′′, (P2)′′′′, (P2)′′′′′, etc.

thinking parts problem. And in the absence of such motivation, the force of the objection diminishes.

At least two rationales for (P2)′ suggest themselves. According to the first, thinking is just what brains do. Most, if not all of our internal organs have some function or other: the heart's function is to circulate blood throughout the body; the function of the kidneys is to remove waste material from the blood and to regulate fluid levels in the body; the function of the lungs is to facilitate bodily respiration by importing oxygen into the bloodstream and by exporting carbon dioxide from the bloodstream; and so on. So too, this line of argument goes, for the brain: the mental function of the brain is to think, i.e. to know, to feel, to believe, to experience, to imagine, to suspect, to calculate, to guess, to infer, to hypothesize, to reflect, to wonder, to understand, etc. It follows, this line of argument continues, that thinking is correctly attributed to all those proper parts of a human animal that include the brain: the undetached head, the brain alone, the animal's upper half, the animal's right-leg complement, the animal's left-leg complement, etc. Call this the "brain function rationale."

A second reason that (P2)′ may seem plausible is that philosophers' fantastical thought experiments and science fiction tell us that if your head were detached from the rest of your body and artificially supported, it would be capable of thinking on its own. Likewise if your head-complement (i.e. all of the parts of your body from the neck down) were gradually pared away, the remaining head could—with the aid of supporting technologies—remain capable of thinking throughout. Since neither detaching your head from your body nor paring away your head-complement could be responsible for *imparting* cognitive capacities to this part, the conclusion that your head is thinking even while it is attached seems difficult to resist. *Mutatis mutandis* for a human animal's brain, its upper half, its right-leg complement, its left-leg complement, etc. Call this the "artificially-sustained-head rationale."

Given the *prima facie* case for the claims on which it relies, and given what it would show if successful, how much should the thinking parts problem worry the animalist? For his part, Olson is very worried indeed. While, he says, "animalists need to solve [it]," he concedes both that the skeptical question lacks an obvious answer and that, if it cannot be answered, "there will be no reason to accept animalism."[11] And in Chapter 2 in this volume, Derek Parfit agrees with this assessment. But whereas Olson remains fairly sanguine about finding a solution to the thinking parts problem, Parfit is persuaded that this objection is decisive: a knockdown refutation of animalism. In fact, on his view, the problem names its own solution. According to his "thinking parts solution" to the thinking parts problem, we are not animals, but proper parts of animals. Specifically, each of us is the smallest proper part of our animal that thinks nonderivatively—as opposed to all of the proper parts (e.g. head, upper half, right-leg complement) that think only derivatively, in virtue of having a smaller part that thinks. Now,

---

[11] Olson (2007: 216). Olson also asserts both that "a solution is not beyond hope" and eventually concludes that the situation "is at least as bad for its main rivals" (ibid.: 219).

whatever the prospects of his solution—the "embodied part view"—what I wish to emphasize here is that, according to Parfit, *the main reason* to prefer his view is that it "is the only view on which the [thinking parts problem] disappears."[12] So, by the lights of animalists and anti-animalists alike, the stakes are very high indeed.

With the fortunes of their standard-bearer argument hanging in the balance, then, how should animalists respond to the thinking parts problem? Generally speaking, there are two sorts of approaches one might pursue. On the first, the animalist concedes the truth of (P1)′ and (P2)′ (at least provisionally, for the sake of argument) and answers the skeptical question directly. Doing so would require providing a principled reason for supposing that you are the entire thinking animal, rather than one or more of its thinking, proper parts. Alternatively, the animalist short-circuits the objection by challenging (P1)′ and/or (P2)′. If one or both of these claims can be shown to be false, then the thinking parts problem cannot even get off the ground.

In Sections 8.3 and 8.4, I will outline some ways that each of these two approaches might be pursued. If even one of them is successful, the chief argument for animalism will be insulated from (what is taken by some to be) its most formidable objection.

8.3. Answering the Thinking Parts Problem

Perhaps the most straightforward answer to the skeptical question raised by the thinking parts problem is also the most direct. You suppose that you are the whole thinking animal, rather than any of its thinking parts, because many of the properties you ascribe to yourself (the self-ascription of these properties being a cognitive act, an instance of thinking) are instantiated by the whole animal but not by its parts. You have two feet, as does the animal; your upper half does not have two feet. You are right-handed, as is the animal; your right-hand complement is not right-handed. Your brain weighs three pounds; you take yourself to weigh exactly as much as the animal weighs, which is much more than three pounds. You are the offspring of your mother and father, as is the animal; your head is not. And so on. What is more, the foregoing list exemplifies the array of properties that your thinking parts *wrongly* ascribe to themselves. Your left-arm complement falsely believes itself to have ten fingers; your undetached head falsely believes itself to be an accomplished guitarist; your brain falsely believes itself to have green eyes; etc. In sum, even if (P1)′, (P2)′, and their cognates were true, none of the thinking, proper parts mentioned in these claims instantiates all of the properties that you do; and all of these parts will self-ascribe properties that they do not in fact instantiate. The whole human animal, by contrast, *does* instantiate all of the properties that you self-ascribe (when these self-ascriptions are true). This is not to say that you are infallible in the properties that you ascribe to yourself, but only that,

---

[12] Parfit, Chapter 2, this volume: p. 40. Parfit regards his embodied part view as the only view insulated from the thinking parts problem because he assumes that nothing larger than the smallest thinking part thinks except in a derivative sense.

when you err, it is not because only a thinking, proper part of the whole animal, rather than the whole animal, instantiates the self-ascribed property.

A similar point can be made concerning your sensory, proprioceptive, and kines-thetic experiences. Whereas all of these experiences are detected in some part of the whole animal, some of the tactile, proprioceptive, and kinesthetic experiences your proper, thinking parts have are detected in parts of the whole animal that are not included in themselves. Both the whole human animal and its upper half have the experience of having their legs crossed, for instance, but only the former has its legs crossed. Both the whole human animal and its brain have the experience of touching a rough surface, but only the former touches anything. And so on. In fact, there is no thinking, proper part of a whole animal that detects only the tactile, proprioceptive, and kinesthetic experiences it has in itself; in principle, any such part can detect at least some of these experiences in parts of the whole animal that are not parts of itself.

These, then, are two reasons for supposing that you are the thinking animal rather than any of its thinking parts. Yet neither of these reasons will, by themselves, worry the critic of animalism one bit. Indeed, the thinking parts problem does not question these facts—that the whole animal has two hands while the undetached head does not, that the whole animal has its legs crossed while the upper half does not, etc.—any more than it attempts to prove that you *are* your animal's undetached head, or your animal's upper half, etc. The thinking parts problem is an epistemic problem precisely because it con-cerns one's *evidence* for claiming to know (P2) in a way that rules out (P2)′ and its cog-nates. The problem stems from the fact that nothing in your experience could supply the evidence needed to ground a claim to *know* that you are the thinking animal, rather than its undetached head, since all of the animal's thinking parts share exactly the same experiences you do. It is this equivalence between the phenomenal evidence for (P2) and the phenomenal evidence for (P2)′ that threatens the animalist's claim to know (P2), and by extension, (C).

All of this is worth belaboring because doing so exposes some of the underlying assumptions embodied in skeptical challenges of this sort. Notably, we see how the skeptical challenge relies on a traditional approach in epistemology, according to which knowledge can be factored into a subjective component (e.g. the whole animal's belief that it has two hands) and an objective one (e.g. the truth that the whole animal does indeed have two hands). In recent years, however, this approach has undergone a series of withering attacks. Perhaps the most provocative and forcefully prosecuted of these comes from Tim Williamson, on whose view knowledge is a *sui generis*, factive mental state that cannot be analyzed further into component parts.[13] Whereas the traditional approach draws a sharp distinction between knowledge and evidence—one's evidence for *p* is part of the analysis of one's knowledge that *p*—for Williamson, "knowledge, and only knowledge, constitutes evidence."[14]

---

[13] Williamson 2000: 185.   [14] Ibid.: ch. 9.

Now, it would take us too far afield to review the array of arguments and considerations that Williamson brings to bear in support of his "$E = K$ thesis". But one consequence of his "knowledge first" view should be registered: if his account of knowledge
is correct, then what Williamson calls the "phenomenal conception of evidence" is
false.[15] According to this mainstay of many familiar skeptical scenarios, a subject's phenomenal state just is her evidentiary state. In other words, two subjects who are in the
same phenomenal state are in the same evidentiary state.

To see how all of this bears on the topic at hand, suppose that you are having the
experience of thinking about your left toe and that, on this basis, you form the belief
that the whole animal currently located where you are is thinking. Your undetached
head is also having the experience of thinking about "its" left toe and, on this basis, it
too forms the belief that the whole animal currently located where it is is thinking. The
undetached head fails to know that the whole animal currently located where it is is
thinking because this belief is based on the experience of thinking about "its" left toe,
and that belief is false: your undetached head does not have a left toe. Yet your evidence
for the belief that the whole animal currently located where you are is thinking is no
different than your undetached head's evidence. And given the phenomenal conception of evidence, it follows that you fail to know that the whole animal currently located
where you are is thinking. But if the phenomenal conception of evidence is false
because knowledge is factive, then this inference does not go through. It follows that
the animalist's claim to know (P2) in a way that rules out (P2)′ and its cognates is not
threatened by the fact that the phenomenal evidence for these claims is identical. In
other words, if Williamson's account is correct, then the considerations raised at the
outset of this section—(a) the properties you ascribe to yourself that are instantiated by
the whole animal rather than its parts, and (b) the fact that the sensory, proprioceptive,
and kinesthetic experiences that your proper, thinking parts have are detected in parts
of the whole animal that are not parts of themselves—do in fact represent a direct
answer to the thinking parts problem: such evidence *just is* the knowledge that you are
the thinking animal rather than any of its thinking parts.

8.4. Short-Circuiting the Thinking Parts Problem

Instead of answering the skeptical question posed by the thinking parts problem, the
animalist might attempt to cut it off at the knees by rejecting one or the other of its two
key claims.

Reject (P1)′?

Let us begin with the first. Ought animalists try to short-circuit the problem by rejecting (P1)′ and its cognates? I think not. Certainly there are views out there that deny the
existence (*sensu stricto*) of proper parts such as heads and hands. But most of these

---

[15] Ibid.: 173–4.

views—including, for instance, so-called "blobjectivism"[16] or mereological nihil-ism[17]—would rule out the existence of not only heads and right-hand complements, but also human animals themselves. And an approach that enables the animalist to reject (P1)′ only at the cost of having to reject (P1) is no help at all.

Possibly the strongest basis for rejecting (P1)′ would be to follow Peter van Inwagen (1990) in arguing that the only composite objects are living organisms. On this view, whereas the activities of the full set of simples together constitute a life and thus the simples compose an object (i.e. the human animal currently located where you are), the subset of simples located where your head is does *not* constitute a life. In contrast with the living organism sitting in your chair, your head—like Dion's foot or Skywalker's hand—is merely an "arbitrary undetached part" and thus does not exist.

But while this strategy *would* allow the animalist to draw a principled distinction between (P1)′ and (P1)—thereby establishing the requisite disanalogy between the thinking animal argument and the thinking parts problem—I believe animalists would do better not to respond in this way. If the thinking animal argument is to con-vince non-animalists, it should do so independently of an animalism-conducive ontology like van Inwagen's. The existence of a human head located where you are looks to be as much of a Moorean fact as the existence of your hands and feet, not to mention the existence of your whole animal.

(P2)′ Proves Too Much

So, rather than (P1)′, let us instead explore some reasons why (P2)′ and its cognates ought to be rejected. First of all, (P2)′ may prove too much. Recall that the original rationale for (P2) appeals to what we know (or take ourselves to know, anyway) not about human animals, but about nonhuman animals, viz. that some of them are think-ers. Earlier I put the point like this: "since it would be odd to deny that human animals think while accepting that many nonhuman animals do, and since we can assume that the human animal sitting in your chair is not atypical of its kind, whatever reasons one has for accepting that various nonhuman animals think apply equally to the human animal sitting in your chair." But if the skeptical question raised by the thinking parts problem is taken seriously, the epistemic status of this rationale for (P2) gets turned on its head (so to say). For if (P2)′ is true, then the skeptical question posed by the think-ing parts problem applies equally to all nonhuman animals ordinarily credited with thinking. Once again, this point would *not* establish that Koko, for example, is not a gorilla, or that Lassie is not a dog, any more than it shows that you are not a human animal. But it *would* show that a parallel thinking animal argument—one concerning Koko the gorilla rather than you the human—could not substantiate a claim to know that Koko is one and the same thing as the gorilla located where she is. In other words, if we fail to know that you are a human animal because of the possible truth of (P2)′, then an equal degree of uncertainty plagues any claim to know that Koko is a gorilla

---

[16]   Horgan and Potrč 2000, 2008.   [17]   Unger 1979.

and Lassie is a dog. "Why suppose that Koko is a thinking animal," we must imagine the critic of animalism also asking, "rather than its head, or its brain, or some other thinking part?" It follows that the critic of animalism cannot consistently doubt that each of us is a thinking animal while affirming that the likes of Koko and Lassie are thinking animals. And for some, this downstream implication of (P2)′ and its cognates may be reason enough not to endorse them in the first place.

(P2)′'s Attribution Error

A more direct objection to (P2)′ is that it commits a kind of mistake—what we might call an "attribution error," and what others have recently labeled the "mereological fallacy."[18] Precisely how to understand the nature of (P2)′'s failure will occupy us shortly. But broadly speaking, the mistake consists in attributing to a part the exercise of capacities appropriately attributed only to the whole. This attribution error was identified as far back as Aristotle, who cautioned that:

to say that the soul is angry is as if one were to say that the soul weaves or builds. For it is surely better not to say that the soul pities, learns, or thinks, but that the human being does these things by virtue of his soul.[19]

In a similar vein, Wittgenstein writes that:

only of a living human being and what resembles (behaves like) a living human being can one say: it has sensations; it sees, is blind; hears, is deaf; is conscious or unconscious.[20]

Just as it is the centipede that walks and not its legs, and just as it is the owl that hears and not its ears, so too it is the human animal that thinks and not any of its parts.

Now, before proceeding any further, note that, even if it *is* a mistake to attribute cognitive and affective capacities to a proper part of a whole animal, nothing said thus far explains *why* it is a mistake to do so. This is important because, while I am sympathetic to the basic charge levied by Aristotle and Wittgenstein—(P2)′ *is* guilty of an attribution error, I believe—there are multiple possible explanations of what makes this attribution a *mis*attribution. I do not endorse all of these explanations, and in fact it is not obvious that all of the explanations could be affirmed consistently. Certainly it is not the case that all of these explanations are available to the animalist at this stage of the dialectic. For instance, the context in *De Anima* in which the remark quoted above appears makes it clear that Aristotle would appeal to his hylomorphism to explain the nature of (P2)′'s attribution error. All things considered, maybe a hylomorphic

---

[18] Bennett and Hacker 2003: ch. 3. For further discussion, see Bennett et al. 2007, Hacker 2007, 2013, Harré 2012, Smit and Hacker 2014.
[19] *De Anima* I 4 408^b 11–15.
[20] Wittgenstein 1953, §281. Hacker and colleagues (e.g. Bennett and Hacker 2003: 71; Hacker 2007: 131–2; Hacker and Smit 2014: 1077–8) frequently reference both of these passages along with an article by Anthony Kenny (1971). Indeed, they regard their mereological fallacy as an adaptation of what they label "Aristotle's Principle" and of what Kenny previously labeled the "homunculus fallacy."

approach is the best way for an animalist to understand the nature of human animals.[21] But even if it were, the animalist's rejoinder to the principal objection to the principal argument for (C) cannot rely on a substantive theory of the relationship between the human animal's mind and its body.

In the current context, there are at least two tenable explanations of the impropriety of attributing cognitive and affective capacities to proper parts of human animals. For Wittgenstein and his recent defenders, the nature of the mistake is conceptual confusion. According to Hacker et al., in ascribing mental properties to a proper part, one effectively subsumes under the concept *human animal* something that does not fall under that concept. An undetached human head, for instance, is not a human animal, but merely an animal part. And its concept, *human head*, is not one of whose instances it makes any sense to apply such psychological predicates as "is thinking" or, for that matter, "is not thinking." Human heads do not know, believe, decide, interpret, hypothesize, calculate, suspect, etc.; human animals do these things. The reason that we have no coherent conception of what it would be for a part of an animal to engage in such activities is that the criteria for their ascription lie in the behavior of a whole animal—behavior that is thoughtful or thoughtless, attentive or inattentive, intentional or unintentional, reflective or unreflective, considerate or inconsiderate, etc.— and animal parts do not behave. An undetached head does not act in ways that license (or fail to license) the ascription of predicates like "is attentive" or "is thoughtless"; only the whole animal of which the head is a part engages in behavior of this sort. In this way, the very expression "thinking parts" reveals its own confusion.

Hacker et al. trace the source of this mistake to "an unthinking adherence to a mutant form of Cartesianism. It was a characteristic feature of Cartesian dualism to ascribe psychological predicates to the mind, and only derivatively to the human being."[22] Even though contemporary neuroscientists and philosophers of psychology have since rejected the dualist outlook adopted by their predecessors, according to Hacker et al., these scientists and theorists nevertheless persist in unreflectively ascribing to the brain the predicates which dualists previously ascribed to the immaterial mind. In so doing, they purport to "explain human perceptual and cognitive capacities and their exercise by reference to the brain's exercise of *its* cognitive and perceptual capacities."[23]

Contra Bennett and Hacker, animalism's critic might respond that (P2)''s talk of an undetached head thinking is just a figure of speech—an innocuous shorthand for describing psychological operations more precisely credited to the organism whose head it is. And indeed, whether *façons de parler* of this type are harmless or whether they reflect one's credulous acceptance of "mutant Cartesianism" is one of the main questions on which subsequent debate over Bennett and Hacker's book has focused.[24] But however that debate goes, it will not help the critic of animalism to qualify the

---

[21] See Hershenov 2008 and especially Toner 2011.   [22] Bennett and Hacker 2003: 72.
[23] Ibid.   [24] See especially Bennett et al. 2007; also Sytsma 2010.

ascription of thinking to an undetached head as merely metaphorical or metonymical. First of all, if (P2)' is to represent a genuine analogue to (P2), it must purport to be true in just the way that (P2) purports to be, viz. literally. Second, recall that the skeptical question raised by the thinking parts problem is motivated (and just to that extent, worrisome for the animalist) only if there is sufficient reason to countenance (P2)'. Two rationales for this claim were suggested, and one of these—the brain function rationale, according to which thinking is the brain's function (just as circulating blood is the heart's function, etc.)—cannot consistently be maintained if, strictly speaking, thinking is *not* the brain's function. In other words, a nonliteral understanding of attributing thinking to proper parts of the human animal undercuts half the case for taking the thinking parts problem seriously in the first place. If this is the preferred interpretation of (P2)', so much the better for the thinking animal argument.

Even so, Hacker et al.'s diagnosis of (P2)''s attribution error leans heavily on the thought (familiar from the *Philosophical Investigations*) that philosophers are led into conceptual confusion by their tendency to misconstrue various uses of language. Many of today's philosophers will be dubious of this methodology, particularly Wittgenstein's notion of a "criterion." So let us briefly consider a non-Wittgensteinian (though certainly complementary) diagnosis of the error of which (P2)' is guilty. I cannot fully defend this suggestion here, but perhaps a sketch will suffice.

The impetus behind this alternative diagnosis lies in the observation that attributions of thinking are not made in a vacuum or in isolation, but are instead embedded in practices of agential understanding and moral concern. Typically it is in our attempts to describe, explain, praise, and blame another being's actions that we credit it with various cognitive and affective capacities and their exercise. Doing so helps us to see why (P2)' and its cognates are mistaken, i.e. because the only behavior eligible for agential understanding and moral concern is the behavior of the whole animal. It is mistaken to ascribe boredom, for instance, to a left-hand complement because it is not this part, but the whole human animal who twiddles her thumbs. It is incorrect to credit an undetached head with feeling thirsty when it is the whole human animal, not his head, who reaches out for a glass of water. It is wrong to attribute to a dog's brain the belief that the squirrel ran up the tree, as it is the whole canine animal who stands barking at the base of that tree. So too, it is erroneous to assign blame to a human animal's upper half on account of impetuous behavior, since it is the whole child who kicked the cat without cause. Such cases illustrate perfectly standard contexts in which attributions of thinking are made. And in these and similar contexts, it is not the proper parts, but the wholes of which they are constituents who act in ways suitable for description, interpretation, explanation, justification, rationalization; for praise and blame; for judgments concerning responsibility and culpability; for attitudes of approval and reproach; and so on. It is in these engagements with the whole being that we credit *it*—not its thinking parts—with various cognitive and affective capacities and their exercise. Likewise when it comes to one's own self-ascriptions and self-knowledge: just as understanding and judging the behavior of another involves ascribing cognitive and affective capacities to the entire system responsible for that behavior, so it is for oneself.[25]

This, then, is how the second diagnosis of (P2)″'s attribution error helps to short-circuit the thinking parts problem: you know that you are the thinking animal, rather than any of its (allegedly thinking) proper parts, because such knowledge is conditioned by widespread practices of understanding human agency and assigning moral responsibility. These practices are also subject to skeptical doubt, I suppose. But in that case, far more than just the thinking animal argument would need to be reassessed in order to accommodate (P2)′ and its cognates. And only one who is already in the grip of an anti-animalist theory would be tempted by that trade-off.

Rationale Autopsy

If (P2)′ is false, then its supporting rationales must be flawed in some way. The brain function rationale errs, I believe, by misunderstanding the import of an admittedly correct observation. Clearly it is the case that most of our internal organs have certain roles to play in contributing to the vital functioning of our bodies. But from this it should not be inferred that each of these organs is the discrete site of the exercise of its particular function, as if in isolation from the rest of the body. Each internal organ plays the role it does only insofar as it operates in concert with the operations of the rest of the body's organs, not to mention its fluids, bones, soft tissue, etc. For this reason, it is not the heart *per se* that circulates blood, but the animal as a whole who does so by virtue of the proper functioning of its heart. Likewise, it is the whole animal who removes waste material from its blood and regulates its fluid levels thanks to the proper functioning of its kidneys; the whole animal who respires due to the proper functioning of its lungs, which import oxygen into the animal's bloodstream and which export carbon dioxide from the animal's bloodstream; and, crucially, the whole animal who thinks by virtue of the proper functioning of its brain.[26] At the very least, this way of understanding the integrated functionality of our internal organs is no less plausible than the one suggested in the brain function rationale. And yet it is an understanding that speaks not in favor, but against (P2)′ and its cognate claims. So the force of the brain function rationale can be neutralized in this way.

The second rationale for (P2)′ appealed to two fantastical cases in which it seemed appropriate to ascribe thinking to a head that was previously attached to a

[25] Admittedly, this alternative diagnosis does not depart radically from the Wittgensteinian one outlined above. The two analyses do differ in where they locate the mistake committed by (P2)′ and its cognates. Whereas Hacker et al. characterize the mistake as conceptual confusion inspired by linguistic misuse, the alternative explanation is less doctrinaire: (P2)′ simply misidentifies the being whose behavior is eligible for agential understanding and moral concern. Still, it is not inappropriate, I think, to construe these two accounts of (P2)″'s attribution error as complementary; the alternative diagnosis simply has been scrubbed of its Wittgensteinian carbuncles.

[26] Further support for this line of thought comes from embodied approaches to the mind, according to which cognition is not simply equivalent to brain activity, but integrally relies on features and activities of the agent's entire physical body. There is a vast literature on embodied cognition, but see, e.g., Gallagher 2005.

head-complement and then subsequently separated and artificially sustained. According to this line of thought, since neither of the separation procedures envisioned could be responsible for causing the head to think, it must have been thinking all along, even while it was attached to the head-complement. Even taking these thought experiments at face value, I am inclined to think (for reasons that will now be obvious) that the "behavior" exhibited by an artificially sustained head is likely to depart too significantly from the norm to ground any strong conviction about whether we would ascribe cognitive and affective capacities to it.[27] Would we take ourselves to understand the behavior of an intelligent agent, a subject of moral concern? Possibly. But even if we did, there would be a decidedly stipulative dimension to any such attitude. We would have to establish, more or less by fiat, that, all things considered, it would be best to interpret the behavior of this otherwise alien being in ways approximating the ways we interpret one another's behavior.

Yet even granting (for the sake of argument) that we would ascribe thinking to an artificially sustained head—even this is not enough to establish the truth of (P2)'. For while it may be true that the separation procedures do not *endow* the artificially sustained head with the cognitive capacities we ascribe to it, nevertheless those procedures *do* make it the case that the detached head *is* and the head-complement is *not* implicated in behaviors whose interpretation would involve such ascriptions. The most that the artificially-sustained-head rationale shows, in other words, is that something smaller than a complete animal may be properly credited with thinking. What it does not show is that this smaller thing is properly credited with thinking *while it is a proper part of the animal.* And given what we know about the conditions under which attributions of cognitive and affective capacities are made, this should come as no surprise.

Indeed, even apart from these flaws in the two rationales for (P2)', in retrospect, there was something telling in the very fact that independent support for this claim was needed in the first place. The skeptical challenge that the thinking parts problem poses to the thinking animal argument trades on the analogy between (P2) and (P2)'. Perhaps we should have recognized that the disanalogy between these two claims lurks in the very fact that (P2) is credible on its face while (P2)' is contrary to commonsense and requires argumentative support. By this I do not mean to suggest that (P2)' is false for the reason that it must be shown to be true; obviously, not all truths are *prima face* truths. I mean only that the plausibility of (P2) derives from our familiarity with associated practices that—we see now—are altogether *un*associated with (P2)', i.e. practices

---

[27] In point of fact, I believe that would-be thought experiments like this are far too underdescribed to ground any assessment whatsoever of the relevant counterfactual judgments and *ipso facto* any assessment of what support they may or may not lend to a claim like (P2)'. I do not pursue this line of criticism here because more philosophers employ thought experiments in this way than do not—including philosophers on both sides of the debate over animalism—and because the methodological discussion required to substantiate this stance would take us too far afield. Here, I simply commend the interested reader to the first chapter of Kathy Wilkes's (1988) underappreciated book on the subject, as well as Williamson 2004 and 2007.

of understanding and judging (whole) human behavior by appeal to our cognitive and affective capacities (according to the non-Wittgensteinian diagnosis) and/or linguistic practices manifesting our concept of the human animal (according to the Wittgensteinian diagnosis).

Remnant Persons Problem

Notably, the considerations brought to bear in this section may harbor the resources needed to reply to another important objection facing animalists. Mark Johnston's "remnant persons problem" invites us to imagine removing the cerebrum of a fully developed human animal—call her Sally—and sustaining it artificially in a vat.[28] Sally's cerebrum, it seems, is not only capable of thinking but also psychologically identical with Sally herself. Animalists deny that the cerebrum—which Johnston calls a "remnant person"—*is* Sally, since a cerebrum is not a human animal. On the contrary, animalists say, Sally is the human vegetable left behind following the operation. But this response—which has struck many non-animalists as counter-intuitive and unappealing—is not Johnston's target. His aim, rather, is to force animalists to answer a related question: When in the course of the procedure described does the remnant person come into existence? The question is challenging because neither of the two answers appears to be open to the animalist. Claiming that the remnant person existed *prior* to the cerebrum's removal would require the animalist to say that two human persons existed all along: Sally, who became a cerebrum-less organism, and the remnant person, who became an envatted cerebrum. But claiming that the remnant person came into existence only *after* the procedure is equally problematic, not least because it carries the absurd implication that a person can be created simply by cutting away sustaining human tissue.

In Chapter 7 in this volume, Olson argues at length that there is no convincing way for an animalist to defend either of these two answers to Johnston's question. But one possibility that Olson does not adequately explore is that there is no answer because there is no remnant person.[29] For if Sally's envatted cerebrum is not properly credited with thinking in the first place, then it is not a person. And if there is no remnant person, then there is no problem.

8.5. Conclusion

I have outlined (without fully exploring) several ways that an animalist might go about resisting the thinking parts problem without renouncing the thinking animal

[28] Johnston 2007: 45. See Chapters 2, 5, 7, and 9 in this volume, by Parfit, Johnston, Olson, and Madden respectively.
[29] I say "fully" because Olson does briefly consider a proposal—inspired by van Inwagen's (1990) answer to the special composition question—he calls "brain eliminativism." But whereas this view denies the existence of remnant people on the grounds that brains do not exist, my view denies the existence of remnant people on the grounds that brains do not think.

argument. We can think of the foregoing as a tactical exercise, the result of which is a menu of avenues open to the animalist to pursue further. I conclude by registering a brief point about strategy.

The fact that the thinking animal argument even appears susceptible to the thinking parts problem reflects, I believe, one reason why animalism's fortunes should not be tied exclusively to that argument in the first place. By this, I mean to suggest neither that the thinking parts problem succeeds in undermining the thinking animal argument, nor that the latter should no longer be considered the primary argument for animalism. I mean only that resting the case for animalism on an appeal to the exercise of our psychological faculties is—besides ironic—injudicious, seeing as it is not the animalist, but the *anti*-animalist who typically insists that these faculties are essential ingredients of our fundamental nature. Indeed, it is precisely our capacity for thought that animalists *deny* is essential to us. On the contrary, animalists say, each of us was once a *non*-thinking fetus, and each of us may yet become a *non*-thinking persistent-vegetative-state patient. Animalists may reply (roughly) that our sameness with these beings existing at other times is a consequence of our present status as human animals, and it is this status that the thinking animal argument establishes. The logic of that point cannot be denied. And yet, it remains peculiar that the line of argument that establishes the truth of our animal nature now could not be invoked to establish the same truth concerning these beings existing at other times.

This peculiarity is one reason why I have offered elsewhere a companion argument that substantiates animalism on altogether different grounds, viz. by showing how the case for (C) can be seen to piggyback on the credibility of evolutionary theory.[30] While this argument is no more immune from criticism than the thinking animal argument,[31] if nothing else, perhaps it adds to the mounting evidence in support of animalism—to a victory through attrition, rather than in a single stroke. Nor are these arguments the only considerations that speak in favor of animalism as against alternative accounts of our fundamental nature.[32] Nevertheless, they suggest that, whatever the fate of the thinking animal argument, maybe Olson overstates the dialectical state of affairs when he remarks that "there will be no reason to accept animalism" if the thinking parts problem cannot be answered. Either way, fortunately, there appears reason to believe that it can be.[33]

[30] Blatti 2012.
[31] See, for instance, Gillett 2013; Daly and Liggins 2013.   [32] See, for instance, Snowdon 2014.
[33] A premature version of this chapter was presented at the Persons and Their Brains Conference, held at St. Anne's College, University of Oxford. A less premature (but still immature) version was presented more recently at the Immortality Project Capstone Conference, sponsored by the Templeton Foundation and held at the University of California, Riverside. Full maturity remains out of reach, but its pursuit was furthered by discussions with Andrew Bailey, Stephen Burwood, Peter Hacker, Eric Olson, Tim Roche, Paul Snowdon, Deb Tollefsen, Somogy Varga, and Eric Yang. Finally, I gratefully acknowledge the support of a Templeton Foundation grant, which enabled some of my work on this project.

References

Aristotle, *De Anima*, ed. and trans. H. Lawson-Tancred (Harmondsworth: Penguin, 1986).

Ayers, M. R. (1991) *Locke: Epistemology and Ontology* (London: Routledge).

Baker, L. R. (2000) *Persons and Bodies: A Constitution View* (Cambridge: Cambridge University Press).

Bennett, M. R., D. Dennett, P. M. S. Hacker, and J. Searle (2007) *Neuroscience and Philosophy: Brain, Mind, and Language* (New York: Columbia University Press).

Bennett, M. R. and P. M. S. Hacker (2003) *Philosophical Foundations of Neuroscience* (Oxford: Blackwell).

Blatti, S. (2012) "A New Argument for Animalism," *Analysis* 72: 685–90.

Blatti, S. (2014) "Animalism," *Stanford Encyclopedia of Philosophy* (Summer 2014 edition) E. Zalta (ed.), <http://plato.stanford.edu/entries/animalism>.

Campbell, S. (2006) "The Conception of a Person as a Series of Mental Events," *Philosophy and Phenomenological Research* 73: 339–58.

Carter, W. R. (1988) "Our Bodies, Our Selves," *Australasian Journal of Philosophy* 66: 308–19.

Carter, W. R. (1989) "How to Change Your Mind," *Canadian Journal of Philosophy* 19: 1–14.

Daly, C. and D. Liggins (2013) "Animalism and Deferentialism," *Dialectica* 67: 605–9.

DeGrazia, D. (2005) *Human Identity and Bioethics* (Cambridge: Cambridge University Press).

Gallagher, S. (2005) *How the Body Shapes the Mind* (Oxford: Oxford University Press).

Gillett, C. (2013) "What You Are and the Evolution of Organs, Souls, and Superorganisms: A Reply to Blatti," *Analysis* 73: 271–9.

Hacker, P. M. S. (2007) *Human Nature: The Categorial Framework* (Oxford: Wiley-Blackwell).

Hacker, P. M. S. (2013) "Before the Mereolgoical Fallacy: A Rejoinder to Rom Harré," *Philosophy* 88: 141–8.

Hacker, P. M. S. and H. Smit (2014) "Seven Misconceptions About the Mereological Fallacy: A Compilation for the Perplexed," *Erkenntnis* 79: 1077–97.

Harré, R. (2012) "Behind the Mereological Fallacy," *Philosophy* 87: 329–52.

Hershenov, D. (2005) "Do Dead Bodies Pose a Problem for Biological Approaches to Personal Identity?" *Mind* 114: 31–59.

Hershenov, D. (2008) "A Hylomorphic Account of Thought Experiments Concerning Personal Identity," *American Catholic Philosophical Quarterly* 82: 481–502.

Horgan, T. and M. Potrč (2000) "Blobjectivism and Indirect Correspondence," *Facta Philosophica* 2: 249–70.

Horgan, T. and M. Potrč (2008) *Austere Realism: Contextual Semantics Meets Minimal Ontology* (Cambridge, MA: MIT Press).

Johnston, M. (2007) "'Human Beings' Revisited: My Body is Not an Animal," in *Oxford Studies in Metaphysics*, vol. 3, D. Zimmerman (ed.) (Oxford: Oxford University Press), 33–74.

Kenny, A. (1971) "The Homunculus Fallacy," in *Interpretations of Life and Mind: Essays around the Problem of Reduction*, M. Grene (ed.) (London: Routledge and Kegan Paul), 65–83.

Mackie, D. (1999) "Animalism vs. Lockeanism: No Contest," *Philosophical Quarterly* 49: 369–76.

McMahan, J. (2002) *The Ethics of Killing: Problems at the Margins of Life* (Oxford: Oxford University Press).

Merricks, T. (2001) *Objects and Persons* (Oxford: Oxford University Press).

Noonan, H. (2010) "The Thinking Animal Problem and Personal Pronoun Revisionism," *Analysis* 70: 93–8.

Olson, E. (1997) *The Human Animal: Personal Identity Without Psychology* (Oxford: Oxford University Press).

Olson, E. (2003) "An Argument for Animalism," in *Personal Identity*, R. Martin and J. Barresi (eds.) (Blackwell): 318–34.

Olson, E. (2007) *What Are We? A Study in Personal Ontology* (Oxford: Oxford University Press).

Olson, E. (2015) "What Does it Mean to Say that We Are Animals?" *Journal of Consciousness Studies* 22: 84–107.

Parfit, D. (2012) "We Are Not Human Beings," *Philosophy* 87: 5–28 (Chapter 2, this volume).

Shoemaker, S. (1999) "Self, Body, and Coincidence," *Proceedings of the Aristotelian Society, Supplementary Volume* 73: 287–306.

Smit, H. and P. M. S. Hacker (2014) "Seven Misconceptions About the Mereological Fallacy: A Compilation for the Perplexed," *Erkenntnis* 79: 1077–97.

Snowdon, P. (1990) "Persons, Animals, and Ourselves," in *The Person and the Human Mind: Issues in Ancient and Modern Philosophy*, C. Gill (ed.) (Oxford: Clarendon Press), 83–107.

Snowdon, P. (2014) *Persons, Animals, Ourselves* (Oxford: Oxford University Press).

Sytsma, J. (2010) "The Proper Province of Philosophy: Conceptual Analysis and Empirical Investigation," *Review of Philosophy and Psychology* 1: 427–45.

Toner, P. (2011) "Hylemorphic Animalism," *Philosophical Studies* 155: 65–81.

Unger, P. (1979) "There are No Ordinary Things," *Synthese* 41: 117–54.

Van Inwagen, P. (1990) *Material Beings* (Ithaca, NY: Cornell University Press).

Wiggins, D. (1980) *Sameness and Substance* (Oxford: Blackwell).

Wiggins, D. (2001) *Sameness and Substance Revisited* (Cambridge: Cambridge University Press).

Wilkes, K. (1988) *Real People: Personal Identity Without Thought Experiments* (Oxford: Clarendon Press).

Williamson, T. (2000) *Knowledge and Its Limits* (Oxford: Oxford University Press).

Williamson, T. (2004) "Philosophical 'Intuitions' and Scepticism About Judgment," *Dialectica* 58: 109–53.

Williamson, T. (2007) *The Philosophy of Philosophy* (Oxford: Wiley-Blackwell).

Wittgenstein, L. (1953) *Philosophical Investigations*, trans. G. E. M. Anscombe (Oxford: Blackwell).

9

Thinking Parts

Rory Madden

9.1. Introduction

Empirical enquiry into the natural world can throw up results that seem to cast doubt on elements of our naïve image of our place in the world.[1] Sophisticated contemporary physics is a source of results of this general sort. But philosophers have sometimes seen our naïve conception of things threatened by rather more modest empirical findings. Hume, for example, took it that knowledge of the occurrence of simple perceptual illusions was a sufficient basis on which to refute the naïve realist view that in perception we are directly acquainted with external objects. Naïve realism about perception has also been criticized on the basis of another empirical commonplace, that proximal stimulation of one's nervous system can bring about sensory experience indistinguishable from the perception of distal external objects.

In this chapter I want to investigate the question of whether a modest empirical truth about the relationship between experience and the central nervous system should cast doubt upon another element of our naïve image of our place in the world.

9.1.1. The Naïve Thesis

We naïvely strike one another as things of a certain, very familiar, form. We seem to be 'humanoid'. We extend through space from head to toe, from fingertip to fingertip. We are bounded by sensitive skin. We are visible to one another, and able to come into contact with one another. In short: we have human form. Let us call the thesis that we have human form *the naïve thesis*, articulating as it does part of the way things naïvely strike us.

How does the naïve thesis relate to animalism? Animalism is the philosophical thesis that we are each fundamentally individuals of a certain biological species (*Homo sapiens*).[2] Animalism is stronger than the naïve thesis that we have human form. In

[1] Ancestors of this paper were presented at CEU Budapest, Cambridge, and York. I should like to thank the audiences on those occasions for their comments and questions. Special thanks to Nick Jones, Mike Martin, Lucy O'Brien, Paul Snowdon, and the other participants of a stimulating research seminar at UCL.
[2] See Snowdon 1990; van Inwagen 1990; Ayers 1991; Olson 1997a.

claiming that we are fundamentally things of the same general category as other biological organisms, animalism employs relatively sophisticated notions of *biological
organism*, and *fundamental kind*. Therefore animalism goes beyond a theoretically
unprejudiced articulation of how things naïvely strike us. Animalism does, however,
entail the naïve view, and extends it in a very simple way to accommodate the discovery that we coincide with humanoid organisms, things sharing a fundamental nature
and origin with other organisms.

But the naïve thesis is not the sole preserve of animalism. The naïve thesis is common ground between animalism and its principal rival in the recent personal identity
debate, constitutionalism. Constitutionalists take a different view of our relation to the
humanoid organisms with which we coincide, claiming that we are distinct from but
'constituted' by such things.[3] Constitutionalism also entails the naïve thesis that we
have human form, because the constitution relation is understood in such a way that
we share the form of the (clearly humanoid) organisms that constitute us, just as the
statue shares the form of the lump of clay which constitutes it. Since the naïve thesis is a
consequence of both animalism and constitutionalism, if an empirical commonplace
poses a threat to the naïve thesis, then it poses a threat to both of these leading views in
the personal identity debate.[4]

9.1.2. A Sceptical Threat to the Naïve Thesis

What is the empirical commonplace that poses a threat to the naïve thesis? It is a finding that has emerged from naturalistic investigation of the subjective states we ascribe
to ourselves and to others. What has emerged is that the local activity of certain *proper
parts* or *subsystems* of a humanoid entity is sufficient for the presence of a conscious
perspective of the sort one now has. The condition of more peripheral parts of a
humanoid has no necessary role in bringing about a conscious perspective of this sort.
For example, it turns out that an amputee with merely 'phantom' limbs will have a perspective subjectively indistinguishable from one's own, just as long as the local activity
of its central parts matches the local activity of one's own central parts.

What are these 'central parts'? The relevant parts of the humanoid coincide roughly
with what we crudely visualize as 'the brain', although perhaps they comprise some
smaller part of the central nervous system, and perhaps they comprise some larger
part of the central nervous system. From time to time slightly different parts are likely
to play the role of guaranteeing a conscious perspective of the sort one has at that time.
What is empirically extremely plausible is just this: that the presence of a conscious
perspective of the sort one has right now is guaranteed by the local activity of parts
significantly smaller than the whole humanoid. For schematic convenience let us call
these parts the *thinking-parts* or *T-parts* of the humanoid. What has emerged from

---

[3] See Shoemaker 1999; Baker 2000.
[4] Certain versions of dualism may also entail the naïve thesis. For example, on the view that one is the
union of an immaterial soul and a material animal, inheriting one's physical shape and extent from one's
material part, one will share the human form of the animal.

naturalistic enquiry is that to possess a conscious perspective of the sort one has now, it is enough to 'have' or in some sense 'contain' T-parts in the right local state.

How does this empirical commonplace threaten the naïve thesis? It threatens it in the following way. Since it turns out that the T-parts are smaller than the whole human-oid, it turns out that the whole humanoid is not the only thing that contains T-parts in a certain local state of activity. Corresponding to an indefinite number of divisions of the humanoid which contains the T-parts, we can pick out an indefinite series of objects, each of which overlap, and in that sense contain, the T-parts. Let us call these objects *overlappers*. The undetached head of the humanoid is an example of an over-lapper that is salient to us, striking us as an object possessed of some degree of causal unity of its own, its parts moving together rigidly and to some extent independently of the rest of the humanoid. But we seem quite able to select for attention overlappers that do not usually attract our gaze: the 'upper-half' of a humanoid for example, or all of a humanoid but for its left leg. As a limiting case we might consider the T-parts them-selves, hidden within the humanoid. These overlappers each lack some peripheral parts that the whole humanoid possesses. But as the possibility of amputees in various states of mutilation reveals, a lack of peripheral parts cannot by itself prevent some-thing from possessing a conscious perspective indistinguishable from one's own; it is enough to 'have' or 'contain' T-parts in a certain local state of activity. But the overlap-pers no less than the whole humanoid meet this condition. So, one might worry, each must have a conscious perspective indistinguishable from one's own.

If this is so, then we have on our hands a dramatic sceptical challenge to the naïve thesis that we have human form. If the overlappers possess a point of view subjectively indistinguishable from one's own, then if one is presented with any evidence for any proposition, the overlappers will each seem to themselves to be presented with evi-dence of the same kind. Suppose that one has the best possible evidence that one could possibly have for the naïve thesis that one has human form. Then the overlappers will each seem to be presented with evidence of the same kind. But the vast majority of them—such as the undetached head—do not even approach human form. So when they believe themselves to have human form, on the basis of what seems to them to be the best possible evidence, they will be in error. So, the sceptic will argue, one's basis for believing that one has human form is unsafe. Even if one does in fact happen to have human form, one's basis for believing this is a basis which in the vast majority of cases leads to error. Knowledge cannot have a basis of this kind.[5]

So the empirical commonplace that the activity of only relatively small parts of a humanoid is needed to guarantee the presence of a conscious perspective threatens the knowability of the naïve thesis that we have human form. On mild assumptions about the closure of knowledge under entailment, this in turn threatens the knowability of both animalism and constitutionalism.

---

[5] For more defence of the plausible view that knowledge requires that one's basis for belief does would lead to error in similar cases, see Sosa 1999 and Williamson 2000.

Moreover, there is a threat to a quite general epistemological thesis, the thesis that one may come to know which particular thing in the world one is. Why? Consider identity statements of the form I = x, where x ranges over the things overlapping one's T-parts. On the naturalistic assumption that one is conscious only if one does in fact overlap T-parts—that one is not for example an unextended soul, or a single tiny material atom—then one of these statements is true. But for any statement to the effect that one is identical with a particular overlapper, one's belief that one is identical with that overlapper is unsafe, even if true. For whatever basis one has for that belief is a basis that leads to error in the vast majority of cases in which a believer relies upon that basis. Therefore the truth about one's identity is unknowable. One's identity is a verification-transcendent fact.[6]

9.1.3. The Plan

Some animalists have explicitly addressed worries about thinking proper parts of animals, but they have tended to be drawn towards the *eliminativist* position of denying the very existence of large undetached proper parts of animals.[7] I do not wish to dismiss this eliminativist position lightly, as it can be motivated to some extent by independent general concerns about material constitution and the conditions under which composition occurs. But the claim that there is no such thing as an undetached head, or brain, or finger, or eye, is at least *prima facie* very unattractive, running counter both to *semantic* appearances, and to *perceptual* appearances.

First, we seem to have the ability to coin a singular term with the overriding intention to refer to one such thing—'let us call this attached finger "Freddy"'—and then to go on to use an atomic sentence containing that term to literally express a truth—'Freddy is now bent'. If these semantic appearances are correct then 'Freddy' achieves singular reference, and we may infer that Freddy exists. If Freddy does not exist then these semantic appearances must be mistaken in some way.

Second, objects such as attached fingers engage our primitive visual capacity to sense collections of low cardinality (1, 2, and 3), a capacity apparently present in even very young children and animals. Arguably the exercise of this 'numerosity sense' constitutes our most basic acquaintance with the cardinal numbers.[8] If, as eliminativism insists, a visible 'three raised fingers' does not really count for three objects, then our pre-linguistic capacity to sense cardinality is simply misfiring. Eliminativists have sometimes sought to sweeten their pill by means of charitable paraphrases of ordinary language.[9] But this effort is beside the point when the conflict lies with pre-linguistic perceptual appearances.

---

[6] See Madden 2013 for a somewhat different argument that first-person reference can generate a divergence between what is true and what is verifiable.
[7] Van Inwagen 1981, 1990; Olson 1995, 1997b; Merricks 2003.
[8] See Giaquinto 2001 for argument for this thesis, and references to relevant empirical studies.
[9] Van Inwagen 1990.

My aim in this chapter is to introduce, and to some extent assess, some non-eliminativist ways of defending our naïve conception of ourselves against the sceptical challenge of thinking parts. These aim to show that we can know that we are possessed of human form without denying the existence of undetached heads and the rest. Eric Olson has helpfully drawn a distinction here between 'psychological' and 'epistemic' species of non-eliminativist solution. A psychological solution would show that 'brains, heads, and other spatial parts of human organisms cannot think, or at least not in the way that you and I can' (Olson 2007: 217). An epistemic solution in contrast would accept that the parts in question 'think our thoughts' (Olson 2007: 217) but show that nevertheless we 'somehow know that we are thinking animals rather than thinking heads or brains' (Olson 2007: 218). All versions of these solutions that Olson surveys he finds unpersuasive, and for this reason considers the problem of thinking proper parts of animals—rightly in my opinion—to be a challenge to animalism 'considerably more troubling' (Olson 2007: 216) than the more familiar ones based on counter-intuitions about our persistence in science-fiction scenarios, such as brain-transplantation, teletransportation, or bionic replacement.

The plan is as follows. In Section 9.2, I shall introduce two new epistemic solutions: an evidential-externalist strategy, and a thought-theoretic strategy. The last in particular seems to be worthy of further investigation, although as things stand it is hostage to the resolution of some difficult issues about first-person thought. I shall then move on, in Section 9.3, to look more closely at the reasons for supposing in the first place that overlappers have a conscious perspective, recommending for further research a *function*-based approach to distinguishing overlappers from humanoids. It will be suggested that this kind of psychological solution is more promising than the more common 'maximality' approach to such problems. However, the recommended approach does not by itself refute a recent 'remnant person' argument endorsed by Johnston and Parfit, an argument which threatens to demonstrate that animalists in particular must face the sceptical threat of at least one conscious proper part of the humanoid. This argument, too, rests on the point that the local activity in parts significantly smaller than the whole humanoid is sufficient for the presence of a conscious perspective. I finish the chapter, in Section 9.4, by explaining how animalists can reject the key presupposition of that argument.

9.2. Epistemic Solutions

A sceptical scenario threatening one's putative knowledge that p is a case meeting two conditions, a 'subjectivity' condition and a 'failure' condition. Designating the subject of a given case by 'one' and whichever case you are now actually in as 'this case', a central kind of sceptical scenario is a case in which (a) things seems to one subjectively no different from this case, and yet (b) one is mistaken in believing p. For example, a classic brain-in-a-vat case threatening one's putative knowledge that one has hands is a case in which (a) things seem to one subjectively no different from this case, and yet (b) one is mistaken in believing that one has hands. As introduced earlier, the cases of overlappers of T-parts seem to include many cases that meet both the subjectivity and failure conditions for a sceptical scenario threatening one's putative knowledge that one has human form. The overlapper cases would include many in which (a) things seem to one no different from this case, and yet (b) one is mistaken in believing that one has human form.

Now, one way of responding to an alleged sceptical scenario would be to try to show that the case does not really meet the subjectivity condition (a)—to show that the case is not really one in which things seem no different from this case. What Olson calls a 'psychological solution' to the problem of thinking parts in effect takes this line, in denying that overlappers think at all. But this is not the usual way in which philosophers have tried to respond to arguments by sceptical hypothesis. It is rare to see the heroic denial that a brain-in-a-vat case could really be one in which things seemed no different from this case. It is far more common to try to find other ways to meet the challenge. In this part of the chapter I shall introduce some new epistemic solutions—an evidential-externalist strategy and a thought-theoretic strategy—neither of which deny that overlappers have subjective perspectives.

9.2.1. An Evidential-Externalist Strategy

An evidential-externalist strategy does not deny that the case of a T-parts overlapper would seem subjectively no different from this case. It also does not deny that the T-parts overlapper would mistakenly believe that it has human form. What the evidential-externalist denies is that this creates an obstacle to one's knowledge that one has human form. The sceptic assumes that it follows from the fact that each overlapper's case is subjectively indistinguishable from one's own case that the evidential basis each has for believing that it has human form is the same as one's own evidential basis for believing that one has human form. If that 'internalist' assumption is correct, then, since these countless beings would be mistaken to think that they have human form, the evidential basis one actually has is a basis that leads to error in a vast majority of cases. So one does not know that one has human form.

The evidential-externalist challenges the sceptic's internalist assumption. What follows from the subjective indistinguishability that we are supposing to be guaranteed by their possession of T-parts in the same state as one's own, is, in the first place, that the overlappers will each *seem* to possess evidence of the sort that one now possesses. It simply does not follow from this alone that they all *do* possess evidence of the sort that one now possesses. So it does not follow that the evidence of the sort that one now possesses leads to error in most cases. So it does not follow that one does not know that one has human form.

But what evidence could one possibly possess that the overlappers do not all possess? Here is one influential way of fleshing out evidential externalism. It is plausible that one may properly use a proposition as a basis for further belief if and only if that proposition is something that one knows.[10] Now consider the proposition that I have hands. It is plausible that the proposition that I have hands is something that I have come to know on the basis of perfectly ordinary empirical channels of visual and proprioceptive self-knowledge. So it is plausible that the proposition that I have hands is part of my evidence, indeed part of my evidence for believing that I have human form. But it is not evidence which most of the overlappers possess. Why not? They do not possess this evidence because it is not even *true* that most of the overlappers have hands. *A fortiori* they are not in possession of the knowledge that they have hands. Thus there is an evidential asymmetry between my case and the case of a handless overlapper. This evidential asymmetry I can use to discriminate my case from the case of every handless overlapper. The evidence I possess—that I have hands—is evidence which clearly settles that I am not a handless overlapper.

Now a serious assessment of this kind of reply to the sceptic would require a very general discussion of the nature of evidence, which cannot be pursued here. What I can do is make a couple of points of clarification about its application to the problem of thinking parts specifically, and then a reason why it is likely to be found unsatisfactory in this context.

First, it is worth noting that for animalists in particular there is *prima facie* a dialectical worry about appealing to the evidential-externalist reply. The problem of thinking parts is potentially especially embarrassing for animalists because it parallels the following 'problem of the thinking animal', which animalists have used to motivate their own position against their constitutionalist rivals.[11] It is plausible that there is a human animal where one is right now, and that such a human animal, like other advanced primates, can think. But if so, challenges the animalist, how could one possibly tell that one is distinct from this animal, even if one is in fact distinct from it? The *prima facie* worry for animalists now is that any sound response to the problem of thinking parts will *mutatis mutandis* furnish a reply to the problem of the thinking animal, which animalists have hoped to use against the constitutionalist view that we are distinct from animals.

In this case, I think, such a dialectical worry would be unfounded. An evidential-externalist reply to the thinking-animal problem on behalf of the constitutionalist looks relatively unpromising. Why? Simply because there is no ordinary piece of self-knowledge—analogous to the perceptually based knowledge that one has hands—which constitutionalists could claim that we, but not thinking animals, possess, and on the basis of which to rule out the epistemic possibility that one is the thinking animal. One's ordinarily empirically accessible properties match those of the animal far too closely. A constitutionalist evidential-externalist reply to the problem of the thinking animal could only be based on intuitions about one's putative possible divergence from

---

[10] See Williamson (2000: chapters 8 and 9) for defence of the thesis that one's evidence is precisely what one knows, and elaboration of the anti-sceptical implications of this thesis.

[11] Snowdon 1990; Ayers 1991; Olson 1997a.

the animal in certain science-fiction and extreme actual circumstances, these being the only respects in which the person and the animal are supposed to fail to match. But, surely, such intuitions do not have the secure status of one's belief that one has hands. The latter is a deliverance of ordinary channels of empirical knowledge. There is a ready answer to the question of how one knows that one has hands. There is no ready answer to the question of how one knows that one would diverge from the animal in science-fiction and other extreme circumstances. It is hardly a 'Moorean' foundation upon which to eliminate the possibility that one is the thinking animal. Therefore an evidential-externalist reply to the problem of the thinking animal looks much weaker than an evidential-externalist reply to the problem of thinking parts.

Here is another clarification of the evidential-externalist reply to the problem of thinking parts. The knowledge that one has hands would allow one to discriminate one's case from every case of a *handless* overlapper, such as an undetached head. But there are many overlappers which do in fact have hands, lacking instead some other peripheral parts (the 'complement' of my left leg, for example). The knowledge that one has hands, then, is not by itself a sufficient basis to discriminate oneself from these subjects. In order to know that one has human form one would need to amass evidence which discriminates one's case from every case of an overlapper who in some way falls short of human form. But it seems plausible that one can amass such evidence. If one can come to know in an ordinary way that one has hands, then one can know in an ordinary way that one has a left leg, and so on for other peripheral parts.[12]

More serious reservations about the evidential-externalist response are likely to revolve around the sense that the response adopts a question-begging, or at least overly casual, attitude towards the sceptical challenge. Isn't the response assuming exactly what is at issue? How can it be legitimate to use elements of one's naïve self-image to refute a sceptical challenge to that very self-image?

Whether this is an apt criticism depends in part upon what exactly a refutation of the sceptic is supposed to achieve. If the aim is to just to undermine the sceptic's argument that one does not know that one has human form then arguably the evidential-externalist can achieve this without assuming the empirical knowledge at issue. The sceptical argument uses as a premise the general philosophical claim that subjective indistinguishability suffices for sameness of evidential basis, and this is a philosophical claim that the evidential-externalist can reject, and can do so without assuming that we in fact have the particular empirical knowledge at issue.

---

[12] Note that I shall not in this chapter consider putative overlappers which differ from a whole human-oid only microscopically. The possibility of such overlappers raises the spectre of Unger's (1980) 'Problem of the Many', and this requires completely separate treatment—for example along the following lines: individual macroscopic continuants are not related one-to-one to precise collections of microscopic parts, but are instead each composed of many slightly different precise collections of microscopic parts. These many collections do not correspond to many near-coincident macroscopic objects, but to one macroscopic object multiply micro-constituted. Jones (2010) explores this promising approach.

But worries will remain if one wants some further positive reassurance that there *is* a difference in evidential basis between the good and bad cases. If in the good case one knows that one has hands then by evidential-externalist lights that would indeed constitute a real difference in evidential basis for the belief that one has human form. But surely one knows that one has hands in turn only if the overlappers' basis for believing that they have hands is not the same as one's own, for otherwise the basis one has for believing that one has hands would be rendered epistemically unsafe by the many nearby handless cases in which that very same basis gives rise to error. To insist now that the basis for believing that one has hands is different because one knows that one has hands really would be to go around in a small circle. On the other hand, what independent reason is there to think that their basis for their belief that they have hands would not be the same as one's own basis? After all, the similarity of basis goes well beyond mere subjective similarity. In contrast to a standard brain-in-a-vat case, the empirical perceptual beliefs of the deluded overlapper not only seem to be the same as one's own, but really do have numerically the same distal environmental causes as one's own, and really do involve stimulation of numerically the same sense organs as one's own. The similarities between the bases are spatial, environmental, and causal, as well as merely apparent.

Until more positive explanations are offered in defence of the claim that there is a difference in evidential basis, few are likely to find the evidential-externalist response a wholly reassuring reply to the epistemic problem of thinking parts, even if it does undermine the sceptic's argument for the conclusion that we do not know that we have human form.

9.2.2. Linguistic and Thought-Theoretic Strategies

An evidential-externalist reply does not deny that the case of an overlapper meets the subjectivity and failure conditions (a) and (b). Before we move on to 'psychological solutions' which deny that an overlapper case meets the subjective similarity condition (a), it is interesting to investigate whether there might be any epistemic solutions which agree that an overlapper case meets (a) while denying that such a case would be a case meeting the failure condition (b), that one would be in error. We can find in the scepticism literature anti-sceptical replies of this general sort. For example, the semantic externalist reply inspired by Putnam's (1981: chapter 1) discussion of brains in a vat can be seen as denying that a brain-in-a-vat case meets the failure condition. The idea is that although the brain-in-vat's case is in some sense subjectively just like this case, the brain-in-vat would *not* mistakenly believe that it has hands. Due to causal constraints on reference, a brain-in-a-vat would be in no position to refer to hands at all. So it would not have a false belief that it has hands. If it has any belief at all, it will have a true belief, to the effect that it has 'hands-in-the-image' or 'virtual hands'.

The only kind of epistemic response to the problem of thinking parts of which I am aware in the literature in effect makes a similar move. It tries to deny that overlapper cases meet condition (b) of a sceptical scenario threatening one's putative knowledge that one has human form. Olson suggests (though does not endorse) a linguistic proposal, according to which personal pronouns such as 'I' are governed by the convention of referring to whole human organisms and not their undetached parts.[13] If this proposal is correct then when the overlappers use 'I' they each refer to the whole human organism. So in fact the overlappers each speak the truth when they say 'I have human form' since they each refer with the pronoun 'I' to the whole human organism, which does indeed have human form. An overlapper's case is not then a case of error after all.

Such a proposal is problematic in two respects. First, the key linguistic hypothesis does not seem plausible. There is no evident reason to think that our use of the first-person pronoun is governed by a convention of referring to any particular kind of object. It is improbable that the standing meaning of a word such as 'I' embodies any restriction on the kind of thing to which it may refer. (This is surely one source of the difficulty of the personal identity debate.) It is much more plausible that 'I' and its cognates, and synonymous words in other languages, are governed by the convention of self-reference, or reflexive reference. They are words by means of which one may intentionally perform the linguistic act any x performs when x refers to x. If it is conceded that undetached parts have the general capacities to conceive, intend, and execute linguistic acts, then it is hard to deny that they could conceive, intend, and execute the act of self-reference by use of 'I'.[14]

A second problem with the linguistic hypothesis derives from the distinction between language and thought. In the first instance the linguistic hypothesis would establish that the conscious overlapping parts would each utter a true sentence when they uttered the English sentence 'I have human form'. But it is not clear how this could establish that they do not nevertheless each have a mistaken first-personal, or 'de se', belief to the effect that they themselves have human form. At most the linguistic proposal would demonstrate that they would be unable to manifest such a belief with a sentence of English. This is a problem because intuitively knowledge requires that the basis one employs could not easily have led to mistaken belief. The linguistic proposal does not show that one's basis could not easily have led to mistaken belief, only that it could not easily have caused the production of a false sentence.[15]

This second problem with the linguistic hypothesis suggests that a more satisfying epistemic solution might question the capacity of the overlappers to *think* about themselves first-personally, to single themselves out self-consciously in thought. If an

---

[13] Olson 2007: 218. Zimmerman considers a parallel reply to an analogous objection to perdurantism about the persistence of persons (2003: 501–3).

[14] See Madden 2011b for more on the intention to self-refer.

[15] See Kearns and Magidor 2008 for more against the idea that plausible counterfactual safety conditions on knowledge can be stated meta-linguistically, in terms of nearby possibilities of truth and falsity of sentences.

overlapper cannot single itself out self-consciously in thought then its does not meet the failure condition (b) for a sceptical scenario: the overlapper would not even mistakenly believe that it has human form.

An immediate concern about the plausibility of such a 'thought-theoretic' solution is that it would fall foul of an equivalent to the first objection to the linguistic proposal: in so far as it is plausible that the word 'I' is a device of reflexive linguistic reference, it is just as plausible that a first-person thought is means for reflexive thought: in grasping a first-person thought x thinks of x. How could overlappers think first-person thoughts without thereby thinking of themselves?

At this point it is helpful to note that there is a kind of solution to the problem of thinking parts that is not clearly classified by Olson's contrast between 'psychological' and 'epistemic' solutions. Such solutions are distinguished by their contrasting attitudes to the claim that overlappers 'can think our thoughts'. But that claim has a strong reading and a weak reading. The strong claim is that overlappers can think *all* of the thoughts that we think. The weak claim is that overlappers can think *some* of the thoughts that we think. A solution could agree to the weak claim while denying the strong claim; a solution could argue that we can know that we are not overlappers on the basis that overlappers think some but not all the thoughts that we undoubtedly do think.

It is not quite clear whether Olson would classify such a solution as 'psychological' or 'epistemic'. But whatever the terminology, it is in exactly this way that we should understand the thought-theoretic analogue of the linguistic epistemic solution. The claim is that we can know that we are not overlappers because there is one kind of thought—first-person thought—that we can think but they cannot think. This forestalls the objection on the basis that first-person thoughts are reflexive thoughts. The proposal is not that overlappers think first-person thoughts but somehow fail to think of themselves, either by thinking of something distinct from themselves, or by thinking of nothing. That would be impossible: first-person thoughts are guaranteed reflexive thoughts if they are anything. The proposal is rather that overlappers do not think first-person thoughts at all.

9.2.3. Self-Acquaintance and Self-Monitoring

To defend such a thought-theoretic proposal one should need to locate some plausible necessary condition of the possibility of thinking a first-person thought—and then show that overlappers fail to meet that condition. A distinguished proposal for a necessary condition on first-person thought is this: x thinks a first-person thought only if x is *self-acquainted*. Some such proposal is found in the writings of philosophers from Descartes to Frege, and much more recently Kripke, who asserts that first-personal understanding requires 'a special acquaintanceship with oneself... more fundamental than anything purely linguistic' (2011: 391). We can think first-personally only 'because each of us is acquainted with her/himself in a special first person way' (2008: 214).

This proposal is no clearer than the notion of self-acquaintance. Although Kripke is confident that 'everyone knows what this type of acquaintance is' (2008: 215) and 'there is nothing mysterious about this' (2008: 214), it would be useful in the present context to say more.

In general one is acquainted with an object only if one has a standing sensitivity to its states and doings, as, for example, one does when an object is immediately present to one's senses. So on one natural filling out of the notion of self-acquaintance, one is self-acquainted only if one has the right kind of standing sensitivity to the states and doings of the object that is oneself. Such sensitivity is realized by a cluster of distinctively first-personal channels of self-awareness: one monitors one's bodily states from the inside, one is visually aware of one's own location in space relative to seen objects, and so on. These are distinctively first-personal channels in the sense that they are channels by means of which one can monitor oneself and no one but oneself. They are by their nature reflexive information channels. In this respect first-personal channels should be distinguished from those which furnish merely accidentally reflexive episodes of awareness, such as the situation in which one is watching the back of the head of someone in a large crowd on a CCTV screen who just happens to be identical to oneself. In such a case one is in some sense acquainted with oneself, but not via a channel that is by its nature reflexive. For one could just as easily have been looking at someone other than oneself by the channel. So the CCTV screen is not a first-personal channel of awareness.[16]

But is it plausible to insist that x can think a first-person thought only if x is self-acquainted in this sense? One might here raise the sort of objection that Anscombe made to the proposal that the word 'I' could be explained as a demonstrative meaning *this body*.[17] She imagines someone struck blind, physically anaesthetized, floating in a sensory deprivation tank of tepid water. It seems intuitive to say that such a subject would remain able to think first-personal thoughts. But the sort of channels of self-monitoring gestured at above are all shut down. So—one might think—self-acquaintance cannot be a necessary condition for first-person thought.

But this objection merely invites clarification of the notion of acquaintance. It can be true that one is acquainted with an object even if one has gaps in one's episodes of awareness of the object. This is obviously the case with one's acquaintance with people and places. So long as one had initial exposure to the object, and one retains standing sensitivity to its states and doings, then one counts as acquainted with the thing. It is only after a long period of separation from a person or place that it can no longer truly be said that one is acquainted with the thing in question. So the kind of temporary blockage of self-monitoring channels envisaged by Anscombe is hardly decisive

---

[16] See Recanati 2010 for an analysis of first-personal acquaintance in terms of a range of 'ways in which I can gain information about no-one else' (2010: 157). Cassam 1997 focuses on bodily self-awareness in particular as foundational of first-person thought, but there is no evident reason to give special weight to any one of these various channels of self-monitoring.

[17] Anscombe 1975: 31.

evidence against the proposal that singling oneself out first-personally requires self-acquaintance.

All this might be agreed. But now how could any of this demonstrate that overlappers are incapable of thinking of themselves first-personally? Let us focus on the element of bodily self-monitoring. It would be immensely implausible to claim that an amputee who is under an illusion of his bodily extent, having a merely phantom left leg for example, is failing to self-monitor, and failing to meet the self-acquaintance condition on first-person thought. Acquaintance with an object is surely consistent with a certain degree of distortion or illusion in one's episodes of awareness of the object. But if this is so, then how could it be claimed that the overlapper who shares all of the parts of the humanoid but for the left leg fails to meet the self-acquaintance condition? Doesn't the overlapper, just like the amputee, have merely distorted bodily awareness of itself; but bodily self-awareness nonetheless?

Why does this seem plausible? In Section 9.3, we shall look at reasons for denying that overlappers have any subjective perspective whatsoever. But the current reply is not taking such a bold stance. It is accepting that the overlapper is in a sensory state similar to one's own. So it has bodily sensations similar to one's own. Since the overlapper's bodily sensations are precisely as reliably causally correlated with the state of its body parts as the bodily sensations of a phantom-limb hallucinating amputee are correlated with *its* body parts, it is tempting to think that the overlapper has first-personal bodily awareness of itself just in so far as the amputee has bodily awareness itself. The amputee surely does have first-personal bodily awareness of itself. Therefore the overlapper too must have first-personal bodily awareness of itself.

But this picture of bodily awareness is questionable. Reliably caused sensation is not in general sufficient for awareness. Suppose, as a result of stroke perhaps, I come to have a certain colourful visual sensation reliably causally correlated with the aroma of coffee in my environment. It does not follow that I am thereby visually aware of the aroma of coffee. I cannot now *see* the aroma of coffee. Why? A plausible answer is that the *function* of the human visual system is to select for attention things other than aromas. Even if the aroma reliably causes my visual sensations, the visual system is still malfunctioning. It is failing in its function of selecting one of its proper objects. That is why I am not seeing an aroma, but instead simply undergoing an unusually caused visual hallucination.[18]

What is the function of body awareness? On one view its function is to select and monitor multiple body parts, just as the function of vision is to select and monitor multiple objects in one's external environment. But this is not the only account of the function of body awareness. One might instead hold that the function of the human somaesthetic system is to monitor the state of the whole organism housing the system.

---

[18] See Davies 1983 for more on the role of function in distinguishing deviant and non-deviant reliable causal chains in perception. See also Burge 2010: part III, on the importance of natural function in understanding perception.

The object of awareness is thus the whole organism. Although various objects may be reliably causally correlated with one's body sensations, the object the human somaesthetic system primarily presents to consciousness is the whole organism, and presents individual parts only to the extent that they are presented as parts of that whole entity.[19]

Is there a reason to prefer one of these views? There is a partly phenomenological reason to prefer the single-object view. Apparent awareness of sensations in a pair of body parts is *eo ipso* awareness of sensations seeming to fall within the boundary of a single whole. If the primary objects of body sense were just individual body parts, then one would expect the phenomenology of body sensation in itself to be neutral over whether a pair of body parts in which one felt sensation were parts of a single whole, or instead parts of distinct wholes. But the phenomenology does not seem to be at all neutral about this. This fact makes it more plausible to take the view that the function of bodily awareness is to make the whole organism present to consciousness and body parts only in so far as they belong to that whole organism. Why? The single-object view makes it unsurprising that no further information or perceptual mechanism could be needed to check that a pair of body parts in which one feels sensation belong to one rather than two wholes. For according to the view on which the function is to monitor the whole organism, the somaesthetic system would at best be malfunctioning if a part causing one's body sensations did not belong to the whole organism. The somaesthetic system furnishes genuine awareness of a body part only if it belongs to the whole organism containing the somaesthetic system. Thus if one is aware of two body parts at all, then one is aware of two parts of the whole organism. That is why there is no need for any further mechanism for tracking whether two body parts of which one is aware belong to one or two wholes.

How does this bear upon the question of whether the overlappers are self-acquainted? Recall the comparison between an overlapper and an amputee. An overlapper is a proper part of a whole organism. An amputee is not a proper part of a whole organism—it is itself a whole organism, albeit one shrunken. Both contain a human somaesthetic system, which, it has been argued, presents the whole organism to consciousness, and parts only in so far as they are parts of that whole. So, although the causal correlation of the overlapper's body sensations with the overlapper's parts is just like the causal correlation of the amputee's body sensations with the amputee's parts, the amputee's body sense gives it a distorted presentation of itself, whereas the overlapper's body sense gives it a non-distorted presentation of the whole organism distinct from itself. Thus the overlapper is not first-personally aware through body sense, despite the fact that it has sensory states similar to those of an amputee who is first-personally aware through body sense. In contrast to the predicament of Anscombe's subject in the sensory deprivation tank, this is not a temporary gap in episodes of

---

[19] The distinction between these single-object and multiple-object views of body awareness, and the style of argument following, is indebted to Martin 1997.

self-awareness consistent with a standing state of self-acquaintance. The overlapper never has been, and never will be, first-personally presented in body sense.

It will clarify the position here to consider an objection. It will be noticed that the single-object view of body awareness does allow that objects distinct from the whole organism can be presented in body awareness, i.e. body parts of the whole organism. But an overlapper is after all a body part of the whole organism. So why exactly can't an overlapper be aware of itself through body awareness? Well, an overlapper can in principle be aware of itself in body awareness. But for an overlapper such awareness cannot in the relevant sense be a first-personal channel of awareness. Why? It is not an essentially reflexive channel of awareness for the overlapper. Suppose that one selectively attends in body awareness to one's left-leg complement. Then indeed one's left-leg complement will in fact be attending to itself. But this is no more a first-person channel of awareness for the overlapper than the awareness that one has when one observes a crowd on a CCTV screen and just happens to attend to the back of one's own head. Looking at the CCTV screen one could just as easily have attended to some other member of the crowd. Likewise, one could just as easily have attended to any one of an indefinite range of body parts of the whole organism. So for any overlapper, body awareness at best furnishes accidentally reflexive episodes of awareness. In contrast, according to the single-object view of body awareness, the whole organism will be aware of itself whenever it is aware of anything in body awareness. So for the whole organism alone, body awareness is an essentially reflexive, first-personal channel of awareness.

That, in outline, is the thought-theoretic strategy for responding to the sceptical challenge of thinking parts. Thinking a first-person thought requires self-acquaintance; the overlappers are not self-acquainted; so the overlappers cannot think first-person thoughts, no matter how similar their sensory states are to our own. They are rather like unselfconscious animals contained within our boundaries. Hence the case of an overlapper is not a sceptical scenario after all. It is not a subjectively indistinguishable case in which one mistakenly thinks that one has human form. It is a case in which one has no first-person thoughts whatsoever.

Now, a full assessment of this thought-theoretic solution to the problem of thinking parts would need to assess whether parallel arguments can establish that channels of self-monitoring other than body sense—such as the proprioceptive aspect of vision—fail in the case of overlappers to furnish them with the self-acquaintance required for first-person thought. In each case the argument is likely to lean rather heavily on the notion of function, and it is a major question how best to understand these notions (although more will be said in Section 9.3).

It would also need to be asked whether, even if overlappers cannot selectively self-monitor themselves as objects, mere introspective awareness of sensory consciousness might be enough to put the overlappers in a position to single themselves out first-personally. Could they, for example, single themselves out as *the subject of this sensory field*, or *the subject causing this mental activity*? Not if it is agreed that the sensory field and activity in question has many subjects. Moreover, as Hume and Lichtenberg famously observed, introspection seems not to acquaint one with oneself as a single entity at all. A faithful report of the content of introspective awareness might better take the subject-less form 'there is thinking', by analogy with reports like 'there is lightning' or 'it is raining'.

A full assessment of the thought-theoretic solution should also ask whether there is a sense in which this solution denies that overlapper cases meet even the 'subjectivity' condition (a) for being a sceptical scenario, let alone the 'failure' condition (b). For if we understand a case's being a case in which things seem to one no different from this case as: a case in which it seems to one *that one is oneself* in such-and-such a situation, then, whatever sensory similarity there is to this case, if one cannot think first-personally then things cannot seem to one no different from this case.[20]

Although these are extremely interesting issues, I want to move on from the thought-theoretic solution, for whatever happens it is likely to remain unsatisfactory in one obvious respect. It concedes that there is a multitude of subjects with sensory points of view—if not first-personal points of view—contained within my boundaries. For those interested in preserving our naïve conception of things this will not be a pleasant point at which to terminate inquiries. So it is time to look much more carefully at the reasons for supposing that overlappers of T-parts have any subjective states whatsoever.

9.3. Psychological Solutions

9.3.1. *Spatial Parts and Causal Parts*

The empirical commonplace which generates the sceptical threat to the naïve thesis that we have human form is the fact that the local activity of the T-parts of a humanoid is enough to guarantee the presence of a subjective perspective similar to one's own. The whole humanoid's consciousness is secured by its bearing certain relations to these central T-parts. But—it might be argued—given that T-parts turn out to be smaller than the whole humanoid, many overlappers also bear these relations to the central T-parts. So the overlappers must be conscious if the humanoid is conscious.

But what are the relations which make this reasoning plausible? First consider the relation of *spatial containment*. In this respect the humanoid and overlappers are similarly related to the T-parts. The spatial region containing the T-parts is a sub-region of the spatial region containing the humanoid. And each overlapper bears the same relation to the T-parts: the spatial region containing the T-parts is a sub-region of the spatial region containing the overlapper.

---

[20] See Peacocke (2008: 141) for argument that one could not seem to oneself to have the capacity for first-person thought without actually having the capacity for first-person thought.

But there is no plausibility to the idea that x's spatial containment of T-parts is by itself sufficient for x to have a conscious perspective. If the city of London spatially contains a humanoid, which spatially contains T-parts, then the city of London also spatially contains T-parts. But the city of London is not for that reason conscious. A thing's spatial containment of T-parts is obviously not sufficient for it to have a conscious perspective.

What is the relevant difference, then, between the city of London and a thing which we do ordinarily take to be conscious, such as a humanoid? Here is *one* relevant difference. In the case of the humanoid, the activity of the T-parts it contains effects an extremely sophisticated causal coordination between the inputs and outputs of the system—between incoming stimuli and outgoing behaviour. The humanoid is in this sense *causally coordinated* by the T-parts it spatially contains. In contrast, London is not causally coordinated by the T-parts of any particular humanoid it spatially contains. The T-parts of a humanoid, although spatially contained in London, do not have that kind of relation to the inputs and outputs of London (whatever they might be).

The principal reason that an overlapper might seem to be a much more serious candidate for having a conscious perspective is that, unlike London, an overlapper spatially contains T-parts that *do* causally coordinate the inputs and outputs of the overlapper, and in a way that exactly mirrors their causal coordination of the inputs and outputs of the whole humanoid. There is of course a certain difference between the overlapper and an ordinary whole humanoid. The inputs into the boundary of some of the overlappers will be more proximal to the T-parts than the inputs into the larger humanoid, and the outputs exiting the boundary of some of the overlappers will be more proximal to the T-parts than the outputs from the whole humanoid. But it is hard to believe that this difference could in itself make a difference to whether an overlapper has a conscious perspective. After all, the local activity of the T-parts of an amputee causally coordinate between inputs and outputs which are more proximal to the T-parts than those of a more typically endowed human. But an amputee is still conscious.

If it is enough for x to be a conscious subject that x has T-parts which causally coordinate in a sufficiently sophisticated way between the inputs of x and the outputs of x, then we have to admit that an overlapper is a conscious subject. But is it enough? I want to suggest a line of thought according to which, while a humanoid and an overlapper match in respect of their spatial and causal relations to the T-parts they overlap, something's bearing spatial and causal relations to T-parts is *not* in fact sufficient for it to be a conscious subject. In order to begin to see how, we can consider an analogy.

9.3.2. Maximality and Functional Parts

What is an *automobile*? Here is a first attempt at an answer: x is an automobile iff x contains parts—principally wheels coupled to an internal engine—which together have the causal capacity to move x around as a whole. Now, here is a *prima facie* problem for this first attempt at an answer. Select for attention the thing which is the whole automobile minus its four doors: call this thing the *sub-car*. The problem is that the sub-car is also an *x* such that *x* contains parts, wheels and internal engine, which cause *x* as a whole to move around. For whenever the wheels and engine move the car around, they inevitably move the sub-car around as well.

Does that mean that we have to accept that what we naïvely took to be the case of a single automobile driving around is really a case of a multitude of automobiles nestled within one another? After all, there is an indefinite number of large undetached parts of a car that lack only 'peripheral' parts—that overlap the wheels and engine, thus each containing parts which move it around.

In reaction to this sort of question some contemporary metaphysicians are drawn to the claim that a property like the property of being an automobile is a *maximal* property: no large proper part of an automobile is itself an automobile.[21] If we conjoin the first attempt at saying what an automobile is with the maximality clause: '…and *x* is not itself a large proper part of an automobile' then we will get the intuitive result that there are no additional automobiles on the scene. The sub-car will not count as an automobile in addition to the large automobile.

But in addition to a certain lack of independent motivation, the problem with this maximality requirement is that it seems not to be true. We can quite easily imagine a kind of automobile which has a quick-escape 'mini-car' built into its structure, designed to detach and drive away in emergencies. That kind of automobile *does* have an automobile as a large proper part. Of course, automobiles do not usually have smaller automobiles as large proper parts. But it seems not to be a necessary truth about automobiles that this must be so. Some kinds of automobiles do, and some kinds of automobile don't, have automobiles as large proper parts.

So how can we diagnose the difference between the sub-car and the mini-car? Each is an *x* such that *x* has parts, wheels and internal engine, which have the causal capacity to move *x* around as a whole. A natural answer is that the mini-car is *designed and built* in just that way. The engine and wheels of the whole which is the mini-car were put together *to* have the joint capacity to move the mini-car around. The parts of the sub-car were not put together to move the sub-car around. They will cause that to happen, but only as a side effect of their assigned function, which is to move the whole car around.

This suggests a way of improving on the first attempt at saying what an automobile is, and without attaching an implausible maximality clause: *x* is an automobile iff *x* contains parts, wheels and engine, which have the *function* of moving *x* around as a whole. The reason that a sub-car is not a car is not that no large proper part of a car can itself be car; a mini-car is a large proper part of a car. The reason that a sub-car is not a car is that the parts of the sub-car do not have the function of moving the sub-car around, although they have the causal capacity to move the sub-car around. They were

---

[21] Sider 2003; Burke 2004.

put together in order to move the whole car around. They are spatial and causal parts of the automobile and sub-car alike, but they are *functional* parts of the automobile alone.

Now we can return to the case of the putative conscious overlappers of the humanoid. Just as a maximality requirement on being an automobile would exclude the various additional sub-cars, a 'maximality' clause on possession of a conscious perspective would exclude the overlappers from being conscious subjects in addition to the humanoid.

But again, a maximality requirement on being a conscious subject is no more plausible than a maximality requirement on being an automobile. Consider the following example. Although the matter is of course controversial, no philosopher has ever given a convincing reason to believe that a sufficiently fast and well-organized 'Chinese nation' of interacting human beings could not amount to a system with a conscious perspective of its own. Even if in the end they do find a reason, it is hardly likely to concern the mere *size* of one of its component people. For suppose that just one of the members of the Chinese nation swells up to colossal size, so that he becomes a spatially large proper part of the whole system. As long as this growth did not disturb the fast and integrated functioning of the system as a whole, it is no less plausible that the system as a whole would be conscious. Why should size matter? In that situation a large proper part of a conscious subject would itself be a conscious subject.[22] The moral, again, seems to be this: even if some kinds of conscious system do not have conscious subjects as large proper parts, others might well do so. The nature of consciousness *as such* seems not to settle the matter.

Now, since a functional version of the criterion for an automobile did better than the original causal criterion with a maximality clause added, the obvious next question is this: Can a functional version of the criterion for a conscious subject do better than the causal criterion with a maximality clause added? The functional version is as follows: x is a conscious subject iff x has parts whose *function* it is to causally coordinate in a complex way the inputs of x and the outputs of x. Just as the functional criterion for an automobile gives a principled way of solving the 'too-many-cars' problem, this functional criterion promises a principled psychological solution to the problem of thinking parts. We might hope to distinguish by its means a thinking large proper part such as the Chinese Colossus from a non-thinking large proper part such as an overlapper. The T-parts of the large proper part of the Chinese Nation have the function of coordinating the inputs of that large proper part. But the T-parts of the overlapper, while they causally coordinate the inputs and outputs of the overlapper, do not have the function of coordinating the inputs and outputs of the overlapper. They have the function of coordinating the inputs and outputs of the whole organism only. The T-parts are spatial and causal parts of the humanoid and overlapper alike, but they are functional parts of the humanoid only.

---

[22]   Thanks to Ian Phillips for this 'Chinese Colossus' example.

9.3.3. Natural Function and the Mind

This approach, as it seems to me, is extremely promising. Its detailed development will be a substantial project. But it is worth indicating in a preliminary why it has motivation quite independent of the personal identity debate.

First note that the analogy with the treatment of automobiles seems immediately to run up against the point that while the purposes, aims, and intentions of a designer can isolate, from among the various causal effects of a part within a system, the function of the part within a system, we cannot seriously appeal to the goals of a designer in distinguishing between the functions and mere effects of parts of a human organism or its overlappers.

But fortunately there has been a great deal of progress made in understanding naturalistically acceptable notions of function. For instance, aetiological theories analyse the function of a part as the effect of the part which explains the current existence of the part in the system.[23] There are also non-etiological theories of function, such as 'systems-analysis' theories, which identify the function of a part in terms of its mention in the analysis of a certain capacity of the whole system. A salient such capacity of an organism is its capacity to perpetuate itself as self-organized system over time.[24]

Still, one might be sceptical, not so much about the prospects for a naturalistic account of function, but about its relevance to the case at hand. Why should function be mentioned at all in a criterion for distinguishing conscious and non-conscious systems?

A positive answer to this question has been a theme of many of the most serious attempts to understand mental representation in naturalistically acceptable terms. A first attempt at a naturalized theory of mental representation might appeal to law-like causal correlations between the representing system and the represented feature. For example, one might take the view that a system represents Fs just in case it has states which are related by causal inputs and causal outputs to Fs. However, there are a number of well-known reasons to be dissatisfied with a simple causal picture of this sort. First, it seems that there should be a distinction, among the many and various causal correlates of a system, between those features which are represented by the system and those which are not. Second, a simple causal picture is not obviously able to cope with the possibility of misrepresentation, a characteristic of genuine intentional mental representation as opposed to mere causal indication.

We can illustrate these points with a tree. This is a system which has parts that 'causally coordinate between its inputs and outputs' in the following sense: as the years pass, its trunk produces tree rings which keep tally with the passing years. But the tree is not

---

[23] See Wright 1973; Millikan 1984; Godfrey-Smith 1994.

[24] Cummins 1975 is a seminal statement of the systems approach. 'Natural design' theories of function claim advantages of both kinds of theory. See Kitcher 1993; Krohs 2009. We should also note that a philosopher might take the view that function is an unproblematic part of nature and yet reducible in none of these ways. See McDowell 1994; Burge 2010.

representing the passing of the years. For a start there is no reason to suppose that it would be representing any of the following in particular: solar rotations, springs, warm spells, or oscillations in the height of the sun in the sky. It is causally correlated with all of these features. And suppose that the tree began to output rings only every other year: there could be no real sense in which it the tree would now be *misrepresenting* the years elapsed. It would simply have begun to causally indicate two-year intervals instead of one-year intervals.

So what is missing for genuine mental representation? An influential answer is that the relevant parts of the tree, although they in fact causally coordinate its inputs and outputs, do not have the *function* of causally coordinating its inputs and outputs.[25] The causal coordination system is a mere by-product of its disposition to springtime growth spurts. It is not in the interests of the tree to indicate the passing of the years in this way; the indication activity is not playing a role in maintaining the organism's structure over time; the tree does not possess the indication system as a causal result of the fitness conferred by such indication upon the tree's forebears; nor as a result of any process of reinforcement learning within the organism. And so on for any reasonable naturalistic account of function. In contrast, when it is the *function* of parts of a system to coordinate between its inputs and outputs in that way, as it is with the cognitive parts of a human organism, then we may speak of the system's genuinely mentally representing some feature. For then we may understand the possibility of the system on occasion failing in its function, as misrepresenting the presence of a feature which is absent. And we may single out the genuinely represented feature from among the various causal correlates of the system, as the feature that it is the system's function to represent.

So this standard naturalistic approach to mental representation suggests that a system is mentally endowed just in case it has parts whose *function* is to causally coordinate its inputs and outputs in a sophisticated way. Thus we arrive at the functional version of the criterion for a conscious thinker, which paralleled the functional version of the criterion for an automobile.

In this light, the task for a psychological solution to the problem of thinking parts will be to argue that the T-parts do not have the function of coordinating the inputs and outputs of the overlappers, although they do have the function of coordinating the inputs and outputs of the whole organism. This has some immediate naturalistic plausibility. We can sketch a couple of ways in which an argument here could be developed.

We might think of an undetached part as a mere aggregate of matter which fills a sub-region of the organism at a time. On that understanding an undetached part can—and soon will—persist in scattered form given the metabolic processes of the organism. And suppose we take the view that the function of a part in a system is an effect which contributes to the persistence of the system over time. Now, the T-parts currently contained with an overlapper causally coordinate its inputs and outputs,

---

[25] Cf. Dretske 1988, 1995; Millikan 1984; Papineau 1984.

just as they causally coordinate the inputs and outputs of the organism. But that coordination makes no contribution whatsoever to the persistence of the overlapper over time: the overlapper will persist whatever happens. So the T-parts do not have the function within the overlapper of coordinating its inputs and outputs. So the overlapper is not a conscious subject by the functional criterion.

But it might be more satisfying to avoid basing an argument on the premise that overlappers are mere aggregates of matter which rapidly scatter and do not change their constitution over time. Whatever one decides about unfamiliar objects like 'leg complements' or 'undetached upper halves' it is surely more natural to view an overlapper such as an undetached head as an object which may persist and retain its form through changes in its matter, and which—like a whole human being—would be destroyed if its matter were scattered. On this way of looking at the overlapper's nature, it is hard to see why the workings of the T-parts don't causally contribute to the persistence of the overlapper just as much as they do the persistence of the humanoid.

However, even on this metaphysical conception of an overlapper, one can still make the case that the T-parts have the function of coordinating the humanoid only. For given that it is the human organism and not the undetached head that is a member of a reproducing population, it is the past success in coordinating the inputs and outputs of ancestors of the organism that causally explains the current presence of the T-parts in the organism. Success in coordinating the inputs and outputs of the 'ancestors' of the undetached head is causally screened off as an explanation of the current presence of the T-parts in the organism.

Why? Suppose, counterfactually, that ancestral T-parts had remained successful in coordinating the organism but had become unsuccessful in coordinating the undetached head—perhaps the undetached head degenerated over time into a mere twitching appendix of the organism. The T-parts would still be present in the organism today, for the coordinated organism is a reproductively fit organism propagating its traits. But the reverse is not true: if somehow T-parts had stopped successfully coordinating the organism, while continuing to coordinate the undetached head alone—perhaps the efferent nerve signals randomizing only upon exiting the boundaries of the undetached head—then the T-parts would not be present today. The organism would have been rendered utterly spasmodic and reproductively unfit. So although the T-parts causally coordinate the undetached head and causally coordinate the whole organism, it is the latter activity that explains why they are there at all. Organism coordination is their function. So by the functional criterion for a conscious subject it is the organism and not the undetached head which is the conscious subject.

This is only a sketch of an argument. The present aim is just to make the point that undetached parts and whole organisms do *not* stand in all the same relations to the T-parts they contain. And moreover, from the perspective of leading naturalistic approaches to mental representation, functional differences of this sort make a psychological difference. So there is a principled way forward here for a psychological solution.

9.4. Remnant Persons

But must an argument for the claim that organisms contain conscious thinking parts depend upon the general presupposition that overlappers and organisms stand in relevantly similar relations to T-parts? No: there is an argument abroad in the recent personal identity literature that aims to pressure animalists in particular into accepting the existence of at least *one* conscious proper part of each organism. This 'remnant person' argument also rests on the point that the local activity in parts significantly smaller than the whole humanoid is sufficient for the presence of a conscious perspective. But the argument seems not to depend on any general presupposition that overlappers are related to T-parts in the right way for consciousness. So if animalists are to resist this route to the sceptical possibility of a conscious proper part, then they need to meet this argument in some other way. I shall finish the chapter by explaining how.

9.4.1. A Dilemma for Animalists

Johnston, recently joined by Parfit, uses the following scenario to force upon animalists a problem of thinking parts.[26]

Let us assume that a human organism can be whittled down to something which is too minimal to count as the original organism, but which is nevertheless nourished and intact enough to sustain a conscious perspective of the sort one has now.[27] We can visualize such a thing as a 'cerebrum-in-a-vat'. Let us follow Johnston in calling such a thing a *remnant person*.

Where did the remnant person come from? Johnston, Parfit—and Olson too[28]—find it incredible that one could bring a new conscious entity into being simply by cutting away surrounding 'tissue that was not functioning to suppress consciousness' (Johnston 2007: 47). But if the remnant person is not a new entity but a thing which was present all along, then the question arises: How did it relate to the animal before the animal was destroyed by the operation? The natural answer is that it was some undetached portion of the animal—the undetached cerebrum say—only now unclothed and exposed.

But a further question now generates a difficult dilemma: Was this undetached thing conscious *before* the whittling operation? If the undetached thing was conscious before the operation, then—since this could happen to any one of us—animalists have to concede that each of us contains a distinct conscious being within our boundaries right now. Thus the sceptical challenge arises: How could one possibly know that one is the whole animal rather than this conscious part of the animal?

---

[26] Johnston 2007; Parfit 2012.
[27] It will be assumed for the sake of argument that this is possible. But it must be said, it is not at all obvious that such a small parcel of tissue, even if it sustained a conscious perspective, would sustain a conscious perspective anything like ours. Our T-parts might be larger than anything which is too small to count as a severely pruned organism.
[28] Olson forthcoming.

On the other hand, if the thing was not conscious before the operation, then, since it was conscious after the operation, it has to be concluded that removing matter from outside the boundaries of the contained entity has somehow bestowed consciousness upon the entity. But that does seem incredible. It seems incredible to suppose that a merely relational change, a 'mere Cambridge' change, could turn something from an unconscious being into a conscious being.

How should animalists react to this dilemma? They might grasp the first horn, and perhaps try to pursue evidential-externalist, or thought-theoretic, epistemic solutions of the sort considered earlier in an effort to show that one may still know that one is the whole animal despite the presence of the conscious part. Or they might grasp the second horn, and somehow come to terms with the consequence that a mere environmental change in an entity can change it from unconscious to conscious.[29]

9.4.2. Creation and Exposure

Fortunately there is a far better solution available to animalists, which is simply to reject the presupposition upon which the dilemma is based. The conscious entity resulting from the whittling operation really is a *new* entity, brought into existence by the operation. Is there any reason not to take this option?

There is, I think, a tendency among philosophers to visualize the living organism along the lines of a familiar kind of wooden block 'anatomical toy'—as if it were a collection of interlocking wooden blocks, any one of which may be freely removed and returned. The casual discussion of brains-in-vats and brain-transplants reinforces this imagery. On this anatomy toy picture, the whittling-down operation which results in the remnant person looks metaphysically not much different from taking a pack of closely nestling snooker balls, and then potting them one by one, until finally only a single snooker ball is left exposed, an entity which undoubtedly pre-existed the process. On this way of thinking of the remnant person the difficult question then arises of whether the pre-existing entity was, or was not, conscious before the operation.

But animalists need not think about the remnant person operation in this way. Conceding that the remnant person is not the original animal shrunk down does not leave as the only, or even the most plausible option, the view that it is a pre-existing object, which has merely been *exposed* by the operation. An equally plausible view is that it is an entity *created* by the operation. After all, there is nothing in itself mysterious about the possibility of having created an entity by 'subtraction'—by the removal of matter external to the matter that comes to compose the new entity. When the sculptor creates a wooden statuette from a block of wood he really *creates* something. The entity standing at the end of the sculptor's labours is not an entity that was there hidden in the wood all along, only now exposed. Likewise, the filet mignon in my frying pan is not an entity that was once riding around inside the living cow. It is an entity the butcher has

---

[29] The radically externalist perspective explored in Madden 2011a in effect grasps the second horn, although the operative environmental change is more complex than mere removal of extrinsic matter.

created, by skilfully carving from the carcass of the cow. Animalists should say something similar about the remnant person: the surgeons have carved a new entity.

Is this creation verdict much less plausible if the remnant operation involved the surgeons prising apart natural membrane boundaries between the cerebrum and the rest of the brain, carving along these pre-existing anatomical planes to some extent? No. The skilful sculptor or butcher will also do their best to carve along the grain of the wood, or between muscle fascia—prising apart strata in the wood or meat. These are nonetheless violent processes of entity creation. No doubt there will be an unclear boundary between cases of entity creation and entity exposure. But is there any reason why animalists should not view the remnant person operation as a clear case of the former?

9.4.3. Continued Participation

There is, one might think, a special reason for an exposure verdict over a creation verdict in the remnant case. It is a reason which is absent, or at least much less salient, in the statuette and filet cases. The reason is this. In neither the case of the statuette created from the lump of wood, nor the filet carved from the beef carcass, is there quite so obviously something that the statuette, or filet, is *now doing*, which the lump of wood, or whole carcass, was also doing before the operation. In stark contrast, the remnant person is now consciously thinking, just as the original organism was consciously thinking. Moreover, the remnant is doing so in virtue of local processes in the cerebral tissue, which we can imagine in principle to have gone on completely undisturbed throughout the operation, processes sufficient at each intervening time for the presence of a conscious thinker at that time.

Why does this matter? It matters because the following *continued participation principle* looks plausible: if x is the thing which is ϕ-ing at a later time, and the local processes which suffice for something to be ϕ-ing have gone on undisturbed since the earlier time, then x must have been ϕ-ing at the earlier time.[30]

Applying the continued participation principle to the remnant person case, we must conclude that since a thing distinct from the original animal is thinking after the operation, and the local cerebral tissue processes which suffice for something to be consciously thinking have gone on undisturbed since before the operation, the thing distinct from the original animal must have been consciously thinking before the operation. Animalists are thus faced with the sceptical conclusion that the operation just had the effect of exposing a rival thinker.

However, while the continued participation principle may seem fairly plausible at first sight, it has counterexamples in cases of entity-creation that are exact, and I think illuminating, analogues of the remnant person operation.

---

[30] Something like this principle seems to be implicit in Johnston's presentation of the remnant person problem (2007: 46–7) and perhaps also in his much earlier anti-animalist argument, based on the metaphor that 'a person cannot be outlived by (what once was) his own mind' (1987: 77).

Suppose that a bush is blossoming. There are petals unfurling on just one stem of the bush. We then engage in the process of 'plant cutting'. This is a horticultural technique of propagating plants by asexual means. Rather than growing a new plant from seed, one creates a new plant by cutting off a small amount of the parent plant. Suitably hydrated and nourished this thing will grow roots and come to flourish in the normal kind of way. It is a genetic clone of the parent plant but it is a new plant nonetheless.[31]

Now, suppose that we happen to take the cutting from the stem of the bush on which the petals are unfurling. Then after the operation the newly created plant will be blossoming in just the same way as the parent plant was earlier, and it will be doing so in virtue of local processes in the tissue of the unfurling petals, processes which have continued undisturbed throughout. But the thing which is blossoming after the operation is not the same as the thing which was blossoming before the operation. It is a new plant, which did not exist before the operation.

So the continued participation principle is simply false. One has brought a brand new 'blossomer' into existence, by separating it away from plant tissue 'that was not functioning to suppress blossoming'. There is nothing conceptually puzzling about this kind of creative practice. Under these conditions a newly created entity can continue the same kind of activity as its distinct parent, even when the local tissue basis of that activity goes on undisturbed. This, I submit, is exactly how animalists should conceive of the remnant person operation. It is an example of entity creation of the same general kind as plant cutting.[32]

9.5. Conclusion

This chapter has introduced some new ways of defending the naïve thesis that one has human form against the sceptical threat posed by the empirical commonplace that the local processes in only relatively small parts of the humanoid are needed to guarantee a subjective perspective. None of these solutions takes the usual, unattractive, animalist step of denying the very existence of undetached parts.

Among epistemic solutions, those of the evidential-externalist and linguistic variety are unlikely to be satisfying. A thought-theoretic analogue of a linguistic solution has been shown to be worthy of further investigation. More satisfying still would be a

---

[31] I am most grateful to Elena Cagnoli Fiecconi for this case. The procedure was well known to Aristotle and was studied in detail by his successor Theophrastus, often credited as the father of botany.

[32] I shall leave unsettled the question of whether the remnant person deserves to be called a new 'animal'. That term is surely polysemous: between (a) an individual of a certain genetic zoological kind, and (b) a fairly well-developed example of such an individual. It would obviously be odd to call the thing an animal in sense (b)—just as it might be odd to call a zygote an animal in that sense. In parallel it would, initially, be odd to call a brand new plant cutting in a glass of water a *bush* (as it would be odd to call a newly sprouting seed a bush). But the cutting, or sprout, is still a new individual of a certain bush-species. In parallel it might be argued that the remnant person is a newly sprouted animal in sense (a), although of course unlikely ever to make it to animalhood in sense (b), at least not without dramatic advances in stem-cell technology.

psychological solution, and I have indicated why a functional approach to the conscious subject promises a much more principled solution than an appeal to maximality. Finally, I turned to the remnant person dilemma, an independent argument which threatens to force animalists in particular into accepting the existence of at least one conscious undetached part of the humanoid, again exploiting the fact that the local activity in parts significantly smaller than the whole humanoid is sufficient for the presence of a conscious subject. We have just seen how the recognition of perfectly ordinary cases of entity creation paves the way for animalists to reject the key presupposition of that dilemma.

Our conclusion is this: the commonplace empirical fact that consciousness is guaranteed to be present by the activity of only relatively small parts of the humanoid is not yet sufficient reason—for animalists or anyone else—to doubt the naïve thesis that one has human form.

References

Anscombe, Elizabeth (1975) 'The First Person'. In *Collected Philosophical Papers, Vol. 2*, pp. 21–36. Minneapolis: University of Minnesota Press.

Ayers, Michael (1991) *Locke*, Vol. 2. London: Routledge.

Baker, Lynne Rudder (2000) *Persons and Bodies: A Constitution View*. Cambridge: Cambridge University Press.

Burge, Tyler (2010) *Origins of Objectivity*. Oxford: Oxford University Press.

Burke, Michael (2004) 'Dion, Theon, and the Many-Thinkers Problem'. *Analysis* 64: 242–50.

Cassam, Quassim (1997) *Self and World*. Oxford: Oxford University Press.

Cummins, Robert (1975) 'Functional Analysis'. *Journal of Philosophy* 72: 741–65.

Davies, Martin (1983) 'Function in Perception'. *Australasian Journal of Philosophy* 61: 409–26.

Dretske, Fred (1988) *Explaining Behaviour*. Cambridge, MA: MIT Press.

Dretske, Fred (1995) *Naturalizing the Mind*. Cambridge, MA: MIT Press.

Kearns, Stephen and Magidor, Ofra (2008) 'Epistemicism About Vagueness and Meta-Linguistic Safety'. *Philosophical Perspectives* 22: 277–304.

Giaquinto, Marcus (2001) 'Knowing Numbers'. *Journal of Philosophy* 98: 5–18.

Godfrey-Smith, Peter (1994) 'A Modern History Theory of Functions'. *Nous* 28: 344–62.

Johnston, Mark (1987) 'Human Beings'. *Journal of Philosophy* 84: 59–83.

Johnston, Mark (2007) ' "Human Beings" Revisited'. In Dean Zimmerman (ed.), *Oxford Studies in Metaphysics Volume 3*, 33–74. Oxford: Oxford University Press.

Jones, Nicholas K. (2010) *Too Many Cats: The Problem of the Many and the Metaphysics of Vagueness*. (PhD thesis, Birkbeck, University of London.)

Kitcher, Philip (1993) 'Function and Design'. *Midwest Studies in Philosophy* 18: 379–97.

Kripke, Saul (2008) 'Frege's Theory of Sense and Reference: Some Exegetical Notes'. *Theoria* 74: 181–218.

Kripke, Saul (2011) 'The First Person'. In *Philosophical Troubles*, pp. 292–321. Oxford: Oxford University Press.

Krohs, Ulrich (2009) 'Functions as Based on a Concept of General Design'. *Synthese* 166: 69–89.

Madden, Rory (2011a) 'Brain Transplants and Externalism'. In Karen Bennett and Dean Zimmerman (eds), *Oxford Studies in Metaphysics Volume 6*, pp. 287–316. Oxford: Oxford University Press.

Madden, Rory (2011b) 'Intention and The Self'. *Proceedings of the Aristotelian Society* 111: 327–51.

Madden, Rory (2013) 'Could a Brain in a Vat Self-Refer?' *European Journal of Philosophy* 21: 74–93.

Martin, M.G.F. (1997) 'Self-Observation'. *European Journal of Philosophy* 5: 119–40.

McDowell, John (1994) *Mind and World*. Cambridge, MA: Harvard University Press.

Merricks, T. (2003) *Objects and Persons*. New York: Oxford University Press.

Millikan, R. (1984) *Language, Thought and Other Biological Categories*. Cambridge, MA: Bradford Books/MIT.

Olson, Eric (1995) 'Why I Have No Hands'. *Theoria* 61: 182–97.

Olson, Eric (1997a) *The Human Animal*. New York: Oxford University Press.

Olson, Eric (1997b) 'Dion's Foot'. *Journal of Philosophy* 94: 260–5.

Olson, Eric (2007) *What Are We?* New York: Oxford University Press.

Olson, Eric (forthcoming) 'Animalism and the Remnant-Person Problem'. In J. Gonçalves (ed.), *Metaphysics of the Self*.

Papineau, David (1984) 'Representation and Explanation'. *Philosophy of Science* 51: 550–72.

Parfit, Derek (2012) 'We Are Not Human Beings'. *Philosophy* 87: 5–28; (Chapter 2, this volume).

Peacocke, Christopher (2008) *Truly Understood*. Oxford: Oxford University Press.

Putnam, Hilary (1981) *Reason, Truth, and History*. Cambridge: Cambridge University Press.

Recanati, Francois (2010) 'Singular Thought: In Defence of Acquaintance'. In Robin Jeshion (ed.), *New Essays on Singular Thought*, pp. 141–89. Oxford: Oxford University Press.

Shoemaker, Sydney (1999) 'Self, Body, and Coincidence'. *Proceedings of the Aristotelian Society*, Supplementary Volume 73: 287–306.

Sider, Ted (2003) 'Maximality and Microphysical Supervenience'. *Philosophical and Phenomenological Research* 66: 139–49.

Snowdon, Paul (1990) 'Persons, animals, and Ourselves'. In Christopher Gill (ed.), *The Person and the Human Mind*, pp. 83–107. Oxford: Clarendon.

Sosa, Ernest. (1999) 'How Must Knowledge be Modally Related to What Is Known?' *Philosophical Topics* 26: 373–84.

Unger, Peter (1980) 'The Problem of the Many'. *Midwest Studies in Philosophy* 5: 411–67.

Van Inwagen, Peter (1981) 'The Doctrine of Arbitrary Undetached Parts'. *Pacific Philosophical Quarterly* 62: 123–57.

Van Inwagen, Peter (1990) *Material Beings*. Ithaca, NY: Cornell University Press.

Williamson, Timothy (2000) *Knowledge and Its Limits*. Oxford: Oxford University Press.

Wright, Larry (1973) 'Functions'. *Philosophical Review* 82: 139–68.

Zimmerman, Dean (2003) 'Material People'. In Michael J. Loux and Dean Zimmerman (eds), *Oxford Handbook of Metaphysics*, pp. 491–526. Oxford: Oxford University Press.

10

Four-Dimensional Animalism

David B. Hershenov

10.1. Introduction

The Four-Dimensionalist recognizes the existence of entities, temporal parts, that the Three-Dimensionalist does not.[1] Your animal will have a temporal part that exists for the first half of its life, another for the first quarter, and even one for the first moment of its life. And your animal will consist of an infinite number of other temporal parts: some composed of only minimally conscious temporal parts, others containing just robustly self-conscious temporal parts, and still others including both thinking and non-thinking temporal parts. Also, unlike many Three-Dimensionalists, the Four-Dimensionalist typically adopts unrestricted composition and thus holds that any collection of objects will compose another. That means there will even be an object consisting of the reader, some sand on the Jersey coast, and the Hanging Gardens of Ancient Babylonia.

The puzzle confronting the Four-Dimensionalist is which of these countless entities that have some thinking parts should be designated a *person*? Since Hud Hudson has thought longer and harder about this topic than anyone else with whom I am familiar, I will concentrate on his solution. He presents an exclusion principle that denies personhood to objects possessing any parts that don't contribute to thought. Thus the human animal is not the human person because it begins life with mindless embryonic temporal parts. I will contest this claim of non-identity, but without rejecting anything else in Hudson's conception of Four-Dimensionalism.[2] So I will accept, though just for the sake of argument, that we persist in virtue of temporal parts, that composition is

---

[1] Informally, a temporal part of an entity will exist only at a time and will then overlap all of the entity's other parts that exist at that time. More formally: something is a temporal part of x during interval T if and only if (i) the object exists at but only at times in T, (ii) it's part of x at every time during T, and (iii) at every moment during T it overlaps everything that's part of x at that moment (Hudson 1999: 59).

[2] Hudson personally favors a version of Four-Dimensionalism that he has named *The Partist View* which replaces temporal parts with an analogue he calls spatio-temporal parts (Hudson 2007: 65). I will ignore his favored version of Four-Dimensionalism for ease of presentation. (He actually does the same for most of his book.) Nothing will be lost, for everything said here about standard Four-Dimensionalism can be translated into the vocabulary of the Partist.

unrestricted, that epistemicism is the appropriate treatment of vagueness, that human persons are complex entities composed of only material parts, and that "person" is maximal and thus there are no persons embedded within other persons.

Section 10.2 will be a response to Hudson's claim that human persons can't be identified with animals who, though mindless at their origins, have the potential for later thought.[3] Hudson argues that if having *later* thinking states were sufficient for being a person, then, assuming unrestricted composition and temporal parts, there would be an infinite number of entities that are persons. I will instead argue that one can identify human persons and human animals on the basis of a gen identity relation that will not extend the title of *person* to other entities that earlier have mindless temporal parts preceding their thinking ones. The key is to appeal to a type of causal relationship unifying temporal parts that is typical of entities that belong to a natural kind.

This will still leave us with two good candidates for the title 'human person': the human animal that is initially mindless and then later self-conscious, and the entity favored by Hudson that is capable of self-conscious psychologically continuous reflections at every stage of its existence.[4] With which of the two candidates for personhood are we to be identified? Hudson argues that just as it is arbitrary and unmotivated to consider an object with unthinking (embryonic) stages to be a person when there is a candidate available with only thinking temporal parts, so too is it unprincipled to view the person as including bodily components of the animal like hair and fingernails that don't contribute to the production of thought. Since Hudson maintains that the parts relevant to production of thought and personhood are found "beneath the skin" in the brain and central nervous system, no animal really has the potential to someday be thinking in the strictest sense.[5] So if a human animal will never come to think in the strictest sense, then we shouldn't consider that animal to be a person in virtue of any potentiality for thought. However, drawing upon ideas of Damasio (1994), Noë (2009), and Olson (1997), I will argue that the thesis that only neurological components beneath the skin of the animal contribute to thought and thus compose the person cannot be sustained. I'll first conjecture why Hudson may have been wrongly led to reduce the size of the person. Even if incorrect as a matter of intellectual biography, my diagnosis will reveal a problem in trying to exclude certain parts of the animal from the person on the grounds that they don't contribute to thought.

Regardless of whether persons are found wholly beneath the skin or not, there will still be a candidate for personhood consisting of just thinking temporal parts overlapping the older perduring animal, the latter including mindless embryonic temporal parts. So it might seem that an exclusion principle will favor the entity with only thinking

---

[3] See Hershenov (2011) and Hudson (1999) for two competing conceptions of the bioethical implications of perduring human beings.

[4] I'm using stages to designate very brief, perhaps momentary, temporal parts.

[5] Perhaps thought could be ascribed to the animal derivatively since it has a part that non-derivatively thinks. The analogy would be to stating the car is noisy in virtue of it having a truly noise-making part, the horn (McMahan 2002: 93).

parts over the entity that possesses parts superfluous to thought. However, in Section 10.4 I will argue that our intuitions about the persistence of persons are best explained by appeal to a biological (or animalist) account of personal identity. Our intuitions that we would survive certain hypothetical changes as indicated by what appears to be prudential concern for the resulting individual can't be accounted for by any criterion of psychological connections and continuity, or even the continuation of the brain's capacity for mere sentience. My contention is that only an appeal to a criterion that identifies us with a future person in virtue of sharing the same biological life can make sense of such responses. Since we take ownership of the thinking temporal parts in virtue of their being biologically related to each other, it would thus be arbitrary and unmotivated to claim the person consists of just the thinking temporal parts of the animal, since these are not unified by immanent *mental* causation. If this is correct, then even if it is wrong to deny that our thought is produced by just a temporal part of the animal's central nervous system, I can still claim that such temporal parts are not linked to each other across time by their realizing psychological continuity.[6] Instead, they are linked by realizing mental states of the same living animal, i.e. they are caught up in the same life processes. Moreover, that same biological relationship linking the various thinking temporal parts also unifies the unthinking parts of the animal with the thinking parts. This provides us with grounds to argue that of the countless Four-Dimensional entities possessing some thinking temporal parts, we are to be identified with the living human animal. Furthermore, if any entities warrant the label of "person," we do, for surely any theory that posits we are not persons is wrong. Then by helping ourselves to Hudson's maximality principle—there are no persons embedded within another person—we can consider any entity with *only* self-conscious temporal parts to be but a proper part of the human person.[7]

10.2. Why Four-Dimensional Human Animals Don't Appear to be Persons

Hudson believes Three-Dimensionalism to be false. He bases this not on an appeal to temporary intrinsics, compatibility with relativistic physics, or considerations about vagueness, but to Four-Dimensionalism's superior handling of well-known problems of material constitution such as fission, embedded parts, and the statue and the clay (2001: 58). Moreover, once one accepts unrestricted composition, Four-Dimensionalism has an appeal that Three-Dimensionalism lacks (2001: 229–31). A Three-Dimensionalist is not at liberty to accept unrestricted composition without some very counter-intuitive results. If one's notion of unrestricted composition includes the idea that any plurality of

---

[6] Thus in Section 10.4.2, the claim that not all of the animal's parts contribute to the person's thought can be added to the list of Hudson's assumptions that are accepted for the sake of argument.

[7] This denial of two kinds of *human* persons isn't meant to rule out there being other kinds of persons such as the robotic, angelic, and divine.

things composes one *and only one* other entity, i.e. there are no spatially coincident entities composed of the same parts, then there is an advantage to advocating a Four-Dimensionalist approach. The reason is that the parts that compose you at any moment will soon be somewhat dispersed as you exhale, perspire, etc. Eventually your composite atoms will be scattered across the region. If you want to avoid having to picture yourself as possessing human shape for but a fraction of your existence, then it is better to understand yourself as composed of temporal parts that are themselves fusions of temporal parts of atoms.

Hudson looks unfavorably on attempts to reject unrestricted composition. He offers a defense that includes both analyzing the intuitions behind those who reject it, and showing the costs of doing so. He conjectures that those who deny unrestricted composition have mistakenly allowed their interests to determine their ontology (2001: 107). While there is no name for the various objects consisting of a grain of sand in the Sahara Desert and a drop of water in the Indian Ocean because there is no human interest in them, Hudson insists that we aren't justified in restricting our account of what exists to what we are interested in. Not only do the interests of human beings change, but there could be non-humans with very different interests. Moreover, there is no principled way to allow some scattered objects and not others (2001: 108). Not only are the United States and its various institutions scattered objects, but its citizens are swarms of scattered microscopic particles. So once one admits Congress and Hawaii into one's ontology, it is very hard to leave out the scattered object consisting of the drop of water and the grain of sand.

Let's now examine Hudson's reasons to claim that if composition is unrestricted, then the person can't be identified with the animal. He insists that the animal is not a person for, at best, human animals and persons would merely share *some* of their temporal parts. The typical human animal consists of thinking stages through most of its life and non-thinking stages during its embryonic months. There is also a distinct perduring creature, perhaps a large temporal part of the animal, whose temporal parts are all capable of thought. Which one is the person? Hudson finds it more compelling to identify the person with the entity consisting of *only* thinking stages rather than something like the animal which also has non-thinking temporal parts. However, such a principle, if left unqualified, would mean that your temporal part that exists for the duration that you are reading this sentence would be a person embedded within you. Since there are countless things that consist of only thinking temporal parts in a Four-Dimensional metaphysics, Hudson contends that the only non-arbitrary selection of stages deserving the label "person" is an aggregate of thinking stages which are *not* embedded within a larger, similar thinking being. Thus "person" is a *maximal* concept.

Hudson further specifies that it isn't any kind of thinking that belongs to the maximal person. For example, *merely* sentient stages aren't sufficient for personhood. What is needed are self-conscious thoughts appropriately related via psychological continuity and connectedness (2001: 122, 130–1, 144). Even that is not enough, since a nuclear explosion could have vaporized Hannah while she was reflecting upon her thoughts, and then in an incredible cosmic coincidence, a psychological duplicate of her could materialize in a far off galaxy (2001: 132). Since Hannah has died rather than suddenly switched locations, the existence of psychologically continuous stages isn't enough to make them belong to the same person. There must also be the right kind of causal connection, an *immanent cause* involving earlier thinking stages bringing about later thinking stages (2001: 134–6).

Hudson contends that appealing to the animal's *potential* to have later temporal parts manifesting thought will not succeed in rendering the animal identical to the person. He acknowledges that might work for a Three-Dimensionalist metaphysics that restricts composition and denies that there exist spatially coincident entities (2001: 125–6, 152–3). On such an account of persistence, it is better to maintain that the mindless embryo is identical to the later minimally sentient newborn, self-conscious adult, senile geriatric, and terminally ill, irreversibly comatose patient. But the Four-Dimensionalist typically accepts unrestricted composition and so there will be countless objects that have thinking stages. There will even be an object that consists of an ancient Egyptian necklace and President Roosevelt. If mindless embryos are persons because they have later thinking parts, then there was an additional person present in ancient Egypt in virtue of the necklace that was an early temporal part of an object composed of it and the later thinking Roosevelt stages. But surely that object isn't a person endowed with the moral status that is typically thought to accompany personhood. When Roosevelt died, the world didn't lose more than one person. If everything that has thinking stages for a time is a person then Roosevelt's death would have involved an infinite number of deaths.

10.3. The Components of a Person

10.3.1. Natural Development

So the problem Hudson presents us with is that if we want to deny a person exists in ancient Egypt due to the necklace existing there and being part of an object that includes the later Roosevelt thinking stages, then we must also deny that the mindless human embryo is a person in virtue of its future thinking temporal parts. My response will involve arguing that there are grounds for claiming that some but not all potential thinkers are themselves persons even when they haven't yet manifested that potential. There is a way to distinguish potential thinkers via the relations unifying the stages of a natural kind in order to then claim that the animal is also a person while other beings that have thinking stages for just some of their existence are not persons. The idea is roughly that the mindless embryonic stages are the same kind of stages of the latter thinking person—i.e. they are all animal stages. There are mindless animal stages linked by life processes to thinking animal stages. They are all living stages of an animal. Their diachronic (as well as synchronic) unity is due to their parts being caught up in the same life processes. They are stages of the same token of a natural kind, not parts of two things of distinct kinds cobbled together in virtue of the principle of unrestricted composition.[8] The gerrymandered entity composed of the ancient necklace and President Roosevelt doesn't have later *necklace* stages that happen to think. This suggests an explanation of why it seems much less plausible to ascribe the capacity of thought to the necklace-Roosevelt entity when only the necklace is present than it is to so ascribe it to the mindless stages of Roosevelt. The capacity is not found in the developmental *telos* of the necklace. It is not the nature of the earlier stages to give rise to later thinking stages. Compare the necklace/Roosevelt composite with Roosevelt himself. One finds a *telos* programmed into all the stages of Roosevelt, even the mindless ones.

So the idea is that there is a principled distinction between things that have thinking parts at one time in their existence but not at another. The mindless animal stages that are part of an entity that later thinks are stages of one and the same animal. The later thinking stages are also animal stages united by life processes. But the mindless necklace stages are not part of an entity that later thinks composed then of necklace stages. I suspect that only the human animal will have its *mindless* and *self-conscious thinking* stages bound by the same unity (gen identity) relation. And the reason there is no *animal* composed of you up to this moment and another reader after this moment is that there is not the appropriate *immanent causation* characteristic of life processes: the earlier stages of a life causing the successive stages of the same life. Likewise for the composite of the scattered gametes and the reader that resulted from their fusion. There are *three* lives involved. The *same* life doesn't link them diachronically or synchronically.

So we can grant that mindless human animals are persons without having to bestow the title on every object which has mindless stages preceding its thinking ones. However, there *may* also be a single relation, psychological continuity, unifying all of the thinking stages of the person. So Hudson could appeal to the existence of a non-gerrymandered, "natural" psychological unity relation in to order apply the label "person" to the perduring object consisting of only thinking stages. Thus my approach might seem to commit us to there being two kinds of persons—some that are mindless for a time, others that are always thinking. And that admission will run afoul of the maximality principle that persons are not to be found within larger persons. However, I shall put forth arguments in Section 10.4 that reveal the best candidate for the label "person" to be the one that was once a very little mindless animal. So it will not be, as Hudson claims, "arbitrary and unmotivated" to identify the human person and human animal.

10.3.2. Contribution Determines Composition

I have so far ignored another Hudson-inspired argument regarding why we should not consider the mindless embryonic animal to be a person on the grounds that it has

---

[8] Hudson admits that appealing to natural kinds is the best option for his rivals who want to identify persons and animals (2007: 233). But he thinks the notion of natural kind is "too obscure" to be effective.

potential to develop into a thinker. Hudson makes the surprising claim that perduring persons are not temporal parts of animals. Rather, persons are "certain proper temporal parts of the brain and central nervous system of living human organisms" (2001: 147). The basis for this claim is that the person is composed only of those parts that contribute to its cognition. The entire animal doesn't produce thought, merely part of it does. So if the mindless animal is never going to develop to where it can *directly* produce thought, there is little reason to identify the person with the animal who will, at best, come to think only derivatively in virtue of some of its parts *really* doing the thinking.

Hudson insists that just as it is unprincipled to identify the person with a perduring animal that possesses non-thinking temporal parts, so too is it to identify the person with any of the temporal parts of the animal since many of the animal's spatial parts have nothing to do with thought production. Hudson explains: "Rather, once again, the only non-arbitrary choice would be an object each of whose parts plays *a contributory role* in supporting a psychological profile constitutive of personhood" (2007: 224). Even though Hudson can't say exactly which parts are so involved, nevertheless, he claims that since he can rule out "such parts as one's forearm" (2007: 219), "some parts of the hand" (2007: 224–5), "finger nails and bone-marrow" (2007, 143–4) as making a contribution to thought, that is enough to sustain his thesis that persons are not temporal parts of animals. This leads Hudson to conclude that the person is not only to be found "within the lifespan" but also "beneath the skin ... of the human animal" (2007: 220).

I am skeptical of the view that only certain parts of the animal contribute to the production of thought and want to offer a rather speculative diagnosis of what might be the source of Hudson's error. Even if I am wrong about the source of his error, the diagnosis will still reveal that "a contributory role in supporting a psychological profile" won't restrict the person's boundaries in the manner Hudson envisions. My suspicion is that Hudson is misled by the truth that the animal could continue to think if reduced in size to the falsehood that such removals show that it is only some of the parts of the animal that produce thought. The mistake is not to appreciate that what earlier made those amputated toes and fingers into parts of the thinking animal are the same life processes that integrate the neurological parts that Hudson thinks produce thought. The animal needs to be alive to think. Following van Inwagen (1990: 81–7), let's give the label *Life* to the event consisting of the biological activities which distinguishes a living human animal from a dead one. *Life* contributes to thought. And *Life* is dispersed throughout the body. Since processes don't think, the thinker is the combined matter caught up in *Life* that makes thought possible. The fact that the event of someone's biological life could configure less material than it does is irrelevant. While it is true that *Life* can involve less matter, i.e. someone can become smaller, that doesn't mean that the life event which makes thought possible was not earlier an event of a larger substance. Since one's thoughts depend upon *Life*, wherever that event is located, so is the thinker of those thoughts to be found.[9] It would be blatantly false to say that the life processes are found only in the central nervous system. We must recognize there are organ systems essential to *Life* that extend beyond the central nervous system, the latter system contributing to thought in virtue of the former providing it with the biochemical necessities for cognitive activities. So it is *Life* that makes thought possible, not a part of it. And the same life that assimilates, maintains, and removes the matter necessary for neurological function, also renders toes and fingers part of the living animal.

The basis for denying that we thinkers are merely parts of animals doesn't just lie in the fact that the living body contributes the life support necessary for any brain activity. The neuroscientist Antonio Damasio argues that the brain's constant monitoring of the body, its receiving and sending of the messages, is necessary for the working of the normal mind (1994: 223–44). Even *partially* cutting off inputs to the brain in those suffering spinal-chord injuries causes changes in the state of mind. Damasio's acceptance of "the idea that the mind derives from the entire organism as an ensemble" (1994: 225) leads him to reject the assumptions underlying one of philosophy's most famous thought experiments—the brain in the vat. He claims the disembodied brain floating in a vat of nutrients, without perfect duplication of the inputs and stimuli outputs, might not even be able to think. For similar reasons we should reject Hudson's view which amounts to considering the person to be "a brain in a living vat." Damasio explains:

In brief, neural circuits represent the organism continuously, as it is perturbed by stimuli from the physical and sociocultural environments, and as it acts on those environments. If the basic topic of those representations were not an organism anchored in the body, we might have some form of mind, but I doubt that it would be the mind we do have ... the body contributes more than life support and modulatory effects to the brain. It contributes a *content* that is part and parcel of the workings of the normal mind. (1994: 226)

It may be that there are other sources of Hudson's claims about the parts of the nervous system being the components of the person rather than the entire organism. He is, after all, a product of the intellectual community that widely holds the view that the brain produces thought much as the stomach's digestive tract produces gastric juices. In Alva Noë's diagnosis, such views are based upon what he calls *The Foundational Argument*. The argument draws primarily upon direct stimulations of the brain and the experience of dreaming as evidence for the claim that the brain's neurology is sufficient for thought. This, in turn, provides reasons to think we persons consist just of the brain's parts. I will briefly sketch the reasons Noë provides to reject it. His preferred understanding is "that brain, body and world together maintain a living consciousness"

---

[9] My stress on the contribution of life processes to thought production should not be interpreted as denying that the non-living can think. If thought could occur after the cessation of life processes, mechanical substitutes would be needed. The brain in the vat envisioned by philosophers needs the vat to function. The thinker, if composed by what contributes to thought production, would then have such mechanisms as parts. If contribution determines composition, we should speak not of a thinking brain in a vat but of a thinking brain/vat composite.

(2009: 42). Consciousness arises from the dynamic activity of the organism with the world. Consciousness "is something we achieve..., more dancing than digestion" (2009: xii).

Noë points out that if our thoughts were just produced by the brain, then one would expect stimulation of the brain to reproduce the thoughts that were realized there. But the plasticity of the brain suggests some reasons to be skeptical of the view that we are found within our skull. Quite revealing are studies of newborn ferrets that had their eyes wired to parts of the brain used for hearing. One would think that such creatures would hear the results. Instead of hearing with their eyes, they saw with parts of the brain previously used to hear. The lesson Noë draws from "the character of conscious experience vary(ing) even though the neural activity underpinning it does not change... (is) that what determines and controls the character of conscious experience is not the associated neural activity" (2009: 53–4). Another revealing experiment enabled the blind to have a vision-like experience. Paul Bach-y-Rita placed a camera that caused vibrations on the torsos of the blind which enabled them to perceive objects, even becoming capable of swatting moving ping pong balls. The vibrations weren't processed by the so-called somatosensory cortex as body touches but as the visual field in front of them. Noë insists that this perceptual plasticity without neural plasticity serves to undermine the dogma that our consciousness is a neural correlate. Noë surmises that "what makes experience the kind of experience it is—is not the neural activity in our brains on its own; it is, rather, our ongoing dynamic relation to objects...We *see* with the Bach-y-Rita system because the relationship that system sets up and maintains between the perceiver and the object is...the sort of relation we bear to things when we see them" (2009: 58–9).

Noë does admit that some stimulus of the brain causes sensations (2009: 173–4). For example, electrodes placed in the brain can give rise to sensations of light or illusions of motion. But he objects that this is no reason to think *all* experiences could be so triggered. One obstacle to such a conclusion is that there is feedback as a result of the body's role in changing its relation to the environment, thus making conscious experience far more than the result of a pattern of brain inputs. Furthermore, such manipulations are affecting existing consciousness, not generating it. However, even if the future brings brain in the vat technologies that create hallucinations corresponding to *all* of our experiences, that still wouldn't mean the brain has produced consciousness. At best, it means that consciousness is produced by the combination of the brain, the vat, and the experimenter. Producing changes in consciousness isn't the same as claiming that consciousness is produced by the brain. Finally, the brain in the vat doesn't have veridical experience so it doesn't capture all experience unless one can maintain the skeptical thesis that the real world is just a virtual world, a Matrix-like creation.

The second part of the Foundational Argument is that dreams are held to show that consciousness is not a dynamic bodily production but something that just transpires inside us (Noë 2009: 177–8). But this may be assuming that every experience can also be dreamt. Noë stresses that normal perceptual experiences have a stability that dreams lack, for it is the world rather than our creative imagination that provides the details. Moreover, it seems that dreams depend upon earlier experiences of the entire waking animal that are the product of dynamic engagement (2009: 180).

Given Noë and Damasio's arguments, I doubt that Hudson can rely upon the notion of "a contributory role" in supporting personhood to so shrink the size of the person. Another explanation of the failure has been offered by Eric Olson, who speaks of *direct involvement* with the production of thought instead of the near equivalent *contributory role*. Olson thinks the real problem with brain-size persons is that little sense can be made of the idea of "direct involvement in a being's thinking" that motivates the position (1997: 91–8). Olson wonders why if the respiratory and circulatory systems are not *directly* involved with thought, we should consider the oxygenated blood vessels in the brain to be so? Olson suggests that someone might maintain that the thought is really produced by the firing of neurons. However, Olson points out that not every part of the neuron is similarly involved in the sending of electrical or chemical messages to other neurons. Some serve other tasks like maintaining structural integrity of the cell or removal of its wastes. This, Olson claims, ought to make "the thinking minimalist uneasy" (1997: 92). Moreover, the neurons won't fire without these tasks being performed. Olson cautions that trying to determine what is *directly involved* in the production of thought is as hopeless as trying to determine which of the many workers, suppliers, managers, tools, and materials is directly involved with the factory production of a knife, or which parts of the body are directly involved with walking. He insists that the problem is not even one of vagueness—it is not that we have a clear application and then boundary cases.[10] Instead, the fault lies in the notion of *directly involved* being unprincipled.

Although Hudson doesn't say much about the crucial notion of *contribution*, perhaps a refined notion can evade or mitigate the criticisms made so far. Perhaps I have been conflating the causal and the constitutive (Clark 2009: 982). A more nuanced conception of *contribution* might distinguish an instrumental causal condition in the past from the neurological basis constitutive of thought in the present. Borrowing from Clark, the constitutive reading of contribution could be limited to the "vehicles of mental states and processes," the physical realization of *information* that governs actions (2009: 966). Moreover, a distinction could be made between content and vehicle (2009: 966). The vehicle is just neurological.[11] Its content may be of extra-neurological states of the body or environment, as Damasio and Noë speculate, but the person is just composed of the vehicle. The body may play an instrumental causal role in the production of thought, but the neurology is sufficiently constitutive of thought. I'm willing to assume, for the sake of argument, that the life support needed for thought need not be

---

[10] So Hudson's epistemicism won't help him.

[11] Even Damasio claimed a brain in the vat with perfect duplication of inputs and outputs of the embodied brain may have the same experiences (1994: 228). But see note 9 for why all that might show that it is the brain/vat complex that is thinking.

simultaneous, i.e. the animal could die but the brain could very briefly continue to function with the resources that life processes earlier delivered. Thus life processes have an instrumental causal role in the production of thought, but are not constitutive of thought. They are more akin to the object dropped on the foot and the damaged tissue that "drives" the later neurological realization of the painful sensation. Let's also assume Olson is wrong and that the notion of "directly involved" is just vague rather than unprincipled, so Hudson's epistemicism will guarantee that the person has precise boundaries within the animal. With such assumptions, Hudson might claim we have good reason to believe that the person's present temporal part consists of whatever parts of the neurology now are the vehicles of the representation, and that a person's later temporal parts will involve the physical realization of psychologically continuous states. However, readers will see in Section 10.4.2 why that won't work even if this refined notion of *contribution* turns out to be able to demarcate the neurological thought producing elements.

10.4. The Human Animal is the Only Person

10.4.1. The Collapse of Psychological Continuity into Biological Continuity

I will now offer a very different line of reasoning for identifying the Four-Dimensional human animal and the human person.[12] I will show that the psychological continuity and connectedness criterion favored by Hudson (2001: 144) *collapses* into animal identity. What I mean by *collapses* is that there are cases which tend to elicit from us descriptions of one thinking entity being identified with another thinker that cannot be explained by a psychological criterion being satisfied. The intuitions we have there about identity can only be accounted for by both thinkers being the same animal. So what we want to say are stages of a persisting person in cases involving the dreaming and the awake, the rational and the demented, divided and reunited minds, can only be construed as such if an appeal is made to the biological persistence conditions of animals.

The first problem for the psychological account of identity involves a twist on Reid's famous critique of Locke's memory criterion (Perry 2008). Locke claimed that one's identity extended as far back in time as one's memories. Reid revealed a failure of transitivity by envisioning an old general who could remember his first military campaign as a young soldier, the young soldier could recall being flogged as a school boy for stealing from an orchard, but the general couldn't remember being flogged. Therefore, the general is *not* identical to the boy, yet he is identical to the young soldier, who is identical to the boy. This absurdity could be avoided by appealing to psychological continuity, i.e. overlapping chains of psychological connections (Parfit 1983: 206–9).

---

[12] The arguments can be extended to Three-Dimensionalist denials of the identity of the human animal and person.

Psychological continuity involves the general being able to remember a time (his first military campaign) at which he could remember being flogged. So an overlap of memories will suffice in lieu of a direct memory connection. But the transitivity problem returns with a modified version of Reid's scenario that Perry named the *Senile General* case (Perry 2008: 19). The senile general could remember being flogged (or remember a time at which he could remember a time that he was flogged). So he is identical to the boy. The young soldier could remember being flogged, so he too is identical to the boy. But the general couldn't remember his more recent experience as a young soldier, nor could he remember any other time at which he then could remember his first military campaign. This renders the general identical to the boy but not identical to the young soldier, who is also identical to the boy. So if they are to be identified, as it intuitively seems they should, an appeal to their being the same animal can do what an appeal to psychological continuity cannot.

I don't think it will work to claim that the general and the young soldier can be identified as long as they both recall, via direct memory or overlap of recollection, the child beaten in the orchard. Advocates of a psychological account of identity generally don't want to say that if Hannah appeared to cease to exist at noon and just by coincidence, a psychological duplicate of her popped into existence a moment later, Hannah would have reappeared elsewhere. As we noted earlier, the reason why Hannah hasn't survived is that there isn't the appropriate causal relationship between Hannah and the duplicate. There is thought to be some kind of immanent causation that must link the psychological states of Hannah at one time with psychological states at a later time.[13] Notice that there would be no immanent causation between the temporal parts in the altered Reid case where the general becomes senile late in life and as a result can't remember or have an overlap of memories (or any other psychological ties), to the young soldier at the time of his first military campaign, but both the general and the young soldier can recall (or have an overlapping chain of memories back to) the child beaten in the orchard for stealing an apple. So even though both the general and young soldier have psychological contents that are immanently caused by the young boy, there is an absence of the requisite causality between the temporal parts linking the perduring general and young soldier. The senile general is psychologically the same as he would be if he had just woken up from a coma that he had been in from the time before his first military campaign as a young soldier to the present time.[14]

Attempting to preserve the identity between the general and the young soldier in virtue of the common memory link to the young thief and the transitivity of identity

---

[13] This relation is more important to persistence than spatio-temporal continuity, so says Dean Zimmerman (1997). Hudson concurs and draws upon Zimmerman's work (2001: 34–7).

[14] It would be a mistake to endorse, as Perry does, Grice's suggestion that the general is the young soldier because he could have remembered the event (Perry 2008: 19–20). That is too promiscuous a criterion. There will be no psychological change that isn't identity preserving because the resulting being could have remembered the earlier events if it wasn't for say the neurosurgeon's intervention in a Parfit spectrum-like case or the comatose could have recalled if not comatose and so on.

220 DAVID B. HERSHENOV

relation would be as illegitimate here as it would be to claim that the two products of fission are the same person because they are both linked to the pre-fission person. The post-fission mental states wouldn't be appropriately immanently causally linked to each other, thus the thinkers are not identical. Likewise for the modified Reid case, in which the young soldier and the general do not have the appropriate causal links between their respective mental contents, neither having access to or causal overlap with the others.

I imagine that someone might object to the analogy because there aren't two concurrent branches in the senile general case as in fission cases. However, fissioned hemispheres and transplantation could be staggered. Someone's upper brain could be divided, one hemisphere removed and frozen and the other transplanted. When the recipient of the first transplant dies, the remaining hemisphere is thawed and transplanted. The Four-Dimensionalist would surely not claim the two post-transplant branching series of stages were the stages of the same person. The Four-Dimensionalist reasoning here isn't fully explained by the fact that two conscious states emerging from fission occur at the same time, rather, it is due to their not being causally related to each other.

A second scenario where a psychological criterion of identity collapses into a biological one involves a temporary division of a mind. Consider Parfit's *My Physics Exam* scenario where there is just a short-term loss of a unified consciousness due to cutting the *corpus collassum* so one person can direct both hemispheres to work on different parts of a test (1983: 246–8). The hemispheres are reunited after the dual work is done. As Parfit himself notes, the most plausible response is that there was one person temporarily cut off from himself. To account for that intuition, something other than a single causal chain of psychological continuity must be relied upon. Four-Dimensionalists usually qualify the criterion of psychological continuity for cases involving fission and fusion so the result is that there are two distinct persons continuous with the same earlier stage. They do so by insisting that psychologically continuous x and y are stages of the same person if there is no stage z that is psychologically continuous with x or y but simultaneous and distinct from either y or x (Brueckner and Buford 2008). So during the exam there are two streams of thought that have stages that are simultaneous but distinct from each other, thus ensuring that there is not a single person despite their both being psychologically continuous with shared earlier stages. But this will deliver the counter-intuitive result that there is not a person with the briefly divided mind but that there were two persons present at that time since they involve simultaneous but distinct stages. If the intuitive response is to be preserved, then it appears that we must appeal to a rather ad hoc modification of the psychological criterion or claim that it must be because it is the same animal doing the thinking.

One can also undermine the psychological continuity criterion for identity by taking issue with Locke's account of Socrates awake and Socrates asleep (Locke 1975: 343). Locke conjectured that if sleeping Socrates was psychologically cut off from waking Socrates then they would not be the same person. Imagine that your waking and dream states are not psychologically connected. You cannot recall your dreams and these dreams don't follow from your waking life. I suspect that few readers would follow Locke and deny that they were states of the same person, interpreting the psychological disconnect as evidence of two people sharing a body. Since there isn't any psychological continuity between the waking and the sleeping, then what makes them the same person must be that they are the same living animal. It might help drive the point home if readers imagine that medical technology reveals that every night they have horrible nightmares though the following day always wake up without any memories of such dreams. I suspect that if readers could prevent these nightmares by doing something when awake, they would. And readers would do so for prudential reasons, not moral concerns about alleviating the suffering of another.[15]

A fourth scenario undermining psychological continuity theories relies upon our reactions now to the possibility of future pain after the onset of amnesia or even more debilitating impairments (McMahan 2002; Unger 2000). Consider the prudential concern many envision having for the being with their brain after a stroke undermines the brain's capacities for rationality and self-consciousness, leaving a mere sentient child-like mind. If told earlier that the being with our damaged brain will suffer horrific pains unless we take on almost as much physical pain before losing our memories and capacity for self-consciousness, most of us would consent to the lesser pain to ensure the greater does not transpire. Such a show of apparently prudential concern for an animal in the future, despite the absence of psychological continuity and the reflective capacities associated with personhood, suggests an adherence to an animalist, i.e. biological, account of our identity.

What I have been hoping to get readers to recognize with the *Sleeping Socrates*, *Physics Exam*, *Senile General*, and future pain scenarios is that there is a divergence between the psychological criterion and our intuitions about our survival. A reliance upon animalist identity conditions can accommodate our judgments of persistence. I suspect, however, that some readers will offer an alternative interpretation. Their response is that it is not psychological continuity that matters to our persistence, but the capacity for mere sentience—minimal thought and feeling. As long as the same brain sustains sentience, then the individual survives despite memory loss and even some mental fragmentation.

Hudson contends that an individual suffering "profound senility" would not be a person (2007: 222). There wouldn't be the requisite self-consciousness and

---

[15] I believe these ideas of one person whose thoughts are cut off from himself can be extended to challenge McMahan's interpretation of the dicephalus—consisting of one animal with two heads—as being two persons (2002: 35–9). It might be argued that while Sleeping and Waking Socrates should not be considered two persons sharing a body, the lesson cannot be extended to McMahan's two-headed case, for Sleeping Socrates and Waking Socrates are not thinking concurrently and the concepts made use of by Sleeping Socrates are acquired from Waking Socrates. I argued that these differences don't undermine the lesson by analogy in Hershenov 2004.

psychological continuity. But our prudential concern in the typical philosophy thought experiments suggests we would survive a loss of mental capacity.[16] So while I think this should lead Hudson to abandon his belief that *we* are essentially self-conscious persons (2007: 218), given unrestricted composition, it need not lead him to deny that there are beings that are essentially self-conscious with psychologically continuous stages. However, if anything deserves the title "person," we do. So given Hudson's commitment to a maximality principle, he should accept that we persons are not essentially self-conscious psychologically continuous thinkers, but merely self-conscious for just a period of our lives. We're persons because of our capacity for self-consciousness, but that capacity need not be actualized during all of our stages. Of course, even if Hudson were to admit this, it still wouldn't commit him to identifying the human person and the human animal. He could instead claim we persons are identical to a maximal being composed of all merely conscious stages rather than only self-conscious, psychologically continuous stages. McMahan and Unger offer Three-Dimensional versions of this thesis (McMahan 2002; Unger 2000), claiming that we survive as long as the same brain produces sentience (consciousness). So what I propose to do in Section 10.4.2, is provide thought experiments which suggest that our prudential concern reveals that we persons believe ourselves to be not even essentially sentient. These thought experiments reveal that the future sentient states we are concerned with can be deemed ours only if they are united by a biological criterion.

10.4.2. *The Collapse of Brain-Based Psychological Identity into Biological Identity*

My contention is that a Four-Dimensionalist can be brought to see that the human animal is the only person by drawing upon our concern for our stages that are devoid of the traits that characterize personhood. Our prudential concern toward our adult conscious animal in the future, including those times when it is without any psychological connections to the present, or even the same cerebrum playing a role subserving our future mental life, suggests that we human people are animals essentially. I will hold that once it is recognized that we could survive certain brain injuries and part replacements, we can resist the intuitive pull of two famous thought experiments that have provided considerable support to psychological accounts of personal identity. The first involves your brain being destroyed and replaced by a new brain. The second thought experiment involves you swapping brains with another person. Most people judge it to be that we wouldn't survive in the first hypothetical scenario but would do so in the second, though in a different body. I shall try to instead elicit intuitions that in neither scenario do we cease to exist or obtain a new body.

---

[16] Hudson assumes that appeals to personal identity thought experiments will end in stalemate (2007: 217). I am more sympathetic to his later "acknowledge(ment) that my dismissal of the fanciful thought experiment defense may have been uncharitable and over-hasty" (2007: 233).

Consider that we have prudence-like concern for the stroke victim that would result from damage to our brain reducing its capacities to realizing mere sentience. Many philosophers believe this shows that it is mere consciousness or sentience, not self-consciousness that is essential to our persistence. I think instead that our prudential responses in such scenarios should actually be construed as showing that it is the criterion of biological identity across time that reveals our persistence conditions. Ask yourself whether your concern for your post-injury self with just a rudimentary mind really is due to your possessing the *same organ* that underlies consciousness or is it rather that it is just the *same animal* that is conscious? I think it is the latter, and this can be seen by pondering the following twist that depends upon the well-known plasticity of the brain. Consider whether your reaction to the prospect of coming out of a stroke-induced coma with pain and pleasure sectors intact but no cognitive capabilities above this will be different if such sentience is a result of different parts of your cerebrum being rewired during the coma to realize pain and pleasure when you awaken? I suspect that most readers would have prudential concern despite different parts of the brain contributing to such sensations.

If you would have prudential concern for the same animal with different physical structures supporting sentience, then why should you react differently to your animal getting an entirely new functioning cerebrum in the thought experiment in which your original cerebrum is destroyed and a new one imparted? Readers might respond that it matters that the different anatomical structures, without which there would be no sentience, are in the *same* cerebrum. If so, consider a second case where, early in someone's life, in the absence of injury and before a web of beliefs and desires arises, different parts of a developing brain play a role in receiving and processing painful and pleasurable signals. Imagine one is in the brainstem, as Shewmon showed is possible (1997: 57–9) and the other is in the cerebrum. Would it be correct to say there were two thinking beings *of the same kind as the reader* in one body? I suspect readers would say it is not. And I doubt readers would assert that there is a new thinking being, one of the same kind as they, produced by fusion if there is the later development of a self-conscious person who provides the respective pain or pleasure reports when either the sector in the brainstem or cerebrum is stimulated. And for all we know, this is roughly what happens in child development. The initially physically dispersed realization and thus psychologically unrelated fragmented mental states of the baby are only later psychologically united as the older child obtains reflective access to the different states. The child can come to say that "I am in pain now and earlier had pleasant experiences," reflectively linking what before had been experienced without the capacity for reflection upon those experiences. We wouldn't maintain that the conscious states prior to the emergence of the unifying self-consciousness capacities didn't belong to the child. Even if such conjectured development is not how we actually develop, our reactions to such a counterfactual assumption about ourselves does illuminate what we take ourselves to be: living human animals, rather than brain-unified thinkers. I don't see any reason to identify ourselves with parts of the consciousness-producing central nervous system (Hudson 2001; McMahan 2002), nor with a larger being only if it *continuously* possesses the same functioning brain-like structure (Unger 2000), rather than holding that these pains and pleasures would be mine because they are subserved by parts caught up in the same biological life and belong to the same animal.

Perhaps you will initially argue that you would survive with *any* parts of your existing brain contributing to the production of conscious states, but would perish if your brain ceased to exist. I believe opposing intuitions can be elicited. Imagine that now and after a debilitating stroke that your pain is received and realized (in some sense) by the upper spine while pleasure has a cerebral basis. I assume that pondering this prospect doesn't eliminate our now having prudential concern for the post-stroke creature in pain that lacks the capacity for self-conscious reflection. It seems that the best explanation of why these would be your pains and pleasures is that the parts involved with producing them are caught up in the same life, i.e. they belong to the same animal.

So it appears that the two most prominent psychological criteria of diachronic identity (*self*-conscious psychological continuity or brain-based persistence of *mere* consciousness) can't deliver the intuitive response—that there is but one and the same thinker in the stroke case. What can do so is the animalist account in which human persons and human animals are identical. Thus it makes sense to claim that the only person in the stories is the animal. As long as our animal can have pleasures and pains into the future, we have some prudential reason to obtain the former and avoid the latter.

Our attitudes of prudential concern provide additional reasons to reject Hudson's idea that the person consists of that which beneath the skin directly produces thought. Thus even if some sense can be made of the proper part of the animal being what directly produces or contributes to thought at this moment, say the neurological realization of some information, it doesn't seem to be the entity for which we have prudential concern. If different parts of our organism would later constitutively contribute to painful sensations, we would be prudentially concerned with preventing these feelings. The neurological states that matter to us are those of the *same* organism, they are not identified by causal connections between earlier and later neurological states that would underlie a psychological continuity or mere (brain-based) sentience thesis.

If you share my attitudes to the individuals with maimed or reduced brains, then why maintain that we would have no prudential reason to care about one's animal if it received a new cerebrum in a thought experiment after the old was destroyed?[17] And if you admit that you have some prudential concern for your animal with a new cerebrum, then you can't also claim to have prudential concern for the being who would receive your cerebrum in a second thought experiment that involves a brain swap between you and your clone. This is not to deny that you can care about the recipient of your functioning cerebrum even though that person will not be you. I don't even have

---

[17]   Likewise, would it not be good for your embryonic child to grow a normal brain? I have elsewhere tried to make the case that mindless organisms have interests in their well-being (Hershenov 2011: 140–2).

to endorse the claim that your commitment to the human animal with your original brain ought to be less than your concern for yourself with a new upper brain. My point is just that you cannot have *prudential* concern for both since prudence is *self-concern*. So I don't have to claim you are irrational to care about the other person/animal who receives your functioning cerebrum in the transplant swap scenario where you stay behind as an animal with a new upper brain. Such concern would be no more irrational than caring more about your spouse or your child than yourself. Nor do I have to follow my fellow animalist, Eric Olson, and treat sympathetically the Parfit–Shoemaker claim that what matters to us is not identity but psychological continuity (Olson 1997: 42–72).[18]

So once readers see that thinkers are best individuated by life processes, it becomes arbitrary to claim that only part of the animal is a person. One can still, on the basis of unrestricted composition, claim that the person consists of only scattered thinking stages of organisms before and after the stroke-induced coma and injury. But the thinking stages of the animal don't have the right causal connections. Such a "person" is an artificial, gerrymandered product of the principle of unrestricted composition, not an entity possessing either a natural biological or psychological unity between its stages. Calling such an entity a person would be as suspect as claiming the first half of my life and the second half of your life would compose a person. There is no immanent *mental* causation between the thoughts of the person who suffers the stroke-induced brain damage and temporary coma, and the later pains and pleasures. Likewise for the other scenarios discussed. If immanent causation is needed, then it would be in the form of life processes unifying sleeping and waking Socrates, the senile general and the young thief, the later stroke victim and the earlier rational self, the merely sentient newborn and the later reflective child, or the divided and then reunified mind studying for Parfit's physics exam. So we see that our prudential intuitions, our belief that we are persons if any entities are, and the maximality principle all serve to indicate that the human animal is the least-arbitrary candidate for the persistence of the person in these cases.[19]

References

Brueckner, Anthony and Buford, Chris. 2008. The Psychological Approach to Personal Identity: Non-Branching and the Individuation of Person Stages. *Dialogue*. 47: 377–86.
Clark, Andy. 2009. Spreading the Joy? Why the Machinery of Consciousness is (Probably) Still in the Head. *Mind*. 118: 472, 962–93.

[18] Part of what I mean by *identity mattering* is that we must be identical to the future subject of our psychology if there is not to be some drop in prudence-like concern for that thinker. I'm not committed by this thesis to our caring prudentially about our later irreversibly comatose organism. But this thesis and my belief that the human person is identical to the human animal does commit me to caring about my animal's future psychology, even if that thinking animal has a new brain and hence no psychological continuity to me now.
[19] I would like to thank Adam Taylor for considerable help with this chapter.

Damasio, Antonio. 1994. *Descartes' Error: Emotion, Reason and the Human Brain*. New York: Penguin Books.

Hershenov. David. 2004. Countering the Appeal of the Psychological Approach to Personal Identity. *Philosophy* 79: 445–72.

Hershenov, David. 2011. Embryos, Four-Dimensionalism and Moral Status. In *Persons, Moral Worth, and Embryos: A Critical Analysis of Pro-Choice Arguments from Philosophy, Law, and Science*. Ed. Stephen Napier, 125–44. New York: Springer.

Hudson, Hud. 1999. Temporal Parts and Moral Personhood. *Philosophical Studies* 93: 299–316.

Hudson, Hud. 2001. *A Materialist Metaphysics of the Human Person*. Ithaca, NY: Cornell University Press.

Hudson, Hud. 2007. I Am Not an Animal! In *Persons: Human and Divine*. Eds. Dean Zimmerman and Peter van Inwagen, 216–34. Oxford: Oxford University Press.

Locke, John. 1975. *An Essay Concerning Human Understanding*. Ed. Peter Nidditch. Oxford: Oxford University Press.

McMahan, Jeff. 2002. *The Ethics of Killing: Problems at the Margins of Life*. Oxford: Oxford University Press.

Noë, Alva. 2009. *Out of Our Heads: Why You Are Not Your Brain, and Other Lessons from the Biology of Consciousness*. New York: Hill and Wang.

Olson, Eric. 1997. *The Human Animal: Identity without Psychology*. Oxford: Oxford University Press.

Olson, Eric. 2008. *What Are We? A Study in Personal Ontology*. Oxford: Oxford University Press.

Parfit, Derek. 1983. *Reasons and Persons*. Oxford: Oxford University Press.

Perry, John. 2008. The Problem of Personal Identity. In *Personal Identity*. Ed. John Perry, 3–30. Berkeley: University of California Press.

Shewmon, Alan D. 1997. Recovery from "Brain Death": A Neurologist's Apologia. *Linacre Quarterly* 64: 1, 30–96.

Unger, Peter. 2000. The Survival of the Sentient. *Philosophical Perspectives* 14: 328–45.

Van Inwagen, Peter. 1990. *Material Beings*. Ithaca, NY: Cornell University Press.

Zimmerman, Dean. 1997. Immanent Causation. *Philosophical Perspectives* 11: 433–71.

PART III

11

Animalism and the Varieties of Conjoined Twinning

Tim Campbell and Jeff McMahan

11.1. Animalism and the Challenge of Dicephalus

There are various theories of what kind of entity we essentially are. Animalism is the view that each of us—each individual of the kind of which we are necessarily and most fundamentally members—is numerically identical to a human organism.[1] Animalism is opposed by a range of theories that insist that the conditions of our identity are not biological but psychological—or, as one of us has argued previously, that they involve certain forms of physical, functional, and organizational continuity of the brain; continuities that, though physical, are nevertheless necessary and sufficient for a minimal form of psychological continuity (McMahan 2002: ch. 1). Some philosophers were earlier persuaded to embrace one or another of these psychological accounts of our identity by thought experiments involving whole-body transplantation, in which one person's brain is transplanted into the decerebrate head of another body, perhaps remaining conscious throughout the process. To many people, it seems obvious that the person whose brain is thus moved from one organism to another would continue to exist in the organism that received his brain, while the organism he animated prior to the transplant would remain behind, either as a corpse or as a living organism sustained by external life support. If, however, the person can survive separation from his animal organism, he cannot have been identical to it.

Some, however, object to the use of science-fiction thought experiments in arguments about personal identity. In earlier work, therefore, one of us sought to reinforce the brain transplantation argument by appealing to an actual case: dicephalus (McMahan 2002: 35–9; McMahan 1998). Dicephalus occurs when a human zygote divides incompletely, resulting in twins fused below the neck. In a case featured in *Life* magazine, Abigail and Brittany Hensel appear as two heads emerging from a single torso; yet they

---

[1] This chapter is a revised version of a paper with the same title that appeared in *Theoretical Medicine and Bioethics* 31 (2010): 285–301.

are clearly separate and distinct persons (Miller 1996). Each has her own private mental life and her own character, each feels sensations only on her own side of the body, and each has exclusive control over limbs on her side. They seem, however, to share a single organism. Although they have two hearts, two esophagi, and two stomachs, they share three lungs, a single liver, a single small intestine, a single large intestine, and single urinary, circulatory, immunological, and reproductive systems (so that any child they might conceive would have three persons as biological parents: a father and two mothers). Their organs are contained in a single rib cage and function together in a harmonious, coordinated manner. The limited duplication of organs would appear to be contingent. Recorded cases of dicephalus show varying degrees of duplication and it is physically possible that there could be an even purer case than that of the Hensel twins, in which there would be virtually no duplication of organs below the neck (for example, only one heart and two esophagi leading to a single stomach). While it is clear that there are two distinct organisms in cases of superficially conjoined twins, in which there is only very limited sharing of nonvital organs but extensive duplication of others, it is implausible to suppose that there are two organisms in cases such as that of the Hensel twins, in which there is only very limited duplication of organs and all the organs function together as a unit.

Before continuing, we should explain our terminology. What is at issue between animalists and us is precisely what kind of entity we essentially and most fundamentally are. This makes it difficult to refer to entities of our essential and fundamental kind in a general way without begging the question. Although we reject the view that we are essentially persons in the familiar Lockean sense (because, for example, we think that it is obvious that you existed prior to becoming self-conscious), we will nevertheless, for convenience, refer to all individuals that are members of the kind to which we essentially and most fundamentally belong as "persons." For the purposes of this essay, all we mean by "person" is "an individual of our essential kind," whatever that kind may be (human animal, embodied mind, Cartesian ego, Lockean person, etc.).

Since animalists claim that we are identical to human organisms, they are committed to the claim that wherever there is one of us, there is precisely one human organism identical to this individual, and wherever there is a human organism, there is one and only one of us identical with it. Dicephalus, therefore, appears to be a counterexample to their theory. This is because each twin is a person and is related to the organism in the same way as the other; therefore, there is no basis for the claim that one is the organism and the other not (though even the claim that one of them is the organism would imply that at least one person is not an organism). Given the transitivity of the identity relation, both persons cannot be identical to the organism without being identical to each other. Since they are not identical to each other, it seems that neither is identical to the organism. Thus, there are persons that are not essentially organisms, and animalism is false. Moreover, since each dicephalic twin is the same kind of entity that we essentially are, none of us is essentially an organism.

The same is true of all conscious nonhuman animals: they are not identical to their organisms either. Transplanting the brain of one animal into a different animal organism would not deprive the original conscious being of a vital organ but would, instead, move it from one organism to another. There are, moreover, cases of dicephalus in nonhuman animals in which, while there are clearly two separate sentient beings, it is reasonable to suppose that there is only one organism between them. If each of these sentient beings is essentially the same kind of entity as every other sentient being, then no sentient being is essentially an organism. We might express this paradoxically by saying that animals, like persons, are also not essentially animals.

11.2. The Too-Many-Subjects Problem

Few animalists have responded to the challenge of dicephalus. Many have concentrated instead on pressing a general objection to theories that deny the central tenet of animalism: that we are identical to animal organisms. We will refer to this objection as the "too-many-subjects problem." It is that if we are not organisms, there must be two entities where you are now: you and your organism. If you are spatially and materially coincident with your organism—that is, located in the same region of space and constituted by the exact same matter—then, since you are conscious and your mental properties supervene on certain of your physical properties, your organism must be conscious as well since it has all of your physical properties. But that is one subject of experience too many. It is absurd to suppose that there are really two subjects of each individual thought or experience occurring in your head (Olson 2007: 29–30).

Some philosophers—coincidentalists—are untroubled by the prospect of coincident entities. They posit them in order to solve certain metaphysical puzzles, such as how a lump of clay sculpted into the shape of Socrates could continue to exist even after being squashed, while the statue could not, even though the statue and the lump are composed of the same matter. They maintain that what makes this possible is the fact that the statue and the lump have different modal properties, even though they coincide spatially and materially before the squashing. But whatever virtues and vices coincidentalism might have in general, special problems seem to arise when it is applied to us and our organisms. As Eric Olson has pointed out, it gives rise to the epistemic problem that one would lack justification for believing that one was identical to the entity with psychological identity conditions rather than the organism coincident with it. If, for example, you were to believe, "I have psychological identity conditions," the organism coincident with you would have this same belief. The organism, however, would be mistaken, for no form of psychological continuity is either necessary or sufficient for its continued existence. And since you and your organism would share the same first-person perspective, you would not be able to tell whether you were the person with the true belief or the organism with the false one.

Olson has noted that animalism might be thought to have its own too-many-subjects problem. If you are an animal organism, it seems that you could continue to exist in the form of a corpse after you die. But many animalists, Olson included, have been reluctant to accept that we usually survive death in this way. They hold that organisms have among their identity conditions a kind of functional unity that is lost at death. So Olson and others have wanted to claim that an animal ceases to exist when it dies. But if that is true, it may seem that what survives the death of the organism is a mere body that has been there all along, coincident with the organism. If so, there must be two coincident entities where you are now: the organism (which is what you are) and your body. And given that the organism is conscious, it seems that the mere body must be as well, since both entities are composed of the same matter.

Olson initially responded to this problem by denying that organisms coexist with bodies (Olson 2004). He suggested instead that there is no body until an organism dies and ceases to exist. When that happens, the matter that composed the organism comes to compose a new and different substance: a corpse or lifeless body that supplants it in the region of space it occupied. Olson finds this proposal attractive because he thinks there is no analogous solution available to his opponents. Those who wish to defend a psychological account of our identity cannot plausibly claim that a human organism exists only before and after one of us exists. So the defender of the psychological approach must give a different response to the too-many-subjects problem.

More recently, Olson has become inclined to accept an eliminativist view of bodies. On this view, there simply are no mere bodies and hence no corpses. When an animal ceases to exist, if its bodily structure remains mostly intact, then although the particles that composed it prior to its death remain in the shape of an organism, they do not compose an organism or a body or corpse. We believe defenders of the psychological approach could with equal plausibility (or implausibility) take an analogous eliminativist stance toward organisms. Suppose that a person's cerebral hemispheres irreversibly lose the capacity for consciousness but that what we call the brain stem and the rest of the body remain functional with minimal external life support. It is open to the defender of the psychological account to claim that the matter that previously composed a person now composes nothing at all. There is no organism but only a set of particles arranged in an organismlike way. If particles arranged in a bodylike way can fail to compose a body, it seems that particles arranged in an organismlike way can fail to compose an organism.

Olson argues for the existence of organisms by appealing to the ontological significance of the functional unity among the parts that compose them:

I claim that if there are any composite objects, there are organisms. The particles that make up a live cat are unified if any particles are … If you don't believe there are organisms, you might as well say there are no composite objects at all. So I feel confident that there are animals if there are any composite objects. I'm a lot less confident about the existence of any of the rival candidates for being me. (Olson 2008: 41)

But a defender of the psychological account might respond that if there is any sort of activity that can be fully explained only by positing a composite object that engages in that activity, consciousness is the most plausible candidate. The claim that there could not be conscious experience without an accompanying subject of that experience is plausible, though controversial. It is harder to believe that we must posit an organism in order to explain the complex biological processes that Olson finds so ontologically impressive. The defender of the psychological account can claim that the complexity of the unity among particles that together generate conscious experience is substantially greater and more impressive even than that among particles whose interactions constitute the life processes of what we take to be organisms. If there are any composite objects, this theorist might say, there are conscious entities; if you do not believe there are conscious entities, you might as well say there are no composite objects at all. So perhaps we should be more confident in the existence of conscious entities (which persist by virtue of psychological continuity) than we are in the existence of organisms. We do not, however, wish to commit ourselves to such a radical eliminativist position. Thus, we are still faced with the too-many-subjects problem.

11.3. You Are a Part of an Organism

Defenders of psychological accounts have offered various responses to the too many-subjects objection as it applies to their view. They have argued, among other things, that psychological properties can be predicated only of psychological continuers and not of organisms, that organisms are incapable of self-reference, and that a person and her organism can be nonidentical yet not numerically distinct.[2] Our own suggestion is to deny that we are spatially coincident with organisms. Each of us is instead a *part* of an organism. We are reluctant to take a position on the issue of the relation between the mind and the brain, but for simplicity of exposition only, we will assume that an identity theory is true. *On that assumption*, there are at least two related but different versions of our view one might develop. One is that a person is identical to those functional areas of her brain that are necessary and jointly sufficient for her capacity for consciousness. The other is that a person is identical to the set of particles whose physical properties constitute the supervenience base for her phenomenal properties (that is, the properties she exemplifies when she is in a state in which there is something it is *like* for her to be in that state). This view assumes that the person possesses a phenomenal core that is genuinely intrinsic, supervening only upon parts of her brain (together, perhaps, with certain parts of her central nervous system).[3] For our present purposes, we will assume the first version.[4] On this view, we are *nonderivative* subjects of consciousness.

---

[2] The first view is defended in Shoemaker (1999) and Shoemaker (2008), the second in Noonan (1998), and the third in Baker (2007).

[3] Olson (2007: 87–98) raises several problems for a view similar to this one. In the same chapter, he also discusses several arguments against what he calls the brain view, which he defines as any view on which we are "something like brains," where this category includes brains, parts of brains, and entire central nervous systems. We take our view to be a version of the brain view—again, on the assumption, on which we take no stand, that an identity theory provides the correct account of the relation between mind and brain.

[4] One of us (Campbell) finds the second view more promising. See Campbell (forthcoming).

Our organisms, by contrast, are conscious only in the derivative sense that they have a part that is conscious, in the same way that a car makes a honking sound only in virtue of having a part—the horn—that makes a honking sound.

This view does not, however, clearly escape the too-many-subjects problem. It would be a mistake to identify the person with a part of the organism whose persistence does not require the capacity for generating consciousness. Such identification would entail that we could survive the loss of this capacity. If, for example, we were identical to our brains, we could survive as dead brains—that is, brains that completely lack the capacity for consciousness. But in our view the capacity for consciousness is one of our *essential* properties. This suggests the need to distinguish between "the functional brain," by which we mean the part of the brain whose persistence requires that it function in a way that is necessary and sufficient for the capacity for generating consciousness, and "the mere brain," by which we mean a part that *could* function in a way that is necessary and sufficient for the capacity for consciousness, but whose persistence does not *require* functioning in this way. Assuming that an identity theory of the relation between mind and brain is correct, we are functional brains. When the functional brain ceases to be functional—that is, when it loses its capacity for generating consciousness—it, and therefore we, cease to exist. But the mere brain could remain as a dead organ, or an organ with extensive areas of necrosis. But this suggests that there might be two spatially coincident entities in each person's head now: the mere brain and the functional brain. The mere brain and the functional brain have different identity conditions and our identity conditions are those of the functional brain. Yet, the mere brain and the functional brain could be composed of exactly the same matter at the same time. It seems that if the functional brain is conscious now then the mere brain, if it is coincident with the functional brain, must be as well (Hershenov 2005).

Hence, again, there are too many subjects of experience. Not surprisingly, the epistemic problem also arises for our view. One could never know if one were the essentially functional brain or the mere brain and only contingently functional. Moreover, it is implausible to suppose that only the functional brain is a nonderivative subject of consciousness, while the mere brain is conscious only derivatively. This response seems to work only for noncoincident entities.

The response we favor to this objection parallels Olson's initial response in defense of animalism. Just as Olson claims that organisms and bodies do not coexist, but that the matter that composes an organism comes to compose a body when the organism dies, so we suggest that functional brains and mere brains are never temporally or spatially coincident, but that the matter that composes a functional brain comes to compose a mere brain when the functional brain loses the capacity to generate consciousness. On this view, the functional brain is not a mere brain in a functional state. It is one substance with a certain set of identity conditions that include the retention of the capacity for consciousness, and the mere brain is a different substance with a different set of identity conditions that do not include the capacity for consciousness.

A second possible solution would be to adopt a version of eliminativism, according to which what exists before and after the existence of the functional brain in the region of space it occupies is merely a collection of particles that has the shape of a functional brain. While one of us (Campbell) is sympathetic to this eliminativist alternative, we agree that we need not commit ourselves to it since the rejection of coincidence is plausible and is a sufficient response to the too-many-subjects objection.

11.4. Objections to the Dicephalus Argument

We now return to the case against animalism, which is an indirect defense of the view we favor. In contrast to the familiar too-many-subjects problem, dicephalus presents animalists with a "not-enough-bodies" problem—or, rather, a "not-enough-animals" problem. Stephan Blatti views the challenge of dicephalus (or the dicephalus objection, as he refers to it) as a version of what he calls a "duplication objection." This kind of objection, he writes, "aims to demonstrate that a view—when correctly applied in a particular case—is committed to claiming of one thing that it is identical to each of two or more nonidentical things," thus violating the transitivity of identity. "Any duplication objection that satisfies this condition has," according to Blatti, "met its prima facie burden" (Blatti 2007: 595, 597).

Blatti compares the dicephalus objection with an objection to the psychological continuity criterion of personal identity that appeals to cases in which psychological continuity takes a branching form. He discusses one such case in which the cerebral hemispheres of a particular person, Peter, are divided and transplanted into the decerebrate heads of two separate bodies. After the transplant, the recipients of Peter's cerebral hemispheres, Righty and Lefty, seem to be two numerically distinct persons, each psychologically continuous with Peter. If psychological continuity is the criterion of diachronic personal identity then Peter should be identical both to Righty and to Lefty. But because Righty and Lefty are not identical to each other, the psychological continuity criterion violates the transitivity of identity. While both the dicephalus objection and the double transplantation objection are construed by Blatti as duplication objections, he claims that only the double transplant objection meets its prima facie burden. Only this objection, Blatti argues, appeals to "a possible circumstance in which the psychological criterion would be committed, by its own lights, to a violation of transitivity" (Blatti 2007: 598). The psychological criterion could avoid such a violation only if it were emended somehow. But, as Blatti points out, animalists are not committed by their own lights to an interpretation of dicephalus that violates transitivity. There are, in fact, several possible interpretations of dicephalus. The most natural interpretation is that there are two persons but only one organism. Call this view (a). Animalism would violate transitivity if (a) were true. The animalist could, however, accept one of the following alternatives. (b) There is only one organism and therefore only one of us—a single person with two minds, or a single mind divided between two brains. (c) There are two of us, and therefore two overlapping or fused organisms, each one a separate person. (d) Dicephalus is what Blatti calls a "borderline case" in which the dicephalic twins instantiate enough of a certain cluster of properties to qualify as a candidate for being a single human organism, but not enough to qualify as a clear instance of a single human organism because they exhibit some properties that are not characteristic of a single human organism—"notably, the presence of two distinct subjects of experience, as well as the overabundance of various organs and appendages" (Blatti 2007: 604). Blatti expresses his view of dicephalus by stating that it involves more than one complete human organism, but fewer than two. There is also a fifth position that Blatti does not explicitly distinguish, namely, (e) that the number of human organisms and therefore the number of entities of our kind is indeterminate.

Blatti's claim that the double transplant objection meets its burden while the dicephalus objection does not is mistaken. For both objections fail to meet their respective burdens *as duplication objections*. We believe, however, that this does not diminish the challenge posed by either objection.

That the double transplant objection does not meet its burden is shown by the fact that there are several different interpretations of the case, none of which is logically incoherent and some of which are compatible with the psychological continuity criterion. (1) The first possible interpretation is that it involves three numerically distinct persons—Peter, Righty, and Lefty—who are related to each other in a way that would violate transitivity if psychological continuity were the criterion of our identity over time. (2) The second is that Peter survives the transplant as a single oddly shaped person with two disconnected cerebral hemispheres, each one controlling a separate body. The names "Righty" and "Lefty" co-refer to Peter, rather than referring to two separate persons or two disconnected parts of Peter, even though each name is associated with only one of his two bodies, just as the names "Hesperus" and "Phosphorus" are associated with different modes of presentation of the object to which they co-refer. On this view, despite appearances, Righty and Lefty *are* identical, and so there is no violation of transitivity. (3) A third alternative would be to claim, following David Lewis, that double transplant involves not three but two persons, each of whom exists both before and after the transplant. Prior to the transplant, these two temporally extended persons share a single person-segment, just as two overlapping roads might share a single segment of pavement before forking off in separate directions. (4) A fourth alternative would be to claim that double transplant is a borderline case in which there are fewer than two, but more than one person. This parallels Blatti's interpretation of dicephalus. (5) A fifth alternative would be to claim that there is no determinate fact about how many entities of our kind are present in double transplant. (6) Finally, there is the view that after the transplant Peter is wholly present at two noncontiguous regions of space which appear to be occupied by two nonidentical persons. Peter is located entirely at Righty's location, and entirely at Lefty's location. Thus, as in view (2), "Righty," "Lefty," and "Peter" are actually three different names for the same person.[5]

---

[5] See Hudson (2001). Blatti (2007) considers views (3) and (5) but treats them as ways of revising the psychological continuity criterion only after the double transplant objection has met its burden. As we

Blatti assumes that the psychological continuity criterion is initially committed to (1) and can avoid violating transitivity only if emended by, for example, the addition of a "no-branching" clause. Yet there is nothing about the psychological continuity criterion *per se* that initially commits it to (1). Rather, Blatti appears to assume that the psychological continuity criterion is initially committed to (1) simply because (1) is more plausible than any of the other interpretations. In this respect, the challenge of double transplant is like the challenge of dicephalus. For, although there are several possible characterizations of dicephalus, (a) is the most natural and plausible interpretation, and it is on this interpretation that animalism violates transitivity. Yet Blatti's comparison of the dicephalus and double transplant objections is illuminating because it reveals that neither objection is plausibly construed as a duplication objection. Rather, both objections challenge their respective targets by posing a dilemma: either the targeted view violates transitivity in a particular type of case, or its proponents must adopt an interpretation of that type of case that is less plausible than the interpretation on which their view violates transitivity. We believe the challenge of dicephalus successfully undermines animalism in this regard, since the most straightforward interpretation of dicephalus, (a), is more plausible than the alternative interpretations, (b) through (e). Consider (b), the view that in dicephalus there is a single person with two minds, or one mind divided between two brains. The problem with this view is that it involves an unacceptable distortion of our concept of a person. As Derek Parfit has recognized, (2) fails as a response to the challenge of double transplant for the same reason. In his well-known discussion of fission Parfit writes that:

we ought to admit as possible that a person could have a divided mind. If this is possible, each half of my divided mind might control its own body. But though this description of the case cannot be rejected as inconceivable, it involves a great distortion in our concept of a person. . . . If a mind was permanently divided, and its halves developed in different ways, it would become less plausible to claim that the case involves only one person. (1984: 256)

One way of highlighting the implausibility of views like (2) and (b) is to consider their moral implications. For example, if (b) were correct, the surgical removal and destruction of one head in the case of the Hensel twins would be relevantly like a hemispherectomy in a normal person—a grave diminishment but not as seriously wrong as the killing of a person. But the removal of one of the heads in a case of dicephalus would clearly be the killing of one of us, and hence an instance of murder.

Views (d) and (e) face a similar objection. (We will consider (c) shortly.) If (d) were correct, removal of one head in a case of dicephalus would result either in a less obvious borderline case, or a nonparadigmatic case of one human organism, but not the killing of one of us, a person. And if (e) were correct, it would be neither true nor false that there had been a killing. Views (d) and (e) deny the existence of a human person.

---

mention below, we think Blatti is mistaken about this. Even initially, the psychological continuity criterion does not rule out any of the views we discuss here.

Blatti might reject our appeal to evaluative judgments as a way of deciding between the different interpretations of dicephalus. He explicitly warns against the use of such judgments as guides for shaping our metaphysical views about personal identity, suggesting that because our evaluative judgments derive from a broader moral framework, attributing

binding metaphysical significance to these judgments... invites analogous determinations regarding other hard cases—cases where our normative intuitions may be... altogether contrary. Consider... the critic who rejects my borderline case view of dicephalus on the grounds that dicephalic twins present exactly two loci of moral status, and the number of such loci correlates with the number of us. Since moral status is typically attributed to an entity in virtue of its psychological capacities (e.g., the capacity to suffer, the capacity for self-consciousness), this critic should also attribute an analogous moral standing to each of the multiple personalities belonging to those who suffer from dissociative identity disorder. (Blatti 2007: 605)

But if an entity has moral status in virtue of its psychological capacities, this fact does not put pressure on Blatti's critic to attribute moral standing to the personalities exhibited by a patient with dissociative identity disorder. To attribute moral standing to an entity's *personality* would involve a rather egregious category mistake. Personalities are not themselves entities with psychological capacities, but are rather sets of dispositions *belonging to* entities with psychological capacities. It is the entity, not the personality, which has moral standing. Interestingly, our attitudes about what counts as acceptable treatment of dissociative identity disorder tell more against views (b), (d), and (e) than they do against the view espoused by Blatti's critic. If, for example, (b) were the correct interpretation of dicephalus and if the memories, beliefs, and desires encoded in one of the two brains were very different from or in conflict with those encoded in the other, one might expect the death of one of these brains to be beneficial for the double-minded or split-minded person, just as the elimination of certain memories, beliefs, and desires associated with a particular personality is commonly considered beneficial for a patient with dissociative identity disorder. Yet this is clearly implausible. The death of one of the brains in a case of dicephalus would constitute a loss precisely because it would be the ceasing to exist of a person.

We agree with Blatti that our moral convictions should not settle the matter about which interpretation of dicephalus is correct. But we also believe that such convictions reflect an antecedent metaphysical conviction that each dicephalic twin is a distinct person. It is because the Hensel twins are two persons—two entities of our kind—that we would view the loss of one of their brains as a much more serious matter than the loss of one of the personalities in a case of dissociative identity disorder.

It is worth noting a final concern about (d), Blatti's suggestion that dicephalic twins constitute more than one organism but fewer than two. We are uncertain whether he would say that this is compatible with (e); but it seems that it is not. The claim about indeterminacy has to be that it is indeterminate whether there is one organism or two. For it is clearly false that there is no organism at all and clearly false that there are more than two. But the claim that it is neither true nor false that there is only one organism, and neither true nor false that there are two, is incompatible with the claim that there is more than one but fewer than two. For according to the latter claim, it *is* false that there is only one, and also false that there are two. Therefore, (d), as we interpret it, does not assert that there is indeterminacy, at least of a kind that one might claim to find in dicephalus.

But if Blatti is not claiming that the number of organisms is indeterminate, then it is hard to make sense of his view. Perhaps the view is that there is one human organism and a determinate fraction of another. But while one can make sense of the idea of a half of a dead organism (assuming, as most people do, that organisms do not necessarily go out of existence when they die), it is hard to make sense of the view that there could be a fraction of an organism that has a fraction of a life, or is fractionally alive. This challenge to the intelligibility of his view of dicephalus assumes that it is a substantive ontological thesis about the number of human organisms and persons in that particular case. Yet some of Blatti's remarks suggest that his account is merely semantic, or perhaps merely conceptual. He might be giving an account of when it is appropriate to apply the concept "human organism" ("human animal") in a particular case, thereby providing an adequate treatment of borderline cases, of which he believes dicephalus is an instance. If this is Blatti's project then he and we may be at cross purposes. For even if Blatti has offered a successful account of the appropriate application of the concept "human organism" we think that, at least with respect to persons, the question "How many are there?" is an ontological one that must be answered by providing a metaphysical account of persons. Such an account would be implausible if it entailed that in the case of dicephalus there was one whole person and a fraction of another.

We turn now to (c), the view that dicephalic twins are really two fused or overlapping organisms. This is the most plausible and the most common animalist response to dicephalic twins. Because, for example, the Hensel twins together have more organs than normally form a single complete set, and some of these organs belong to one twin rather than to the other, it is plausible to suppose that each of them is identical to a numerically distinct organism, but that each organism shares a large number of parts with the other. Thus, Matthew Liao notes that "each twin has her own stomach and heart; they have distinct brainstems and distinct spines that are only joined at the hips; and they have partially distinct organs that are united. This suggests that in fact, there are two organisms here although they are not fully independent organisms" (Liao 2006: 341).

Robert George and Patrick Lee echo Liao's view about the duplication of organs but also claim that each twin has some organs of her own, and that the twins' organs cannot all be parts of a single organism:

The...difficulty in McMahan's argument concerning dicephalic twins is that if his interpretation of their situation were correct, then none of the organs in the twins could be assigned to one individual rather than the other. Each set of eyes, each set of ears, and so on, would not belong biologically more to one girl than to the other. Each of these organs would have to be a part of a single larger organism, subservient to the survival and functioning of this one organism. But this plainly is not the case. It is indisputable that each one biologically has not only her own brain, but also her own skull, eyes, ears, and many organs, while sharing many other organs. (George and Lee 2008: 47)

Yet most of Abigail and Brittany's organs do serve both of them equally. This is true of all the duplicated organs below the neck, such as the esophagi, stomachs, and hearts. If, for example, the heart on one's side of the body were to die, the other heart would presumably be sufficient to continue to circulate blood to the whole of the organism, including the head on the side with the nonfunctional heart, since there is only one circulatory system and the areas to which the remaining heart would need to pump blood are not abnormally extensive. But a few of the duplicated organs serve only one of the two persons. Unsurprisingly, they are certain organs on that person's side of the body (where "body" refers to the single organic mass and does not presuppose that this mass constitutes only one organism). Thus, we say that one sibling's eyes "belong" to her because they are the ones that she sees with. That is exactly what one would expect when two persons are sustained by a single organism. Compare a case of highly asymmetrical conjoined twinning, when there is clearly only one person and one organism—for example, a case in which the only vestige of the second twin is a third leg. Assume that the conjunction was the result of the incomplete fusion of two embryos. In that case, there is a sense in which the third leg "belonged" to the twin that was largely absorbed in the process of fusion. But it is now part of the organism that sustains the one person. Similarly, in dicephalus, one sibling's eyes transmit signals that are received only by her and not by the other sibling, but these eyes are still part of the organism that sustains both siblings; both sets of eyes are caught up in the organism's life-sustaining processes.[6]

11.5. Craniopagus parasiticus

There is another actual type of conjoined twinning that resists description as two fused or overlapping organisms.[7] In craniopagus parasiticus, there is what one would naturally describe as one complete and fully developed human organism with a head in which the brain generates consciousness and both controls and receives signals from the body in the normal way. Yet, at the top of this head, there is a second head that is attached by a continuous growth of cranial bone and is thus upside down in relation to the primary head and the body. This second head has failed to develop a body and thus terminates in a truncated neck. As the name for the phenomenon implies, the second

---

[6] Mark Reid (Chapter 12, this volume) provides an example in which two persons use all and only the same organs, except that each is located in his own single cerebral hemisphere. This example is not vulnerable to George and Lee's objection.

[7] For an earlier discussion, see McMahan (2009: 286–98).

head draws life support from the organs below the primary head, yet it contributes nothing to their regulation, control, or functioning. There is no duplication of organs apart from those in the second head.

History records very few instances of craniopagus parasiticus, but at least two have occurred in the twenty-first century. In one of these, the parasitic head was surgically removed but the remaining twin died a little over a year later from an infection of the brain. Before the parasitic head was removed, it was observed to smile and blink, but we have been unable to determine whether it was carefully tested for consciousness or whether its anatomy was examined in detail after the separation. But whatever may be true of the recorded instances of craniopagus parasiticus, the fact that a second head, with its own brain, can develop in this way, and, as in one recorded instance in the eighteenth century, can remain alive for years, suggests that it is possible that there could be a case in which the brain in the parasitic head developed normally and thus would be capable not only of consciousness but also of self-consciousness. Suppose, then, that there were a case of craniopagus parasiticus in which the parasitic head contained a normally developed cerebrum, cerebellum, and brain stem, but in which the nervous system was truncated at the brain stem. Assuming that the cerebrum in the second head was physically and functionally entirely separate from that in the primary head, so that neither brain had any direct conscious access to the mental states of the other, each head would be a fully distinct, separate, and independent center of consciousness. Both heads would be self-conscious and each could speak through its own mouth.

It would be highly implausible to deny that in such a case there would be two persons—that is, two entities of the kind of which we are essentially and most fundamentally members—and that both would be persons in the Lockean sense as well. But if animalists were to concede that there would be two of us present, they would also have to accept that there would be two animal organisms.

Suppose that animalists recognize that this is the most plausible understanding of the hypothetical case of craniopagus parasiticus that is open to them. They might argue that it is entirely reasonable to suppose that there would be two persons and two organisms in this case, and that this is shown by the fact that they would be separable. The parasitic head could be surgically separated and kept alive, either by being artificially perfused with blood or by being grafted on to a headless cloned body. This could also be done, of course, with either of the heads in a case of dicephalus. There have in fact been actual cases in which the head of a higher animal has been surgically severed and then attached to the body of another living animal of the same species, remaining alive and demonstrably conscious for a short period following the transplant.

In the hypothetical instance of craniopagus parasiticus, the severing of the parasitic head is the only feasible way to separate the two persons. The severed head would be self-conscious and capable of sight, hearing, and speech. Its subjective experience would be indistinguishable from that of a person who has suffered high cervical transection of the spinal cord. It would clearly be a person and therefore, according to

242 TIM CAMPBELL AND JEFF MCMAHAN

animalism, must also be a human organism. And that is precisely what some of the leading animalists, such as Peter van Inwagen (1990: 169–81) and Eric Olson (1997), have claimed.

11.6. Severed Heads and Headless Bodies

Suppose that surgeons sever the head of a person with normal anatomy, maintaining the head alive and conscious throughout the process of separation, and then sustain it indefinitely through the provision of blood from an external source. Suppose further that they also provide the support necessary to keep the remainder of the original organism in a functional state. Is the head really a human organism? And is the remainder of the original organism now an organism as well?

There are six possible views about this case, which we will call the *Severed Head Case*. (1) One might think that the head sustains the original organism that has now been pared down to its minimal or almost minimal form, but that the headless body, even if its component parts continue to function, is not an organism. It might be a dead body—what some in the medical profession call a "ventilated corpse"—or merely a collection of particles. (2) Another possibility is that the head and body are each associated with a separate living organism. On this view, the surgical separation of the head and body is an instance of biological fission. (3) Although the head sustains a person— that is, one of us, or an entity of our kind—it is nevertheless not a human organism. Rather, the headless body is the original organism, which remains alive. (4) Neither the head nor the body sustains a human organism. On this view, the separation of the head from the body causes the biological death, and therefore the ceasing to exist, of the organism. (5) The head and body remain the constituent parts of the original organism, which survives as a "scattered object" whose parts now occupy noncontiguous regions of space. (6) The organism becomes a "multi-locator"—that is, an object that is wholly present at two separate regions of space—and thus survives the procedure as both the head and the headless body (Hudson, 2001). Of these six views, all are compatible with animalism except (3). Which is most plausible?

Since the notion of multi-location at a time strains at the boundaries of coherence and, as far as we know, has not been defended by any animalist, we merely note it as a possibility and will discuss only the other five views. View (1) consists of two claims that are both implausible.

Consider first the claim that the living though isolated head sustains a human organism. The reason that animalists give for thinking that the organism survives with only a head is not that it retains the capacity for consciousness. For they claim that our identity conditions are not psychological but biological. There is no more reason to suppose that the existence of an organ that generates consciousness is sufficient for the existence of an organism than there is to suppose the same about the existence of an organ that pumps blood. Rather, animalists tend to follow biologists in identifying organisms with collections of organs, tissues, and cells that function together in an internally integrated way to maintain collective biological homeostasis. And they tend also to adopt the familiar position of those who argue that a fully developed human organism dies if and only if its brain dies because the brain, and in particular the brain stem, is what regulates and coordinates the functions of the various organs, so that the processes they individually sustain together constitute a life. On this view, the brain, or even just the brain stem, is the biological core of the organism, the internal integrator of the processes that are constitutive of the organism's life, and thus of its existence. Animalists therefore argue that an organism may be pared down to an isolated head or an isolated brain or even an isolated brain stem; but in the absence of a functional brain, all the other parts that once composed an organism will no longer do so, even if they all individually remain alive.

Suppose, for the sake of argument, that the brain stem really is the regulatory center and thus the biological core of a human organism, and that it is therefore possible to pare such an organism all the way down to a functional brain stem—that is, that a human organism can survive in the form of a brain stem but not as any other collection of parts that does not include the brain stem or some functionally equivalent part (van Inwagen 1990: 45, 140). But then suppose that we modify our earlier hypothetical case of craniopagus parasiticus so that the parasitic head has a fully developed cerebrum but a truncated, or only a partially developed, lower brain. Suppose, for example, that the areas of the reticular formation, which is necessary for consciousness, that extend into the brain stem are present and functional, while other areas of the brain stem that would normally serve to regulate certain somatic functions are not developed at all, as is true in such a case of all the other areas of the central nervous system that normally form below the brain stem. If the parasitic head were then surgically removed, remaining conscious throughout the operation, and were then sustained indefinitely by the external provision of a blood supply, it would be a person but not, in the absence of a brain stem, a human organism. That, however, is not a possibility that can be recognized by animalists who claim that a human organism requires an internal regulatory center. They must give up either the claim that a functional brain stem is necessary for the existence of a human organism or the claim that a person could survive with only a severed head.

We reject the claim that an organism could survive with nothing but a severed head composed of living organs, including an intact brain stem. Neither the brain stem nor the brain as a whole is either necessary or sufficient for the regulation and integration of the functions of the other bodily organs. That the brain and brain stem are not necessary is demonstrated most clearly by a case reported by Dr. Alan Shewmon. A boy of four was diagnosed as brain dead but, because his mother refused to accept that he was dead, was transferred to her home where, with only mechanical ventilation, the provision of nutrition and hydration, and basic nursing care, his body continued to function normally except, of course, in the generation of consciousness. More than fourteen years later, Shewmon was permitted to perform an examination, which revealed that "the entire brain, including the stem, had been replaced by ghost-like tissues and disorganized proteinaceous fluids." Yet, Shewmon observed, "while 'brain dead,' he has grown, overcome infections and healed wounds" (Shewmon 1998: 136). What this case shows is that even in the absence of any brain at all, a human body can remain comprehensively functional for years with no more external life support than that required by many fully conscious and uncontroversially living human beings. The basic biological functions of the boy's body remained internally coordinated; it is just that the integration was decentralized, with organs responding to signals from other organs, rather than centralized in the activities of the brain stem.

Animalists might argue that what is necessary for a human organism to continue to exist is not that it retain a functional brain stem, but that it continue, with minimal external support, to be self-regulating and self-sustaining. According to van Inwagen, a living head satisfies that condition, while a headless body does not:

Give the severed head the proper environment and it will maintain itself, but the headless body will need a constant supply of "instructions" in the form of electrically transmitted information. Unlike the head, it will not be able to coordinate its activities. A life-support system for the head will be no more than an elaborate pump. A mechanical life-support system for the headless body must involve the functional equivalent of a computer. (1990: 177–8)

But neither of these empirical claims is true. As Shewmon's case vividly illustrates, a headless body can remain functionally integrated with the assistance of little more than a pump, albeit one that supplies oxygen rather than blood. A severed head, by contrast, requires a great deal more than a pump. The blood that the pump carries to the head has to be continuously renewed, a function that can be performed by the bone marrow in a headless body but not by the head itself. The blood must also be cleansed of toxins and supplied with immune cells and oxygen—functions that again can be carried out by a brainless body, such as the one described by Shewmon, but not by a severed head. Indeed, a living but isolated head has no internal regulation or integration, even of a decentralized sort. The regulatory capacities of the brain stem are idle since they are concerned with areas of the body to which the head is no longer connected. The constituent organs of the head, such as the brain and the eyes, may signal one another but they do not cooperate in maintaining biological homeostasis or sustaining themselves as a unit. Almost everything they need for survival must be externally supplied. If self-regulation and self-sustenance are necessary for being an organism and if, despite having a fully functional brain stem, an isolated head is neither self-regulating nor self-sustaining, then having a fully functional brain stem is not sufficient for being an organism.

The second of the two claims that together constitute view (1) of the Severed Head Case assumes that a living organism could not persist as a headless, ventilated, and fully functional body. This claim is also refuted by Shewmon's actual case, which shows that a body can be self-sustaining with no more life support than is required by a person whose spinal cord has been severed at the neck. The only significant function that a person in this condition can perform that the boy in Shewmon's case could not is the exercise of consciousness and mental activity. That makes it hard, especially for the animalist who claims that the capacity for consciousness is inessential to our existence, to deny that the boy is a living human organism. Yet the boy's head could be removed without any effect at all on the life processes occurring below the neck. Thus, both of the claims made by the first of the four positions cited earlier appear to be false.

The second of those positions, which is also compatible with animalism, is that both the severed head and the headless body would each sustain a separate organism, so that their initial surgical separation is an instance of biological fission. If, however, we are right that a human organism cannot survive with only an isolated head, then this position is also untenable, even though it is correct in its assumption that an organism can exist with only a headless body. But it is worth noting three further objections to this second position, since there are bound to be some who are unpersuaded by the arguments we gave to show that a human organism cannot survive with only an isolated head. First, this position, as it is understood by animalists, implies that one of us, indeed that each of us, could in principle survive without a head. We find that counter-intuitive, though animalists may not. Second, if the separation of the head from the body is an instance of fission, the animalist seems committed to one of three conclusions about what happens to the original person. The most plausible options for the animalist are: (i) that the original person goes with the head, while an entirely new individual of our kind comes into existence as a headless organism; (ii) that the original person survives with only the headless body, while a new person comes into existence and is sustained by a severed head; and (iii) that the original person ceases to exist but is replaced by two entirely new individuals of our kind. None of these claims seems plausible.[8]

Third, and finally, if the separation of the head and the body is an instance of fission, we must ask what would happen if they were surgically "reunited." There are in fact two possible modes of unification, which animalists must treat quite differently. The head and body might be connected in just the way that they (or the bits of matter that were physically continuous with them) were connected prior to separation, so that they would function together as a unit in an internally integrated way. This would seem to be an instance of biological fusion, in which the head-organism and the body-organism would both cease to exist and be replaced by a single new organism that might be

---

[8] It is worth noting that there are at least three other options available to animalists. They could say (iv) that there are two organisms collocated prior to the fission, and that the person is identical to one of them, although we do not know which; (v) that there are two organisms collocated prior to the fission, and that the person is identical to the one that has the severed head after the fission, while the other survives fission with the headless body; and (vi) that there are two organisms collocated prior to the fission, and that the person is identical to the one that has the headless body after the fission, while the other organism survives fission with the severed head. We find these alternatives less plausible than (i) through (iii). Moreover, we doubt that animalists will want to defend any of these alternatives, since they all seem vulnerable to a version of the too-many-subjects problem, on which the collocated animals share the same mind prior to the fission event.

qualitatively indistinguishable from the original pre-fission organism, apart from a few surgical scars.

The other mode of reunification is quite different. Recall that both the severed head and the headless body have external life support systems. It is possible that the head could be surgically attached to the body and partially neurologically connected with it while both would retain their external life support systems. Suppose, for example, that the head would continue to receive cleansed, oxygenated blood from an external source, and that the brain would be able to receive sensory signals from the body and to control its movements, but that the body would continue to receive external ventilation and that its integrated functioning would continue to be decentralized rather than governed by the brain stem. This, it seems, would not be a case of fusion but of conjunction, in the manner of superficially conjoined twins—that is, a case of two distinct organisms, each self-sustaining, conjoined at the neck, and sufficiently neurologically integrated that, apart from any visible life-support mechanisms, they would appear indistinguishable from a single ordinary person. That is, on the assumption that the separated head and body are both organisms, their continued biological independence after reunification means that they would continue to be distinct organisms. Even though we began with only one of us, when we separated the head and body we created two organisms and thus, according to animalism, two of us. Uniting these organisms neurologically but not biologically leaves both of them in existence, so the animalist must accept that there are two of us even though the head and body act together in the manner of a single person, and even though the conscious subject in the head would think of the conjunction as his being reunited with his body and would regard himself and his body as constituting a single person, or a single entity of our kind. Indeed, he might, in defense of this perception, urge animalists to consider that his condition could be replicated in any person simply by severing certain connections between the brain stem and the body and providing the head and the body with independent life support systems. That, he might claim, would not be an instance of personal or biological fission and would certainly not constitute his ceasing to exist and the simultaneous creation of two new human organisms and hence two new persons. And he would be right.

If, as we have argued, Shewmon's case establishes that a human organism can survive without a brain, the fourth of the six positions cited at the beginning of this section is also false. This leaves only the third and fifth positions.

The fifth position—that the organism survives with the head and body as spatially separate parts—seems incompatible with the view that an organism is a collection of parts that all function together in an internally integrated way to maintain collective biological homeostasis; for after their separation, the head and body do not interact at all. This view is, therefore, unlikely to appeal to those animalists who claim that organisms are essentially alive. But there is a more serious objection to any version of animalism on which the head and body continue to compose a human organism even after they are biologically disconnected. Suppose the severed head were attached to a third animal body so that they interacted in the same way that most human animals' heads and lower bodies interact. If the head and the new animal body were fully integrated in this way, animalists would have to regard them as parts of a new organism. But there is no reason to suppose that its attachment to a new body would cause the head to cease to be a part of the old organism. For two or more organisms can share parts, as occurs, for example, in superficially conjoined twins. But if the head remains part of the original organism after it has been separated from the rest of the body and would not cease to be part of that organism if it also became part of a numerically distinct organism, then the old and new organisms would share the same brain. Two distinct organisms would therefore share every mental state produced by that brain—a bizarre version of the too-many-subjects problem.

Of the original six positions concerning what would happen if a human head were separated from its body and both were kept functional by means of external life support, only the third remains. We believe it to be correct—that is, we believe that the original person would be a part of the severed head, which would not sustain, or be a part of any organism, while the original organism would survive with the headless body. If this is right, we are potentially separable in this way from our animal organisms, and so cannot be identical with them. Animalism is false.

11.7. Cephalopagus

This conclusion can be reinforced by consideration of another form of conjoined twinning: cephalopagus. A brief and perhaps tendentious description of this phenomenon is that there is one head with two bodies—the antithesis of dicephalus. In one case, reported in 2008, a single head contained a single cerebrum but two cerebella and two brain stems. In addition to four arms and four legs, there were two spinal cords, two hearts, four lungs, two livers, two spleens, four kidneys, and so on. If the duplication of organs indicates the presence of two organisms, there would seem to have been two in this case. There was, however, only one esophagus and one stomach, and the cerebrum was formed from four fused cerebral hemispheres (so that there was also fusion of the faces) and so may not have been capable of supporting consciousness (Hovorakova et al. 2008).

In another case that is more promising for our purposes, there was a single head containing a single cerebrum composed of two cerebral hemispheres, but two cerebella and two brain stems. Although there were two hearts, two spinal cords, two spleens, and two bladders, there were only two lungs, and only one esophagus, one stomach, one liver, and one pancreas (Kokcu et al. 2007).

The report of the first of these cases does not mention whether or for how long the conjoined twins survived birth. In the second case they died twenty minutes after delivery. There is no mention in either case of whether there were signs of consciousness. So, neither of these actual cases is a clear instance of a single subject of consciousness resident in the area of overlap between two distinct human organisms. But these cases occupy positions on a continuum of actual and possible cases—a continuum that includes more possible than actual cases because cephalopagus is extremely rare. If the phenomenon were more common, there might by now have been an actual case that, like the second case we cite, had a single normally formed cerebrum with two cerebella and two brain stems, as well as a single face, mouth, and throat, but that, unlike that case, had two esophagi diverging from the single throat, each leading to a different stomach, as well as the normal complement of other organs and appendages in each half of the total bodily mass below the neck. There is, as far as we can tell, no reason to suppose that such a case is a physiological impossibility. If there were such a case, and if it, or they, were to survive long enough to experience not only consciousness but also self-consciousness, and if consciousness is confined to the cerebrum and is not generated in the cerebellum or brain stem, then it seems that it would be a clear case in which there would be only one self-conscious mind but two human organisms.

That there would be two organisms is suggested by the fact that they would be separable, perhaps even with technologies that already exist or will exist soon. They might, for example, be separated asymmetrically, with one taking the cranium, the cerebrum, and one each of the cerebella and brain stems, and the other taking only a cerebellum and brain stem and thus requiring an artificial cranium to house them. This would result in two self-sustaining organisms: one relevantly like a normal person, the other, without a cerebrum, relevantly like a patient in a persistent vegetative state whose cerebrum had been destroyed but who could remain biologically alive with little external support other than nutrition and hydration. Alternatively, these hypothetical cephalopagus twins might be divided symmetrically, with each taking part of the cranium, one cerebral hemisphere, one cerebellum, and one brain stem. Each would then be relevantly like a patient who has received a hemispherectomy, although each would require a partial artificial cranium. (In our view, though not that of the animalist, this would be a case in which one of us would undergo fission.)

This hypothetical though not unrealistic case of cephalopagus combines with dicephalus to present a formidable challenge to animalism. Earlier we distinguished several options available to animalists with regard to dicephalus. Of these, the one that is clearly most plausible is to accept that because there are various duplicate organs and two wholly independent brain stems, there are two overlapping organisms and therefore two of us. Next recall what options are available to animalists with regard to our hypothetical case of cephalopagus. They can accept that because there would be only one cerebrum, there would be only one mind and therefore only one person, or one of us. That would oblige them to say that there would be only one organism. But that seems impossible to reconcile with their most plausible interpretation of dicephalus, namely, that there are two overlapping organisms. Every reason that animalists have cited in favor of the view that there are two overlapping organisms in a case of dicephalus—that there is considerable duplication of organs, that there are two functional brain stems, etc.—counts equally or even more strongly in favor of the view that there are two overlapping organisms in a case of cephalopagus. There is no prin-cipled reason for treating dicephalus as two organisms but cephalopagus as one. If, therefore, animalists accept that there is only one person, and thus only one organism in cephalopagus, it seems they must accept that there can be only one organism, and thus only one person, in dicephalus. It is, however, very difficult to believe that the Hensel twins are only one person. So it seems that animalists must accept that there are two organisms in cephalopagus.

That is highly plausible. What is implausible is what that view entails according to animalism, namely, that in our hypothetical case of cephalopagus there are two of us. If the cerebrum in that case has matured to a point at which the mind it sustains is fully self-conscious, there would undeniably be a person present, someone who, with his single mouth, could engage with us in rational discourse while punctuating his asser-tions with multibrachiate gestures. But it is highly implausible to suppose that there are two persons present. There is only one cerebrum—one consciousness–generating entity—and therefore a single unified mind, exactly as in the case of any ordinary person. How many limbs or organs there are below that single center of conscious experience seems irrelevant to how many persons, or individuals of our sort, there are.

Perhaps animalists could claim that although there are two organisms and therefore two of us, only one of the two entities of our kind would be a person *in the Lockean sense*. This is possible because, according to animalism, we are not essentially Lockean per-sons. Personhood is just a phase through which most of us contingently pass. But the problem with this response is that both organisms are related to the cerebrum in exactly the same way. Anything that might give one organism a claim to be a Lockean person would be equally true of the other. There can therefore be no reason to suppose that one organism rather than the other is the person. Animalists might try to argue that one organism is the Lockean person but that we cannot know which one it is, or that it is indeterminate which one is the person, but these are strategies of desperation with little credibility.

This leaves animalists with yet another form of the too-many-subjects problem. Unless they are willing to accept that in dicephalus there is only one organism, in which case their view will be refuted by dicephalus, they have to accept that there are two organisms in cephalopagus. Their view therefore entails that there are two of us in cephalopagus, and indeed two Lockean persons if the cerebrum has achieved self-consciousness, despite the fact that there is only one center of consciousness, just as there is in any ordinary person. For every thought generated by the single cerebrum, animalists must say that there are two thinkers. These are not thinkers of different kinds—for example, an animal and a person—but two thinkers of the same kind: human animals. They are also not spatially coincident but are animals that are physic-ally overlapping in the consciousness-generating regions.

Because animalists typically argue that the brain stem is the "control center" and therefore the essential core of a human organism, they might try to argue that in ceph-alopagus there are two control centers for a single organism, just as a single airplane might have duplicate controls for two pilots. This might be plausible if both brain stems in cephalopagus cooperated in regulating the entire bodily mass below the neck. But, in fact, each is connected to the central nervous system below it in only one half of that mass. Each, in short, has regulatory capacities with respect to only one of the two fused bodies. There is, it seems, no plausible basis for the claim that cephalopagus is a single organism. And this is true quite independently of that claim's implication that there is only one organism in dicephalus.

While it seems that animalists must accept that cephalopagus is a case of two persons who share the same mind, we think it is a case in which the operations of a single cerebrum sustain a single unified and self-conscious mind, which is, as in all other cases that satisfy this description, the mind of a single Lockean person. There is no one else who thinks this one person's thoughts. In this case, however, this one person is sustained by and controls two overlapping human organisms. Yet one person cannot be identical with two nonidentical organisms. Since anything that might suggest that one organism was identical with the person would be equally true of the other, there is no reason to suppose that one of the organisms but not the other is the person. It seems, therefore, that neither organism is identical with the person. In our hypothetical case of cephalopagus, there are three distinct or nonidentical individuals: an individual of our kind—a person who is, we are supposing, made up of the matter in the consciousness-generating areas of the brain—and two human organisms. If this is the correct description, animalism is false.

Animalists might be tempted to assert that the debate between them and their opponents ends in a draw. They have shown that theories that claim that we are not identical to but are spatially coincident with entities such as organisms or brains face a difficult too-many-subjects objection, and we have now shown that animalism faces one as well. But defenders of psychological accounts of our identity have a variety of resources for addressing their too-many-subjects problem. They have argued variously that only psychological continuers can have psychological properties, that only psychological continuers are capable of self-reference, that we and our constituting organisms are nonidentical yet not numerically distinct, that we are parts of our organisms, that there are no brains but only functional brains, and that we are identical with functional brains that have different identity conditions from those of mere brains and are never spatially coincident with mere brains. It is worth noting that there are no parallels to these responses that are available to animalists in addressing the too-many-subjects problem we have just advanced against their view. This is because animalism's too many subjects are of the same kind rather than spatially coincident entities of different kinds. It does not help, therefore, to claim that only biological continuers can have psychological properties or refer to themselves, since both organisms in cephalopagus have biological identity conditions. Nor is it possible to claim that the two organisms in cephalopagus are nonidentical but numerically one, or that one, which thinks nonderivatively, is a proper part of the other, which thinks only derivatively; for each has proper parts that the other lacks. Eliminativist strategies are also unavailing because the two alleged subjects in cephalopagus are of the same kind; hence, any proposal that would eliminate one would also eliminate the other. Finally, there is no parallel to our favored solution, which is to deny spatial coincidence by claiming that the same matter composes different entities at different times. For in cephalopagus, the two organisms undeniably exist simultaneously.

It seems, therefore, that the too-many-subjects problem to which animalism is vulnerable is far more intractable than the one that faces the rival psychological accounts. Those who have thought that animalism is the frontrunner in the debate about our identity on the ground that it is uniquely exempt from this objection are badly mistaken.[9]

References

Baker, L. (2007). *The Metaphysics of Everyday Life*. Cambridge: Cambridge University Press.

Blatti, Stephan (2007). "Animalism, Dicephalus, and Borderline Cases," *Philosophical Psychology* 20: 595–608.

Campbell, Tim (forthcoming). "The Minimal Subject."

George, H. and Lee, P. (2008). *Body–Self Dualism in Contemporary Ethics and Politics*. Cambridge: Cambridge University Press.

Hershenov, David (2005). "Persons as Proper Parts of Organisms," *Theoria* 71: 29–37.

Hovorakova, M., Likovsky, Z., and Peterka, M. (2008). "A Case of Conjoined Twins: Cephalothoracopagus Janiceps Disymmetros," *Reproductive Toxicology* 26: 178–82.

Hudson, H. (2001). *A Materialist Metaphysics of the Human Person*. Ithaca, NY: Cornell University Press.

Kokcu, A., Cetinkaya, M.B., Aydin, O., and Tosun, M. (2007). "Conjoined Twins: Historical Perspective and Report of a Case," *The Journal of Maternal-Fetal and Neonatal Medicine* 20: 349–56.

Liao, M.S. (2006). "The Organism View Defended," *The Monist* 89: 334–50.

McMahan, Jeff (1998). "Brain Death, Cortical Death, and Persistent Vegetative State," in Kuhse, H. and Singer, P. (eds.), *A Companion to Bioethics*, 254–5. Oxford: Blackwell.

McMahan, Jeff (2002). *The Ethics of Killing: Problems at the Margins of Life*. Oxford: Oxford University Press.

McMahan, Jeff (2009). "Death, Brain Death, and Persistent Vegetative State," in Kuhse, H. and Singer, P. (eds.), *A Companion to Bioethics*, 2nd edition, 250–60. Malden, MA: Wiley-Blackwell.

Miller, Kenneth (1996). "Together Forever," *Life* (April): 44–56.

Noonan, Harold (1998). "Animalism v. Lockeanism: A Current Controversy," *The Philosophical Quarterly* 48: 302–18.

Olson, Eric (1997). *The Human Animal: Personal Identity Without Psychology*. New York: Oxford University Press.

Olson, Eric (2004). "Animalism and the Corpse Problem," *Australasian Journal of Philosophy* 82: 265–74.

[9] We are grateful to Derek Parfit, Jacob Ross, Huiyuhl Yi, Dean Zimmerman, and especially Mark Bajakian for comments on an earlier draft of this chapter. Funding from the Swedish Research Council is gratefully acknowledged.

Olson, Eric (2007). *What Are We?* New York: Oxford University Press.

Olson, Eric (2008). "Replies," *Abstracta* 4 (Special Issue I): 32–42.

Parfit, Derek (1984). *Reasons and Persons*. Oxford: Clarendon Press.

Shewmon, Alan (1998). "'Brain-Stem Death,' 'Brain Death,' and Death: A Critical Re-evaluation of the Purported Equivalence," *Issues in Law and Medicine* 14: 125–45.

Shoemaker, Sydney (1999). "Self, Body, and Coincidence," *Proceedings of the Aristotelian Society* 73: 287–306.

Shoemaker, Sydney (2008). "Persons, Animals, and Identity," *Synthese* 162: 313–24.

Van Inwagen, P. (1990). *Material Beings*. Ithaca, NY: Cornell University Press.

12

A Case in which Two Persons Exist in One Animal

Mark D. Reid

12.1. Introduction

Animalism holds that we are each numerically identical to a particular human animal, and three of its implications are that we existed as mindless embryos, that we would continue to exist in an irreversibly comatose state, and that if one's cerebrum were transplanted, the recipient would have all of one's memories and character traits but not be oneself.[1] According to animalism, one would remain the decerebrate human animal.[2]

One might suppose that a case involving the gradual transformation of a human person into a nonhuman person, such as a chimpanzee, would be a counterexample to animalism, since the result would be a different animal but arguably the same person as the original human person. But animalism opposes the traditional view that there are psychological conditions for a person's survival (Snowdon 1995: 73). Moreover, species change, as well as teletransportation and the erasure of all of a brain's psychological contents are conceivable but *purely* hypothetical and thus weak counterexamples to animalism.

Better counterexamples to animalism are actual cases or realistic but hypothetical cases. Actual cases include split-brain patients (Nagel 1979; Snowdon 1995), dicephalus (McMahan 2002; Blatti 2007), and dissociative identity disorder (DID) with multiple personas (Olson 2003). McMahan and Blatti also consider realistic hypothetical cases of dicephalus, and Olson considers realistic hypothetical cases of DID with two personas.

[1] I especially thank Jeff McMahan for his mentoring, discussions, and for extensive comments. I thank Ray Martin for discussions and mentoring. I thank Fredric Schiffer for many discussions.
[2] Animalism's rival is the better-known, more widely endorsed psychological approach, according to which we are each numerically identical to a particular human person. This approach defines a person at a time by psychological unity and defines a person over time by psychological continuity. Because embryonic and irreversibly comatose human animals lack a psychology entirely, they are not persons. The psychological approach thus holds that we do not exist when the animals that are us exist at these times. Because a transplanted cerebrum would be psychologically continuous with us, this approach says that we become its recipient.

In this chapter, I present a realistic but hypothetical counterexample to animalism in which two persons exist in one animal. This example is an actual possibility, as it requires only presently available techniques. It asks us to consider the administration of anesthesia to only one hemisphere at a time, so that when one hemisphere is unconscious, the other alone is conscious and free to exercise exclusive control over the human animal. If applied to one hemisphere after the other in succession, this technique would cause there to be two fully independent hemispheres, each of which could be conscious on alternating days. This case could produce two persons, one per hemisphere, without changing the number of animals. Animalism, however, denies that this is possible.

The logic of the argument against animalism based on this example is as follows. If each of the two persons were identical to the animal, they would be identical to each other, but they are not. Because each is a person with an equal claim to be identical to the animal, neither is identical to it. Because they are identical to no other animal, they are not identical to any animal, which means that it is unlikely that any person is identical to an animal. Even if only some of us are not identical to animals, animalism is false.

Animalists and their opponents can agree about the particular mental and nonmental facts of my case but disagree about the number of persons. And the animalist, it seems, must resist the claim that there are two persons, but I will show that this is implausible.

12.2. Duplication Objections

Counterexamples to animalism often involve duplication. A duplication objection challenges a claim of numerical identity between two entities, *a* and *b*, by presenting an example where one of them, *a*, relates to two numerically distinct entities in the way that it usually relates to just one entity by duplicating *b* so that there are *b1* and *b2*.[3] If we suppose that the original entity, *a*, could somehow be numerically identical to both entities (such that *a* is *b1*, and *a* is *b2*), then the transitivity of numerical identity would require there to be a relation of numerical identity between *b1* and *b2*. Because *b1* and *b2* are numerically distinct, the duplication of *b* into *b1* and *b2* proves that *a* cannot be numerically identical to *b* (since *b* is the same kind as *b1* and *b2*) and therefore that the claim of numerical identity is false.

To consider the duplication objection that split-brain patients might pose for animalism, Paul Snowdon (1995) asks how the animalist ought to interpret their behavior. Nagel says that he cannot imagine what it would be like to be a split-brain patient, but Snowdon claims that Nagel's failure suggests that a split-brain patient is actually two subjects if we grant Nagel's assumption that there must be something that it is like to be a split-brain patient. Once we identify and question that assumption, he

---

[3] Duplication objections have been around since at least Aristotle, but Stephan Blatti (2007) was the first to depict duplications in this manner.

suggests, it becomes more plausible to interpret split-brain patients as persons with divided minds. He argues that a split-brain patient is obviously one human animal and that a behavioral and psychological account of that human animal (including attributions of beliefs, desires, experience, and so on) is generally more useful and valid than an account involving more specific attributions of each hemisphere.

Another example of a duplication objection is dicephalus—a case of conjoined twins that appears to be a two-headed human being, a "spectacle of two heads sprouting from a single torso" (McMahan 2002: 35–6). Jeff McMahan argues that in the pair of dicephalic twins, Abigail and Brittany Hensel, there are clearly two persons, each with her own character and experiences, but only one organism. Offering dicephalus as a counterexample to animalism, McMahan argues that "they cannot both be identical with the organism, as that would imply that they are identical with each other, which they are not, [so] neither is identical with the human organism they share" (2002: 35). He concludes that "if dicephalic twins are not human organisms, this strongly suggests that none of us is an organism" (2002: 35). Stephan Blatti (2007) claims that McMahan fails to discredit various alternative descriptions of dicephalus that are compatible with animalism, such as "one animal with a divided mind" and "two fused animals." He argues that dicephalus is a borderline case of an animal— more than one but fewer than two human animals. Since "it is obvious neither that there is one animal nor that there are two of us...the animalist criterion does not straightforwardly apply to cases of dicephalus" (2007: 595).[4] The only reasons not to consider dicephalus to be a borderline case, a case of two minds (but one person), or two fused organisms, Blatti argues, might be normative considerations, but these should not decide ontology.[5]

Another type of duplication objection is "split-personality," or DID with multiple personas. If there is reason to believe that each persona in a case of DID is a distinct person, animalism is again threatened. If a human animal contains multiple persons and if each of us is a person, we cannot each be numerically identical with a particular human animal, since some of us share a single animal with another person. Olson argues that, assuming that materialism is true, there could never be a case of DID where two or more persons exist in one human animal.

The classic example of fission in which a person splits into two people is a well-known duplication objection against the psychological approach to personal identity. As Parfit presents it (1984: 254–5), each of a person's two cerebral hemispheres is transplanted into a separate person with the amount of psychological continuity holding

---

[4] In Blatti's analogy, replacing *unity of consciousness* with *mind* may achieve a better analogy, since commissurotomy may threaten the concept *unity of consciousness* itself, whereas dicephalus threatens not the concept *human animal* itself but only its countability (the case of dicephalus being undoubtedly *human animal*, as opposed to nonhuman or nonanimal).

[5] Blatti may convince the nonanimalist that "cases of dicephalus present us with more than one but less than two complete animals" (2007: 602) without convincing her that whatever the numbers of animals and persons, they are equal.

between the original person and each of the two new persons that someone's normal persistence contains. Fission poses a challenge for the psychological approach because the two persons cannot both be the original person. If either new person is numerically identical with the original person, then, because they bear the same relation to the original, both must be, in which case, by the principle of the transitivity of identity, they must be numerically identical to each other. But they are numerically distinct. Fission therefore destroys the original person and creates two persons. This forceful objection to a psychological criterion of personal identity has no force against animalism that is not already had in the cerebrum transplant case. Since according to animalism we are not the recipient of our cerebrum, we are certainly not the recipient of half of it.

Briefly reviewing these counterexamples, we see that the case against animalism that appeals to them is inconclusive. I will now present a duplication objection that is stronger than any of those previously considered.

12.3. A Case in which Two Persons Exist in One Animal

Split-brain patients, dicephalus, DID, and realistic variations of these cases gain strength by avoiding objections that some philosophers advance against *purely* hypothetical examples.[6] In contrast to a *purely* hypothetical example, which is practically or metaphysically impossible, a *merely* hypothetical example may be consistent with our best scientific and metaphysical principles, neuroscientific findings, basic principles of psychology, and known physical laws, in which case it is not vulnerable to the objections to *purely* hypothetical examples. The following *merely* hypothetical example can inform us about the metaphysics of personal identity and the plausibility of animalism.[7]

A pre-operative test for brain surgery devised by Juhn Wada in 1949 involves the sedation of one cerebral hemisphere while the other remains conscious. Known as the "intracarotid amobarbital procedure" (IAP), Wada's test is essentially a reversible hemispherectomy (Wada and Rasmussen 1960). Moments after the barbiturate amytal or propofol[8] is injected into one of the two carotid arteries, which supply blood to the left and right cerebral hemispheres, respectively, the patient is able to engage in physical or mental activities using only half the body and half the brain.

Various known facts, together with certain proven techniques, help to ensure the feasibility of a *prolonged* IAP. People with epilepsy take barbiturates safely every day for years. In Wada testing, rhesus monkeys tolerate a dose of amytal fourteen times that used for humans (Wada and Rasmussen 1960). Brassel et al. (1996) successfully

---

[6] Some examples may or may not be possible, e.g. brain transplants.

[7] I adapt this case from cases used to argue for the existence of quasi-memory, Reid (2005).

[8] Based on having fewer side-effects, propofol appears to be a better drug than amytal for the Wada test. See Mikati et al. (2009).

inserted permanent tiny catheters within the carotid arteries of human patients. In the hypothetical prolonged IAP, surgeons implant a drug-supply module with refillable cutaneous ports that can deliver amytal or propofol with precision through ascending catheters to either the left or the right hemisphere.

A prolonged *alternating* IAP is feasible, as well. Because a microchip controlling the supply module could ensure that one hemisphere is always under complete anesthesia, so that the two are never conscious at the same time, the cerebral hemispheres could be conscious in turns. For example, one could be conscious one day, the other the next, and so on, throughout life. If this process were begun during the late period of fetal gestation, when the hemispheres have just acquired the capacity for consciousness, the corpus callosum would probably fail to mature as a result of disuse. But to ensure against any possibility of memory access and direct communication between the hemispheres, surgeons could sever it before birth along with other forebrain commissures. (In order to consider an objection, I later discuss a case in which they leave it intact.) The impossibility of the hemispheres sharing experiences or memories is thus overdetermined by the commissurotomy and the fact that they are never co-conscious. The neural tissue that sustains the psychology of one is entirely distinct from that which sustains the psychology of the other. These conditions ensure that any mental content (representational or experiential) that arises from the normal functioning of one hemisphere is excluded from that which arises from the normal functioning of the other hemisphere, and vice versa.

Each hemisphere is functionally similar to the hemisphere that remains after a human being has received a hemispherectomy at birth; hence the two hemispheres are relevantly similar to the single hemispheres of two different people who each received a hemispherectomy at birth. Each hemisphere, therefore, supports a different person in just the way a spared hemisphere that remains after a hemispherectomy at birth does. Call the person supported by the left hemisphere "Lefty," and the person supported by the right hemisphere "Righty." Lefty and Righty are two distinct persons. Apart from the fact that each of them is unconscious every other day, they are relevantly like two people who each had a hemispherectomy at birth. The difference is that, unlike hemispherectomy patients, Lefty and Righty have a "timeshare" arrangement with respect to the occupation of a single human animal.

Here is what it might be like for you to be Lefty. You awaken in Righty's duplex wearing your favorite T-shirt and pair of Levis that Righty dirtied before undergoing anesthesia. Briefly feeling groggy from the day of propofol, you stumble to your duplex next door. After catching up on yesterday's events by reading two daily newspapers, you read an email from Righty. Unfortunately, Righty reinjured your knee and failed to bathe again. During your shower, you contemplate how to explain to someone whom you recently began dating why you failed to return any phone calls yesterday. Your experience since birth is that you receive anesthesia on alternating days and awake to different conditions after loaning your body to someone for a day. Events, experiences, and statements that others share with you remain with you privately.

Alternating IAP from birth, or even earlier, is similar to cases where there are unquestionably two persons. For example, suppose that at birth one identical twin sister receives a left hemispherectomy, while the other receives a right hemispherectomy. They each receive anesthesia on alternating days so that, like Lefty and Righty, only one twin sister is ever awake at a time.[9] Although Lefty and Righty share one human animal, while each twin sister coexists with her own animal, it is nevertheless hard to find a difference between Lefty and Righty and the twins that is relevant to the question of how many persons there are. One might want to claim that the difference between the twin sisters and Lefty and Righty is precisely that Lefty and Righty share a body (and some noncerebral brain tissue, including the brainstem). Although it is true that Lefty and Righty share a body and brainstem, while each of the twin sisters has her own, offering this fact as the relevant difference seems to beg the question, since the example was devised specifically to address this difference. Without a reason to believe that sharing a body is a reason to count what are otherwise two persons as one, Lefty and Righty are relevantly the same as the twin sisters about whom there is no basis at all to argue that they are a single person. A comparison with the twins, therefore, helps confirm that Lefty and Righty are two distinct persons.

Although when begun before or at birth, prolonged alternating IAP provides a stronger counterexample to animalism, it provides a practicable case of fission even when it is begun in adulthood. One difference between these two versions of the procedure is that the plasticity of the brain is sufficient to overcome any paralysis if the procedure is begun at or before birth, whereas recovery from paralysis would be limited if it were begun in adulthood. When applied in adulthood, moreover, it seems that after only a few weeks, or even months, it would not produce two persons. But continued for many years, it arguably would. IAP fission differs from Parfit's case of fission in that the IAP fission descendants share a human animal, whereas the fission descendants in Parfit's case occupy separate human animals.

12.4. Features of Personhood

Several further considerations help to confirm that Lefty and Righty are two distinct persons.[10] These include the conditions of Lefty's and Righty's persistence, the bases of their rational self-concern, fairness, and moral responsibility.

Concerning survival, since a right hemispherectomy merely removes brain tissue that is of no use to Lefty, Lefty survives it. Indeed, since there would then be no reason to anesthetize him every other day, this would benefit him. But because the hemispherectomy removes all the neocortical tissue that is involved in Righty's conscious mental life, it causes him to cease to exist. Conversely, a left hemispherectomy kills Lefty and spares Righty. Since each may survive when the other ceases to exist,

---

[9] I thank Jeff McMahan for suggesting this type of example.

[10] The term 'features of personhood' is Marya Schechtman's (1996). Also, see Reid (1997).

the survival of each is separable from that of the other, which is the situation of two persons.

Lefty is anxious when he thinks about a speech he will give later in the day. His pulse quickens, his palms moisten, and he shows all the signs of someone anticipating his own future action. If, however, Righty will give a speech the following day while Lefty is under anesthesia, Lefty will not anticipate giving it, and he will not remember it afterward. The pattern of self-concern here is that of two distinct persons.

Suppose that Lefty is a diligent worker and Righty is a lazy glutton who benefits from Lefty but contributes nothing. This situation contains an unfair distribution of benefits and burdens, as Lefty ends up paying for most of their rent and so on. They are not like one person since issues of compensation do not arise where a person has days of leisure because of her prior diligence. Since these issues do seem to arise for Lefty and Righty, this suggests that they are two distinct persons.

Concerning moral responsibility, if Lefty committed a crime, Lefty alone is morally responsible for it. Since Righty was under anesthesia during the crime and for hours both before and after it, punishing him would be unjust. He did not intend or even foresee the crime and has no memory of it, but Lefty remembers committing the crime and feels guilt. Punishing Lefty and sparing Righty is possible simply by administering the punishment while Lefty is conscious. Selective corporal punishment is easy to imagine. Imprisonment is more difficult but possible. A simple hemispherectomy could administer capital punishment. Lefty and Righty are, therefore, distinct moral agents on both theoretical and practical grounds.

12.5. Objections

Objections are likely to appeal to counting persons or animals, and I consider objections of both sorts.

(i) Objections that appeal to counting persons are that Lefty and Righty are not two persons but merely "two subjects of experience," "two minds," or "one divided mind," which are Blatti's alternative descriptions of dicephalus in the debate between Blatti and McMahan (Blatti 2007: 600).

The comparison with the single-hemisphere twin sisters case shows that Lefty and Righty are two persons and not merely separate subjects of experience, since they are like the twin sisters in all respects other than the "timeshare" arrangement. In addition, they have independent conditions of survival and separate self-concern. Issues of fairness arise between them, and they are independent moral agents, making the claim that they are *merely* two subjects of experience implausible.

One might object that prolonged, alternating IAP is like commissurotomy with separate streams of consciousness that are staggered in time, so that in both cases there is one person with either two minds or one divided mind. A commissurotomy patient has neocortical independence between the hemispheres and yet virtually all believe her to be one person. It does seem that a commissurotomy patient is two streams of consciousness and one person, and Snowdon's defense of animalism against objections based on split-brain patients is credible. The same kind of defense of animalism, however, does not easily carry over to Lefty and Righty.

The hemispheres of a commissurotomy patient were commissurally intact until surgery, and even after surgery, a split-brain patient's two minds (or one divided mind) work together, cooperatively. Except in rare or experimental situations, they experience the same events and stimuli at the same time. Even in rare cases where a split-brain patient's hemispheres have different information, they strive for unity (whether or not they succeed) by thinking and solving problems to support the psychology of one person in as integrated a way as possible. The autonomy of the hemispheres that support Lefty and Right respectively is simply not attainable for the hemispheres of a commissurotomy patient. This suggests that the descriptions "two minds but one person" and "one person with a divided mind" inaccurately describe Lefty and Righty, who are never conscious at the same time, share no neocortical tissue, and have no conscious or recollective access to the other's mental states.

One may object that Lefty and Righty are not two fully fledged persons but two personas similar to those found in DID. In DID with multiple personas, the psychiatrist reduces dissociation with the aim of integrating the patient. This aim reflects a view that DID is an affliction of a single person with a fragmented psychology rather than an instance of multiple persons. One might claim that we should view Lefty and Righty in the same way that we view two personas in a case of DID.

Sufferers of DID, however, share neocortical tissue, contain personas that are capable of undergoing integration, are sometimes conscious with other personas, and may appear in other personas' dreams. In addition, they result from trauma, and their various phases of activation and deactivation seem to result from efforts by a single self to cope with extreme forms of stress. None of that is true of Lefty and Righty. In addition, a persona may be eliminated by ordinary therapeutic means, which would seem to be insufficient to cause a person to cease to exist. Also, the personas do not survive equally. The host usually survives the process of integration, whereas the alter personas are usually eliminated. To eliminate Lefty or Righty, however, hemispherectomy is required. Even permanent anesthesia of the left hemisphere, for example, is compatible with Lefty's continued existence. Considering these major differences, the claim that Lefty and Righty are merely personas is implausible.

Olson (2003) argues against the "cohabitation claim," which says that if two personas were sufficiently independent and separate, then two persons would cohabit one human animal. Olson argues that regardless of their degree of independence and separation (i.e. regardless of the psychological facts), two personas in a DID patient could never constitute two persons in one animal. Olson argues, first, that for the two personas to be two persons, they would have to differ mentally. Second, a nonmental difference must account for their mental difference. Third, their being the same human animal with the same surroundings, evolutionary history, and so on, means that they cannot have a mental difference (at least assuming that two sets of the same physical facts imply the same mental facts, i.e. assuming weak psychophysical supervenience). It is thus impossible for there to be two persons—two thinking subjects—for one human animal. Any materialist who believes that the cohabitation claim is true, he says, will have to challenge his argument's third premise and claim that there must be some nonmental difference (or the assumption that being the same human entails having the same physical properties).

Olson's argument straightforwardly applies to cases of DID with two personas that are nonmentally the same, but Lefty and Righty are obviously nonmentally different. Against a case of DID with two personas that are nonmentally different, Olson's argument is complex. He argues that there is no way to make sense of a nonmental difference in a way that is consistent with materialism.

Olson considers two possible spatial differences that might explain the two personas' mental difference.[11] One—that each persona is a different part of the brain—Olson dismisses as absurd (2003: 342). The other is that each of the two personas is the entire animal except that which is specifically involved in the mental life of the other. Applying this proposal to my case would mean that Lefty would be the entire animal except the right cerebral hemisphere, while Righty would be the entire animal except the left cerebral hemisphere. Olson dismisses this because, he claims, there is no theoretical justification for it.

Put simply, then, Olson's argument is that we can consider any possible case that is most favorable to the cohabitation claim, and two personas cannot both be material beings because there is no room for two material beings both to be one human being.

We must distinguish between a need to provide an intelligible materialist account of how two persons might exist in one animal and a need to do so in a way that the animalist will accept. Olson's arguments make it seem that this is a distinction without a difference, but I have shown that it is possible to provide an intelligible materialist account of how two persons can exist in one animal.

Lefty and Righty are *merely* hypothetical, but nothing metaphysical depends on whether the procedure has actually been carried out. Could believing that Lefty and Righty are two persons require one to give up materialism, as Olson and Snowdon have implied? I am not convinced. The question is whether it is consistent with materialism to suppose that two persons can exist in one human animal. I suggest that this is indeed possible, because the persons can *share* the animal between them.

The simplest possibility is that we are our cerebral hemispheres, so that Lefty and Righty are the left and right cerebral hemispheres, respectively. This, although conceivable, seems implausible because it is difficult to believe that we are our brains. At minimum, it would require a major adjustment in how we understand ourselves as material beings.

---

[11]   Olson considers nonmental differences related to space and time. I find it implausible to suppose that the ontology of two persons being one animal can consist in temporal differences because this would imply intermittent existences, i.e. a person or animal popping in or out of existence at different times.

Another possibility is that, in the coarsest-grained analysis, Lefty and Righty share a human animal, while at a finer grain, Lefty and Righty share a human animal, and Lefty bears a relation to the animal's left hemisphere that is similar to the relation that we bear to both our hemispheres, while bearing a relation to his right hemisphere that we bear to a vestigial, dispensable organ, such as the appendix.

Ultimately one must decide whether it is more plausible to accept that two persons can cohabit one animal by sharing it (for instance, in the way that I sketched) or to deny that Lefty and Righty are two different persons, despite their leading different lives, never being conscious at the same time, never experiencing an event together, having different sets of memories and separate memory systems, independent egoistic self-concern, mutually separable conditions of survival, independent moral responsibility, and independent deserts, and who share no neocortical tissue.

Olson might object that it would nevertheless be implausible to suppose that there are two persons even if the nonmental difference is different, nonoverlapping brain tissue, because that would mean that Lefty and Righty weigh less than the animal, an amount equal to the brain tissue that is solely devoted to each one's mental life. To show why this is implausible, Olson provides an example in which a part of one person's brain contains cortex that supports memories that only another person can access. In this case, Olson says that it is implausible to suppose that the person with this strange cortex weighs less because only another person uses this cortex. Again, we may analyze these examples consistently with materialism with the notion of sharing.[12]

One may object that being a person is a matter of societal recognition and that society would refuse to recognize two persons in what is, in most respects, a person like everyone else. Accurately predicting society's view of Lefty and Righty might be difficult. After understanding the physical conditions of Lefty's and Righty's existence, people would have sufficient reason to believe that they are two persons, and society might suffer from believing that they were the same person. Lefty and Righty would make a poor juror for multi-day trials, for example, since two persons who do not communicate would be taking turns in one juror's chair.

One might object that the two hemispheres could be activated together and the fact that the result would be a fusion product who is Lefty and Righty proves that Lefty and Righty are the same person. (We might imagine either that the hemispheres are surgically provided with a corpus callosum or that their original corpus callosum was never severed.) It is possible, however, that Lefty and Righty would remain two distinct persons even when both hemispheres would be conscious at the same times, and even with access to each other's mental states via the corpus callosum. In that case, the removal of the IAP device would merely introduce a lot of confusion into each person's mental life. But it would not challenge the claim that they are distinct persons. It seems likely, however, that if the hemispheres were to become conscious and unconscious at the

---

[12] Olson's specific example, however, seems to strain the notion of sharing since it is unclear what physical connection, if any, there is between him and the brain tissue whose mental content only he accesses in your head.

same times and had conscious access to each other's mental states via the corpus callosum, there would, at least after a period of time, be only one person rather than two. This would, in other words, be a case of fusion. But would this show that all along Lefty and Righty had been only one person?

If fusion is possible, then Lefty and Righty have equal claim to be the product of fusion. If one of them is numerically identical with it, then, by the transitivity of identity, both must be. But that would mean that they are numerically identical to each other. Since they are instead numerically distinct, neither Lefty nor Righty is the fusion product, and fusion therefore causes both of them to cease to exist. Fusion, therefore, does not threaten the thesis that Lefty and Righty are distinct persons. Instead, it helps to clarify it by showing that Lefty and Righty were two distinct entities that fused.

There is, however, another way to understand fusion. According to Lewis's (1976) multiple occupancy thesis, a person contains as many occupants as were fused into him, or that he will fission into, with fission and fusion never changing the number of occupants or violating the logic of identity. The objection is thus that Lefty and Righty's fusion product, which clearly is one person, contains Lefty and Righty as occupants, which means that Lefty and Righty are merely occupants before fusion, as well. A potential objection, therefore, describes Lefty and Righty as "two occupants but one person," which is a description that may be compatible with animalism. Drawing an analogy, Lewis claims that occupants are like highway routes that may merge and split. For instance, Route 1 and Interstate 95 merge and later divide, just as an occupant can fuse and split with another occupant.

Once we consider what happens when the IAP apparatus is reapplied after fusion, however, it is easy to see that Lewis's analogy is a poor one. If the IAP apparatus is reapplied for a number of years, fission is likely to result. The fission descendants will initially be similar to each other. Because neither has a special claim to be the fusion product or the fusion predecessors, they must be two persons (each carrying the original Lefty and Righty as occupants). A better understanding is thus to see fusion as integrative, analogous to the mixing of two masses of clay. For example, Lefty is a blue mass, while Righty is a yellow mass, and they fuse into a green mass. Fission splits the green mass into two green masses, not the original blue or yellow, which means that the merging and division of highway routes has no place in explaining the fission or fusion of human persons. Someone might object that we would want to identify the pair of fission descendants with Lefty and Righty because in each case, the cerebral hemispheres are the lines of division. If Lefty and Righty actually fused, however, it would be a mistake to identify the fission descendants with Lefty and Righty, as the clay analogy suggests.

(ii)   In the debate over dicephalus, McMahan counts the Hensel twins as one animal with organ duplication (2002: 36), but since the organ duplication includes the brain, Blatti argues that it is as plausible to count two fused animals with shared organs (2007: 602). One might object that Lefty and Righty are "two fused animals" with all organs, except the two hemispheres, shared.

But if Lefty and Righty are two fused animals, then the IAP apparatus must create two animals from one. Because IAP neither involves nor causes any anatomical changes apart from the severing of the corpus callosum and because a change in the number of animals would require, at a minimum, major anatomical changes, applying it to a single animal will not create two animals.

Another possibility is that two animals exist alternatingly with the activation and deactivation of the hemispheres. But to suppose that whenever Lefty or Righty awakes, one animal ceases to exist while another comes into existence, is implausible. In a driver's education car with two steering wheels and sets of pedals, one car does not go out of existence with another coming into existence when the student driver takes control.[13]

Nagel (1979) contends that a split-brain patient is midway between a single individual with an intact brain and a pair of individuals who are behaviorally coordinated. Blatti adopts "an analogous stance... with respect to cases of dicephalus" (2007: 603). According to Blatti, Nagel's point is that a split-brain patient presents us with a borderline case of our concept *unity of consciousness* (or a single mind). One might argue that Lefty and Righty are a borderline case of human animal. But there are so few grounds on which to claim that Lefty and Righty are a borderline case of human animal that it is incumbent on the animalist to provide one.

A final objection is to grant that the procedure is possible but claim that the entities that it produces are sufficiently dissimilar to us that the example does not serve as a reliable guide in the metaphysics of personal identity.

This charge is unfounded because Lefty and Righty are each relevantly similar to a human individual who has received a hemispherectomy at birth. We know from such cases that the remaining hemisphere has sufficient plasticity at that early age to take on virtually all of the functions that are normally distributed between the hemispheres. Individuals who receive a hemispherectomy very soon after birth typically develop into normal people with no obvious psychological deficits. In order to make the parallel even closer, one could anesthetize such a person on alternating days, as in the earlier case of the twins.

I conclude that my practicable case of prolonged, alternating IAP produces two persons in one human animal. That the case demonstrates how two persons can be one animal in a way that does not violate materialism suggests that animalism's core claim is false. We can remain materialists and deny animalism's claim that we are each identical to a particular human animal.

References

Blatti, Stephan. (2007). Animalism, Dicephalus, and Borderline Cases. *Philosophical Psychology*, 20, 595–608.
Brassel, F., Weissenborn, K., Ruckert, N., Hussein, S., and Becker, H. (1996). Superselective Intra-Arterial Amytal (Wada Test) in Temporal Lobe Epilepsy. *Neuroradiology*, 38, 417–21.

[13] I thank Jeff McMahan for this example.

Lewis, David K. (1976). Survival and Identity. In A. O. Rorty (Ed.), *The Identities of Persons* (pp. 17–40). Berkeley: University of California Press.

McMahan, Jeff. (2002). *The Ethics of Killing: Problems at the Margins of Life*. Oxford: Oxford University Press.

Mikati, M., Naasan, G., Tarabay, H., Yamen, S., Baydoun, A., and Comair, Y. (2009). Intracarotid Propofol Testing: A Comparative Study with Amobarbital. *Epilepsy & Behavior*, 14, 503–7.

Nagel, Thomas. (1979). Brain Bisection and the Unity of Consciousness. In *Mortal Questions* (pp. 147–64). Cambridge, England.

Olson, Eric T. (2003). Was Jekyll Hyde? *Philosophy and Phenomenological Research*, 66, 328–48.

Parfit, Derek. (1984). *Reasons and Persons*. Oxford: Oxford University Press.

Reid, Mark D. (1997). Narrative and Fission: A Review Essay of Marya Schechtman's *The Constitution of Selves*. *Philosophical Psychology*, 10, 211–19.

Reid, Mark D. (2005). Memory As Initial Experiencing of the Past. *Philosophical Psychology*, 18, 671–98.

Schechtman, Marya. (1996). *The Constitution of Selves*. Ithaca, NY: Cornell University Press.

Snowdon, Paul F. (1995). Persons, Animals, and Bodies. In J. Bermudez, A. Marcel, and N. Eilan (Eds.), *The Body and the Self* (pp. 71–86). Cambridge, MA: MIT Press.

Wada, Juhn and Rasmussen, T. (1960). Intracarotid Injection of Sodium Amytal for the Lateralization of Cerebral Speech Dominance: Experimental and Clinical Observations. *Journal of Neurosurgery*, 17, 266–282.

13

Animalism and the Unity of Consciousness
Some Issues

Paul F. Snowdon

For the purposes of discussion in this chapter I shall understand animalism as the thesis that each of us is identical with an animal. Many questions could, no doubt, be raised about this formulation, and also about the truth of the formulated claim, which I shall not pursue here. The thing I wish to stress is that animalism so defined is not well characterized as a thesis *about* personal identity. First, if providing a theory of personal identity means providing a specification of what constitutes our remaining in existence over time, animalism does not explicitly provide that. The thesis implies that we have the same requirements for persistence as the animals we are, but it does not say what they are. Determining that is a matter for further debate. Second, and more significantly, as I shall argue, the animalist thesis has implications about matters other than personal identity. In particular I shall develop the claim that it has implications about how we should think about the unity of consciousness and the unity of psychological subjects. The point can be put more generally: animalism identifies us with a certain type of natural object—human animals—and so it implies that the understanding of any important features that we may possess must be consistent with the idea that it is an animal that possesses them. There is really no limiting in advance what implications this idea has. We are, in fact, currently at the stage of working out these implications. In the light of our estimate of them we shall either accept them as correct, or alternatively reject animalism.

In a single chapter it is impossible to consider all the implications that animalism might have for the issue of unity of consciousness and of mind. In order, then, to make a start with the issue in the space available I propose to consider what animalism implies about actual split-brain cases—but also about imagined and more extreme extensions of such cases. By a split-brain case I am thinking of a case where we start with an ordinary human being and in an operation its corpus callosum is severed. Having tried to work out what the implications are I shall ask whether there is anything wrong in supposing that the implied verdicts are *actually* correct.

Puzzles of Commisurotomy

In his excellent book *Commisurotomy, Consciousness and the Unity of Mind*, Charles E. Marks (1981) uses a clear and simple case, which I shall repeat, to illustrate the kind of thing that has been discovered.[1]

In commisurotomy patients the corpus callosum, which joins the two hemispheres of the cerebral cortex, has been severed. This was actually done to prevent epileptic fits which start in one hemisphere from spreading to the other one, thereby diminishing their severity. Patients to whom this has been done revealed in normal circumstances no (or, at least, hardly any) detectable abnormalities of behaviour. In fact, in controlled experiments extraordinary abnormalities are generated. If it is ensured that chunks of input reach one hemisphere and other chunks reach the other then, because the two hemispheres control different parts of the body, very strange behaviour can be produced. Marks describes the following experiment. The word 'key ring' is flashed for a tenth of a second in front of the patient. The brevity of the time prevents the subject moving his or her eyes. Therefore, the word 'key' is projected onto only the right side of each retina. (The light from it passes through the lens, and so ends up on the right.) The word 'ring' is projected to the left half of each retina. The left half of the retina feeds to the left hemisphere of the cortex, and the right to the right hemisphere. However, the left hemisphere controls speech, whereas the right hemisphere controls the left hand. If the subject is instructed to *point with their left hand* to the kind of thing named by the seen word he will point to a key, and certainly not to a ring. If asked to *say* what the seen word picked out the subject will say that it was a ring, and deny that it was a key.

Clearly this reaction is very puzzling, and it is undeniable that there is an immediate intuitive pull in favour of saying that the left hemisphere (or the subject located in it) saw one thing and the right (or the subject located in it) another.[2] The implication of this seems to be that there are two subjects of consciousness and not just one. When this reaction is articulated there is not always agreement over what count noun to use in expressing the verdict. Candidate nouns are 'minds', 'selves', 'consciousnesses',

---

[1] Marks' illustration in fact itself comes from Sperry (1974). It is also used in Tim Bayne's book (Bayne 2010), where its origin is revealed. Bayne's treatment of split brains in chapter 9 of his book is very well informed and also highly interesting. It is undoubtedly the best place to discover the actual findings about split-brains.

[2] It is worth noting that the existence of this tendency is, to some extent, an embarrassment for Professor Mark Johnston. (See Chapter 5, this volume.) He subscribes, and invites us to do so also, to a principle that says, more or less, that you cannot create a new subject (or person) by destroying matter, unless that matter served to prevent experiences. But the tendency of people to judge that commissurotomy results in two subjects rather than one, seems to indicate they do not accept Johnston's principle. Now, I am not suggesting here that these cases in fact show that Johnston's principle is untrue, since I do not accept pluralism. The appeal to many of pluralism shows, rather, that there is nothing obvious about Johnston's principle to many people.

'centres of consciousness', 'subjects of consciousness', and 'persons'. I shall choose, at this stage, 'subjects (of consciousness)'. I choose that because it seems to me to be both a (term for a) notion about which it is true to say that I *am* one (of that kind) but which is also less restrictive and philosophically clouded than the noun 'person'.

We can initially pick out two possible attitudes to such cases, and give them labels. The first reaction of supposing that there are two subjects can be called the 'pluralizing option'. The contrasting option of claiming that there is still only one subject, albeit a rather unusual one, we can call the 'singularist option'. Now, I highlight these not because they are the only options, but because initially in thinking about such cases one's thinking tends to alternate between them. They are the two alternatives to which we *tend* to adhere, or between which we veer.[3]

The Animalist Treatment

I wish to ask first: what should an animalist say about the number of subjects (of consciousness) in such a splitting case?

To begin with there are two important features of the concept, subject of experience, which need to be specified. The first is that all experiences are conceived of as belonging to a subject. If there is an experience of pain (say) then there is some subject (someone) in pain. Our commitment to this is evidenced by our intuitive revulsion to Hume's conception of experiences as self standing entities, out of which persons might be constructed. It is evidenced too by our tendency in thinking about these sorts of cases to unhesitatingly regard it as important to decide how many subjects there are. It has to be agreed, indeed affirmed, that many questions can be raised about the principle and its grounds, but I propose to rely on it here.[4]

The second principle is that token experiences can have only *one* subject. As soon as an experience has been allocated to a subject, there is no question of allocating it also to *another* subject. I shall refer to it as the Single Subject Assumption. There is a complication in relation to this assumption, since there are currently quite a few people who do not accept it. It is an assumption that is abandoned in an argument against animalism based on the problems generated once we agree that as things are there is one subject with the extension of the animal, but that there are also others which are the sub-parts

[3] In Nagel's original treatment of this problem (in Nagel 1971) he introduces a greater number of possible responses. The terminology of 'singularism' and 'pluralism' is a useful one to employ in debates about animalism. Thus one style of argument against animalism rests on claims that in some scenarios although there is one animal there is a plurality of persons, so persons cannot be the animal. In response, animalists need to affirm singularism about subjects or persons. However, in other cases animalism is challenged by claims that there is a single person over developments where there is not a single animal. In that kind of example animalists need to pluralize the number of subjects or persons.

[4] We should not rush to agree that the subjects that experiences require must be a new type of thing— say, things which are essentially mental subjects. The principle may be best understood as saying: if there are experiences then there are things, of some sort, having those experiences. Animalism supplies one sort of thing: animals.

of that total physical structure which contain the brain where experiences occur, such parts as the head, or the upper body. This argument is investigated by Blatti and Madden in Chapters 8 and 9, this volume. The best response, I think, is to understand the Single Subject Assumption as saying that once an experience (or mental state) has been assigned to a subject it cannot be assigned to another subject (unless one is required to do it on the basis of considerations to do with parts and the location of mental processes). Given the restriction it can be applied in the arguments relevant here.

There is a further assumption, this time about animals, which needs to be specified. The assumption is that merely by slicing the connections between the two halves of the cortex one does not *destroy* the animal. The existence of the animal is no more threatened by this injury than it would be by slicing the muscles in its left calf. Split brains, at least in their actual form, do not raise issues about animal persistence. This is an important but surely plausible assumption.

Given these principles, the animalist will argue as follows. Let 'P' designate the person who is the patient and who undergoes the commisurotomy. Let 'A' designate the human animal with which, according to animalism, P is identical. The animal survives the operation, and so, therefore, does P. Clearly, though, A is having the experiences induced after the operation. It follows that P is having those experiences. So, P is the subject of those experiences. Since no experience has more than one subject, P is the one and only subject of them. There is, therefore, a single subject in the post-commisurotomy case.

This simple argument appears strong, and it seems to mean that an animalist should be a singularist. If it is sound, however, it would seem that such an argument also blocks acceptance of pluralizing accounts, as far as the animalist is concerned, in *any* possible case where the animal remains as a subject of (or locus of) consciousness. So, the animalist seems to be committed to supporting the following claim; there are no possible circumstances in which this animal A exists and has experiences, *however internally disconnected A's brain*, in which P is not the subject of those experiences. This is a strong modal thesis, and it needs a suitable defence against the counter-claim that we can envisage *possible* cases in which there is this single animal but more than one subject associated with it, each having different experiences.

The argument just developed allows, as far as I can see, one escape route. It cannot be denied that A, and hence P, survives the split, but it might be claimed that A is not having the post-operative experiences. If this is denied, the animalist thesis implies nothing about the number of subjects. This denial, however, can have two sources. The first ground might be the perfectly general claim that the animal never has experiences (or mental states).[5] This general claim deserves consideration because it might form part of a position designed to avoid the standard arguments for animalism. It cannot, however, be used to block the derivation of consequences from animalism, since it is clearly incompatible with animalism. However, it is highly implausible to defend the

---

[5] Professor Sydney Shoemaker, in effect, defends this thesis in Chapter 6, this volume.

claim by simply denying that the post-operative animal is having the experiences. For, if we allow that before the experiment the animal is having experiences, then it seems that after it the animal fulfils as well as before any conditions on having experiences.[6] I do not see how a case could be made for that restricted claim. I shall therefore assume that animalism is committed to singularism and so I want to articulate and to assess (some of) the objections to singularism.

Unity Requirements

The singularist ascribes all the psychological states and occurrences which in some sense are occurring within the human animal A to a single subject. There will be a problem with this if the proposition that the states belong to a single subject implies that there is a certain relation Rel holding amongst those states which, given the peculiarities of the disconnection in the split-brain cases, fails to hold amongst them. Intuitively Rel is a relation of what might be called *unity*. So I shall call suggested principles of the form 'if psychological states S1...Sn belong to a single subject then Rel (S1...Sn)' *unity principles*.

   Unity principles can be classified in accordance with the *types* of states they concern. So we can distinguish between *experiential* unity principles, which lay down relations amongst experiences, and *propositional attitude* unity principles, which specify relations amongst so called propositional attitudes, beliefs, desires, etc. There may, of course, be unity principles with a single structure which apply to both.[7] The crucial question is: are there *true* unity principles which have the consequence that despite the states belonging (in some sense) to a single animal they cannot be ascribed to a single subject? In effect, with any suggested principles, the proponent of singularism has two options; accept the principle but argue that it is fulfilled in split-brain cases, or deny the soundness of the principle.

   It is important not to think that the strategy of this chapter is to deny that there are any true unity principles. The crucial issue is whether there are any unity principles which require psychological links amongst all the psychological states of a single subject which the commisurotomy procedure destroys. It is also important to distinguish such unity principles from the more limited idea, which strikes some as plausible, that for there to be a subject with mental states at all there must be a multiplicity of such states amongst which some strong unity relation holds. If some such principle is true it cannot generate problems for the singularism that the animalist needs to defend.

   There is one final clarification. When people talk about *the* unity of consciousness, we can distinguish, it seems to me, a number of different things that might be meant,

---

   [6] How can it be denied that animal A might be hurt, or can see well enough to feed itself and move around the world successfully, or act, and so on?

   [7] This distinction between two types of functional unity principles reflects a fairly conventional twofold division of mental states. Should it be felt, as it very reasonably might be, that this has left out other important sorts of mental states, then other types of unity principles would need recognizing.

which it is important to keep separate. The first just is the simple idea that a group of experiences are had by a single subject. We might call this the unity of *ownership*. (The experiences are, as we might say, owned by a single *unit*.) The second is the idea of what we might call *functional* unities amongst such experiences. This is the kind of unity which is envisaged in the arguments about to be considered. Now, crucially it is entirely *open* whether unity of ownership *entails* any *functional* unification. It is easy to overlook this gap. Here is a remark by John Mackie in which he appears to do so: 'All its simultaneous experiences must be co-conscious, because it is just one subject of consciousness at any one time'.[8] Co-consciousness represents a functional unity, which Mackie clearly thinks follows from what I have called unity of ownership. In fact, I suggest, it is not obvious that it follows. There is also a *third* use of talk of unity, where by unity of experience is meant a type of unity at the level, as one might say, of *content*. Thus it might be said, along lines associated with Kant, that the experiences of a *single subject* must present a *unified spatial world* to that subject. Again, it is completely open whether such unity of *content* is entailed by unity of *ownership*. I shall hereafter ignore suggested content unities, and concentrate on what can be said about functional unities.

There is, though, a fourth thing worth picking out that can be meant when theorists talk about spelling out the unity of experience (and explaining it). Their idea is that in fact with normal human subjects there is something properly described as unified about their experiences and mental lives; the task is to specify this and, further, to explain its presence. Someone committed to this totally respectable research task is not laying down necessary conditions for experiences to belong to a single subject. They are trying to spell out a unity that can be said to be there, at least in normal cases, and to explain it. That is a fascinating problem which I shall here ignore.

What I now want to explore is whether there are any significant difficulties in holding that there is a single subject in such split-brain cases.

The Possibility of a Consistent Interpretation

I shall first consider the objection that it is impossible to provide a consistent psychological account when the number of subjects is limited to one. The objection, as I shall interpret it, alleges that if we try to offer a psychological explanation for the behaviour (or behavioural dispositions) on the assumption that there is only one subject we shall find ourselves forced to make inconsistent ascriptions to the single subject. That is, we shall end up having to say both 'F(P)' and '¬F(P)', for some psychological value of 'F' (and 'P').[9]

To see whether a case can be made for this claim I shall take *belief* as the value for 'F', and consider Sperry's experiment. I shall let 'K' stand for 'P saw "key"'; 'R' stand for

---

[8] Mackie (1976: 194).
[9] In filling out this line of thought I am proposing arguments that seem to me to resemble those that I have heard offered.

'P saw "ring"; and 'KR' stand for 'P saw "key ring"'. I shall call the patient 'P'.[10] What ascriptions must we make to explain the behaviour of P? We can say that P verbally expresses his conviction that R, and so PB(R). We can also say that P expresses, by pointing action, his conviction that K, so PB(K). P also verbally expresses his conviction that ¬K, and so we can say PB(¬K), and we could also get expression of the conviction that ¬R, so we must say PB(¬R). We therefore end up affirming:

1. PB(R)
2. PB(¬R)
3. PB(K)
4. PB(¬K)

Further, despite the truth of KR we can get P to express the conviction that ¬KR, so we shall also 5. PB(¬KR).

Explaining P's expressive behaviour, it is clear, requires us to ascribe inconsistencies to P. That, however, does *not* amount to an inconsistency in *our* psychological theory of P. So far, P is inconsistent; we, the interpreters, are not. The argument has not reached the conclusion that is required.

There are, as far as I can see, two ways for the proponent of this argument to continue. The first way is to claim that, although the psychological ascriptions are not formally inconsistent there are principles governing psychological theories which make it an unacceptable defect in a psychological theory to characterize a subject as himself (or herself) *so* inconsistent, or perhaps irrational, as this. I shall return to this general thought.

The second way of pursuing the objection arises from noting that, as initially presented, the critical argument fails because it tries to generate an inconsistency from a sequence of positive belief ascriptions.[11] But no contradiction can arise that way. It is necessary therefore to generate some negative ascriptions, by, presumably, isolating principles for negative psychological attributions, and showing how they are fulfilled in our example. (We might call such principles—negation introduction rules for psychological claims.) It then needs to be shown that for some proposition Q, there are grounds, on the assumption of a single subject, for affirming that PB(Q) and also for affirming ¬PB(Q). It could then be concluded that we cannot consistently maintain a single subject interpretation.

How do we ground negative belief ascriptions? I want to explore two ideas that might be suggested. To develop the first I shall employ an intuitive notion, which is that of a piece of behaviour being *expressive of* a belief. Here is an example. If P is asked whether Q and says, manifestly sincerely, 'yes', then that verbal behaviour is expressive

---

[10] It should be obvious that there is something shorthand about the assignment of interpretations in the text. When I say that 'K' stands for 'P saw "key"' I mean that to be a first-person proposition, and not third personal.

[11] I mean that the belief ascriptions themselves are positive. The content of the ascribed beliefs might be negative.

of his belief that Q. Employing this notion someone might suggest the following principle:

NB1; if P fails to exhibit behaviour expressive of Q then ¬(PB(Q)).

This principle is obviously false. Here are some counterexamples. P might be incapable of expressive behaviour at all at a certain time, because knocked out, without losing his beliefs. P might not be being prompted to express his belief that Q. P might be being prompted to expressive behaviour, but have reasons not to express his belief that Q (say, he might win a large amount of money if he remains silent). Finally, P simply cannot express *all* his beliefs at any one time, since there are too many. So, instead, the following principle might be suggested:

NB2; if P is capable of expressive behaviour, and whatever the prompting and circumstances might be would not engage in any behaviour expressive of Q, then ¬(PB(Q)).

This principle might be plausible, but it cannot yield any results in our case. P does engage in behaviour expressive of both the belief that K and the belief that not K. It is clear that NB2 is useless, for P must exhibit some expressive behaviour to ground the positive ascription of belief which is needed for the contradiction, and so the antecedent of NB2 cannot be fulfilled. It seems therefore that the following principle (or something like it) is needed:

NB3; if P is capable of expressive behaviour of type T, and whatever the prompting and circumstances would not engage in behaviour of type T which is expressive of Q, then ¬(PB(Q)).

If NB3 is true then we get a contradiction. P is capable of expressive behaviour using speech, but would not engage in such behaviour expressive of the belief that K; so it would follow that ¬(PB(K)). However, a belief that K is expressed by different expressive behaviour. So there is also belief that K.

The reply which I wish to make to this version of the argument is that, despite seeming plausible, NB3 is *not true*. P might be capable of expressive behaviour of type T, in that he can express *some* of his beliefs that way, without being capable of expressing *all* his beliefs that way. If so, failure to express the belief that Q by type T behaviour does not mean that there is no belief that Q; it may be that he cannot express the belief, as held there and then, *in that sort of way*.

It will be replied that the restriction that I have just suggested does indeed block the attempted use of the principle, but that NB3 would surely command unqualified assent by anybody who is not keen to defend a singularist account. This claim is, in fact, not true, but even if it were it would not support acceptance of an unqualified NB3. Split-brain cases precisely provide a reason for caution about accepting NB3, and would do so even if they were the only cases of which we could think. There are though other counterexamples to NB3. For example, maybe P can engage in type T behaviour to express belief, but something about P's belief that Q means that prompting expression of it makes him unable to engage in type T behaviour; perhaps it induces temporary, hysterical paralysis of limb L (for some reason). People who stutter may be capable of verbally expressing some beliefs which are expressible in sentences they can utter but be incapable of expressing verbally other beliefs which are expressible in sentences they cannot utter.

Along these lines, then, we have not discovered a basis for generating a contradiction. The second approach to grounding the ascription of negative beliefs starts from the intuitive idea that if someone sincerely denies that they believe something then it is legitimate to assert that they do not believe it. Putting it more precisely, the suggested principle, NB4, is: if P sincerely denies believing that Q then P does not believe that Q. Now, if NB4 is correct then we can generate a contradiction. P will sincerely deny verbally that he saw the word for a key. According to NB4 this means that P does not believe that he saw it, yet since P apparently sincerely also affirms by pointing that he did see such a word we must attribute to him that belief. A contradiction is generated.

The way to avoid this contradiction is to abandon NB4. Thus, suppose that someone, P, is asked, by an interrogator whispering in his or her left ear, whether they believe that Q? Assuming no other influences, this input will trigger some search mechanism that P uses to determine whether there is such a belief. How can it be ruled out that the search mechanism itself that this particular query stimulates or triggers might fail to pick up on the presence somewhere in P's psychological system of a belief that P? After all, the causal consequence of this particular query might well be a mechanism that has, for some reason, limited access to the belief system. I am suggesting therefore that we cannot rule out the possibility that a certain belief might not be expressible in a certain way because what I am calling the search mechanism, triggered by the query and generating the expression, does not, or cannot, detect that belief. Sincere denial that one has a belief does not mean that one lacks the belief. This kind of case also counts against the correctness of NB3. One form of sincere belief expression is to sincerely answer a query as to whether one thinks something. But one might have a belief and fail to express it in such a way because what I am calling the search mechanism might not detect the belief.[12]

I conclude, therefore, that if singularism is to be criticized on the basis of the psychological theories it might endorse, it is necessary to argue that the degree of inconsistency it must ascribe to subjects *itself* contravenes some constitutive principles internal to, or definitive of, psychological theorizing.

---

[12] What we have here is the psychological analogue of the insight that negative existential claims cannot be verified. As critics of verificationism pointed out, that we do not find an X does not establish—or verify—that there are no Xs. We may have simply missed it. Similarly, that we cannot find a belief (or find evidence for the belief) does not mean there is no such belief. Of course, this possibility is not of practical significance unless we start getting evidence that we do overlook our own beliefs. We cannot, though, deny that as a possibility.

Other Constraints

Are there *other* constraints on psychological ascription which make a single subject account impossible?

The conception of psychological ascription which might ground the conviction that there are such constraints is familiar, popular, and not unpersuasive. Subjects at a time possess many psychological states. They have, and must have, many beliefs. It is also in the nature of beliefs to evolve under the influence of observation and reflection. Belief is dynamic. Finally, one important interactive aspect of belief is that, in response to related desires and goals, they generate behaviour, attempts to do things. However, both the patterns of co-occurrence and development must be psychologically intelligible, which is to say rational. Beliefs must conform to a pattern of rationality.[13]

These observations are extremely general and if we remain so general there is no reason to suppose a single subject treatment falls foul of a rationality constraint. Is P irrational? Given what can be described as the *trick* played by the experimentalists on P's perception, it is rational for P to believe K and to believe R. It is also rational for P to believe ¬K and ¬R. In forming these beliefs P is displaying no irrationality. Further, given these beliefs the communicative behaviour P exhibits is also rational. Since he believes R, for example, it is rational to express it. Finally, there is no irrationality in P's believing (say) R and believing ¬R, for P is unaware that he believes contradictory propositions, so, in sustaining these beliefs he is not being irrational. He remains unaware, of course, because his brain has been tampered with. P's reactions and beliefs would strike an *uninformed* observer as irrational; but an *informed* observer can recognize that P's responses are as rational as possible in P's circumstances. I do not see, therefore, that simply stressing the requirement of rationality generates any problems for singularism.

For the objection to continue, more specific constraints on psychological ascription than simple rationality must be articulated. There is however an argument to show that there can be no specific constraints with which a single subject account is inconsistent. Thus, we do not have a way to detect items which are beliefs. We do not say or think (in regular circumstances, where we are dealing with a single human being, even if one who has been subjected to a variety of surgical insults) that somewhere hereabouts is the belief that P and also the belief that Q, the only question is: is it the same believer or a different one? Rather, we detect the *beliefs of a certain subject*. Conditions for belief are, therefore, conditions which a believer must satisfy. These conditions, relative to the envisaged subject, must already be satisfied for the belief ascriptions to be (properly) made. To determine that a believer satisfies certain conditions we must, already, have a conception of the location and extent of the believer. Now, consider the extent of the object which must fulfil the conditions for the psychological states which it is

---

[13] I am, of course, alluding to the ideas about constraints on interpretation imposed by considerations of rationality that Davidson has promulgated and which have been widely accepted in recent philosophy.

agreed must be ascribed in our case (with their agreed degree of inconsistency). Surely the object which satisfies the conditions has the same extension as the human being. That is the size of the object we start off dealing with and to which we ascribe the states. This makes it plausible to say that the whole large object must fulfil all the conditions, whatever they are, for the ascription of beliefs. But if so, there cannot be any *further* legitimate constraints with which a single subject account is inconsistent.

Inferential Conditions

Whatever one's attitude to the previous argument, further conditions do, and no doubt will, continue to be suggested which would create problems for the singularist approach. I want to glance very briefly at one such suggestion. Tim Bayne proposes that genuine I-thoughts should display certain properties; they are, roughly, that if a single subject thinks 'I am F' and also thinks 'I am G' then that subject should think 'I am F and G', and also a single subject should not think both 'I am F' and 'I am not F', and, finally, if a single subject wants to G and believes that the way to G is to F then that subject will (tend to) G. Bayne himself uses these in commenting on a more extreme case than split brains, but it is fairly clear that split-brain patients (and certainly more extreme imagined cases of brain-splitting) will not conform to these requirements.[14] The simplest response to this style of suggestion is to ask why it should be counted a strict necessary condition for a subject having such mental states that they conform without exception to these requirements. There is a significant missing step in moving from the observation that in normal people these conditions are fulfilled to the claim that they must be fulfilled to have such attitudes and thoughts. I cannot see what fills that gap. But, second, do we actually know that even in normal cases such conditions are satisfied? What investigations that can be cited should convince us that we know that about normal cases? It may seem to us to be so, but that is not very hard data. My conclusion is that there is no entitlement to rely on such principles to criticize singularism.

I propose that the attributions of propositional attitudes that are warranted to split-brain patients are neither inconsistent in themselves, nor are there principles of interpretation or understanding that disallow their application to a single subject. How, though, do things stand with experiences?

Unity of Experience Principles

In Marks' (or Sperry's) little story it seems there is a sighting of the word 'key' and a sighting of the word 'ring'. The question is: are there any reasons to deny that a single subject enjoyed both sightings? Is that claim inconsistent with some deep truths about experience and subjects?

[14] See Bayne (2010: 271–5).

I want to develop my answer to this question by scrutinizing Nagel's famous answer to it in his classis paper on brain bisection.[15] Nagel gives profound expression to a version of the view I wish to oppose and scrutinizing it enables me to put forward an alternative.

Nagel's overall purpose is to suggest that the 'personal, mentalist idea of a human being' may not be consistent with an 'understanding of humans as physical systems'.[16] Nagel says that 'it is the idea of a *single* person, a single subject of experience and action that is in difficulties'. He is, though, tempted by the thought (which is, at an abstract level, Humean) that although the idea is in difficulties it may be an idea that we simply cannot abandon. It may be part of our cognitive nature to think in that mistaken way. The main premise in Nagel's argument is that in split-brains cases 'there is no whole number of individual minds that these patients can be said to have'.[17] Now, it is not obvious that his conclusion about *split-brain* cases *shows* that the idea of a single subject is in difficulties in *all its applications*.[18] Nagel suggests, however, that 'consideration of these very unusual cases should cause us to be sceptical about the concept of a single subject of consciousness as it applies to ourselves'.[19] Nagel claims that we think of our own unity as 'in some sense numerically absolute, rather than relative and a function of the integration of its contents'.[20] This, he says, is 'quite genuinely an illusion'. How well, though, does Nagel argue for his verdict about split brains? The verdict implied by animalism is that there is a single subject, the human animal, which is also the person. It is not as such committed to any further theoretical description of the case. When Nagel discusses the issues he does so in terms of 'how many minds' the patients have. However, the relation between questions about the number of minds and the number of persons or subjects is not straightforward. Does it, for example, make sense to suppose that a single subject, or person, has *two* minds? The significance of 'mind' talk in philosophy is, I believe, deeply obscure. However, Nagel evidently assumes that the principle, one mind per person, is unquestionable, and it is better, therefore, to read his arguments, which are explicitly designed to establish difficulties with *mind*-counting, as directly bearing on *subject*-counting and to reformulate the conclusion correspondingly.

Nagels' strategy is to consider five hypotheses about the number of what I am calling subjects and to reject them all. Three of them are consistent with the claim, to which animalists are committed, that there is a single subject. The first two, however, preserve that claim by relegating, in rather different ways, all the occurrences in the right hemisphere to the status of not being experiences. This is not, I take it, an appealing manoeuvre, so I shall treat the third single-subject option which Nagel discusses as the one which corresponds to the animalist verdict. Nagel states it thus: 'they [i.e. the

---

[15] See Nagel (1979: 147–64).   [16] Nagel (1979: 146).   [17] Nagel (1979: 163).
[18] It does not obviously follow that human beings in general do not satisfy the requirements of the concept of a single subject. It does not follow either that there are no such things anywhere 'in heaven and earth'.
[19] Nagel (1979: 163).   [20] Nagel (1979: 163).

patients] have one mind, whose contents derive from both hemispheres and are rather peculiar and dissociated'.[21] Why, according to Nagel, should we *not* say this?

Nagel's answer is contained in the following lengthy passage:

This makes it difficult to conceive what it is like to *be* one of these people. Lack of interaction at the level of a preconscious control system would be comprehensible. But lack of interaction in the domain of visual experience and conscious intention threatens assumptions about the unity of consciousness which are basic to our understanding of another individual as a person. These assumptions are associated with our conception of ourselves, which to a considerable extent constrains our understanding of others. And it is just these assumptions, I believe, that make it impossible to arrive at an interpretation of the cases under discussion in terms of a countable number of minds.

Roughly, we assume that a single mind has sufficiently immediate access to its conscious states so that, for elements of experience or other mental events occurring simultaneously or in close temporal proximity, the mind which is their subject can also experience the simpler relations between them if it attends to the matter. Thus we assume that when a single person has two visual impressions, he can usually also experience the sameness or difference of their coloration, shape, size, the relation of their position and movement within his visual field, and so forth.[22]

Nagel's line of thought is that there is a principle about experiences which are enjoyed by a single subject (or mind) which requires that they are, in some sense, experienced together, and hence can be compared by the subject. Not all the experiences of the split-brain patient are so linked. They cannot, therefore, be the experiences of a single subject. The principle upon which Nagel's argument relies is, roughly, this: if a subject P has experiences E1 and E2 at t then the experiences occur to P in such a way that, if P is able to make cognitive judgements, P will be able to know easily and immediately some truth which concerns both E1 and E2.[23]

Some Problems

It seems that if the principle is accepted we cannot suppose that all the experiences in a split-brain patient are enjoyed by a single subject. There are pairs of experiences which will not be known about together. The question to ask is: is the proposed principle *true*? Indeed, I think the question we should ask is: where does the sense that such a principle is true *so much as come from*? Since a lot depends on whether it is true, proponents of it are under an obligation to give it a substantial justification. It cannot be good enough simply to cite it as a *plausible intuition*.

---

[21] Nagel (1979: 155).   [22] Nagel (1979: 160).

[23] I include the condition 'if P is able to make cognitive judgements' so as to enable the condition to apply to creatures with experiences but without judgement. How one knows that such a complex conditional property applies to them is of course another matter.

Now, in Nagel's advocacy of a such a principle it is a little unclear whether his view is that it is, simply, a basic commitment that we have, or whether it is a commitment derived from, or held in place by, aspects of experience and of subjects. If Nagel's view is the former, then it faces two immediate challenges. The first is to be told what the evidence is that we do have a basic commitment to such a principle. Maybe we would think it is true prior to any serious thought or consideration of evidence, but that cannot be transformed into the idea that we simply cannot abandon it. The second challenge is to say why we should not consider abandoning it. Why cannot we develop an acceptable view which does not endorse it?

We clearly need more if we are to commit to the principle. What is there? One process of thought which, I suggest, typically leads to acceptance of the principle is that of imagining a subject S (perhaps oneself) having experience E1, and experience E2, and, on that basis, being inclined to think that S *must* be able to compare E1 and E2. Although the widespread acceptance of such unity principles is testimony to the psychological power which such imaginative thought processes have, when described for what it is it *seems* a remarkably flimsy basis for accepting the principle. The imaginer, by knowingly imagining two experiences, is in a position to compare them, but is there not a risk of confusing the imaginer's capacity with the capacities, if any, of comparison in the subject which we are aiming to determine? How can thinkers who are impressed by this little act of imagination be confident that they have not confused what they are capable of with what *the subject* must be capable of?

What Experience Must Be Like

Having posed the above question, which raises the allegation that acceptance of the disputed principle rests solely on a confusion between what the *imaginer* is capable of and what the subject is capable of, how is a defender of the principle to keep the argument going? I think that one response that might be offered, and there are traces of this in Nagel's discussion, is the claim that experiences are, in their very nature, things which it is like to undergo or enjoy. They are, therefore, things which can be represented by another as like something to undergo. Imagining accurately what experiences are like just is representing them properly. So, what is involved in imagining them must correspond to how things are for the subject.[24]

There are, of course, obscurities in this defence which I have credited to defenders of the principle. But assuming its drift is clear enough, I wish to suggest that it does not provide a cogent basis to accept the principle. The crucial difficulty is this: suppose that we agree with the principle that any experience E1 is (in its nature as an experience) such that it is like something for the subject to undergo, it does not follow, from considerations of general logic, or anything else that I can see, that for any *pairs* of experiences E1 and E2 which a single subject is enjoying it is like something to *jointly* experience

---

[24] I have tried to formulate a response which Nagel's remarks suggest that he might make.

them. We simply remain without a reason to accept that.[25] Moreover, if the singularist approach to split-brain patients is correct then, of course, some experiences of such patients are counterexamples to the principle. There is nothing it is *like* to have a split brain, and for some pairs of experiences enjoyed by a split-brain patient there is nothing it is like to conjointly have them. It is, therefore, akin to begging the question simply to affirm that the simultaneous experiences of a single subject must be something it is like to undergo as a whole. We are still without a reason to accept that principle.

To this I want to add two things. The first is that it is obvious that in general understanding another does not require us to ground that understanding in 'knowing what it is like' for them. This is obvious in many cases of cognitive deficits or quirks which life can throw up. Thus, it is not possible to understand blind-sight by knowing what it is like for the subject. Rather, they have limited experiences but an extra cognitive capacity ungrounded in those experiences. There is, it is surely obvious, nothing in what it is like for them which explains or aids in the explaining of their capacity. With such people we can describe their capacities and understand them by locating the physical mechanisms at work. This case shows that psychological understanding cannot be equated with 'knowing what the condition is like for the subject'.

The second point is that our understanding of others even in relation to what their experiences mean or do for them is not necessarily centred on knowing what these experiences are like for the responding subject. The example I wish to use to illustrate this point comes from Humphreys and Riddoch (1987). They describe a patient, John, suffering from a type of agnosia. He looks at a drawing of a nose, which depicts the outline, nostril, and inner edge. He sees the different lines, which he can draw with relative ease, but fails to see it *as a nose*.[26] In fact, he takes it to be a drawing of a ladle. Suppose we ask: what was John's experience like when he saw the drawing of a nose that explains why he failed to recognize it? It seems to me that we have grave difficulties in answering that question, difficulties which are so grave that we should be inclined to deny there is any chance of explaining John's deficit by saying what it is like for him. For what can be said? It cannot be said that John had an experience which was like the experience *we* get on seeing those lines, because part of our experience is recognizing it as a nose-drawing. That is what John did not do. It cannot, for two reasons, be said that it was like our experience minus the recognition. First, this subtraction does not pick out what it was positively like. Second, this description simply says what went on, when the aim was to render what went on intelligible in the light of what it was like for the subject. There seems to be no other way of picking out what it was like. I conclude that in such a case we have no understanding grounded in knowing what it was like.

---

[25] I am trying to generate some scepticism about the principle that Nagel's argument relies on without, here, being sceptical about the link between experience and what-it-is-likeness. My views on that link are presented in Snowdon (2010).

[26] See Humphreys and Riddoch (1987: 59–61).

For these two general reasons it seems to me to be an illusion to seek to explain psychological capacities and responses in terms of what it is like. This means that adopting a singularist account of split-brain patients which prevents us explaining what is going on in terms of what it is like, does not, in any way, threaten the application of something that is essential to our normal mode of understanding others.

I conclude that defending Nagel's principle by appeal to the explanatory role of knowing how what was going on was like is quite unpersuasive and that we lack any other good reason to accept it. At this point we should give expression to the weakest remark that might be made on behalf of the principle. It might be pointed out that it is at least true that we do assume *in normal circumstances* that subjects can 'compare' in some respects their joint experiences. The response to this remark is obvious. Even if we do assume it, that gives us no reason for thinking it represents a necessary condition for a single subject to have multiple experiences *whatever has happened to that subject*.

Conclusion

I have been trying to generate some scepticism about the conviction that there are principles about the unity of mental states that a single subject enjoys which count against the singularist verdict in split-brain cases. I have done little more than scratch the surface here. But it does seem to me that the animalist treatment remains undefeated, and also that unity principles along the lines investigated here lack good support.

Here is one bit of evolutionary make-believe to strengthen this present approach. Imagine the time when nervous systems were evolving. Let us suppose a type of animal emerged that had a nervous system rather like the one that patients who have had a commissurotomy end up having in terms of its general organization, but which is not as advanced as human patients. There is, it seems to me, nothing odd in the above description. I myself cannot see that this description generates any worries. Moreover, such types of creatures could have remained in existence, and, indeed, might still be in existence. Do we know there are no such animals? That an operation has rendered some humans like this seems equally untroubling.

How then should we think about subjects and unity? Here is a sketch. We should explore, it seems to me, the idea that our understanding of unity of ownership is grounded in the presence in our world of subjects to which we ascribe a multiplicity of mental states, the obvious cases being advanced animals and the manifestly animal-like things that we are. We perceive them and ourselves as complex mentally endowed entities. Our understanding of things having a range of simultaneous mental states is grounded in this predicative practice. It then becomes an empirical question to what degree the mental states owned by such single objects are functionally unified. We tend to have simple assumptions about that, but on reflection should hold that we do not know what degree of functional unity there is. We should stand prepared to recognize that it might quite generally be, and certainly can in unusual cases be, restricted and limited. We really have no vantage point from which to declare that split-brain cases conflict with the implications of unity of ownership. I see this as an illustration of the potential insights generated by animalism.[27]

References

Bayne T. (2010) *The Unity of Consciousness* (Oxford: Oxford University Press).

Humphreys G. W. and Riddoch M. T. (1987) *To See but not to See* (Hove: Taylor and Francis Group).

Mackie J. L. (1976) *Problems from Locke* (Oxford: Oxford University Press).

Marks C. E. (1981) *Commisurotomy, Consciousness and the Unity of Mind* (Cambridge, MA: MIT Press).

Nagel T. (1971) 'Brain Bissection and the Unity of Consciousness'. *Synthese* 22: 396–413.

Nagel T. (1979) *Mortal Questions* (Cambridge: Cambridge University Press).

Snowdon P. F. (2010) 'On the What-it-is-likeness of Experience'. *The Southern Journal of Philosophy* 48(1): 8–27.

Sperry R. W. (1974) 'Lateral Specialization in the Surgically Separated Hemispheres' in Schmitt F. O. and Worden F. G. (eds), *Neuroscience*, 3rd Study Programme (Cambridge, MA: MIT Press).

[27] I wish to thank Stephan Blatti for help and support in writing this, and Jonathan Dancy and Marie McGinn for discussion a few years ago which improved my understanding of these issues.

14

Animal Ethics

Jens Johansson

14.1. Introduction

I am an animal. But don't misunderstand: I am not suggesting that I should be on a leash, served as dinner, or prevented from voting. Rather, I want to give a rough formulation of a certain view of personal identity, the doctrine often called "animalism." While animalism is much more popular nowadays than it was until about twenty years ago (a development largely due to Olson 1997; Snowdon 1990; van Inwagen 1990), most philosophers still reject it. One important reason to do so is that the theory has counter-intuitive ethical consequences—especially in cases where a person's psychology is transferred to another organism. In such a case, animalism seems to yield the odd result that I should have prudential concern about someone else's future and not about my own, and that I am morally responsible for what someone else has done but not for what I myself have done. In this chapter, I shall discuss this sort of objection against animalism, with special attention to Eric Olson's responses (1997: ch. 3). While I find these somewhat wanting, I shall suggest at the end of the chapter another kind of animalist response. As I will note, it has some similarities with the most influential argument in favor of animalism, the "thinking animal" argument.

14.2. Animalism: What It Is, and Isn't

"I am an animal." This is true if animalism is true. Still, it will hardly do as a precise formulation of the theory. For instance, animalism does not depend logically on my own existence, whereas "I am an animal" does so depend (nonexistent things are not animals). What, then, would be a more adequate formulation of the view?

A natural approach is to define animalism as the thesis that all people are animals.[1] This does not work, however, because the animalist can happily accept the existence of

---

[1] Like Olson and most non-philosophers, I use "people" as the plural of "person." Many participants in the personal identity debate prefer "persons," which perhaps sounds more dignified and flattering. (If mice, teeth, and feet were discussing their own nature, maybe they would similarly prefer the terms "mouses," "tooths," and "foots.")

non-animal people, such as Martians, computers, robots, angels, and gods. For example, animalist Peter van Inwagen's otherwise sparse ontology includes angels and the God of Christianity. Animalism does not say anything about such people; it is concerned with people like you and I (the reader and author of this paper), Queen Elizabeth II, Gabriel García Márquez, and Rafael Nadal—not with the Queen of Mars or Archangels Gabriel and Raphael.

This consideration suggests that animalism could instead be defined as the view that all *human* people are animals (Olson 2003: 320). While the issue is complex (see Johansson 2007), this formulation is good enough for the purposes of the present chapter. It must be emphasized, though, that the term "human person" should not here be regarded as synonymous with "person who is an animal of the species *Homo sapiens*." That would render animalism trivial; even the most uncompromising Cartesian dualist will grant that anything satisfying *that* description is an animal. Instead, we should take "human person" to mean the same as "person whose body is an animal of the species *Homo sapiens*." This makes animalism a nontrivial view. For the theory's opponents—"anti-animalists," as I shall call them—can now contend, without incoherence, that although I am a human person, I am not an animal. I am intimately related to an animal, they'll concede, but I am not it, but instead (to list some of the alternatives) a soul; a compound of soul and organism; a material object that is "constituted" by but not identical to an organism; a temporal part of an organism; or a bundle of perceptions.

Some take animalism to include modal elements. For instance, it is sometimes asked, "Are we essentially people or essentially animals?"—and animalism is then identified with the latter answer, that we are essentially animals (e.g. Holtug 2010: 60, 70). In my opinion, this is a bit misleading, and slightly biased against animalism. It gives the impression that anti-animalists can accept the animalists' attractive claim that we are both people and animals, and that animalists and anti-animalists disagree only when we turn to modal issues. This picture is dubious for several reasons. I certainly do not deny that animalists should believe that we are essentially animals. For whether or not animalism is true, it is very plausible that animals—including human animals, animals of the species *Homo sapiens*—are essentially animals. But precisely for that very reason, there is little space for the view that we are animals contingently. Moreover, if we are animals (essentially or not), we can hardly be people essentially, or even essentially have mental features. For example, each human animal has once been an embryo, which at that point lacked psychological properties altogether (see also Section 14.3). So it seems clear that being a person is not essential to any human animal.

There is also another, related source of confusion. According to some philosophers, the anti-animalist can hold that we are animals, so long as she denies that we are *identical* to animals. We can realize this, it is suggested, if we take note of the distinction between the "is" ("be," "am," "are") of identity and other kinds of "is" ("be," "am," "are"), such as that of predication, or that of constitution. The "is" of identity is the one that occurs in "Elizabeth II is the present Queen of the United Kingdom" and "I am the author of this paper"; the "is" of predication is the one that occurs in "Elizabeth II is a queen" and "I am an author"; the "is" of constitution is, supposedly, the one that occurs in "This statue of Elizabeth II is a piece of marble" and "This copyright assignment is a piece of paper," used by someone who holds that the statue and the copyright assignment, respectively, are constituted by but numerically distinct from the pieces of marble and paper. The idea is that while the animalist accepts "I am an animal" in the identity sense of "is," the anti-animalist is free to accept it in one of the other two (Baker 2000: 54–7; Campbell 2006: 348; DeGrazia 2002: 106; Shoemaker 2008: 318; not all these writers appeal to both latter senses).

Maybe English does contain the "is" of constitution, in which case some anti-animalists are indeed allowed to say that I am an animal in that sense—if they really must. One may wonder, however, what the point is in speaking in such a misleading way, instead of saying "I am constituted by but not identical to an animal." (For less mild complaints, see Olson 2003: 319; 2007: 24.) In any case, the rest of the proposal is doubly puzzling. First, the animalist has no reason to think that "I am an animal" involves the "is" of identity. The "is" of identity is flanked by singular terms, and "an animal" is not a singular term. If animalism is true, I am an animal in the predicative sense of "is"—in exactly the same sense that I am an author. Second, it holds quite generally that if x is predicatively an F, then x is *identical* to an F: namely, x. If I am predicatively an author, I am identical to an author—myself; if I am predicatively an animal, I am identical to an animal—myself. (Note that this does not imply that the "is" in "I am an animal" is that of identity. Not even "I am identical to an animal" involves the "is" of identity; "identical to an animal" is not a singular term.) Consequently, there is no room for the proposed view that I am predicatively an animal but not identical to an animal.

Maybe some anti-animalists insist on saying "I am an animal" because they do not want to be thought of as denying that we are much more closely related to animals than to the bodies of Martians, computers, robots, angels, and gods. And indeed, if we use the term "animal" in some suitably loose sense—e.g. as meaning "individual whose body is a member of some biological species"—then the sentence "I am an animal" will be true even if animalism is not (cf. Shoemaker 2008: 318). (Of course, "I am identical to an animal" will also be true in this loose sense of "animal," even if animalism is false.) This also would be a misleading way of talking. In any event, it has nothing to do with different senses of "is," but with different senses of "animal."

14.3. The Persistence of Animals

Animalism is in conflict with a widely endorsed theory of what it takes for us to persist through time. I shall briefly (and wholly unoriginally; see Olson 1994; 1997; van Inwagen 1997) explain why the conflict is there, as it underlies much of the discussion to come.

I was once a schoolboy. What makes it the case that I am identical to him; in virtue of what are he and I one individual rather than two? According to the most popular view of personal identity over time, the "psychological approach," the answer is that I am the person who is now psychologically continuous with the schoolboy, as he was then. Alternatively put, I am the person whose current mental features—memories, beliefs, desires, intentions, personality traits, etc.—have, in the right kind of way, grown out of those that he had at that earlier point.[2]

The definite article ("*the* person") is intentional. As we shall see, a person can be psychologically continuous with two (or more) future people. For this reason, standard versions of the psychological approach contain a "non-branching" requirement: if there had been two people who are now psychologically continuous with the boy as he was at the earlier time, he would not have existed now.[3] The theory can be refined in various other ways as well, an opportunity that has not been left unexploited in the debate (e.g. many writers are busy specifying what the "right kind of way" is). We can largely ignore such complications here, because all versions of the view are in conflict with animalism.

For if animalism is correct, psychology is utterly irrelevant to our persistence. Admittedly, this does not follow logically from animalism itself: animalism is after all not a theory of personal identity over time—not even of the identity over time of *human* people. Still, it does logically imply that we have the persistence conditions of animals. And animals persist by virtue of purely biological processes—metabolism, respiration, digestion, etc.—that have nothing to do with psychology. (We need not deny that psychological states are biological. Even if they are, it is not in virtue of these that animals persist through time.) While this claim is not a component of animalism, it seems clearly true nonetheless.

First, psychological continuity is not *necessary* for animal identity over time. As noted earlier, each human organism has once been an embryo, which at that time did not have any mental states whatever, and thus failed to be psychologically continuous with anything. Moreover, a human organism can enter a permanent vegetative state, where it is still alive but has lost its psychology. According to a more controversial argument (rightly so, in my opinion), every human organism loses its psychology *and* life at death, but—unless the death is extraordinarily violent—still continues to exist for a while as a corpse (e.g. Feldman 1992: ch. 6; 2000; 2013; Mackie 1999).

Second, psychological continuity—even non-branching psychological continuity—is not *sufficient* for animal identity over time. To substantiate this judgment, we can consider a more extravagant scenario, with its roots in Locke's case of a prince and a cobbler (cf. Olson 1997: 42–4). Imagine that the cerebrum of a prince, call him

---

[2] Some think that the concepts of memory and intention presuppose identity over time. I use "memory" and "intention" (and related terms) in an identity-neutral way here, however, meaning what others mean by "quasi-memory" and "quasi-intention."

[3] The main alternative to the "non-branching" requirement is to espouse David Lewis's "multiple occupancy" thesis (Lewis 1976). On this view, if a person is psychologically continuous with two future people, then there is another person where she is right now, sharing her present matter and psychology.

"Charles," is transferred in a reliable way to (what has at least until now been) shoe designer Cesare's head, whose earlier cerebrum has been taken out and destroyed. Because the cerebrum is that part of the brain which is responsible for mentality, this procedure has the result that the cerebrum "recipient" is, after the transplant, psychologically continuous with the "donor" animal—the animal from which Charles's cerebrum has been removed—as the latter was prior to the transplant. However, the recipient is decidedly not identical to the donor animal: the surgeons have not moved an animal, only an organ. (This case also provides additional support for the thesis that psychological continuity is not *necessary* for animal identity over time. So long as the relevant biological processes continue, the "donor" animal still exists, despite its loss of the cerebrum and of all its royal thoughts.)

Did Charles himself lose his cerebrum and psychology (instead of being moved to a new body) when the surgeons performed the transplant? Did Cesare acquire an entirely new psychology? Have I been an embryo? Can I enter a permanent vegetative state? If animalism is true, the answer to each of these questions is "Yes." If the psychological approach is true, the answer to each of them is "No."

If animalism were compatible with the psychological approach, the problems we shall now discuss—about prudential concern and moral responsibility—would not arise. But the incompatibility is there; and they do arise.

14.4. Two Arguments from Prudential Concern

Personal identity over time seems to be of crucial importance to the justification of "prudential concern" (Olson 1997: 52–3). Prudential concern is the kind of concern that an individual ordinarily has for herself and for no one else. If you tell me that someone is going to be tortured tomorrow, I may well feel sad, and even be prepared to make several sacrifices in order to prevent the torture. This is not *prudential* concern, however. On the other hand, if you add that this future torture victim is *me*, I am immediately filled with a remarkably different set of attitudes. I anticipate the experience "from the inside" and with no small amounts of horror. Even if I couldn't care less about, for instance, my friends' suffering in having to watch the torture, I would be willing to do almost anything to avoid it. *This* is prudential concern.

Arguably, not only is this how I actually react to your additional piece of news; my prudential concern also seems *justified*, in the sense of being appropriate or fitting: the future torture *merits* or *deserves* my prudential concern. (My prudential concern may or may not also be justified in a "practical" sense: my prudential concern might have good consequences. But this practical sense is not what is at issue here. Compare: it may well be fitting for me to be ashamed of my singing voice, even if this shame only brings me pain; and it may well fail to be fitting for you to admire me, even if I'll kill you if you don't.) By contrast, if *you* have prudential concern about my future suffering, knowing fully well that you are going to be miles away when it takes place, then your attitude does not seem justified.

Whence this difference? Plausibly, the answer has a lot to do with personal identity over time—more specifically, with the fact that I am going to have the painful experience in question, whereas you are not. The following principles suggest themselves:

PC1.   If a person would be justified in having prudential concern for a future experience, then she is going to have that experience.

PC2.   If a person is going to have a future experience, then she would be justified in having prudential concern for that experience.[4]

These principles have a good deal of initial plausibility. And this fact ought to worry the animalist. To see why, let us return to the strange case of Charles and Cesare.

Suppose that, prior to the operation, a not particularly uplifting announcement is made. We are informed that, when Charles's cerebrum has been successfully transferred to Cesare's head, the resulting person—the one with (what has at least up to the time of the transplant been) Charles's psychology—is going to be mercilessly tortured. Surely both Charles and Cesare, as well as everyone else, would be justified in finding this fact highly regrettable. But it also seems that Charles would be justified in having *prudential* concern, before the operation, about the future torture. If the news terrifies him and he wishes to escape to the other side of the earth, his reaction seems perfectly fitting. PC1 thus tells us that he is going to experience the torture (this is also the verdict delivered by the psychological approach). But if animalism is true, he is not; the instruments will not touch him. Indeed, if animalism is true, Charles is never going to experience anything at all after the transplant (unless, of course, another cerebrum is placed in his empty skull).

Cesare, on the other hand—who does not have more in common psychologically with the torture victim than he has with you or me—would apparently not be justified in having prudential concern about the future pain. PC2 then dictates that he is not going to experience it. Yet if animalism is true, this is precisely what he is going to do. This is too bad—not for Cesare, but for animalism.

14.5. The Problem Spreads

Too bad for animalism, indeed; however, it might be worth noting in passing that far from all anti-animalists have reason to be pleased. For analogous problems will confront any view of what kind of thing we are that is inconsistent with the psychological approach. And there are plenty of such views, including some that are very distant from animalism (Merricks 1999; Olson 1994; van Inwagen 1997; 2002).

---

[4] The subjunctive "would" is there because the principles should not only cover cases in which the person actually does have prudential concern. The important thing is under what circumstances it is true that prudential concern *would* be justified *if* the person were to have it. For simplicity, I've left that antecedent—i.e. "if the person were to have it"—implicit in the principles. (It is the antecedent of PC1's antecedent and of PC2's consequent.)

Consider, for instance, the dualist thesis that we are immaterial souls. Seemingly, just as an animal can be psychologically continuous with another individual than itself, so can a soul. Suppose that Charles's psychological features will somehow move from his current soul (the soul that he is identical to, on this dualist view) to Cesare's, whose current psychology will be erased. If Charles and Cesare, before this process has begun, are prudentially concerned about a future pain that the "recipient" soul is going to be subjected to, it seems that Charles's prudential concern is justified, while Cesare's is not. Given PC1 and PC2, then, Charles is going to experience the pain, and Cesare is not. But this is incompatible with the dualist thesis. Charles's soul simply loses its psychology; it does not become the "recipient" soul. No matter how impressive a soul might be in several ways, it is not capable of becoming identical with something other than itself.

Similar points apply to many other anti-animalist views as well, e.g. the rival dualist thesis that I am a compound of soul and organism. Not even the view that I am a cerebrum will escape the difficulty. For cerebrums do not seem to persist by virtue of psychological continuity: if cerebrums have beliefs, memories, intentions, and so forth, it seems that these can be transferred from one cerebrum to another.

Thus, animalism is not uniquely vulnerable to the problem. But of course, this does not mean that it is not vulnerable to it.[5] How should the animalist respond?

14.6. Help from an Unexpected Source

One strategy would be to argue against the contention that Charles's prudential concern about the torture is justified and that Cesare's is not. While this is not an obviously hopeless strategy (cf. Williams 1970), it will not be pursued here.

Eric Olson, in his defense of animalism against this kind of criticism, reminds us that many philosophers—especially adherents of the psychological approach—have been convinced of the truth of what he calls the "Parfit–Shoemaker Thesis" (Olson 1997: 54). According to this thesis, justified prudential concern does not always follow personal identity over time. The anti-animalist objections from prudential concern, on the other hand, apparently presuppose that it does.

So far as I can see, Olson himself neither affirms nor rejects the Parfit–Shoemaker Thesis. Rather, he seems to make the more modest point that, because the Parfit–Shoemaker Thesis is fairly plausible independently of animalism, the anti-animalist arguments from prudential concern are unpersuasive. But this more modest point is still of substantial interest.

Why, then, is the Parfit–Shoemaker Thesis fairly plausible? The principal argument for the thesis appeals to so-called "fission" (e.g. Parfit 1984: §§89–90; 1993; 1995).

---

[5] Things would be different if *no* view of what kind of thing we were were compatible with the psychological approach. But some are, especially those that take us to have temporal parts (see, again, Merricks 1999; Olson 1994; van Inwagen 1997; 2002).

Consider first a simpler case, which does not involve fission. The left half of my cerebrum is reliably transferred to another organism (whose former cerebrum has been
removed), and the right half is destroyed. After the transplant, the resulting person, "A,"
is psychologically continuous with me as I was before the transplant; half a cerebrum
suffices for this. It seems that I would be justified in having pre-transplant prudential
concern about A's post-transplant experiences. Thus far no strong support for the
Parfit–Shoemaker Thesis: most philosophers hold that I am A in this scenario (animalists disagree, of course).

But consider next a slightly more complicated variant of this story, one that does
involve fission. Let the case be as before, except that the right half of my cerebrum is
not destroyed, but instead reliably transferred to yet another, third organism. After the
transplant, each of the resulting people, "B" and "C," is psychologically continuous
with me, as I was earlier. Apparently, I would be just as justified in having pre-transplant
prudential concern for the post-transplant experiences of B as I was, in the simpler
case, in having pre-transplant prudential concern for those of A. After all, my relation
to B does not differ, intrinsically speaking, from my relation to A. The fact that there is
also another person, C, to whom I stand in the same kind of relation, does not make
my concern for B's future experiences any less fitting. And for similar reasons, it seems
that I would also be justified in having prudential concern about the future experiences of C.

However, I cannot be identical to both B and C. For this would imply that B is identical to C, which is clearly not the case: B and C are two individuals, not one. (Hence the
non-branching requirement of standard versions of the psychological approach.) The
fission scenario, then, seems to involve justified prudential concern in the absence of personal identity over time. If it does, the Parfit–Shoemaker Thesis is correct; if it is, the anti-
animalist objections from prudential concern fail.

14.7. But Hardly Enough

This is too quick. The separation between prudential concern and personal identity
that the Parfit–Shoemaker Thesis sanctions seems significantly less radical than the
one that animalism leads to (cf. Unger 2000). This can be brought out particularly
clearly if we compare the fission argument's consequences for animalism to those it
has for the psychological approach.

First, section IV contained two anti-animalist arguments from prudential concern,
and the fission case undermines at most one of them. It may well refute the argument
based on PC1, i.e. the principle that personal identity over time is *necessary* for justified prudential concern. However, since the fission scenario does not involve personal
identity over time in the absence of justified prudential concern—only the reverse—it
leaves standing the argument based on PC2: the principle that personal identity over
time is *sufficient* for justified special concern. (The same point applies to the other
common arguments for the Parfit–Shoemaker Thesis, e.g. appeals to teletransportation.)

While PC2 thus continues to threaten animalism, it sits pretty well with the psycho-logical approach. One important lesson that the fission case seems to teach us is that psychological continuity—which obtains between me and each of the fission products, B and C—is sufficient for justified prudential concern. If this is indeed so, *non-branching* psychological continuity is of course also sufficient for justified prudential concern. Thus, given the psychological approach, whenever there is personal identity over time, prudential concern would be justified—just as PC2 says.

Second, even if PC1 does not work, it seems that it can be modified in light of the fission scenario. Recall first that, according to the psychological approach, psycho-logical continuity is a necessary condition of personal identity over time. And this is so in a rather strong sense of "necessary condition." In a weaker sense, a relation is a necessary condition of personal identity over time just in case, necessarily, if I am iden-tical to someone who exists at another time, then that relation holds between him and me. In this sense, there are lots of relations that are, uncontroversially, necessary condi-tions of personal identity over time: e.g. *being either identical with or numerically dis-tinct from*. But in the stronger sense I am thinking of, a relation is a necessary condition of personal identity over time just in case, necessarily, if I am identical to someone existing at another time, then this is at least partly *in virtue of* the fact that this relation holds between us; the relation is part of what *grounds* personal identity over time. Trivial relations, such as *being either identical with or numerically distinct from*, do not satisfy this stronger requirement. However, on the psychological approach, psycho-logical (but not biological) continuity satisfies it; and if animalism is true, biological (but not psychological) continuity satisfies it.

With this in mind, consider this revision of PC1:

PC3.   If a person would be justified in having prudential concern for a future experience, then she stands in a relation that is a necessary condition (in the stronger sense specified above) of personal identity over time to someone who is going to have that experience.

On the psychological approach, I do stand in such a relation—psychological continuity—to each of B and C in the fission case. Therefore, while the fission case might falsify PC1, it does not prevent advocates of the psychological approach from embracing PC3. And this is an advantage of the psychological approach, because PC3 seems to preserve quite a lot of the intuitively attractive idea that justified prudential concern is intimately connected to personal identity over time.

By contrast, animalism does not sit significantly better with PC3 than it does with PC1. On animalism, I do not stand in any relation to B or C that is a necessary condition (in the stronger sense) of personal identity over time. Moreover, on ani-malism, in contrast to the psychological approach, it is not the case that Charles before the transplant stands in such a relation to the torture victim. The fittingness of Charles's prudential concern, therefore, is still troublesome for animalism—even without PC1.

Third, it is somewhat attractive to say that it is *indeterminate* what happens to me in the fission case. This is Parfit's view (Parfit 1993; see also Johansson 2010). More precisely, Parfit maintains that each of the following four theses is neither true nor false: (i) I cease to exist at fission; (ii) I am B; (iii) I am C; (iv) I am the fusion of B and C (that is, after fission I am a mentally and spatially scattered object, composed of both B and C). Though Parfit says that (i) gives the "best description" of what happens, he emphasizes that this does not mean that (i) is true.

Clearly, the psychological approach can be construed so as to yield this result. Such a view could be stated roughly as follows: if there is non-branching psychological continuity between me and someone existing at a future time, then it is true that I am him; if there is no psychological continuity between us, then it is false that I am him; and if there is branching psychological continuity, then it is indeterminate whether I exist at that future time and, if so, which individual existing then I am identical to.

Given such a view, it seems natural to endorse the following principle:

PC4.   If a person would be justified in having prudential concern for a future experience, then it is not false that she is going to have that experience.

This principle too should embarrass the animalist. For in the case of Charles and Cesare, the animalist must say that it *is* false that Charles is going to experience the torture. Likewise, in the fission case, the animalist must say that it *is* false that I am going to have B's or C's experiences.

We can go further. There is considerable intuitive force to the idea that I am justified in having prudential concern about a future experience only if I exist at that future time—i.e. only if I am identical to someone existing then. This also could be accommodated by the psychological approach. We could say that in cases of branching, it is true (not indeterminate) that I am identical to some individual who exists at the future time (namely, someone with whom I am psychologically continuous), but it is indeterminate which individual this is (Williams 2008: 151; cf. Johansson 2010). This implies that, in the fission case, I am identical to B or C, but for each of them, it is neither true nor false that I am identical to him. Friends of this view could affirm a stronger principle than PC4:

PC5.   If a person would be justified in having prudential concern for a future experience, then she exists at that future time and it is not false that she is going to have that experience.

Animalism is even less congenial with this principle than with PC4. Suppose that the "donor" animal—the animal from which Charles's cerebrum is removed—ceases to exist before the torture. Then animalism implies that both conjuncts of PC5's consequent fail to hold in this case.

Of course, indeterminacy of personal identity is far from unproblematic (especially since indeterminate identity in general is far from unproblematic; see e.g. Evans 1978). But nor is it an uncommon or obviously false idea. Arguably, one thing that speaks in its favor is the very fact that it accommodates substantial portions of the intuitive view that justified prudential concern is very closely connected to personal identity over time. So it does seem to strengthen the case against animalism that certain forms of the psychological approach go nicely together with PC4 and PC5, whereas animalism does not.

This section's three main points suggest, I think, that the animalist cannot find as much comfort in the fission case as one might have thought. It is not that I accept any of PC1–PC5. But my reason for doubting them (see Sections 14.11–14.12) is not the same as Olson's.

14.8. Two Arguments from Moral Responsibility

Personal identity over time also seems to have considerable bearing on moral responsibility (Olson 1997: 57–62). If I stole a magazine from my local store yesterday, I am now morally responsible for this action: I deserve blame and punishment, and my bad conscience is perfectly appropriate. It seems equally clear that you, who had nothing whatsoever to do with the theft, totally lack moral responsibility for it. Whence this difference? Plausibly, the answer has a lot to do with personal identity over time—more specifically, with the fact that I performed the action in question, whereas you did not. The following principles suggest themselves:

MR1.   If a person is now morally responsible for a certain earlier action, then she has performed that action.

MR2.   If a person has performed a certain earlier action, then she is now morally responsible for that action.

Each of these two principles poses a serious threat to animalism. Again, this can be illustrated by the case of Charles and Cesare. One day before the operation, let us suppose, both of them acted in ways that fell somewhat short of moral perfection: Charles insulted his mother at a royal family gathering, and Cesare kicked his neighbor in the leg. After the transplant, it seems, the person who has ended up with Charles's pre-transplant cerebrum and psychology—call him "D"—is morally responsible for the insult. He deserves blame for it, and owes Charles's mother an apology. If this is right, MR1 judges that D has delivered the insult. But this is incompatible with animalism: if animalism is true, D was not even present when the insult was uttered and has probably never even met Charles's mother.

Furthermore, it seems that D has no moral responsibility for what Cesare did before the transplant. So far as the kick is concerned—an action that D doesn't have the faintest recollection of, and which is entirely contrary to his character—D's conscience is clean; and this seems wholly appropriate. If so, MR2 tells us that D didn't kick Cesare's neighbor. Animalism, on the other hand, tells us that he did; animalism tells us that D *is* Cesare.

As Olson points out (1997: 58), the scope of these principles may have to be restricted, for reasons independent of animalism. MR1 may fail in some cases of unequal relations: for example, parents might be morally responsible for their children's actions, and the Queen for the Queen's Guard's. MR2 may fail in some cases involving lack of "moral competence": for example, I might be without moral responsibility now for an earlier action if I was then, or if I now am, mentally deranged. However, with the scope of MR1 and MR2 suitably restricted—i.e. to cases where such factors are not present—the principles look plausible. And the restrictions do not help animalism, for we can unproblematically assume that these factors are absent from the case of Charles and Cesare.

14.9. A Continuous Copy?

According to Olson, the Parfit–Shoemaker Thesis speaks against these objections from moral responsibility. Arguably, there is a strong link between a future individual's being an appropriate object of my prudential concern and his being morally responsible for my actions. Hence, if justified prudential concern need not follow personal identity over time, presumably moral responsibility need not do so either. However, Olson suggests that the arguments can be answered even if we suppose that the Parfit–Shoemaker Thesis is false. Let us focus on this latter line of defense.

Start with the argument that is based on MR1, the principle that a person is morally responsible only for actions she herself has performed. (The other argument, based on MR2, is assessed in Section 14.10.) Olson says that when we are inclined to regard D—the person ending up with Charles's cerebrum—as morally responsible for what Charles has done, this is because we are impressed by the facts that D has clear memories of insulting Charles's mother, that D possesses the character traits that Charles had when the insult was made, and so forth.[6] More precisely, we are inclined to subscribe to the following principle:

> MR3.   If a person is psychologically continuous now with someone who has performed an earlier action (as that individual was then), then she is now morally responsible for that action.

But MR3, Olson contends, is incompatible with MR1. If he is right, the argument is clearly in danger. For its premises are then in tension with each other: one of them (MR1) is inconsistent with the main thought (MR3) underlying one of the others (i.e. that D is morally responsible for the insult).

In support of the incompatibility charge, Olson offers a variation of the story. Suppose something goes wrong in the operation's initial stages: Charles dies before

---

[6] Olson's examples do not contain the same individuals or kinds of actions as mine; for ease of exposition, I am taking the liberty of writing as if they did.

the transplant would have begun, and his cerebrum stops functioning. By consulting the detailed information gathered during the preparations, however, the doctors manage in a few days to construct an exact duplicate of Charles as he was shortly before the operation. This creature, "E," has thus very clear memories of Charles's life, except the last moments prior to the operation. According to Olson, MR3 implies that E is morally responsible for the insult. This implication is not entirely absurd, Olson seems to think. But he emphasizes that it is in conflict with MR1, as E is obviously not the same individual as Charles.

In short: if MR3 is true, then E is morally responsible for the insult; if E is morally responsible for the insult, one can be morally responsible for actions one has not performed; and that's just what MR1 asserts that one cannot be.

Is this convincing? It seems to me that Olson's remarks too are in tension with each other. If it is obvious that E is not Charles, then this indicates that MR3 does *not* have the result that E is morally responsible for what Charles has done. For if E and Charles are obviously numerically distinct, they are hardly psychologically continuous with each other—at least not in the sense that proponents of the psychological approach are likely to require for personal identity over time. There are several features of the case that make it strikingly different from that of Charles and D (not to mention more ordinary cases): for instance, considerable time has passed between the mental states that Charles had before his demise and those that E has right after the doctors' work is finished; the latter states are not directly caused by the former; and Charles had a few mental states immediately after those that E's mental states are continuations of. Unless any of these three factors, or some other factor, prevents Charles from being psychologically continuous with E in the sense required by the psychological approach, that approach becomes a little too easy to refute.

Admittedly, it is hard to deny that E is psychologically continuous with Charles in some looser sense. But is there any reason to believe that, when we regard D as morally responsible for Charles's insult, this is because we accept MR3 taken in this looser sense? Such a reason would exist if we were also inclined to believe that E is morally responsible for Charles's insult. For my own part, I lack that inclination, and Olson does not seem to suggest that he or anyone else has it. However, without such a looser reading of MP3, the conflict with MR1 does not arise.

14.10. Mary's Loss of Memory

Turn now to the argument that relies on MR2: if a person has performed some action in the past (and was morally competent then and is morally competent now), then she is now morally responsible for that action. The problem for animalism here was that D does not seem morally responsible after the transplant for Cesare's earlier action (kicking the neighbor); yet if animalism is right, D *is* Cesare (and no lack of moral competence is involved).

Olson does not deny that D is without moral responsibility for the kick, and focuses instead on MR2 (or rather on a slightly stronger principle).[7] Someone could suggest the following counterexample, he says. When Mary was thirty-five she cheated on her income taxes. Now, recently turned forty-five, she completely loses all her memories of what she was up to during her first four decades; she is, however, still morally competent. Is she morally responsible now for her past crime? If she is not, MR2 fails. If she is, as Olson is inclined to think, then this is according to him because she is now psychologically continuous with herself as she was when she committed the crime. (It would be misguided to object that Mary's recent loss of memories must have brought about psychological discontinuity. There's no reason to think that her current mental states—memories and others—cannot have grown out of those she had when she was thirty-five.)

In Olson's view, this shows that a genuine counterexample to MR2 instead has to consist of a case where someone still exists but is no longer psychologically continuous with herself as she was when she performed the relevant action. And whether there is such a case depends on whether a person can persist in the absence of psychological continuity. But, he emphasizes, that is one of the crucial issues in the controversy between animalism and the psychological approach. If animalism is correct, cases like that of D and Cesare constitute counterexamples to MR2. Therefore, Olson seems to hold, the argument from MR2 does not provide any independent ground to reject animalism.

So far, this seems to be a weak response. What Olson has done is to first present a possible counterexample to MR2—Mary's tax crime—that even he himself suspects is unsuccessful, and then call attention to the fact that MR2 however fails if animalism is true. In other words: if MR2 is true, then animalism is false. But that's exactly as it should be in an argument against animalism; an attack on a view cannot only invoke premises that are friendly to that view. Whether the argument offers independent grounds to reject animalism rather hinges upon whether MR2 is plausible for reasons which do not appeal to the falsity of animalism. Arguably, this condition is satisfied. For one thing, MR2 is intuitively attractive taken all by itself. For another, it seems reasonable to include it in explanations of many specific ethical truths, which do not concern controversial issues of personal identity: for example, my being morally responsible now for stealing a magazine yesterday.

However, the matter does not end here, for Olson also suggests an alternative principle, which he says is weaker than but at least as plausible as MR2 (or rather the slightly different principle that he focuses on). Consider:[8]

---

[7] The principle Olson discusses is: (1) Someone is now morally responsible for something he did earlier if and only if he is morally competent now and he was morally competent at that earlier time (1997: 60). But it seems distracting to focus on an "if and only if" principle here; the present objection to animalism needs only MR2.

[8] The principle Olson actually suggests is: (1*) Someone is now morally responsible for something he did earlier if and only if he is morally competent now and he was morally competent at that earlier time,

MR4.   If a person has performed a certain earlier action and is psychologically continuous now with herself as she was when she performed the action (and was morally competent then and is morally competent now), then she is now morally responsible for that action.

The requisite psychological continuity does not hold between D and Cesare. Thus even if D, after the transplant, is without moral responsibility for the kick, MR4 does not have the consequence that D hasn't kicked Cesare's neighbor. Unlike MR2, then, MR4 leaves animalism unscathed.

As MR2 entails MR4, MR4 is indeed in one way at least as plausible as MR2. But this does not show that we should not accept MR2. As a moral principle, MR2 has a clear advantage over MR4: it is simpler. It explains instances of moral responsibility by appealing to one factor (personal identity over time) instead of two (personal identity over time and psychological continuity). Admittedly, this difference is not very big if the psychological approach is true: on this view, the two factors are intimately related; one of them holds partly in virtue of the other. Given animalism, on the other hand, there is no such close connection between the two factors.

Of course, simplicity is just one virtue among others. If there are cases where MR2 gives the wrong result and MR4 does not, we should abandon MR2 in favor of MR4. To be sure, if animalism is true, there are such cases; but again, this is just to say that MR2, unlike MR4, is unfriendly to animalism. If even champions of the psychological approach had to acknowledge the existence of such cases, on the other hand, this would be much worse for MR2. But they don't. On the psychological approach, whenever the first conjunct of MR4's antecedent holds, so does the second; hence whenever MR2's antecedent holds, so does MR4's.

14.11. Don't Forget the Animals

Olson's discussion might not provide sufficiently good reasons for denying the intuitive idea that justified prudential concern and moral responsibility are intimately connected to personal identity over time.[9] But let us make another attempt.

We can begin by noting that, in our midst, there are plenty of individuals who seem to be much like ourselves, and whose identity over time apparently lacks the ethical relevance that the anti-animalist arguments attach to personal identity over time. I am thinking of human organisms: the beings that we are identical to according to

and he is now psychologically continuous with himself as he was then (1997: 62). However, (1*) is in fact not weaker (as Olson claims at 1997: 61) than the principle in note 7, (1) (or than MR2, of course). For (1*) entails something that (1) does not: that a person is now morally responsible for something he did earlier only if he is now psychologically continuous with himself as he was then. By contrast, MR4 is weaker than MR2.

[9] Olson points out that the animalist can say that I am the "same person" as any future person who is an appropriate object of my prudential concern and who is morally responsible for what I have done (1997: 65–70). But as he makes clear, "same person" does not here imply identity.

animalism, and that are our bodies even according to anti-animalists. Consider for instance the following principle, analogous to PC1:

> PC6.   If a human animal would be justified in having prudential concern for a future experience, then she is going to have that experience.

Call the "donor" animal, the one in which Charles's cerebrum resides before the operation, "F." Arguably, because Charles and F have exactly similar brain states up to the time of transplant, they have exactly similar mental states until then. Admittedly, it is controversial whether human animals have mental features at all even if animalism is false (Shoemaker 2008 and dualists deny this); here I can only point out that my argument assumes that they do. Given this assumption, when Charles is terrified by the upcoming torture, so is F. Now, so far as the future torture is concerned, there does not seem to be anything irrational going on inside Charles's head; it does not seem that there is one justified prudential concern there (Charles's) and one which is not justified (F's). While PC6's antecedent is thus apparently satisfied here, the consequent undoubtedly is not: organism F is not going to be tortured. Hence, PC6 is a dubious principle. And it is easy to verify that the same kind of reasoning can be applied to the various modifications of PC1 we discussed earlier (PC3–PC5; Section 14.7).

Consider also this principle, analogous to PC2:

> PC7.   If a human animal is going to have a future experience, then she would be justified in having prudential concern for that experience.

Call the "recipient" organism, the one in which Cesare's cerebrum resides before the operation, "G." Arguably, if Cesare has pre-transplant prudential concern about the future torture—in spite of his complete lack of psychological continuity with the tortured D, as D is during the torture—G does as well. There do not seem to be, inside Cesare's head, one unjustified prudential concern (Cesare's) going on and one justified (G's); rather, each seems unjustified. This speaks against PC7, for G is going to be tortured.

The following principle of moral responsibility is analogous to MR1:

> MR5.   If a human animal is now morally responsible for a certain earlier action, then she has performed that action.

MR5 is questionable. If we, after the transplant, blame and punish D for Charles's earlier insult, we also blame and punish G. Apparently, we are then doing nothing inappropriate at all; in particular, there does not seem to be any individual involved who is undeservedly blamed and punished. And yet, G's history does not contain any insult to Charles's mother.

The following principle is analogous to MR2:

> MR6.   If a human animal has performed a certain earlier action (and was morally competent then and is morally competent now), then she is now morally responsible for that action.

MR6 is also questionable. Animal G has kicked Cesare's neighbor, and seems morally competent both after the transplant and at the time of the kick. MR6 thus tells us that G is morally responsible for this action. This seems wrong, however. If we spare person D blame and punishment for the kick—which seems entirely appropriate—we do not thereby also let some responsible individual escape blame and punishment.

Initiated readers might have noted that the above remarks have some similarities with what is by far the most important argument for animalism, the "thinking animal" argument. Briefly put, that argument says that the anti-animalist must hold, implausibly, that there are two rational beings thinking my thoughts (the animal and I), making it impossible for me to know which one I am (e.g. Olson 1997: 80–1; 100–9; 2003; 2007: 29–39). Observe, though, that my remarks do not at all aim at such ambitious conclusions. I do not here want to cast doubt on the view that Charles is numerically distinct from D, and Cesare from G. My remarks are the beginning of an answer to an attack on animalism; they are not meant to provide positive support for the view.

Some might want to defend these principles. It may be argued that precisely because organism G, but not organism F, is going to be tortured, G but not F would be justified in having prudential concern about the torture; and precisely because G has kicked Cesare's neighbor, but not insulted Charles's mother, G is morally responsible for the former but not the latter action. However, this would be a dangerous move to make for the anti-animalist. For if individuals, who in many ways are remarkably similar to us, can have justified prudential concern and moral responsibility in the absence of psychological continuity, it no longer seems so hard to swallow that we ourselves—human people—can have that as well.

But, you might impatiently wonder, even if these principles about organisms are untenable, how is that supposed to affect the anti-animalist arguments from prudential concern and moral responsibility? After all, those arguments are not based on these principles, but on principles about people. We'll come to that now.

14.12. Us and Them

The anti-animalist needs to explain why the identity over time of human organisms does not have the ethical relevance that the anti-animalist arguments ascribe to personal identity over time. If personal identity over time is strongly correlated with justified prudential concern and moral responsibility, why isn't human organism identity over time this as well? After all, it is the same relation that obtains in both cases: numerical identity (that it is "over time" only means that its relata are picked out by reference to different times). And again, the beings in question—human people and human animals—are strikingly similar.

It seems to me that the answer must be that human organisms have non-psychological identity conditions. They persist, as noted earlier (Section 14.3), by virtue of purely biological, non-psychological continuity. If their identity over time had obtained in virtue of psychological continuity, it would have been intimately linked to justified prudential concern and moral responsibility—the four principles of Section 14.11, or some slight modifications thereof, would have been correct—but it doesn't. (Some might prefer the answer that human animals, unlike human people, are not people— even though they are rational beings with mental features like those that people have. But why aren't they people? Arguably, the reason is that they don't have psychological persistence conditions. So this answer would come down to the same thing.)

In that case, however, the anti-animalist arguments' appeal to identity over time seems to be a red herring. Identity over time is said to correlate with justified pruden- tial concern and moral responsibility in those cases where it obtains in virtue of psy- chological continuity, but not in those cases where it obtains in virtue of biological continuity. However, there is then a very small step to the view that it is psychological continuity that possesses the entire ethical relevance: the important thing for justified prudential concern and moral responsibility is not identity over time—not even in the case of people—but psychological continuity. It is because of the presence and absence of psychological continuity, nothing else, that Charles and F, but not Cesare or G, would be justified in having prudential concern for the post-transplant torture, and D and G have post-transplant moral responsibility for the insult but not for the kick. Importantly, this position is fully compatible with animalism. Of course, it is still fully possible that the ethical principles that the anti-animalist arguments are based on are correct—namely if personal identity over time obtains by virtue of psychological con- tinuity. But the latter idea presupposes the psychological approach, and that would be an illegitimate assumption to make in an argument against animalism.

Alternatively put: identity over time appears crucial to justified prudential concern and moral responsibility when we only consider the principles that are utilized in the anti-animalist arguments. By contrast, the very same relation, identity over time, does not appear at all relevant when we consider analogous principles about human organ- isms, even though these organisms are very similar to ourselves. Why not? The sugges- tion was that their identity over time does not have anything to do with psychological continuity. But then the most reasonable conclusion seems to be that the important thing for justified prudential concern and moral responsibility is not identity over time (including personal identity over time), but psychological continuity.

I have emphasized, however, especially in the discussion of Olson's arguments, that it is intuitively attractive to hold that personal identity over time is tightly connected to justified prudential concern and moral responsibility. The present animalist defense strategy rejects this tight connection. From where, then, comes the temptation to accept it? I presume that the psychological approach is attractive for non-ethical reasons. Probably, many people have a strong metaphysical intuition that, for example, Charles is D, simply because of Charles's psychological continuity with D. This intu- ition need not stem from any ethical opinions. If it is thus tempting for non-ethical reasons to think that personal identity over time is closely connected to psychological continuity, and also tempting to think that psychological continuity is closely con- nected to justified prudential concern and moral responsibility, then it is unsurprising that it is tempting to think that personal identity over time is closely connected to justi-fied prudential concern and moral responsibility.

Of course, the animalist must deny that Charles is D, and that Cesare isn't D. This seems to be a cost. As I think the support in favor of animalism is strong, I believe this is a price worth paying. Needless to say, this cannot be argued here. More important in this context is that it is a cost that does not derive from any ethical shortcomings of animalism.

References

Baker, L. R. 2000. *Persons and Bodies: A Constitution View*. Cambridge: Cambridge University Press.

Campbell, S. 2006. "The Conception of a Person as a Series of Mental Events," *Philosophy and Phenomenological Research* 73: 339–58.

DeGrazia, D. 2002. "Are We Essentially Persons? Olson, Baker, and a Reply," *Philosophical Forum* 33: 101–20.

Evans, G. 1978. "Can There Be Vague Objects?" *Analysis* 38: 208.

Feldman, F. 1992. *Confrontations with the Reaper*. New York and Oxford: Oxford University Press.

Feldman, F. 2000. "The Termination Thesis," *Midwest Studies in Philosophy* 24: 98–115.

Feldman, F. 2013. "Death and the Disintegration of Personality," *Oxford Handbook of Philosophy and Death*, eds. B. Bradley, F. Feldman, and J. Johansson, 60–79. Oxford: Oxford University Press.

Holtug, N. 2010. *Persons, Interests, and Justice*. Oxford: Oxford University Press.

Johansson, J. 2007. "What Is Animalism?," *Ratio* 20: 194–205.

Johansson, J. 2010. "Parfit on Fission," *Philosophical Studies* 150: 21–35.

Lewis, D. 1976. "Survival and Identity," *The Identities of Persons*, ed. A. Rorty, 17–40. Berkeley: University of California Press.

Mackie, D. 1999. "Personal Identity and Dead People," *Philosophical Studies* 49: 369–76.

Merricks, T. 1999. "Endurance, Psychological Continuity, and the Importance of Personal Identity," *Philosophy and Phenomenological Research* 59: 983–96.

Olson, E. T. 1994. "Is Psychology Relevant to Personal Identity?" *Australasian Journal of Philosophy* 72: 173–86.

Olson, E. T. 1997. *The Human Animal: Personal Identity without Psychology*. New York & Oxford: Oxford University Press.

Olson, E. T. 2003. "An Argument for Animalism," *Personal Identity*, eds. J. Barresi and R. Martin, 318–34. Malden, MA: Blackwell.

Olson, E. T. 2007. *What are We? A Study in Personal Ontology*. New York: Oxford University Press.

Parfit, D. 1984. *Reasons and Persons*. Oxford: Clarendon Press.

Parfit, D. 1993. "The Indeterminacy of Identity: A Reply to Brueckner," *Philosophical Studies* 70: 23–33.

Parfit, D. 1995. "The Unimportance of Identity," *Identity: Essays Based on Herbert Spencer Lectures Given in the University of Oxford*, ed. H. Harris, 13–45. Oxford: Clarendon Press.

Shoemaker, S. 2008. "Persons, Animals, and Identity," *Synthese* 162: 313–24.

Snowdon, P. 1990. "Persons, Animals, and Ourselves," *The Person and the Human Mind: Issues in Ancient and Modern Philosophy*, ed. C. Gill, 83–107. Oxford: Clarendon Press.

Unger. P. 2000. "The Survival of the Sentient," *Philosophical Perspectives* 11: 325–48.

Van Inwagen, P. 1990. *Material Beings*. Ithaca, NY: Cornell University Press.

Van Inwagen, P. 1997. "Materialism and the Psychological-Continuity Account of Personal Identity," *Philosophical Perspectives* 11: 305–19.

Van Inwagen, P. 2002. "What Do We Refer to When We Say 'I'?" *Blackwell Guide to Metaphysics*, ed. R. Gale, 175–89. Oxford: Blackwell.

Williams, B. 1970. "The Self and the Future," *Philosophical Review* 79: 161–80.

Williams, J. R. G. 2008. "Multiple Actualities and Ontically Vague Identity," *The Philosophical Quarterly* 58: 134–54.

15

The Stony Metaphysical Heart of Animalism

David Shoemaker

> I'm an animal…I've got to satisfy
> I'm an animal…never been known to lie
> I'm an animal…animal life
> I'm an animal…animalism
> I'm an animal…human system
> Breath, flesh, flesh and blood,
> physique, strength, power,
> vigor, force, spring,
> elasticity, tone, and grace…
> Dumb animal, dumb friend, dumb creature, brute
> I'm an animal
> Let me be your best friend
> I'm an animal
> Let me be your best friend
>
> The Animals, "I'm an Animal"

> I am not an animal! I am a human being! I am a *man*!
>
> John Merrick, in David Lynch's *The Elephant Man*

Animalism, by the forthright acknowledgment of many of its own adherents, does poorly at accounting for our identity-related practical concerns. The reason is straightforward: whereas our practical concerns seem to track the identity of psychological creatures—persons—animalism focuses on the identity of human organisms who are not essentially persons. This lack of fit between our practical concerns and animalism may thus be taken to pose the following serious *Challenge* to animalism: (1) animalism lacks the proper fit with the set of our practical concerns; (2) if a theory of personal identity lacks the proper fit with the set of our practical concerns, it suffers a loss in plausibility; thus, (3) animalism suffers a loss in plausibility (in particular to psychological criteria of identity).

There are two very general replies to *Challenge*. First, one might deny (1), showing that animalism doesn't in fact lack the proper fit with our practical concerns. One might tack this response in one of two directions: either (a) appeal to the fact that animal continuity is at least a *necessary* condition for instantiation of the relevant (psychologically grounded) practical concerns (and so is sufficient for delivering a "proper fit"), or (b) show that our understanding of the relevant practical concerns is overly narrow and that our person-related practical concerns may actually define the "persons" to whom they apply in much broader—humanesque—terms, such that the theory of identity that fits best with them in the end is actually, surprisingly, animalism. The second general response to *Challenge* is to deny (2), showing instead how a lack of fit with our practical concerns is not a plausibility condition for theories of personal identity.

What we have, then, are actually three attempted responses to *Challenge*, and these may be drawn from the work of, respectively, David DeGrazia, Marya Schechtman, and Eric Olson. It is my first aim in this chapter to explain and evaluate them. I will find the first two responses problematic and the third, while on the right track, to be significantly incomplete. I will then attempt to fill in the gaps of the third response to render it viable. In doing so, I will show that and how our practical concerns do not consist in a monolithic set; rather, there are distinctly different *types* of practical concerns, and while some are clearly grounded on psychological relations, some are actually grounded on others, including animalistic and humanistic relations; furthermore, their actual connection to identity is tenuous at best. What these concerns are, how they divide up, and what they are grounded on in each instance—these are the issues it is my second aim in this chapter to take up. I begin with a more thorough explication of *Challenge*.

Challenge

Consider the following awful short story, *The Party*:[1]

As I lie awake in bed this morning and think about how embarrassingly drunk I was when I got into bed last night, I start again to anticipate tonight's party, as many of my old friends will be there (I hope we will recognize one another!). I know that everyone else will be concerned about what they look like, but I am especially concerned about what *I* will look like: which ascot should I wear? I am also worried about what I will say to the host. She owes me money for some improvisational bricklaying I did at her house last week, and so she had better pay me soon.... When I arrive at the party that evening, I wind up speaking too harshly to the host about what she owes me, and her lummox of a boyfriend confronts me, so I overreact and

---

[1] From my never-to-be-forthcoming collection of very short stories, *Teatime for Troglodytes, and Other Tales*.

punch him in the spleen. She blames me for this rude display and kicks me out of the party. I did not get a chance to catch up with my old friends. It is hot, and I am sad.

Contained in this dreadful display of writing are the essential identity-related practical concerns to which various theorists point: anticipation, first-person recognition and concern, third-person recognition and concern, general social treatment, emotional patterns (e.g. embarrassment), compensation, and responsibility.[2] These are the concerns that are ostensibly grounded by personal identity: I can justifiably anticipate only my own future experiences; I justifiably have a special sort of concern only for my own future self; I can be justifiably embarrassed, regretful, or proud of only my own past actions or attitudes; I can justifiably be compensated with benefits only for my own burdens; I can justifiably be responsible only for my own past actions; and I am justified in responding to others I claim to recognize in certain ways only if they are the same people I believe them to be.

Taken as a set, these concerns have struck most theorists as being about psychological relations. To take just two examples from the list, anticipation consists in current projective imagination into someone's future experiential states, and responsibility ties some current psychological/moral agent (the target of praise or blame, say) to some past psychological/moral agent (the doer of the deed). The presumed link to identity then goes as follows: if I can justifiably anticipate only my own future experiences and I am responsible only for my own past actions (etc.), and if what makes those experiences or actions my own is that I am numerically identical to the future or past entity to which they are attributable, then if the ownership relation is a psychological relation, so too is the numerical identity relation providing it.

Thus do we arrive at *Challenge*. If animalism is true, goes the worry, there is a missing link between the ownership of actions/experiences and identity. According to animalism, what makes X (a person) identical to any individual Y at any other time is that X and Y are one and the same biological organism, one and the same human animal (a sameness typically consisting in biological continuity).[3] But anticipation (say) is a relation between two *experiencers*, and so there seems a crucial gap between animalism and the ownership of those experiences, for the animalist would have us saying that what makes the experiences I anticipate *mine* is ultimately that the experiencer to whom they are attributable will be biologically continuous with me. But what could biological continuity alone have to do with the experiential—psychological—relation that obtains between us? How could the continuity of *meat* serve to explain a relation of *minds*?

Surely, goes the objection, if the ownership relation is psychological, then so is its grounding numerical identity relation. That is to say, whatever makes some experience or action mine must be just what renders me identical to that experiencer or agent.

---

[2] Compiled from DeGrazia 2005; Locke 1975; Martin 1998; Olson 1997: esp. ch. 3; Schechtman 1996; and Shoemaker 2007.

[3] See, e.g., Olson 1997; and DeGrazia 2005.

Consequently, if what justifies my anticipation of some future experience is that that experience is mine, and it is mine in virtue of my bearing some psychological relation to that experiencer, then that psychological relation is just what *makes him me*. The fundamental assumption driving *Challenge*, then, is that the plausibility of a criterion of identity depends, at least in part, on how tightly that criterion is tied to the ownership of actions and experiences relevant to our practical concerns. This assumption thus yields the result that, if animalism falls prey to *Challenge*, psychological criteria of identity are thereby favored in the plausibility race.

I have already laid out the two general animalist replies to *Challenge*: either deny that animalism in fact does poorly at linking the ownership of our practical concerns to identity, or deny that such a link is necessary. Turn now to a consideration of the first, which comes in two forms.

Accounting for our Practical Concerns, 1.0: DeGrazia's Realism

DeGrazia 2005 offers a defense of animalism against a variety of attacks.[4] One of the more pressing is that animalism cannot account for our practical concerns. DeGrazia's key response is that, *in the world as we know it*, animalism can indeed account for our practical concerns, *at least in virtue of being their necessary condition*. He deals explicitly with some of the concerns mentioned earlier—responsibility, prudential concern, and social treatment—as well as more loosely related concerns such as self-knowledge, interest in the afterlife, and what matters in survival. With the exception of our interest in the afterlife,[5] animalism does rather well as long as we scale back our expectations for success. Consider, for example, moral responsibility, which, again, seems to be grounded on psychological continuity. DeGrazia points out that, in our world—the real world—psychological continuity itself depends on biological continuity: you need continuity of your biological life to support continuity of your psychological

---

[4] See DeGrazia 2005: ch. 2.

[5] This is a very odd concern to include on the list anyway, for it functions quite differently from the others. Take responsibility, for instance. Here, "both ends" of the concern are in place, as it were: we've got someone before us whom we hold responsible for the actions of some past person. Both persons exist, and we are just trying to figure out what metaphysical relations obtain between them that will justify our responsibility-concern. Or consider self-concern: on the assumption that there will exist a person exactly like me getting out of my bed tomorrow, my concern for my well-being extends to him, so what metaphysical relation grounds it? In these cases, then, we stipulate the existence of two person-stages and then explore the metaphysical relation between them, *given the antecedent concern that obtains*. Our interest in the afterlife, though, functions very differently. Here, we have *hopes* about the *possibility* of our surviving the deaths of our bodies. So we aren't—indeed we can't be—stipulating the existence of some heavenly person-stage for whom we already have concern and then trying to figure out the relevant metaphysical grounding relationship. Instead, we simply have a prudential interest in there existing some such heavenly person-stage who is us, but this interest isn't built on any metaphysical relation at all. To hope for the mere *obtaining* of some metaphysical relation, therefore, is just not to have the sort of concern that is relevant to the type of interaction between our practical concerns and identity that is at issue here. Thanks to Shaun Nichols for discussion of this issue.

life (DeGrazia 2005: 60–1). And similar replies attach to the other concerns. With respect to prudential concern and planning, biological continuity is necessary for them as well in the world as we know it. Furthermore, we may plan or have prudential concern for our future comatose selves, something a story about psychological continuity cannot account for very well while animalism can. And with respect to social treatment, while it's true that people often treat one another as ongoing psychological beings, it's also true that we typically reidentify one another via our bodies, and, further, our socializing extends beyond psychological persons to newborns and those in demented states (DeGrazia 2005: 60).

There is one last, more subtle, response here. We may allow that a psychological continuity theory does *better* at accounting for our practical concerns without inferring that animalism *cannot* account for those concerns thereby. And accounting for them as it does is nothing to sneeze at. As DeGrazia puts it with respect to what matters in survival, "[T]he practical concerns under discussion all presuppose or depend on our continued existence; so does what matters in survival, even if we agree that what *most* matters in survival is psychological continuity or the continuing capacity for consciousness" (DeGrazia 2005: 63, emphasis mine).

There are two general responses here, then: animalism accounts for our practical concerns (a) by providing (at least) their necessary condition in the world as we know it, and (b) this provision is sufficient to stave off *Challenge*, i.e. sufficient to prevent a decrease in the plausibility of animalism. Sure enough, it is *possible* that, with various forms of radical technological advances, we will be able to engage in the kind of activities (e.g. fission) wherein animalistic identity could diverge from our practical concerns, but these are "presently hypothetical cases," and that such diverging might occur in this remote future "is an acceptable price to pay for a theory that otherwise seems more coherent, more metaphysically plausible, and more consonant with educated common sense than its competitors" (DeGrazia 2005: 64).

Whether or not these responses are successful depends entirely on what it means for some theory of numerical identity to "account" for our practical concerns. This is a difficult issue, one that DeGrazia sometimes seems to want to sidestep entirely.[6] But the account he has nevertheless offered doesn't actually give us what we want. I suggest that what the advocates of *Challenge* are looking for when investigating the alleged relation between numerical identity and our practical concerns is a robust, informative explanation of the justificatory role played by numerical identity *qua* necessary condition for our practical concerns. To see what I mean, consider moral responsibility (MR). There is a platitude at work here, evident from my earlier discussion of *Challenge*: I can be morally responsible only for my own actions.[7] So insofar as the nature of ownership here is presumably cashed out in terms of numerical identity (i.e. what

---

[6] As he puts it, "The biological view is a theory of human identity…, a metaphysical and conceptual theory. Strictly speaking, then, it is not responsible for tracking all of the concerns we tend to associate with identity" (DeGrazia 2005: 63).

[7] See Shoemaker 2011a.

makes some past action my own is just that I am numerically identical to the person who performed it), such identity is a necessary condition in the justification of attributions of MR: you are justified in judging or holding me morally responsible for A only if I am numerically identical to the person who performed A. What the *Challenger*s are looking for, then—beyond precisely what numerical identity itself consists in—is an informative explanation for *why* numerical identity plays this justifying role. Indeed, this is the respect in which various proposed criteria of identity may be thought to fall short: if the role they would play in justifying attributions of responsibility failed to illuminate those attributions in any real way, they would fail to be *relevant* to the practical concern in the way many have thought identity to be.

It is with respect to this desideratum that DeGrazia's "account" falls short, for he fails to provide on behalf of animalism any sort of illuminating explanation of its justificatory role with respect to our practical concerns. Consider again the way many view MR: ostensibly, I am morally responsible for A only if I am identical to the individual who performed A. Now if this is our starting point, then we have already assumed that the relation between identity and MR consists in the former being a necessary condition of the latter. Consequently, to propose, as DeGrazia does, that animalism could account for MR by being a necessary condition for it is just to reaffirm that starting point. But animalism had *better* be a necessary condition for MR, for that is just what the relation between them *has* to consist in (given our starting assumption). Now perhaps it might be thought that animalism's ability to serve as a necessary condition for MR at least gives us some (as opposed to no) kind of relation to MR, albeit not as robust a relation as we might have liked given that it doesn't deliver a *sufficient* condition. But no one could plausibly think identity could ever be a sufficient condition for MR anyway—there are surely epistemic and control conditions one must meet in addition to identity—so identity can serve as no more and no less than a necessary condition for MR. DeGrazia's response (a) is, therefore, redundant.

It is also unilluminating. On the methodology I have outlined, to test the plausibility of animalism with respect to MR, we are supposed to plug its criterion of numerical identity into the platitude as an explication of the nature of my ownership of some past action. So on the proposed view, I am morally responsible for A only if I am biologically continuous with the individual who performed A, and you are justified in judging or holding me responsible for A only if I am biologically continuous with that individual. Let us then ask the fundamental question of the enterprise: what explains how biological continuity plays this justifying role in MR? And to this question the only reply is that it supports or enables the psychological continuity that is actually relevant to MR in the world as we know it. But consider the primary constitutive elements of animal persistence: continuity of a functioning brain and brain stem, continuity of a functioning heart, the intake of nutrition, continuous blood circulation, and regular ventilation. Each of these is individually necessary for real-world psychological continuity, but none of them is relevant to an *explanation* of the justifying relation from identity to MR, and that is because none of them is relevant to explaining what makes some past action *my own*. What makes that action mine must have something to do with the relation between a past agent's volitional network and my own: the desires, beliefs, and intentions that produced that action must bear some sort of relation to my current desires, beliefs, and intentions.[8] But these are entirely psychological relations. So while there may be multiple non-psychological relations that support or enable these psychological relations, they are simply not the relevant *types* of necessary condition to play the justificatory role in attributions of MR presumed by the *Challenge*rs.

This is precisely why we would get divergence in hypothetical worlds in which fission and other technological marvels occur, where psychological continuity could be prized apart from biological continuity. In such worlds we would presumably still have a robust explanation of how psychological continuity justifies attributions of MR even in the absence of biological continuity. That biological continuity could drop out of the picture with no loss in explanatory value, however, suggests that, even in the world as we know it, biological continuity is not what's doing the explanatory work. So while it may indeed be a necessary condition for MR in our world, it fails to offer the right *kind* of necessary condition to be explanatorily relevant for our investigation into the relation between identity and the practical concerns. If this is a story that is broadly applicable to the remainder of our practical concerns, then DeGrazia's point (b) remains in doubt as well: the plausibility of animalism could still be downgraded by its ineffectiveness in providing the *right* kind of grounding relation to those concerns.

Accounting for our Practical Concerns, 2.0: Schechtman's Expanded Persons

In a recent article and book, Marya Schechtman offers what might be construed as a different way to show how animalism could account for all our practical concerns, a way providing a more plausible route to rescuing the theory from *Challenge* (Schechtman 2010 and 2014; although she doesn't pitch it in these terms and may, as we will see, ultimately reject it being put in these terms!). Her story begins with what she diagnoses as a fundamental problem for both psychological and biological theories of numerical identity with respect to their alleged bearing on our practical concerns: they both rely too heavily on a Lockean conception of robust personhood. On Locke's view, a person is an intelligent, self-conscious and self-reflective being, one that thus requires some rather sophisticated psychological capacities. These are the capacities, Locke thinks, that ground personhood's "forensic" nature: "person" is a thoroughly normative concept serving as an umbrella term for those creatures that, due to their sophisticated psychological capacities, are both prudentially concerned and morally responsible. Tracking these prudential and moral creatures across time is a matter of tracking the

---

[8] As astute readers may have noticed, why *psychological* continuity explains this relation any better than biological continuity is something about which I have said nothing just yet. I address this issue in the final section of this chapter, as well as in Shoemaker 2011b.

persisting instantiation of those sophisticated forensic capacities, i.e. psychological continuity. Thus is born the psychological criterion of identity.

However, if the psychological criterion is explicitly coupled with the view that we persons are *essentially* persons, then it seemingly cannot account for some rather obvious truths, such as the fact that I was once a fetus, or that I could fall into a permanent vegetative state (PVS) (given that I who am essentially a person could not have been otherwise, whereas fetuses and those in PVS are indeed otherwise; they are non-persons).[9] Animalism here rides to the rescue: I was once a fetus and I could fall into PVS precisely because what I am essentially is an animal compatible with all sorts of phases, including my current personhood phase. But animalism gains in plausibility on the essentialist score only seemingly to undermine the presumed connection to practical concerns. The concerns are attached (so the Lockean story goes) to personhood, to sophisticated psychological capacities, but as it turns out the story about personhood is a story about what we *do*—we reason, reflect on ourselves, form intentions, etc.—whereas animalism is a story about what we *are*, so if the animalists are right, it looks like the forensic aspect of persons just can't be about *identity* in the end.[10]

Schechtman reveals why this story is still problematic, however, by considering a bioethical issue having grave practical importance, namely, advance directives. The difficult issue seems to be whether or not the patient before us with severe dementia who needs extraordinary measures to keep her alive is identical to the person who signed the advance directive (AD) five years ago stating that no extraordinary measures were to be taken to keep her alive.[11] The advocate of the psychological criterion will likely say that the severely demented patient just isn't a person, so the AD no longer applies (although what's in the best interest of the patient may still dictate not deploying extraordinary measures, or the previous person's "surviving interests" as laid out in the AD may determine what is to be done with her living "remains").[12] This response is unsatisfying, however, because it suggests that there remains no rational grounding for the concerns we may have for this patient persisting in the face of this verdict. Suppose my mother was the one who signed the AD. If my mother is truly no longer in existence now, why should it bother me as it does to see the demented person before me in this way? Indeed, what grounds could I have for continuing to care for this woman, for treating her with love and affection (Schechtman 2010: 275–6)? There are, it seems, concerns that (reasonably) persist toward those whose psychological robustness has considerably waned.

Alternatively, the animalist at least gets the identity part of the story right: this is indeed my mother before me (and so she is identical to the signer of the AD), albeit *sans*

---

[9] See, e.g., Olson 1997: ch. 4.

[10] More precisely, it can't be about *numerical* identity. Olson 1997's insightful discussion in chapter 3 (about which more below) offers the possibility of a "same person" relation that accounts for the forensic features of persons but can't meet the logical demands of the numerical identity relation.

[11] I argue against this reading of the issue in Shoemaker 2010.

[12] See, e.g., Buchanan 1988: esp. 286–7.

(robust Lockean) personhood. But if animalism goes on to divorce completely what we are from what we do, its truth has no practical implications for my interactions with this woman in these circumstances. As Schechtman puts it:

The animalist need not deny that we might for some reason decide to place practical significance on the brute fact of the continuation of a single individual, but on this view, it is somewhat mysterious why we should ever decide to do so. In our actual lives, however, we do not seem to need an extra step to explain why it should be of practical significance to me that the individual suffering in a hospital bed is the mother I loved; nothing feels more natural than that it should. Animalism thus fails to capture a direct and immediate connection between identity and practical concerns that is a forceful part of our lived experience. (Schechtman 2010: 276–7)

That she is my mother is sufficient to explain my ongoing affection for her, goes the thought; her life is simply intertwined with mine. But we cannot squeeze out what ought to be this practical implication from the stony metaphysical heart of animalism.

The overall problem that Schechtman identifies, then, is that advocates of both animalism and psychological criteria think that our practical concerns are associated solely with a robust conception of Lockean personhood. If we are essentially such persons (and so our persistence conditions are psychological), then we get the desired practical implications, but only at the cost of metaphysical implausibility. If we are essentially animals (and so our persistence conditions are biological), then we gain metaphysical plausibility, but only by losing the desired practical implications. Schechtman's solution is thus to broaden the (forensic) understanding of personhood so as to incorporate the metaphysical insights of animalism in a way that allows that theory to produce the desired practical implications.

She does so by taking our practical concerns and commitments as foundational and then recognizing that humans aren't the only animals to have such concerns and commitments. Other animals also care for their young and have friendly relations with others and seek out pleasure and avoid pain, etc. Now we happen to have concerns in addition to these that are unique to our biology and way of life, but the set of concerns in itself is continuous with those of other animals. We are *human* animals who typically live certain sorts of lives, various elements of which are the targets of our practical concerns. Schechtman thus proposes to understand "person" as a creature living a "person-life" and a person-life as the "kind of life typically lived by an enculturated human" (Schechtman 2010: 278; cf. Schechtman 2014: ch. 5). But there is a wide variety of concerns attaching to this sort of life, including the various ways we have of loving and treating Lockean non-persons such as infants, adults with cognitive disabilities, and those in PVS. It is true, of course, that we treat full-fledged moral agents in additional sorts of ways—we hold them responsible, for one thing—but this sort of treatment is simply continuous with the sort of treatment just mentioned. It is just one form our practical interactions may take, one we reserve for those with certain more developed sorts of human capacities.

Person-lives will be very closely associated with the animal-lives targeted by animalism, but there are some crucial differences. It is not solely, primarily, or even necessarily in virtue of our biological nature that we have person-lives; it is, rather, in virtue of our *anthropological* nature that we do so (a feral human child may not have such a nature). The relevant lives are the lives of *enculturated* humans, after all (and so it is possible that non-humans could also have such lives). Nevertheless, the standard case is one in which these sorts of person-lives just overlap with our animal lives, such that the end-points of both are the same, as are the biological conditions of their preservation. So insofar as the two sorts of lives typically share these features, the relevant gap might be bridged between identity and the practical concerns: *that she is my mother*, for example, will indeed be sufficient to explain and ground my ongoing affection for the demented patient before me, given that such concern is a direct implication of her being the same person—the same enculturated human animal whose life is intertwined with mine—as the woman who took care of me as a child. Animalism thus may be altered and adopted to resist *Challenge*. The continuity of our animal life, in the world as we know it, would be a crucial constituting element of our personhood in this broader sense. The key would be to ground our practical concerns in the *types* of animals we are. That we are animals is thus important, but it is not what matters most, which is that we are *human* animals. To the extent that our animal identity is a constituting component of our person-life identity, though, it at least may be said to be a constituting component of the practical concerns targeting that life.[13]

This seems a more plausible route to resisting *Challenge* than DeGrazia's in two respects. First, insofar as biological continuity is a necessary condition for our practical concerns in both approaches (in typical cases), it at least plays a more directly relevant constituting role in the person-life view, for our humanity is much more directly a function of our animality on Schechtman's picture. Second, the appeal to "the world as we know it," is far less *ad hoc* on Schechtman's view, for the world as we know it is precisely the world in which we have evolved the relevant practices, the practices central to our enculturated humanity. Restricting the analysis to "the world as we know it" on Schechtman's approach thus at least *explains* why appeals to hypothetical future teleporters and fissioners are less relevant to our enterprise, for who are those future beings to us and our concerns? We can plausibly speak only about who *we* are and what *we* care about (see Schechtman's own discussion of fission in Schechtman 2014: 159–66).

I find Schechtman's overall discussion of this issue sensitive and insightful. But whereas DeGrazia's reply to *Challenge* gives an account of the "proper fit" between identity and our practical concerns that is too tight (providing a very constricted explanatory story), the Schechtmanian account embodied in this sort of reply to

---

[13] This should be flagged as my own liberal extrapolation from Schechtman's earlier (2010) view, a view that itself is not intended to rescue animalism from any challenges at all. Indeed, Schechtman rejects animalism in favor of her own distinct person-life view in her 2014: ch. 7.

Challenge is too loose.[14] To see what I mean, consider the following analogy. Suppose our family has a dog, and as our young daughter sees the dog and me interacting in various ways, she asks for an explanation. "Why do you take him out to pee?" she asks. "Why do you feed him this kind of food?" "Why do you play with him by throwing the tennis ball in the yard?" "Why does he bark when the doorbell rings?" "Why is he walking outside with his nose to the ground?" "Why do you take away his toys when he chews up your papers?" Suppose that I reply to each of these queries in precisely the same way: "Because he's a dog." In each case my reply is true, and in each case it is equally uninformative. That's because every one of my daughter's questions is tracking a different *aspect* of our dog's nature and his relation to us—e.g. his protective instincts, his sensory capacities, his doggy discipline, his digestive nature, his toilet abilities— and my answer conflates these importantly distinct elements of dog-ness for the sake of a simple explanation.

I believe the Schechtmanian reply to *Challenge* does the same thing.[15] There are importantly distinct elements of our personhood (or person-lives) that are being glossed on this story. Every answer to a question about what grounds the different practical concerns appeals simply to the sameness of the person-life at issue. So "Why do you care about the demented patient before you?" "Because she's living the same person-life as the woman who raised me." "Why should we hold this guy responsible for that past action?" "Because he's living the same person-life as the guy who performed it." "Why should we compensate this woman for the injuries to that fetus in the ultrasound picture?" "Because she is living the same person-life as that fetus." "Why am I justified in anticipating the experiences of some partygoer next week?" "Because the person whose experiences you are anticipating will be living the same person-life as you." And so on. But each of these questions is, I suggest, asking about a different distinct element of those person-lives: we want to know what it is about the person-life that grounds our concern *in each specific case* (just as my daughter was surely asking what it is about our dog's dog-ness specifically that grounds our various interactions with him in each case). So while the Schechtmanian answer to each question may be true, it doesn't seem to give us what we want. As I said earlier, when investigating the relation between identity and our practical concerns, what the *Challenge*rs are looking for is a robust, informative explanation of the justificatory role played by identity *qua*

---

[14] And again, I use "Schechtmanian" here because it is not Schechtman's aim to respond to *Challenge* at all.

[15] Here is the spot where Schechtman herself would get off the boat, I think, for she merely takes her account to provide a unifying story about the *locus* of such questions and concerns, i.e. what is the thing which all these questions and concerns are tracking, and what unifies that thing for these purposes? (See, e.g., Schechtman 2014: chs. 1–2.) Consequently, if we just want to know what it is to be a (domesticated) dog, the answer could well be that it's a creature that has protective instincts, sensory capacities, a digestive nature, certain toilet abilities, discipline, etc., and what unifies these various features has to do with facts both about canine biology *and* domestication *and* the sorts of lives such dogs lead (as informed by evolution in particular sorts of environments, say). This all seems right to me. What I object to, then, is the *extension* of this view to ground our specific practical concerns in a way that allegedly vindicates animalism.

necessary condition for those concerns. While certainly robust (it purports to explain all of our practical concerns), the Schechtmanian answer seems uninformative: it doesn't yet explain the presumably crucial connection between identity (of these more broadly construed "persons") and the practical concerns, the connection that also presumably renders a theory of identity more or less plausible.

Now the response just given should be taken as merely suggestive and preliminary, for I have not yet shown that our questions about the practical concerns really *are* distinct from one another or that they really track more specific aspects of our person-lives. This will be the task of the final section of the chapter. But before embarking on that project (and also to motivate it further), I need to explore the possibility of a very different response to *Challenge*, namely, that the degree of "fit" between a theory of identity and our practical concerns is actually independent from the plausibility of that theory. If this response is correct, then the tightness or looseness of some purported fit between them will be irrelevant.

Divorcing Animalism from Our Practical Concerns: Olson and Transplants

In making his case for animalism, Eric Olson is first concerned to undermine the most powerful argument in favor of its rival, what he calls the Psychological Approach. What seems to do the most work in its favor is the reaction people have to the following story: suppose Prince's cerebrum were transplanted into Cobbler's skull, resulting both in someone with Cobbler's body but Prince's psychological characteristics ("Brainy"), and someone else more or less in a persistent vegetative state with Prince's body and no cerebrum ("Brainless"). What happened to Prince when his cerebrum was transplanted into Cobbler? Most people's strong intuition here is that Prince survived in Cobbler's body, that Prince is Brainy. This is what Olson calls the *Transplant Intuition*, the hunch that persons go where their cerebrums (preserving psychological continuity) go (Olson 1997: 42–3). If our intuition is that Prince survives the transplant as Brainy, then it seems we are therefore committed to the Psychological Approach to personal identity.

Not so fast, though, argues Olson. Instead, he suggests, we can have the Transplant Intuition without accepting the Psychological Approach. This is because the Transplant Intuition actually may just be tracking our practical concerns, and so may be prized apart from a commitment to any particular theory of numerical identity. Consequently, it may well be equally compatible with both the Psychological Approach *and animalism*.

In making this point, Olson explains and defends what he calls the "Parfit–Shoemaker Thesis," the view that our practical concerns don't always track numerical identity.[16] Olson specifically considers three such concerns: prudential concern, moral responsibility,

---

[16] See Olson 1997: 54, for this formulation with respect to prudential concern.

and social treatment. Regarding the first, in the fission case I might well have the special sort of prudential concern for my fission products that is typically reserved only for myself. So were I about to undergo the division (resulting in two people who would be exactly similar to me), it could be perfectly justifiable for me to have special concern for the prospects of both, despite the fact that neither (on the standard story) could be me (Olson 1997: 54–5).[17]

Regarding the second concern, one might well be justifiably held accountable for the actions of someone else. If Prince performed some bad action pre-transplant, it seems we could hold Brainy accountable for Prince's action, regardless of whether or not Brainy was Prince. Now one might still insist that the accountability here obtains precisely *because* Brainy is Prince, but then consider a different case: Prince dies during the initial operation, and several days later technicians build a perfect replica of him and install Prince's preserved cerebrum into the replica's head. Prince is certainly dead; this is merely a duplicate (call him Duplicate). Nevertheless, it could well be appropriate to hold Duplicate accountable for Prince's actions. Accountability seems to depend on psychological continuity, but this relation could obtain independently of numerical identity. Indeed, it would surely obtain without numerical identity if animalism were true (Olson 1997: 57–62).

Finally, consider social treatment. Presumably everyone will treat Brainy as Prince once they find out what happened or they talk with him a bit: the hospital will allow visitations for Brainy from Prince's wife and the Queen, Brainy will have access to Prince's bank account, Prince's friends will view Brainy as Prince, Brainy will raise Prince's kids and pay his bills, and so on. Additionally, Olson turns the screws by considering the duplication case again: everyone would likely treat Duplicate in this way too, but that means that numerical identity and this particular practical concern are surely prized apart. Thus the fact that social treatment seems to track psychological continuity neither increases the plausibility of the Psychological Approach nor decreases the plausibility of animalism, as it is equally compatible with both.

In each case, then, the practical concerns may be divorced from numerical identity. Olson's thought (what he calls the "bold conjecture" (Olson 1997: 69)) is that the Transplant Intuition is really about our practical concerns (which "are closely connected with psychological continuity" (Olson 1997: 70)), and not about numerical identity. So we may think that, because Prince would be warranted in having special concern for Brainy, and because Brainy would be accountable for Prince's actions, and because others would treat Brainy as if they would have treated Prince, the psychological continuity that grounds those practical concerns delivers numerical identity as well, insofar as identity is thought to have practical importance. But given that these concerns could be grounded (on psychological continuity) regardless of whether or

---

[17] On a four-dimensionalist ontology, however (an ontology Olson later rejects), there may be a way to preserve the tracking relation between prudential concern and numerical identity even in the fission case. See, e.g., Lewis 1976 and Sider 2001.

not numerical identity obtains, we may deny the view that numerical identity has practical importance, and thus effectively block *Challenge*. Animalism could be true *despite*
its failure to account for our practical concerns in the robust, informative sense.

I am less concerned here to evaluate Olson's success in disabusing the Transplant
Intuition of its force in establishing the Psychological Approach than I am in evaluating the success of an approach like his (call it Olsonian) in resisting *Challenge*.
And on this point, a genuine worry remains: even if the Transplant Intuition is really
tracking our practical concerns and not numerical identity, that doesn't yet mean
that numerical identity has no practical importance, that the plausibility of a theory of
numerical identity doesn't increase or decrease depending on the extent to which it fits
with our practical concerns. In other words, just because our practical concerns *might*
track a relation—psychological continuity—which itself may not hold uniquely (in
fission) or may obtain in duplicates, that doesn't yet show (a) that psychological relation isn't *what matters in* numerical identity, and therefore (b) that psychological relation
isn't (at least) a necessary condition for numerical identity.

This is a subtle but important point. Olson draws primarily from Parfit, adopting
the motto that "identity is not what matters," i.e. numerical identity has no practical
import (Parfit 1984: ch. 12). But this motto may be taken in one of two ways. On the
one hand, it might mean that there are two necessary aspects of numerical identity—
psychological continuity (let us stipulate) and uniqueness—and where psychological
continuity without uniqueness obtains, numerical identity is absent, but so what?
Everything that matters (i.e. psychological continuity) still obtains, so nothing of
importance is lost when numerical identity in this sense is lost, i.e. when uniqueness is
absent. This is Parfit's own take on the motto (Parfit 1984: 262–4). On the other hand, it
might mean that *none* of the relations or elements in which numerical identity consists
matter, so that the correct theory of personal identity will contain nothing of relevance
to our practical concerns.[18] The most Olson has done is support the first interpretation.
What is needed to thwart the second premise of *Challenge*, however, is support for
the second, stronger interpretation.[19] Otherwise, it remains open to an advocate of
Challenge to say, "True enough, my intuitions may be tracking the practical concerns
grounded in psychological continuity, and psychological continuity on its own isn't
sufficient to establish numerical identity, but *it still must be the primary necessary
ingredient in identity* because of its connection to our set of practical concerns, so the
Psychological Approach nevertheless gains in plausibility over animalism."[20] It is my

---

[18] I am stipulating away here non-reductionism about personal identity, the view that the facts of personal identity simply don't consist in more particular facts about brains, bodies, and series of interrelated
mental and/or physical events. See Parfit 1984: 210 and throughout part III for discussion.

[19] And I should make it clear that, for Olson's own purposes, what he has done is sufficient. Again, I'm
taking up a possible *Olsonian* response to *Challenge*, and for that to succeed, it will have to involve a
stronger thesis than Olson's.

[20] Consider how this would work with respect to what Olson takes to be his knock-down case, wherein
Duplicate resides. The advocate I have just described might simply deny Olson's stipulation that Duplicate
is indeed a duplicate. To the extent that psychological continuity (with any cause) can bridge gaps in its

aim in what remains to rebut this last challenge by supporting the stronger interpretation of "identity is not what matters."

The Pluralism of the Practical

Olson's version of the practical unimportance of numerical identity stems from consideration of three practical concerns (prudence, responsibility, and social treatment) that are assumed to be (a) the only relevant practical concerns at issue, and (b) unified in virtue of being grounded in psychological continuity. Both assumptions are mistaken, however.[21]

Regarding (a), I have already noted that there are several other possible person- or identity-related practical concerns at issue, including compensation, anticipation, and emotional patterns. These could be relevant to bolstering the strength of the Transplant Intuition, as we might also be thinking of how Brainy could be compensated for burdens underwent by Prince, or how Brainy could justifiably feel pride at the past actions of Prince, or how, if he knew the transplant was coming, Prince might justifiably anticipate the experiences of Brainy. Alternatively, they might be thought to bolster the *Challenge* that, by also tracking psychological continuity, they still track *what matters in* numerical identity. My only point in reminding us of the additional practical concerns, though, is that their presence, in addition to those discussed by Olson, actually makes my main case, which is against (b), more stark.

Let us turn, then, to that case. The basic assumption I want to argue against is that our practical concerns constitute a unified set that is grounded on psychological continuity. What is actually the case, I will urge, is that the grounding relation is neither psychological continuity nor, ultimately, identity; it is, rather, *ownership*, which itself takes multiple forms, and so is not capturable under any kind of explanatorily robust, single rubric. In order to see both the meaning and force of this point, however, we need to examine each of the relevant practical concerns in more detail.

To provide a glimpse into what I think of as the pluralism of the practical, we may start by considering one of the practical concerns Olson himself discusses: social treatment. While we may at first be inclined to go along with his thought that social treatment in the Prince/Cobbler case tracks psychological continuity, further reflection suggests that the matter is far more complicated than he lets on. Indeed, it turns out that by emphasizing different possibilities we may come to think that social treatment actually

---

biological underpinning, it could still preserve what is necessary to numerical identity, and given that uniqueness also obtains in this case, Duplicate may well be me as a result.

[21] In a way, Olson recognizes this point. In an insightful speculative passage, he briefly mentions that it might be implausible to believe that the three concerns he discusses "always go together" (Olson 1997: 66), and he admits that there may be "additional relations of practical concern associated with personal identity besides the three we have discussed" (Olson 1997: 68). But in neither case does he sufficiently explore what this might mean for the general thesis that our practical concerns are not necessarily connected at all with personal identity, such that the plausibility of animalism isn't dependent on how it accounts for them. It is my aim in what follows in the text to take up this burden.

tracks *biological* continuity. For example, consider someone who, due to some traumatic brain injury, undergoes radical psychological discontinuity. She will still be
treated as the owner of the pre-transformation-person's car and other property, and
she will also be treated as the spouse of the pre-transformation-person's spouse, the
daughter of her parent, and so forth. Indeed, parenthood provides an excellent general
case: expectant mothers often treat their fetuses in loving ways from early in pregnancy,
and while their specific *expressions* of love may change for that growing organism in
ways rendered appropriate by its different phases, there remains an ongoing target
of these expressions, and they are clearly tracking biological continuity. The ongoing
specific love is targeted at a human animal, from fetushood through infancy, toddler-
hood, adolescence, adulthood, senescence, and even, perhaps, to a vegetative state
(I take it that both DeGrazia and Schechtman advance versions of this point as well).
That the Queen would thus so blithely switch her loving expressions from Brainless
(Prince's body *sans* cerebrum) to Brainy is actually no foregone conclusion. The special
concerns of parenthood are tied tightly to our biological natures.

One might respond to these examples by embracing pluralism about our social
treatment concerns but only in order to embrace a pluralism about identity, suggesting
that different sorts of identity relations obtain depending on the form of treatment in
question.[22] Such a response would maintain the view that personal identity is what has
practical importance. In what follows, I hope to undermine this response by focusing
precisely on the details of each practical concern in question, and so by investigating
what really is being tracked in each case.

Responsibility:[23]   The relevant platitude is that *I can be responsible only for my own
actions*, and what is thought to make an action my own is that I am numerically identical to the person who performed it. But there is a conceptual wedge we can introduce
here: my ownership of some action is distinct from my identity with its agent. The
straightforward reason is just that each involves two different relata: ownership is a
relation between an agent and an action, whereas numerical identity is a relation some
individual bears to itself (*qua* individual). And what I take the actual lesson of the fission case to be is a revelation of how *ownership* of this sort may be prized apart from
identity. If I perform A and then divide, A may still be properly attributable to both of
my fission products despite their not being numerically identical to me (on pain of their
being numerically identical to one another).[24] But we can also see this phenomenon at

[22]   For instance, one might think that a biological criterion is true of us *qua* moral patients (e.g. as children)
but that a psychological criterion is true of us *qua* moral agents (e.g. as bearers of various financial and
parental obligations). I don't know of anyone who has held a view like this, but it's not *prima facie* implausible.
(Perhaps Locke's view—distinguishing between man and person, with different identity conditions for
each—comes closest.)
[23]   The arguments in this paragraph are drawn from Shoemaker 2011a.
[24]   If a four-dimensionalist is unhappy with this treatment of the case, she could instead imagine a
version of Olson's duplication case, where my duplicates may still properly be thought to own my previous
actions, despite clearly not being me.

work in real world cases: I may be the joint owner of actions produced by a joint agent. When we have sex, or sing a duet, or rob a bank, or win a game, we contribute to joint acts of joint agents; these are actions a *we*, not an I, performs. But even though I am not identical to that joint agent (on pain of being identical to all the other contributors to it), I may own that agent's actions for purposes of responsibility.[25] So here is another reason to distinguish ownership from numerical identity: ownership isn't a uniqueness (1–1) relation, whereas numerical identity is. Finally, there are real life cases in which ownership of actions is divorced from performance of them. If I order my children to run around breaking valuables in your house, those actions are attributable to me (I own them), despite the fact that I didn't perform any of them and so cannot be identical to their agent.[26]

So what does ownership-with-respect-to-responsibility consist in? As we have seen, theorists on both sides of the personal identity divide are at least united in agreeing that this ownership relation consists in psychological continuity. As it turns out, though, psychological continuity is neither necessary nor sufficient for ownership in this arena. It is not sufficient, because if I gradually go into and out of a fugue state during which my values and volitional make-up are radically changed, I will, post-fugue, be psychologically continuous with that person in the fugue state (because of the gradual nature of the transformation) *without his actions being mine*. It is not necessary, because it is possible to undergo psychological discontinuity (from a blow to the head, say) while preserving ownership of the pre-trauma action just in case the small number of values or concerns constructing one's volitional network at the time of action have been preserved post-trauma. What all of this suggests instead, then, is that responsibility-ownership consists in something like the preservation of the psychological elements contributing to one's volitional network, but this may be very different from psychological continuity full stop.[27]

---

[25] One might think that in such cases I have only *partial* responsibility, tracking my limited degree of attributability as it coincides with my limited degree of participation in the original joint action. I don't think this is correct. Instead, I think individual members of joint agents are often *fully* responsible for their joint action. Suppose there are five of us who rob a bank. One of us points a gun at the tellers, one of us shoves the money into a bag, one of us keeps a gun on the security guard, one of us serves as a lookout, and one of us awaits in the getaway car. The joint action—robbing the bank—strikes me as fully attributable to each of us individually. Suppose, for example, that only one person robbed the bank. The degree of ownership (and subsequent responsibility) attributed to him will be equal to that assigned to *each* of us in the joint robbery case (to the extent it makes sense to talk in terms of degrees of attribution). This doesn't mean there's *more* responsibility (five times as much) in the joint robbery case; rather, it means that the notion of full responsibility (which presupposes full ownership) isn't additive. I take what I'm saying here as akin to Harry Frankfurt's example of our simultaneously flipping two light switches at either end of a room that control the same bulb. As he puts it, "Neither person is solely responsible for the light's going on, nor do they share the responsibility in the sense that each is partially responsible; rather, each of them is fully responsible" (Frankfurt 1988: 25, n.10).

[26] It's not just my *ordering* them to break the valuables that I am responsible for; it is, I maintain, their actual actions. This is because what they've done is directly dependent on my will. This is also why, for example, a general who orders his troops to take the bridge may be responsible for that action if they are successful. That the children or the troops are able to refuse the orders may render them also complicit in the actions, and so co-owners of them as well.

[27] This final suggestion is fleshed out in Shoemaker 2011b.

Anticipation: The assumed platitude regarding anticipation is that *I am justified in anticipating some set of future experiences only if they are mine*. And again there is thought to be a connection between the ownership of those future experiences and numerical identity: what makes those experiences mine is just that I will be the person who experiences them. This seems once more to suggest a psychological continuity theory of identity. But anticipation-ownership is a relation between an experiencer now and some future *experiences*, whereas identity (as it is relevant here, anyway) is a relation between experiencers. And anticipation-ownership clearly seems divorceable from identity: were I about to undergo fission, I could certainly anticipate the experiences of each product, viewing them both as mine, whereas identity between us would not obtain. Relatedly, were I to entertain undergoing *fusion*, I might be able to antici-pate the experiences of the fused experiencer, despite that experiencer (likely) not being me.[28] Anticipation-ownership is not a uniqueness relation, whereas numerical identity is.

So what does anticipation-ownership consist in? Once again, psychological con-tinuity (prized apart from identity) might be thought at least to be what matters, but that is actually too broad. Instead, all that seems to be needed is some kind of properly connected stream of conscious awareness. Perhaps one might want to insist on the additional persistence of relevant values (in order for the various features of the antici-pated experiences and the actual experiences to be viewed in sufficiently similar evalu-ative light and so themselves to be sufficiently similar for the process to count as anticipation), but this doesn't seem necessary either, given that it ought to be possible for a wanton—someone who values and cares about nothing—to anticipate future experiences as well. But I leave this possibility open for future analysis.

Self-concern: Here what may seem to be going on is that I have a special sort of concern only for the person in the future who is *me*. Isn't this, then, clearly an identity-directed concern? "Self-concern" is what Mark Johnston calls the clearest example of "a wider pattern of self-*referential* concern, directed outwards from one's present self to one's future self, one's friends, family, acquaintances, neighbourhood, and so on" (Johnston 1997: 156; emphasis mine). True enough. But then what really unites all of these var-ieties of "special" concern is the *mineness* attached to them: the concerns are for *my* self, *my* friends, *my* family, etc. This suggests again, though, that the grounding relation is ownership, which could well run independently of identity.[29] Were I destroyed as I sleep tonight and a duplicate put in my place, it seems that the *mineness* of the self, friends, family, and acquaintances with respect to special concern could be preserved

---

[28] For a similar argument applied to Don Marquis's anti-abortion argument, see Shoemaker 2010: 485–6.
[29] Johnston's point (Johnston 1997: 158–9) is that these self-referential concerns are ungrounded, or at least self-grounded independently of the metaphysics of identity. What I am suggesting, however, is that even if the latter is true, they may still have to answer to the metaphysics of *ownership*. In other words, my having this sort of special concern for someone to whom I don't bear the mineness relation would likely be unjustified (or at least very weird).

in the duplicate despite the loss of identity, and despite the fact that the duplicate didn't *make* any of those friends or acquaintances, say, or wasn't around for the genesis of the family or the original self. Consequently, it seems that this sort of ownership consists in yet another psychological relation, a kind of persistence or resemblance relation between the values and attitudes directed toward the relevant object (the entities filling the roles of self, friends, family, etc.), along with connections of memory (or q-memory), intentions, beliefs, desires, and goals relevant to those cared-for objects. This sort of ownership, then, does indeed start to sound like robust psychological continuity.

Compensation: This requires a more complicated analysis. Here is the relevant platitude: *I can truly be compensated with a benefit for a burden only if the burden underwent was my own.* This platitude is then taken to entail the view that compensation presupposes personal identity: some burden could be my own if and only if I am numerically identical with the person who underwent it.[30] This entailment does not obtain, however. Some past burden may be mine without my being numerically identical to the one who was burdened. In science fiction cases, this could be true of one of the fission products with respect to some pre-fission burden, and it could also be true of Duplicate with respect to some burden underwent by me. In real world cases, I may be legitimately compensated for a burden undergone by a joint agent to which I contributed. For example, for the sacrifices made by a *team* on which I myself personally sacrificed very little (perhaps I was injured or rode the bench), I may still warrant compensation equal to everyone else. But I am not identical to that joint agent, that *team*, on pain of being identical with every other player who would ostensibly be identical to that joint agent as well, despite the team's sacrifice being (partially) mine.

   It may seem that compensation-ownership consists in psychological continuity, but I believe this is false. Suppose Johann suddenly enters a fugue state. Call the radically psychologically discontinuous "fuguer" Sebastian. Suppose that I had broken Johann's wrist prior to the fugue state but that I now have the medical equipment and expertise to completely heal it and, indeed, make it stronger than before (i.e. to "rejuvenate" it). When I rejuvenate the wrist I broke, it is Sebastian's. Does what I have done count as compensation? It certainly seems so, despite the psychological discontinuity between Sebastian and Johann. This is because the kind of burden I attempted to rectify was to Johann's animal self, and while physical setbacks are, at most, merely instrumental to well-being—on any account of well-being, I think—if they persist across multiple psychological beings, they may be instrumental in reducing the well-being of *whomever* they are attached to. To rejuvenate the specific wrist I broke (attached to a living human being) is to make right a burden I caused.

---

[30] Parfit explicitly takes to be "clearly true" the view that compensation presupposes personal identity (Parfit 1984: 337), and Diane Jeske agrees, saying that "if you are to compensate *me* for a burden imposed on me, then you must provide *me* with some counterbalancing benefit" (Jeske 1993: 560).

Whose burden did I rectify, however? We could say that I clearly burdened Johann, so I must have compensated him. Alternatively, we could say that I clearly compensated Sebastian, so I must have burdened him. If we take only one of these construals to be true, though, we are overly attached to the thought that compensation presupposes *personal* identity, i.e. that it tracks the identity of psychological beings. But there remains another, more plausible, option: there is a persisting animal here, call him Bach, whose interests were set back when his wrist was broken but whose injury was made right when his wrist was later rejuvenated. That he underwent radical psychological discontinuity during this period is irrelevant, for his interests *qua* animal were sufficient to generate the grounds for compensation for the injury to his animal body.

This last way of construing matters might suggest that identity is actually still grounding compensation, but now just *animal* identity. This would be too quick, however, for compensation may also coherently cut across different animals. This is presumably the case in the Prince/Cobbler scenarios. Suppose I psychologically injured Prince, causing certain traumatic flashbacks to occur, but I was able to eliminate such flashbacks by fiddling with the cerebrum from which they were produced. Doing so when the cerebrum is installed in Brainy strikes me as compensation for the burdens of Prince, despite the lack of animal continuity between them.

We might, therefore, ultimately be tempted to say this: yes, compensation-ownership may sometimes be grounded in animal continuity and may sometimes be grounded in psychological continuity, but in either case it would still be grounded in *numerical identity*, which would preserve the original assumption that compensation presupposes identity. To explain, we could say that when the injury is to one's (non-psychological) physical self, a benefit may compensate for that burden if and only if the benefited individual is the same animal as the burdened individual, whereas when the injury is to one's psychological self, a benefit may compensate for that burden if and only if the benefited individual is the same person—psychological entity—as the burdened individual. On this construal, then, compensation-ownership still presupposes identity, but because there are different kinds of compensation, there must be multiple identity relations grounding ownership for each kind.

This response will not work, however, for we cannot be pluralists about numerical identity; we can only be pluralists about ownership. If the numerical identity we are talking about is identity of individuals like us, then the proposal just given could require that I am both identical with, and not identical with, some past or future individual. This could be the case, for example, with respect to an injury caused to Johann pre-fugue, an injury affecting both his physical and psychological selves, e.g. if I stabbed him in the brain, causing him both physical trauma and psychological trauma. Suppose the stabbing caused both impaired motor skills and the loss of a central value, perhaps the love of cats which had guided the projects of his adult life. He then enters the fugue state and Sebastian is "born." In this state, given his radical psychological discontinuity from Johann, Sebastian embarks on a very different life project, pursuing a brand of stand-up comedy that centrally involves making fun of cats and cat lovers. Suppose

I have the ability to heal the portion of the brain I had destroyed. Were I to do so, I would compensate Sebastian with respect to his physical (animal) self—restoring his motor skills—but would not compensate Sebastian with respect to his psychological (personal) self, for introducing a love of cats would probably undermine his stand-up comedy dreams. On the above proposal, then, Sebastian both is and is not identical to Johann, the individual who underwent the original burden: to the extent Sebastian is (physically) compensated for the injury to Johann, they are one and the same; to the extent he could not be (psychologically) compensated by the very same treatment for that very same injury, they are not.[31]

I think, then, that this last-ditch effort to preserve some relation between compensation and numerical identity must be abandoned.[32] If all we are tracking when we are distributing a compensatory benefit to someone is that the burden it outweighs was *his*, it is just irrelevant whether or not that compensation-ownership relation happens to correspond to some numerical identity relation or other. All that matters is whether or not compensation-ownership in any particular instance is attached to the agent's physical or psychological self, and this in turn will be determined by the specific nature of the benefits or burdens in question.

While we cannot coherently be pluralists about numerical identity, therefore, we nevertheless can and ought to be pluralists about compensation-ownership (and ownership generally). Individuals like us are numerically identical only to ourselves, whereas, given the wide variety of physical and psychological elements we have, individuals like us may be many different kinds of owners.

This point returns us to the heart of my worry about the implications of the Schechtmanian proposal: expanding the notion of personhood in the way suggested there glosses over the wide variety of relations that *actually* ground our person-related practices, and so fails to do any real explanatory work. What is doing the explanatory work instead is the ownership relation, with its multiple and varying instantiation conditions, whereas talk of identity doesn't help and may actually hurt (by distracting our attention away from the actual conditions of ownership). Identity is the reddest of herrings.[33]

[31] Perhaps there were really two injuries, one to his brain and one to his psychology? Perhaps, but it seems more plausible to describe it as one injury with multiple manifestations. For example, if I break your hand, it will hinder you as a driver and as a cook. But there is only one injury, namely to your hand; it would be odd to say that I injured your driving hand and I also injured your cooking hand. At any rate, though, what matters most here is the form of compensation: I undid to Sebastian's brain precisely what I did to Johann's brain. That this only counts as compensation for one of the injury's manifestations is what generates the contradiction when tied to identity.

[32] And I think similar contradictions could be derived for the previously discussed practical concerns as well.

[33] Perhaps, though, there are some other practical concerns for which identity is important? The only ones that would seem to have a chance are the concerns surrounding third-person reidentification. I actually believe that considerations of ownership are more fundamental in such cases too, although space constraints prevent me from laying out this case in any detail here. The basic idea, though, is that where we have concerns regarding reidentifying others, they are often—albeit definitely not always—with respect to an extension of the sort of special concern we have for ourselves. I have already cited Johnston's plausible

Conclusion

The *Challenge* to animalism is that it is rendered less plausible in virtue of its lacking a proper fit with our practical concerns. After exploring and expressing worries about two attempts to show how animalism might not lack the relevant practical fit, I turned to an Olsonian defense of the view that lacking this fit has no effect either way on the plausibility of animalism. While Olson's own attempt at making this case does defend against a weaker interpretation of *Challenge*, it doesn't defend[34] against a stronger interpretation, according to which the psychological continuity assumed to ground and unify our practical concerns must still be at least the primary necessary ingredient of numerical identity. In the final part of the chapter, I tried to undermine this case by showing that (a) our practical concerns are not a unified set; (b) different concerns are grounded on different relations, most of which (perhaps all) are *not* psychological continuity; and (c) because at least some individual practical concerns (e.g. compensation) themselves are grounded on multiple, competing forms of ownership, there can be no entailment from ownership to numerical identity without contradiction.

Because of the surface similarity of the view I have expounded to previously articulated views of others, I want to spend the remainder of my concluding time here noting those similarities in order to spell out what I take to be some new and crucial differences. It may seem, first, that my view is simply a revisiting of Parfit's "Identity Doesn't Matter" view, according to which what matters instead (given thought experiments like fission) is just psychological continuity and/or connectedness (Relation R); the uniqueness relation that combines with R to deliver numerical identity is unimportant (Parfit 1984: 253–66). What I have tried to show, by contrast, is that not only does uniqueness not matter; neither does Relation R. Now Parfit's is officially a story about what matters in *survival*, but he takes this mattering to extend across the board to all of our practical concerns. Nonetheless, what matters in survival may well not be what matters for anticipation, responsibility, compensation, self-referential concerns, and so forth.[35] Indeed, we have good reason to believe that these concerns are grounded in

understanding of self-concern, which is just the most central case of self-referential concerns like those extended to one's family, friends, acquaintances, loved ones, and so on. But the identities of those who fall into these categories may change: the set of "my friends" includes different people at different times. What makes them my friends depends primarily on who they are, not who they have been. Indeed, my affective concern for them depends on features of them that affect our relationship (where these features may also include our shared history). To the extent I want to reidentify one of them, then, this often involves establishing or ensuring that they have the same relation to me now that grounded my affective concern in the past. Depending on the nature of our friendship, then (i.e. what it is that warrants my affective concern), the relevant ownership relation may be delivered by (a) psychological continuity on their part, (b) one aspect of psychological continuity (perhaps just continuity of character, or persistence of beliefs/desires/goals), (c) some combination of physical and psychological continuity, or (d) mere physical continuity (for those who are seriously shallow). And while all of these may still fall under the general rubric of human identity, that characterization completely glosses over what is fascinatingly different about each, marking very different construals of both friendship and ownership.

[34] Nor was it meant to.

[35] I'm unsure psychological continuity is even what matters in *survival*, but this is a story for another day.

different relations, and furthermore it is doubtful that for *any* of these concerns psychological continuity/connectedness is actually what matters. Instead, sometimes there are subsets of the psychological relations making up continuity/connectedness that are relevant, sometimes it is mere physical continuity that matters, and sometimes all that matters is my current relation to some other person (so continuity of any sort is irrelevant). What this suggests, then, is that, not only does identity not matter for our practical concerns, but also the relation Parfit thought mattered *in* identity is irrelevant to our practical concerns. So perhaps what I am advocating should be labeled the "Identity *Really* Doesn't Matter" view.

The second surface similarity my view bears is to an aspect of Schechtman's position in her early book *The Constitution of Selves*. There she makes an important distinction between two different questions identity theorists might pursue. The first is the *reidentification question*: what makes X at t1 identical to Y at t2? The second is the *characterization question*: what makes various thoughts, experiences, actions, and events properly attributable to some agent (Schechtman 1996: e.g. 73)? Pursuit of the latter question involves pursuit of identity of a different sort, she thinks, having to do with the sense relevant to an "identity crisis," according to which the identity discovered will consist in " 'the set of characteristics that make a person who she is' " (Schechtman 1996: 76). For Schechtman, the best unifying account of this sort appeals to narrative: what makes these various characteristics properly attributable to me is their being incorporated into the self-told story of my life (Schechtman 1996: ch. 5).

I take myself in part to be reminding us of the importance of the characterization question. The relation on which our various practical concerns are grounded is not numerical identity but is instead what I have referred to as the ownership relation. The relevant question then becomes what such ownership—characterization—consists in. And this is where I depart significantly from Schechtman. Whereas early-Schechtman believes that our various practical concerns are unified via narrative identity, and later-Schechtman believes (in addition?) that our various practical concerns are unified in targeting person-lives, I believe that the practical concerns *just aren't unified*, that what each of their relevant ownership relations consist in are simply different. I advocate pluralism regarding our person-related practical concerns in virtue of their plural grounds.[36] To force a unity upon this set under some umbrella rubric is to overlook precisely those fascinating and important pluralities, and it also may run headlong into contradiction (where, as in the compensation example, the benefited agent both is and is not identical to the burdened agent). So while my view is distinguished from Parfit's in denying the importance of what ostensibly matters in numerical identity (which addresses the reidentification question), it is also distinguished from Schechtman's in denying the importance of narrative or person-life identity as providing a unified answer to the characterization question. Perhaps, then, mine should be labeled the "Identity Really *Really* Doesn't Matter View."

---

[36] See Schechtman's discussion of an earlier sketch of my position in her 2014: 82–8.

I close by returning to the epigraphs. Contrary to John Merrick's animated cry he is—we all are—animals. But beyond the Animals' song, we are also human beings. And we are also persons (to translate Merrick's "man"). To the extent there are characteristics specific to each, we own them in that specific capacity.[37] As an animal, I have "breath, flesh, flesh and blood, physique, strength, power, vigor, force, spring, elasticity, tone, and grace." As a human being, I participate in a way of life giving rise to various sorts of self-referential concerns, friendships, and views of others generally that are expressed in uniquely human ways. As a person, I am a self-conscious moral agent producing actions and attitudes that are properly attributable to me for purposes of responsibility. Our practical concerns are distributed across these categories, some of them attached to our animality, some of them attached to our humanity, and some of them attached to our personhood. And while most (all?) of the concerns in the set do at least track what is *ours*, the conditions of said ownership are different enough in each case to thwart genuine unity in anything but name. Animalism indeed does poorly in accounting for our practical concerns, but then again, so does *any* theory of personal or human identity, or, for that matter, any theory purporting to account for the set as a whole. Revealing the thoroughgoing pluralism of our practical concerns should finally expose the sham that their marriage to identity has always really been.[38]

References

Buchanan, Allen. 1988. "Advance Directives and the Personal Identity Problem." *Philosophy and Public Affairs* 17: 277–302.

DeGrazia, David. 2005. *Human Identity and Bioethics* (Cambridge: Cambridge University Press).

Frankfurt, Harry. 1988. *The Importance of What We Care About* (Cambridge: Cambridge University Press).

Jeske, Diane. 1993. "Persons, Compensation, and Utilitarianism." *The Philosophical Review* 102: 541–75.

Johnston, Mark. 1997. "Human Concerns Without Superlative Selves." In Jonathan Dancy, ed., *Reading Parfit* (Oxford: Blackwell Publishers), 149–79.

Lewis, David. 1976. "Survival and Identity." In Amelie Oksenberg Rorty, ed., *The Identities of Persons* (Berkeley: University of California Press), 17–40.

Locke, John. 1975. "Of Identity and Diversity." In John Perry, ed., *Personal Identity* (Berkeley: University of California Press), 33–52.

Martin, Raymond. 1998. *Self-Concern* (Cambridge: Cambridge University Press).

[37] Are we *essentially* one or the other? This is irrelevant to the question of ownership, it seems. I may own something *qua* any variety of phase sortals.

[38] This chapter was a long time coming out, and I've learned a lot from many people about the relevant issues over the years. For feedback on various drafts and presentations of the material, I'm grateful to Stephan Blatti, Victor Kumar, Shaun Nichols, Eric Olson, Marya Schechtman, David Silver, and Hannah Tierney. I am also grateful for helpful discussion of some of the material herein with the participants in my seminars on Personal Identity and Ethics at Bowling Green State University in 2011, and Tulane in 2011 and 2015, as well as the audiences at my presentation of this material at Ohio State and the University of Arizona.

Olson, Eric. 1997. *The Human Animal* (Oxford: Oxford University Press).

Parfit, Derek. 1984. *Reasons and Persons* (Oxford: Oxford University Press).

Schechtman, Marya. 1996. *The Constitution of Selves* (Ithaca, NY: Cornell University Press).

Schechtman, Marya. 2010. "Personhood and the Practical." *Theoretical Medicine and Bioethics* 31: 271–83.

Schechtman, Marya. 2014. *Staying Alive: Personal Identity, Practical Concerns, and the Unity of a Life*. Oxford: Oxford University Press.

Shoemaker, David W. 2007. "Personal Identity and Practical Concerns." *Mind* 116: 317–57.

Shoemaker, David W. 2010. "The Insignificance of Personal Identity for Bioethics." *Bioethics* 24: 481–9.

Shoemaker, David W. 2011a. "Moral Responsibility and the Self." In Shaun Gallagher, ed., *Oxford Handbook of the Self* (Oxford: Oxford University Press), 487–520.

Shoemaker, David W. 2011b. "Responsibility Without Identity." *Harvard Review of Philosophy* 18: 109–32.

Sider, Theodore. 2001. *Four-Dimensionalism* (Oxford: Oxford University Press).

Index

agency 83, 135, 174–5, 259, 305, 311, 318, 319, 321, 323, 325–6
animals:
 nature of 2–3, 10–11, 15, 47, 50, 65, 86, 104, 106, 150, 172, 177, 181, 283, 318
 nonhuman 16, 40, 54, 57–8, 60, 102, 126, 128–9, 136, 163, 170–1, 173, 216, 231, 253, 255–6, 283, 313
Anscombe, Elizabeth 191, 193
Aquinas, Thomas 103, 127
Aristotle 53, 124, 157, 171
attribution error 171–4
Ayers, Michael 3, 13, 102, 163

Baker, Lynn Rudder 13, 33, 51–4, 56, 58, 61–2, 137, 285
Bayne, Tim 23, 267, 276
belief 20, 23, 44, 48, 55, 95, 107, 132, 135, 145, 154–5, 165, 168–9, 173, 183, 187–9, 231, 238, 255, 270–6, 286
Bennett, Karen 79
Bennett, Max 172
biotechnology 58–61
Blatti, Stephan 19–20, 235–9, 253, 255, 259, 263–4, 269
brain 2, 6, 12, 16, 18–20, 22–3, 32, 35–42, 57–60, 93, 98, 105–6, 108–15, 117–25, 135, 145–60, 164–8, 171–4, 181, 183–5, 204, 209, 214–18, 220–5, 229, 233–5, 240–1, 243–4, 246–7, 250, 258, 261–3, 269, 275, 298, 323
 bisection 23–4, 111, 218, 220, 225, 235, 237–8, 248, 253–60, 263–4, 266–71, 273, 276–8, 280–2
 cerebrum and cerebral hemispheres 12, 17, 18, 23–4, 36–9, 40–2, 46–8, 60, 110–15, 122, 124, 125, 128–30, 134–7, 149, 152, 176, 202, 204, 220, 222–5, 232, 235–6, 240–1, 243, 247–50, 253, 255–8, 261–4, 267, 278, 286–90, 292–5, 298, 315, 318, 322
 cerebrum in a vat 41, 176, 202
 damage and death 34, 61, 93–4, 225, 238, 243–4, 318, 322
 in a vat 107, 111–12, 117, 148, 153–5, 157, 159–60, 176, 184–5, 188, 203, 215–17
 stem 36–7, 41, 46–8, 106, 129, 232, 241, 243–4, 246–50
 transplant, see transplant
brain-based psychological criterion 32, 35, 37, 222, 224

brain view 18, 39, 160, 233
branching 220, 235, 237, 286, 290–2
Brancazio, Nicolle 26
Brassel, Freidhelm 256
brave general 218–21, 225
Buchanan, Allen 310
Burge, Tyler 70
Burke, Michael 77, 156
Byrne, Alex 128

Campbell, Scott 285
capacities 5, 16, 19, 38, 65–7, 82–3, 93, 111, 117, 165, 171–6, 221, 223, 238, 280–1, 309–11, 313
Carter, William 18, 40, 42, 102, 107, 163
Cartwright, Helen 70, 78
Cartwright, Richard 75
Cassam, Quassim 191
causation 14, 17, 22, 81–5, 111–12, 114–15, 118, 120, 131–3, 135–7, 139–40, 182, 187–8, 192–3, 195–201, 209–10, 212–13, 217–20, 224–5
central nervous system 5, 83, 107, 180–1, 209–10, 214–15, 233, 241, 243, 250, 281
Clark, Andy 217
clone, see replica
coincidence 64, 130, 140, 235, 251
commissurotomy, see brain: bisection
composite objects 102, 158, 170, 213, 232–3
composition 18, 57–8, 74, 82, 85, 114, 158, 208–13, 215, 222, 225
concepts 14–15, 34, 60–1, 67–70, 79–80, 83, 91–2, 96–100, 106, 172, 176, 211, 237, 239, 264, 268, 277 (see also substance: concepts)
conjoined twins 41, 230, 240, 246, 247, 255
 cephalopagus 247–51
 craniopagus parasiticus 240–1, 243
 dicephalus 221, 229–31, 235–41, 248–51, 253, 255, 256, 259, 263–4
consciousness 10, 16, 20–1, 33, 36–48, 51, 69, 92–4, 96–7, 105–6, 110, 115, 119, 146–8, 154, 156, 159, 171, 181–4, 189, 193–6, 198–204, 206, 208, 215–16, 222–4, 229, 231–4, 240–50, 254–7, 259–60, 262–4, 267–71, 277–8, 320
 self-consciousness 65, 156, 189–90, 208–12, 221–4, 230, 241, 248–50, 309, 326
 unity of 23, 220, 255, 257, 264, 266, 270, 278

constitution 13–14, 20, 23, 33, 38–9, 42, 50–63, 64, 70–80, 82–6, 103, 107, 108, 110–21, 123, 125, 129–31, 133, 140, 145, 148, 153, 155, 158–60, 162, 170, 173, 181–3, 187, 201, 210, 214, 217–18, 224, 233, 238, 242–4, 246, 250, 284–5, 308
content 60, 154, 195, 215, 217, 219, 220, 253, 257, 271, 277, 278
continuity 2, 10, 25, 32–49, 51, 61–2, 66, 83, 90, 96–103, 106–7, 112–15, 117, 119, 122, 129–30, 139–40, 145–52, 204–5, 209–15, 218–25, 229, 231, 233, 235–7, 244–6, 250, 253, 255–6
  biological 33–6, 41–2, 46, 48, 51, 68, 130, 140, 152, 204–5, 229, 244–6, 250, 300, 304–9, 312, 318, 322
  causal 139–40
  physical 10, 61–2, 100, 103, 106–7, 112–14, 117, 122, 138, 324
  psychological 25, 32–5, 37–8, 48–9, 66, 68, 83, 90, 96–103, 106–7, 112–14, 117, 119, 127, 129–30, 145–50, 209–13, 219–22, 224–5, 229, 231, 233, 235–7, 250, 253, 255–6, 286–7, 289–92, 294–300, 306–11, 314–22, 324–5
  spatiotemporal 139–40
corpse 17, 67, 124–5, 138–40, 214, 229, 232, 239, 242, 286
creation and destruction 16, 18, 21, 23, 37–8, 62, 77, 111–12, 114–15, 117–18, 125, 149–53, 155–7, 159, 176, 203–5, 246, 256, 264, 267
Cruzan, Nancy 41
Cummins, Robert 199

Damasio, Antonio 209, 215, 217
Davidson, Donald 23, 154
death 13, 48, 61, 67, 92, 94, 117–18, 123–7, 138–40, 160, 212, 232, 242 (see also brain damage and death)
DeGrazia, David 25, 162, 285, 304–9, 312, 318
Descartes, René 5, 43, 45, 69, 115, 163, 190
dicephalus, see conjoined twins
dissociative identity disorder 238, 253, 255, 256, 260–1
divided mind, see brain: bisection
dualism 15, 66, 69, 82, 140, 172, 181
duplication objections 236–7, 254–6
Dupré, John 105

eliminativism 18, 20, 157–8, 183, 235
embodied mind view 39–40
embodied part view 38–43, 167
embodied person view 12–13, 40–4, 46, 48
embryo 33, 34, 37, 103, 122, 208, 209, 211, 212, 224, 240, 253, 284, 286–7 (see also fetus)
essence 80, 82, 85–6, 100, 105

Evans, Gareth 292
evolution 11, 51, 55–6, 82, 85–6, 177, 260, 281

Feldman, Fred 286
fetus 33, 34, 110, 130, 149, 177, 310, 313, 318 (see also embryo)
Fine, Kit 73
first-person perspective 50–1, 54–7, 60–2, 181–2, 184–5, 192, 195–6, 198, 202, 205, 231
first-person reference 12–13, 32, 43–7, 51, 54–5, 110–11, 114, 125–6, 154, 157, 163, 167–9, 173–4, 189–95, 233, 250, 276, 320, 324–5
fission 256, 263
Forster, Michael 126
four-dimensionalism 14, 22, 72–3, 117, 208, 210, 263
Frankfurt, Harry 319
Frege, Gottlob 190
fusion 213, 220, 223, 240, 245–7, 262–3, 292, 320

Geach, Peter 75
Giaquinto, Marcus 183
Gibbard, Allan 70, 77, 79
God 9, 13, 57, 61–2, 148, 284, 285
Godfrey-Smith, Peter 23

Hacker, Peter 171–4
Harré, Rom 171
Hawley, Katherine 156
hemispherectomy, see brain: bisection
Hensel, Abigail and Brittany, see conjoined twins: dicephalus
Heraclitus 79, 82
Hershenov, David 21, 22, 151, 234
Hudson, Hud 208–15, 217–19, 221–2, 224, 242
human:
  animal 2, 5–6, 8, 12, 14, 18–19, 23, 33, 36–9, 41–7, 58–9, 65–6, 68, 85, 100–1, 106–14, 121, 127, 145, 147, 151–2, 162–4, 166–8, 170–3, 176, 186, 208–11, 213–14, 218–25, 230, 239, 253–5, 257–8, 260–4, 269–70, 277, 285, 298, 305, 312, 318
  form 180–2, 184–90, 194–5, 205–6
  Homo sapiens 2, 15, 100, 102–4, 162–3, 180, 284
  nature 65
  person 47, 54, 66, 68, 76, 85, 89, 122, 148, 150, 158–9, 165, 208–9, 213, 222, 225, 237, 253, 284
humanity 312, 326
Hume, David 116, 140, 180, 195, 268, 277
Humphreys, Glyn 280
hylomorphism 171, 284, 289

identity:
  conditions 82, 90, 96
  diachronic 82, 224, 235
  gen 209, 213
  and nonidentity 208
  numerical 31–2, 49, 53, 56, 92, 95–6, 100–1,
    162, 229, 233, 235–6, 250, 253–6, 285, 291,
    295, 299, 305, 307–10, 314–25
  personal 2–16, 24–6, 31–2, 42, 48, 60–2,
    67–9, 74, 83, 90–3, 95–103, 106–7, 109–10,
    112, 117–18, 120–1, 125, 127, 129–30, 162,
    181, 189, 199, 208, 210, 222, 229, 235, 238,
    255–6, 264, 266, 283, 286–97, 299–301,
    303–5, 314, 316–19, 321–2, 326
  qualitative 19, 31–2, 35
  relation 1, 26, 32, 70, 73–4, 101, 209, 213, 220,
    230, 234, 254, 291, 299–300, 305, 310, 318,
    319–20, 322–3
  synchronic 82
  thesis (of animalism) 4, 7–10, 18–20, 22,
    266, 287
  token 118, 121
  transitivity of 219–20, 230, 235–7, 254, 256, 263
  type 118
  what matters in, see Parfit-Shoemaker thesis
implantation 59 (see also biotechnology)
intracarotid amytal procedure 23, 256
    (see also brain bisection)
intuition 10, 15, 24, 41, 65, 69, 74, 78, 82, 91–3,
    95–6, 98, 102, 137, 140, 184, 186–7, 210–11,
    218, 220–2, 224–5, 238, 278, 316
    (see also transplant: intuition)

Johansson, Jens 10, 22, 24–5, 284, 292
Johnston, Mark 6, 8, 15–16, 17, 37, 39–42, 45,
    69, 80–2, 119, 148–51, 156, 159, 176, 184,
    202, 267, 320

Kant, Immanuel 271
Kearns, Stephen 63, 189
key distinction, the 53, 56 (see also properties:
    derivative and non–derivative)
kind 51–4, 56–8, 60, 61, 62, 65, 67–9, 72, 78–86,
    100, 125, 128, 130–7, 181, 229–31, 236, 238,
    241, 242, 245–6, 249–51, 254, 268
  natural 80, 105, 209, 212–13
  phase and substance (see also sortal) 14–16,
    78, 82, 84, 86, 89, 91, 100–12, 114, 117–18,
    120–2, 125–7, 249
knowledge 19–21, 61, 80, 91–2, 96–102, 105,
    154, 168–9, 173–4, 180, 182, 185–7, 189, 306
Koko (gorilla) 170–1
Kripke, Saul 86, 105, 190–1
Krohs, Ulrich 199

language 55, 57, 74, 78, 84, 99, 183, 189
LaPorte, Joseph 103

Leibniz's Law 75
Leslie, Sarah-Jane 97
Lewis, David 2–3, 32, 70, 72, 75, 79, 84,
    86, 236, 263
Liao, Matthew 239
Lichtenberg, Georg Christoph 45, 195
life, see processes: biological and life
life support 98, 124, 215, 217, 229, 232, 241, 244,
    246–7
Lim, Joungbin 122
link thesis 60–1
Locke, John 2–3, 9–10, 12, 32, 67–9, 110–11,
    122, 126, 140, 149, 152, 156, 218, 220–1,
    286, 309, 318
Lockeanism and neo-Lockeanism 3, 7, 10,
    12–13, 16, 32–4, 36–8, 40–8, 64, 68–9, 83,
    230, 241, 249–50, 309–11
  memory criterion 218

McDowell, John 18, 33
Mackie, David 102, 286
Mackie, John 271
Mackie, Penelope 73
McMahan, Jeff 6, 11, 22, 23, 38, 39, 47, 221, 222,
    224, 229, 239, 253, 255, 259, 263
Madden, Rory 7, 18, 20–1, 154–5, 269
Magidor, Ofra 189
Maker, see God
Marks, Charles 267, 276
mass nouns 79–80
materialism 255, 261–2, 264
    (see also physicalism)
matter 5, 13, 14, 70–2, 85, 87, 90, 108–9, 111,
    119–20, 121, 122, 131, 133, 139–40, 154, 158,
    200–1, 203, 214–15, 231–2, 234, 245, 250–1
maximality 209, 210, 211, 213, 222, 225
memory 218–19, 221, 257, 259, 262, 295, 321
    (see also memory criterion)
mental state 23–4, 33, 55, 60, 62, 68, 82–3, 129,
    132, 168–9, 209–10, 217–33, 241, 247, 260,
    262–3, 269–70, 275–6, 278, 281, 286,
    295–6, 298, 305
mereological fallacy, see attribution error
mereological nihilism 158, 170
    (see also eliminativism)
Merricks, Trenton 288
method of cases 15, 69, 90, 91–2, 96–8, 103,
    105, 110, 111
microentities 132–3
Miller, Kenneth 230
Millikan, Ruth 199, 200
mind 21–2, 40, 42, 59, 92, 96–7, 99, 103, 106,
    118, 121, 126, 163, 172, 174, 204, 208–9,
    212–15, 218, 220–1, 223–5, 230, 233–5,
    237–8, 245, 248–50, 253, 255, 259–60, 264,
    266–7, 277–8, 305 (see also embodied mind
    view; too many minds problem)

modality 6, 14, 73, 79, 86, 231, 269, 284
monism 73
Moore, G. E. 65, 170, 187
moral:
    competence 294, 295
    convictions 238
    responsibility 24, 25, 40, 173–4, 258–9, 262,
        287, 293–4, 296–301, 305, 306, 308, 314,
        318, 326
    standing and status 212, 238

Nagel, Thomas 24, 122, 253, 254, 264, 277–81
naive realism 180
narrative 325
natural selection, see evolution
Newton, Isaac 79
Noë, Alva 209, 215–17
Noonan, Harold 2, 13, 73, 79
normativity 25, 55, 157, 238, 255, 309
Nozick, Robert 96, 98, 99, 127

Okasha, Samir 103
Olson, Eric 3, 13, 14, 16–18, 20–1, 24–7, 31, 32,
        35, 37–45, 47, 49, 51, 56–9, 66, 70–3, 79,
        107, 129–30, 140, 147, 158, 160, 163, 165–6,
        176, 177, 184, 185, 189–90, 202, 209,
        217–18, 225, 231–4, 242, 253, 255, 260–2,
        283–9, 293–7, 299–300, 304, 314–18, 324
ontology 21–2, 56–8, 64, 74–5, 77–9, 116, 170,
        211, 255, 284
organism 17–19, 37, 50, 52, 54–5, 61–2, 89,
        90–2, 98, 103, 106, 114, 116, 119–25, 129,
        138, 145–59, 162, 170, 172, 176, 181, 184,
        189, 192–4, 198–204, 214–16, 224–5,
        229–51, 255, 283–4, 286, 289–90, 297–300,
        303, 305, 318
overlappers 20–1, 76, 125, 182–90, 192–202,
        209, 218–20, 235–6

pain 128, 132, 134, 218, 221, 223–5, 268, 287–8,
        289, 311
Parfit, Derek 1–3, 6, 10, 12–13, 21, 24, 49, 158,
        160, 162, 166–7, 176, 184, 202, 218–20, 225,
        237, 251, 255, 258, 292, 316, 321, 324–5
Parfit–Shoemaker Thesis 3, 10, 24, 48–9, 225,
        289–90, 294, 314, 316–17, 324–5
Peacocke, Christopher 195
perception 180, 275, 284
perdurance 209, 211, 214, 219
Perry, John 32, 218, 219
persistence conditions 8, 10, 15–17, 50–1, 60–1,
        65, 78–82, 85, 89, 95–6, 98, 118, 126,
        128–31, 134, 136, 138, 140, 218, 221, 223,
        234, 258, 286, 300, 311
persistent (permanent) vegetative state 36, 41,
        46, 98, 100, 103, 106, 122, 177, 248, 286,
        287, 310, 314, 318

person:
    as forensic term 10, 34, 309–11
    brain-size 152–3, 158, 209, 214, 217
    person-life 25, 311–13, 325
personhood 25, 51, 69, 111–14, 130, 208–9,
        211–12, 214, 217, 221–2, 249, 258, 309–13,
        323, 326
    maximal 156–7
phantom limb 181, 192
phenomenology 19, 93–4, 168–9, 193, 233
Phillips, Ian 198
physicalism 16–17, 64, 130–1
        (see also materialism)
plasticity 216, 223, 258, 264
practical concern 25–6, 303–26
        (see also prudential concern, self-concern)
predication 13, 127, 128, 281, 284–5
and the pure predicative view 121
processes:
    biological and life 5, 14, 66–7, 81, 83, 109,
        116, 123, 138, 200, 205, 210, 212–15, 218,
        225, 233, 243, 245, 286–7
    mental 20, 45, 59, 121, 204, 216–17
properties:
    biological 133–40
    derivative and non-derivative 52–3, 56,
        137, 157
    essential 52–3, 85–6, 234
    extrinsic and intrinsic 84–6, 134–5, 137, 154
    maximal 85, 156, 197
    mental 17, 51, 129–38, 145, 148, 156–7, 159,
        172, 231
    modal 6, 14, 50, 59, 79, 146, 231
    phenomenal 233
    physical 5, 17, 42–3, 62, 130–7, 231, 261
    primary-kind 52–3
    psychological 4, 133, 233, 250, 284
    relational 135, 137
    thick and thin 17, 130–40
proprioception 19, 135, 168–9, 194
prudential concern 22, 24–5, 210, 221–5, 283,
        287–94, 297–301, 306–7, 309, 314–15
        (see also practical concern, self-concern)
Putnam, Hilary 82, 105, 188

Quine, Willard Van Orman 67
Quinton, Anthony 32

rationality 5, 34, 47, 127, 156, 221, 258, 275
realization and realizability 17, 68, 83, 86, 119,
        136, 191, 223–4
    mental 129, 131, 137, 138–9, 210
    microphysical 132–4, 137
    neurophysical 216–18
    property 132
    of relations 81
    of thought 153–4

reason, *see* rationality
Recanati, Francois 191
recognition 20, 105, 116, 121, 128, 262, 280, 305
reductio argument 53–4, 62
reductionism 33, 72
Reid, Mark 240, 256, 258
Reid, Thomas 218–20
remnant:
  cerebralism 18, 155, 159
  persons 17–18, 21, 89, 111–13, 115, 117–21, 124–7, 148–60, 176, 184, 202–6
replica 205, 224, 241
representation 80, 199–201, 215, 218, 257
responsibility 10, 24–5, 34, 173–4, 258–9, 262, 283, 287, 293–301, 305–9, 311, 313–14, 317–19, 324, 326
resurrection 61–3, 68, 127
Riddoch, M. Jane 280

Schechtman, Marya 25, 309–14, 318, 323, 325
Schiavo, Terri 60
self-acquaintance 21, 191–2, 194
self-ascription, *see* first-person reference
self-concern 225, 258–9, 262, 305, 306, 315, 320–1, 323–4 (*see also* prudential concern)
self-consciousness, *see* consciousness: self-consciousness
self-knowledge 105, 173, 186
self-monitoring 190–4
sentience 54, 210, 221–4
severed head 16, 19, 113–15, 117, 122, 124–6, 162, 166, 242–7
Shewmon, Alan 152, 223, 243–6
Shoemaker, Sydney 2, 15, 16–17, 24, 32, 33, 48, 49, 105, 107, 112, 163, 285
Shoemaker, David 25–6
Sider, Ted 197, 315
simples 57–8, 114–16, 158, 170
Smit, Harry 171
Snowdon, Paul 3, 8, 18, 23, 32–3, 49, 50, 53–4, 60, 102, 107, 149, 163, 253, 254, 260, 261, 283
social treatment 305–7, 315, 317–18
Socrates 220–1, 225
somaesthetic system 192–3
sortal 9, 34, 52, 67–8, 73, 77–86, 326 (*see also* kind: substance)
Sosa, Ernest 182
soul 32, 43, 48, 62, 69, 89–90, 92–8, 101, 102, 107, 127, 141, 171, 183, 284, 289
special composition question 18, 176
species 55, 65, 86, 90, 102–5, 131, 162–3, 180, 241, 284, 285
  migration 103–4
Sperry, Roger 271, 276
split-brain, *see* brain bisection

stages 22, 74, 77, 117, 131–2, 139–40, 155, 156, 162, 209, 211–12, 218, 220, 222, 225, 306
Strawson, P. F. 2, 13
subject 84, 94, 134, 191, 193, 198–201
  of experience 8, 17, 19–24, 40, 42, 101, 107, 115–16, 120–1, 125, 132, 134, 136, 154, 169, 184–5, 194–6, 206, 225, 231–5, 246, 254, 259, 261, 266–72, 274–81 (*see also* too many subjects problem)
  of mental properties 134
  of moral concern 175
subjective perspective, *see* first-person perspective
substance 16, 34, 48, 62, 64, 66, 69, 73, 77–86, 89, 91, 93–4, 100–10, 112, 114, 118, 120–2, 125–7, 151, 214, 232, 234
  concept 15, 67–8 (*see also* kind; sortal)
supervenience 81, 84–5, 106, 112–17, 125, 131, 132, 231, 233, 261
Sytsma, Justin 172

teletransportation 31–2, 44, 90, 97–9, 127, 184, 253, 290
temporal:
  boundaries 67, 77, 81, 85
  partitions 73
  parts 70, 72, 117, 148, 208–12, 214, 218, 219, 236, 284
  relations 84
  unity 51, 81, 86, 139–40
tense 34, 84–5
thinking animal problem (thinking animal argument) 18–19, 70, 162–5, 167–77, 186–7, 283, 299
thinking parts 12, 19–20, 38–40, 46–7, 156, 164–77, 181–90, 192–202, 208–15, 217–18, 223–4, 242, 268–9
Toner, Patrick 151, 172
too many minds problem 16, 56, 130, 138, 140, 162–3
too many persons problem 33, 46, 56, 62
too many subjects problem 231–5, 245, 247, 249–51, 261
too many thinkers problem 12, 16, 33, 38–9, 42, 46, 56, 62, 70, 108–10, 121, 126–7, 130, 162–3, 198
torture 287–9, 291–2, 298–300
transplant
  brain or head 2, 6–7, 12, 15–18, 24–5, 34–8, 40, 60, 76, 105–7, 110–12, 120–1, 129–30, 132, 134, 136–7, 145–60, 184, 203, 225, 229, 231, 241, 253, 287–95, 297–300, 314–17
  hemispheric 149, 220, 235–7, 255–6, 290
  intuition 6, 12, 15, 25–6, 35, 89–90, 105–6, 112, 300, 314–17

truth 8, 66, 93, 183
  truth-conditions 13, 78
two lives argument (two lives objection) 4, 33, 162

Unger, Peter 2, 16, 128, 221, 222, 224, 290
uniqueness 32, 34, 51, 54, 56–7, 316, 319–20,
    324, 326
unity 8, 23–4, 52, 59, 80–2, 133–6, 140, 182,
    212–13, 225, 232–3, 253, 255, 260, 264, 266,
    270–1, 276–82, 325–6
universalism 57–8, 158

vagueness 66–7, 77–80, 85, 209, 210, 217–18
value theory 3, 9, 10, 24

van Inwagen, Peter 4, 16, 18, 57–8, 61–2,
    114–17, 122, 124–5, 140, 152, 158, 170, 214,
    242–4, 283–5, 288

de Waal, Frans 4
Wada, Juhn 256
Wiggins, David 3, 14, 70, 75, 80, 89, 100–1
Williams, Bernard 2, 34–6, 289, 292
Williamson, Tim 19–20, 168–9
Wittgenstein, Ludwig 19–20, 109, 171–4, 176
Wollheim, Richard 102
Wright, Larry 199

Zimmerman, Dean 78, 80